SERMON
OUTLINES

AND

ALL-AGE
TALKS

*for every Sunday of
Common Worship*

SUSAN SAYERS

kevin
mayhew

The material in this book was originally published in the Living Stones Programme for Common Worship.

kevin mayhew

First published in Great Britain in 2015 by Kevin Mayhew Ltd
Buxhall, Stowmarket, Suffolk IP14 3BW
Tel: +44 (0) 1449 737978 Fax: +44 (0) 1449 737834
E-mail: info@kevinmayhew.com

www.kevinmayhew.com

9 8 7 6 5 4 3 2 1 0

ISBN 978 1 84867 769 2
Catalogue No. 1501469

Cover design by Rob Mortonson
© Images used under licence from Shutterstock Inc.
Edited by John Cox
Typeset by Richard Weaver

Printed and bound in Great Britain

Contents

About the author

A teacher by profession, Susan Sayers was ordained a priest in the Anglican Church and, before retirement her work was divided between the parish of Southend-on-Sea, the local women's prison, writing, training days and retreats.

Susan is the author of many popular resource books for the church including our ever-popular *Living Stones* and *Confirmation Experience* ranges. Her most recent publication for Kevin Mayhew is *The Holy Ground Around You, Reflective services for taking the church outside*.

Through the conferences and workshops she is invited to lead, she has been privileged to share in the worship of many different traditions and cultures.

Foreword

Since the day it was published, Susan Sayers' all-age programme for Common Worship has proved invaluable to people who are responsible for leading worship.

Susan's biblical and spiritual insights retain the value they have always had and her ideas for sermons for adults and for talks for younger members of the congregation continue to encourage and inspire.

Those reflections and ideas are gathered together here in one convenient volume. The content is based on the readings for each Sunday of the three-year cycle as set out in the *Common Worship Lectionary*.

It is inevitable that some of the illustrations offered emerged from particular events or the popular culture of the time and those who use this book may wish to update them while ensuring that they do in fact illuminate the point being made. The insights offered retain their value and are as fresh and stimulating as ever.

YEAR A

Advent 1

Thought for the day

We are to wake up and make sure we stay ready for the second coming.

Reflection on the readings

Isaiah 2:1-5
Psalm 122
Romans 13:11-14
Matthew 24:36-44

The Church begins its new year on Advent Sunday with the alarm clock jerking us out of sleep. There isn't even a snooze button. There is rather a sense of urgency as we listen to the readings.

First we have the vision seen by Isaiah of the last days, with the holy hill of Jerusalem a centre of pilgrimage for people from every nation. It is a picture of two-way traffic; the pilgrims streaming towards the city from all directions in order to understand and know God better, and the Word of God pouring out from Jerusalem in all directions to teach, explain and transform lives.

From our position in time we can appreciate the typical and extraordinary nature of such prophecy, since in Jesus the Word of God has indeed been pouring out from Jerusalem to the rest of the world, and to the rest of time during this last age before the end of all. And it is to him that the people come in every generation to have their lives transformed.

The Isaiah passage ends with a summons and an invitation to walk in the light of the Lord, and Paul takes this up in his letter to the Romans. The armour of light that will protect us from evil is the life of love spelt out by Jesus both in teaching and example. So, as we begin our preparation for Christmas, we are reminded of Jesus' humility in coming to live among us and show us the

Way, and also of the future, when he will return in glory as righteous judge.

In the Gospel we have Jesus' own teaching about the last days, and discover that one thing we can be certain of is that the second coming cannot be predicted. No last-minute revision will be possible, then, and the regular coursework format is a more helpful model. We have to live our lives in constant readiness so that we are not taken by surprise. This is partly so that we can be prepared for death or the second coming, and partly so that we can enjoy that quality of eternity which means God is constantly coming to us even while we live out our earthly lives. We need to be ready to receive him at every moment of every day.

All-age talk

Begin by explaining that today is Advent Sunday, the first Sunday of the year as far as the Church is concerned. Advent means 'coming', and over the next four weeks we will be getting ourselves ready for the coming of Jesus which we celebrate on Christmas Day.

Today's readings tell us to keep ourselves ready and alert for God's coming, which happens all the time and will happen in a very dramatic way at the end of time when Jesus returns in all his glory. The children will be helping to show us all how to make sure we don't miss out by being unprepared for this.

Invite all the children and young people to walk quickly around the centre aisle, changing direction every time you clap your hands or blow a whistle. Two claps or whistle blows means stand still and listen to a new instruction. Give them a few goes at changing direction, and then make the standing-still and listening signal. Explain that one clap will now mean change direction, two will mean walk backwards, and three will mean stand still and listen. Try this out for a short while and then, when they are standing still and listening, thank them for their demonstration and ask them to sit down where they are.

Explain that if we are to keep ourselves ready and alert while we get on with our lives, it will mean listening out all the time for the good and loving direction that God whispers to us to follow, just as the children were doing so well. As they walked about their lives, they were listening out, so that whenever there was a need to change direction, they were ready to do it straight away. If they hadn't listened so carefully, they wouldn't have been able to do it nearly so well.

Tell the children that this time when they hear the signal it will mean 'Go back to your seat'. As you start them moving about the aisle again, remind everyone to keep listening to God's loving direction as they walk about through life, so they are always ready. Make the last signal, and thank the children for their help as they go back to their seats.

Advent 2

Thought for the day
Get the road ready for the Lord!

Reflection on the readings
Isaiah 11:1-10
Psalm 72:1-7, 18-19
Romans 15:4-13
Matthew 3:1-12

Before any real changes can take place in our spiritual development, we have to come to the point of recognising where we are and wanting it to be better. All addicts and their families are painfully aware of the necessity to acknowledge the addiction and find it unbearable, before there is any real hope of kicking the habit. It is at the point when a situation finally becomes intolerable that we are galvanised into taking action to change things.

Living in exile, the people of Israel became acutely aware of their nation's need for good leadership, justice, integrity and peace. In today's passage from Isaiah we sense their longing, as they look forward to God providing what they know they need. Typically, the prophecy was fulfilled in far greater measure, since the kingdom of justice, peace and love – the kingdom of God proclaimed by Jesus – is still growing throughout the entire world.

John the Baptist's message of repentance once again recovered the urgency for people sorting their lives out, since the coming of the Messiah was imminent and they wanted to put things right and be ready, much as we might rush round clearing up the house just before guests are due to arrive – especially those guests we want to impress, or those who we know will notice the clutter! Often the clearing will be something we know has needed doing for ages; the arrival of guests simply reminds us that it has to be done.

So what about all that spiritual clutter and grime which we know needs sorting? Today the Gospel helps to nudge us into urgent action, recognising that we don't want things to stay as they are, and the effort of changing whatever needs changing is well worth it. God comes and knocks at the door of our hearts all the time – not just at the end of the world.

All-age talk

In the aisle lay down some 'holes' (cut from black paper) and some blocks (chairs with cardboard boxes or trays leaning against them).

Talk about John the Baptist coming out of the desert and urging everyone to 'Get the road ready!' Some people may have seen a new road being built, with some parts being banked up and others tunnelled through, in order to cut out the steep hills. Most people will at some time have been stuck in traffic jams while roads are being mended, or widened.

John the Baptist was imagining us getting a nice new road ready so that God can travel straight into our lives without finding any holes to fall down, or blocks in the way. He was saying to the people, 'You need to get yourselves ready like a good straight road.'

Ask a couple of volunteers to inspect the 'road' in the aisle, finding all sorts of blocks and holes along it that need putting right. This is a bit like our lives, and the lives of the people John was talking to nearly two thousand years ago. There are 'holes' of selfishness and meanness, and gaping holes in our loving. They need to be filled in with loving kindness and thoughtfulness. Perhaps there are gaps in our honesty, because we don't always tell the truth, or live the truth. These holes need filling up with truthfulness and integrity. There are perhaps holes of superiority, because we sneer at people who aren't like us, or as clever or handsome or rich as us.

Then there are those roadblocks which block God from getting through to us: blocks such as 'I don't need God', 'I'm fine as I am, thanks', 'I don't want to change', and 'It's not my fault I'm bad-tempered so you'll have to put up with it'. (The blocks can have these labels written on them clearly.)

When today we hear John the Baptist rushing out of the desert and shouting, 'Get the road ready for our God!', it's a good idea to listen to him, look at our own life-road, see where the holes and blocks are, and ask God to help us put them right straight away, so that God can come to us easily without any hold-ups.

Advent 3

Thought for the day

Great expectations. Jesus fulfils the great statements of prophecy.

Reflection on the readings

Isaiah 35:1-10
Psalm 146:5-10 or Canticle: Magnificat
James 5:7-10
Matthew 11:2-11

John the Baptist's task had been to prepare people for the coming of the Messiah, and that placed him, with all the prophets before him, in the age before the coming of the kingdom. We recall how John had urged people to sort out their lives, stressing the possibility of judgement as the all-seeing God came among his people in person, and it is easy to see how John's enthusiasm had polished his hopes into a specific shape. This is something we are all prone to do.

While it helped the urgency and focus of John's message, the side effect was that when Jesus' ministry started to look different from his expectation John began to wonder if he'd been mistaken. The frustration and suffering of his imprisonment must have added to the undermining negatives.

What Jesus does is hold up the Isaiah prophecy as a checklist. If these signs of the kingdom are indeed happening, then John can trust that the promised Saviour is indeed at work, even if the style of his ministry is different from what he had imagined. It's all to do with our expectations. If we get into the way of fleshing these out completely through our imagination, we may find that we don't recognise the real thing when we see it.

So it is as well to stay flexible, holding on to what we do know for certain and keeping our minds open about the details. This is true for us when we try to imagine God, heaven, or the end of all things. They may look like the paintings and frescoes of the Old Masters, and they may not. We mustn't let our expectations become stunted or narrowed by a particular artist's impression. That is what happened when people expected the astronauts to see God above the clouds and were disappointed. Our great expectations of God will be fulfilled far in excess of anything we might imagine and entirely in keeping with his nature.

All-age talk

Beforehand wrap some objects as presents. Some should be obvious, such as a tennis racket, a balloon and a bottle of wine. Others should be harder to guess from the shape, such as a boxed toy and a book.

Display the wrapped presents, and talk about the way Christmas is getting nearer and we're all getting our presents ready. Perhaps some of us are really hoping for a particular present, even though we know it's the thought that counts and we'll be happy with whatever we get because it means someone has thought of us.

Draw attention to the wrapped presents you have brought in, and pick up the first group of obvious presents, asking people to guess what is inside. Then go on to the second group, discovering that some things are harder to guess – we might look at the parcel and expect something completely different to be inside.

John the Baptist knew that God was coming to his people, and he had done a good job of getting them ready. But exactly how this would happen was like a wrapped present – still hidden from view because it hadn't happened yet. Perhaps John was expecting Jesus to be more of a mighty warrior, judging everyone and destroying those who didn't make the grade.

What *did* Jesus do? We heard about it in the first reading from the prophet Isaiah: he was going around healing the sick, making the deaf hear again, the blind see again and the lame walk again. He was letting the weak and downtrodden know that God was on their side and loved them.

Once Jesus pointed out that he was doing these things, John could see that it really did fit in with the 'shape' he had been expecting, even though it wasn't quite the same, rather like our wrapped-up bottle of red wine which we had perhaps been expecting to be white wine, or sherry. Or like the boxed game that you might have expected to be 'Guess Who' and it turned out to be 'Mr Pop'.

As we wrap our presents, let's remember that God's ways are often hidden and unexpected – he is a God who sometimes takes us by surprise. But the surprises will always be true to his good and loving nature.

Advent 4

Thought for the day

Through the willing participation of Mary and Joseph, God is poised to come among his people as their Saviour.

Reflection on the readings

Isaiah 7:10-16
Psalm 80:1-7, 17-19
Romans 1:1-7
Matthew 1:18-25

Matthew, writing for a Hebrew audience, is keen to show the Jewish people that Jesus is indeed the promised Messiah. He draws attention to Isaiah's prophecy spoken to King Ahaz, and sets out Jesus' credentials. Through Joseph, Jesus is a descendant of King David; through Mary, this son, born to a virgin, fulfils the ancient prophecy and turns out to be 'Immanuel' or 'God with us'.

It is not unusual for prophecies about short-term, immediate events to turn out to have resonances far in excess of their original meaning. One familiar example is the call to St Francis to 'repair my Church, which is in ruins'. It was far more than one stone chapel which was eventually 'repaired'; the whole Church of God became refreshed and invigorated.

The expectant atmosphere of today's readings attunes us to God's way of orchestrating events and working in co-operation with his people. The stage is set, the timing is right, and the focused light of all the hopes and longings of generations is about to shine out in the person of Jesus. Typically, we find God delighting in using the ordinariness of good people so that extraordinary things can be accomplished. Typically, he allows individual people to know their own part in the action exactly as and when they need to know it.

It is because Joseph is expecting God to be God that he is prepared to alter his sensible and considerate plan to make no loud accusations about Mary when divorcing her for assumed unfaithfulness. Whatever that dream was, it made him think again. Perhaps Mary had tried to tell him the truth and he hadn't been able to believe her before. We can only guess at how Mary felt before Joseph changed his mind.

God will still speak to us through our dreams, memories and feelings, if only we take the trouble to notice. They can often be our own personal parables, able to put us in touch with our true selves; enabling us to recognise God's ways forward which we haven't been able to see before.

All-age talk

Ask for two volunteers. Stand one on a chair and have the other lie down on the floor. Talk with the volunteers about what they can see from their particular viewpoint. Although nothing else in the church has changed, the descriptions will be different because of where the volunteers are.

You could also suggest that everyone looks at something central, first through one eye and then the other. They can then all notice the change of view even when looking out from the same head!

What our readings today are reminding us is that we need to get into the habit of looking at everything from God's point of view. What we then see may sometimes come as a surprise to us, because we are so used to looking from our own point of view. Take Joseph, for instance. He was in for a surprise. He thought he had worked out the kindest way of dealing with the embarrassing problem of Mary expecting a baby before they were married. He had it all worked out. He'd divorce Mary without a big fuss, so that she needn't be noticed too much.

But through the dream God helped him look at things from another point of view. Joseph saw that Mary's baby was all part of God's plan, and, rather than divorcing her, he had an important job to do – to look after Mary and this very special baby. Joseph must have been a very brave man, as well as a good and kind one. He knew people would think he was stupid; perhaps they would stop being friends with him; his life would never be nice and straightforward again. But he did that brave, good thing because he had seen the situation from God's point of view and was happy to go along with that.

It was the same with Mary. If she had only seen the angel's message from her own point of view she might have refused to go along with God's plan, which was bound to turn her own hopes and dreams upside down. But she saw it from God's point of view – that the people of our earth needed a Saviour; God needed to be born as a human baby so he could rescue humans as an insider. And a baby needed a mum. So she agreed and that made Christmas possible.

Christmas Day

(Set 3)

Thought for the day

The Word of God is made flesh. In the birth of Jesus we see God expressed in human terms.

Reflection on the readings

Isaiah 52:7-10
Psalm 98
Hebrews 1:1-4 (5-12)
John 1:1-14

The well-loved reading from Isaiah resounds with hope. It is not wishful thinking, talking about impossible dreams, but rings with utter surety that God has revealed to his attentive prophet, so that the good news can be shared with all the people of Israel. There is a great sense of excitement, like the stirring in a great crowd as word gets round that the famous and adored person they have been waiting for is about to arrive. Today God has arrived in person to live with the people of his creation, sharing their humanity in order to save them.

The writer of Hebrews chooses this to introduce his whole teaching: in the past God had spoken through his prophets, but from the Incarnation onwards we are looking at an entirely new and dynamic experience, as God speaks to us in person, through Jesus, the Son of God.

The introduction to John's Gospel helps us to see the extraordinary depth of the meaning of God's 'Word', flinging us back to the emerging creation from chaos, and forward to the streams of people through the generations who choose to receive the light of God's life to transform them and the world they inhabit. Stretched out across it all is the person of Jesus, expressing God's creative and redeeming love in a way we, as humans, can understand. No darkness can ever extinguish the hope of this light.

All-age talk

Begin by getting different people to say, 'Happy Christmas, everyone!' in whatever way they like. A group of friends might like to shout it together; someone might like to stand at the front; others will choose to say it quietly to their neighbour.

Point out how all the 'Happy Christmas!' messages are much appreciated, and they all show the wonderful way we're all different. You don't have to be a particular sort of person to be a Christian. The only sort of person you have to be is yourself! God loves you that way.

Today we've been expressing ourselves when we spoke our Christmas messages, and Christmas is about God expressing himself: Jesus being born as a human baby is God saying to all of us, 'I love you!'

Christmas 1

Thought for the day

Jesus, the expression of God's love, lives as a vulnerable boy in the real and dangerous world we all inhabit.

Reflection on the readings

Isaiah 63:7-9
Psalm 148
Hebrews 2:10-18
Matthew 2:13-23

One of the truths recognised in our readings today is that the work of redemption cannot be done at arm's length. No rescue operation can be carried out successfully without someone being prepared to brave the dangers and go in to share the conditions of those who need rescuing; only by being this close can the rescuer bring the trapped to freedom. As the Isaiah passage acknowledges, 'It was no messenger or angel but his presence that saved them', and in the person of Jesus, being born into the human condition to live a human life with human temptations and dangers, this presence became a practical reality.

There is a wonderful sense in Psalm 148 of the entire created world welcoming God's creative Word, and the passage from Hebrews emphasises the special link Jesus has with the rest of us. We share flesh and blood with the incarnate One – God made human. And the side effects of that involvement are itemised clearly in the events following Jesus' birth, as told by Matthew. Although the Christmas cards usually show an idyllic scene of peace and joy, the real and dangerous world we all know is just outside the stable door.

In today's Gospel we find that Jesus has been born into our familiar world of ruthless ambition, cruelty and despair, of rejection and wandering, of isolation and fear. It reminds us that our God does not hold himself remote from our sufferings but is part of them, prepared to share with us the vulnerability of a baby refugee, bundled up in the night and taken off to a strange country in a life and death situation. It is God's willingness to be utterly immanent that means we really can trust him through the searing pain of life as well as its light and comfortable times.

Joseph gives us an inspiring example of committed attentiveness to God's leading, so that God can use his gifts of practical and efficient organisation to keep this child and his mother safe.

All-age talk

If you have a member of the congregation whose job involves rescue (for example in the fire, ambulance, lifeboat or mountain rescue services), ask if they would be willing to take part in a brief interview before the talk. Talk with them about the kind of dangers they themselves have to accept in order to rescue people, and the way they get alongside the people who need rescuing in order to help them. If you are not having a live interview, talk briefly about these rescuers.

Explain how Jesus is a rescuer, who comes in person to save us and help us. Stand someone on a paper island in the middle of a flood. God doesn't stand a long way off and shout to us. (Stand a long way off and shout to them to get into a boat and sail away.) That's no good, because the person feeling drowned by sadness or guilt or evil can't do what you are shouting even if they wanted to. We can't rescue ourselves; only God can set us free by accepting us, loving us and forgiving us. So instead of being a long way off and telling us what to do, God came in person to rescue us. (Pretend to row over to the person and then rescue them.) That's what happened at Christmas – God came to live among us in the person of Jesus, and he is still with us now. We are all his brothers and sisters.

Christmas 2

Thought for the day

The grace and truth revealed in Jesus show God's freely-given love; through Jesus, God pours out his blessings on us and gives us real freedom.

Reflection on the readings

Ecclesiasticus* 24:1-12 (* also called Sirach)
Canticle: Wisdom of Solomon 10:15-21
Ephesians 1:3-14
John 1:(1-9) 10-18

It is an amazing thought that there was never a time for God when he was not yearning for all his creation to be brought into a close, loving relationship as family members. There is the breathtaking cosmic breadth of such a harmony, and at the same time the intimate, personal invitation to each person throughout all time and space. Even as our world was forming, God was longing for you and me and our loved ones to be his own sons and daughters, enjoying his love and responding to it.

The moment of Incarnation, which we celebrate at Christmas, marks a new stage in the journey towards the fulfilment of that longing and outreach. As Jesus, in the ordinary, messy process of childbirth, emerges into the world of human existence, the possibility is there for our salvation. The Law, given through Moses, was of great value, but with Jesus we have what the Law could never give – God's freely-given grace in a totally loving human life, to sort out our sin once and for all.

Mary and Joseph were happy to receive this child into their home and their lives, and the receiving was very costly. There have always been many who consider that receiving Jesus Christ into their lives is too costly and they are not prepared to make that commitment. It is right that we sit down and count the cost before committing ourselves, and it is true that receiving Jesus is likely to be disruptive and is, in worldly terms, complete foolishness.

Paradoxically, receiving Jesus is also the way to such blessings and freedom of spirit that those who have taken the plunge would not have anything any different. Living in that close relationship with the God who is Father, Son and Spirit, allows us into a completely new dimension of living; quite apart from all the many blessings and joys, there is the underlying sense of it being profoundly good and right and true, and the place we were created to live in.

All-age talk

Bring something with you to offer as a small gift – a chocolate bar, a sticker, a few flowers or a piece of fruit, perhaps.

Over Christmas we have all been busy giving one another presents. Explain that you have brought something with you to give away today, so that we can understand a bit more about God's Christmas present to us. In Jesus we see God giving himself to set us free from sin and evil because he loves us so much.

Show everyone what your gift is, and ask them to put their hands up if they would like to be considered for it. Choose someone using some random method, such as their name being first in the alphabet, or their birthday coming up this week. When God gives us his present no one has to get left out. Everyone who asks, gets.

Stand a short distance away from the person chosen, and hold out the gift. Can they receive the gift without moving? No, they can't. If we are going to receive a gift we have to change our position a bit. (The person can demonstrate this and receive the gift.) It's the same with us all receiving God's gift – we are bound to change if we receive Jesus into our daily living.

Just as Joseph and Mary's lives changed when Jesus was born into their family, so our lives will change. As we reach out to receive Jesus, we shall find we are able to reach out to one another in a more loving, positive way; we shall find we are more concerned about justice and mercy being written into our social system; we shall find we are wanting to be more truthful to others and ourselves.

So be prepared – if you don't want to change into a happier, more loving person, freed from guilt and able to be truly yourself, then don't take God up on his offer!

Epiphany

Thought for the day
Jesus, the hope of the nations, is shown to the world.

Reflection on the readings
Isaiah 60:1-6
Psalm 72:(1-9) 10-15
Ephesians 3:1-12
Matthew 2:1-12

Beginning with one person (Abraham) and developing to embrace one family and eventually one nation, God has painstakingly planted the seed of salvation and nurtured it until the whole earth is involved. Isaiah had sensed that day in terms of a sunrise dawning with the light of day on a world of darkness, with all the hope and joy and relief that a new day can bring after a long, dark night. Probably this was one of the prophecies these magi had read as they studied the signs of the sky and wondered about life's meaning. And perhaps it was then that they felt stirring in them a profound calling to be, in person, those visitors who could symbolise the light dawning on the wider world. Certainly they must have been inspired by a powerful sense of urgency and necessity to make such a journey. And as they travelled, both physically and spiritually, towards Bethlehem, bearing the gifts laid down in those ancient scriptures, perhaps they were drawn by much more than a star. Jesus later proclaimed that anyone who sets out to search always finds.

Paul also knows himself to be commissioned to explain God's nature to the Gentiles. He is overwhelmed by the extraordinary way that the Christ has enabled us to approach the great and awesome God with freedom and confidence – as one of the family.

And for all of us who are Gentiles, the feast of the Epiphany is particularly one to celebrate, since it marks the truth that we too are part of God's salvation and can share the light of dawn.

All-age talk

Beforehand arrange for a knitter to bring a completed garment to church, together with a ball of wool and needles. Also prepare a large paper cut-out of a similar garment, which is folded up so that the first bit that would be made is the only piece showing. Alternatively use the actual garment, folded up at that point.

Begin by showing everyone the wonderful garment that the knitter has made and asking how long it took to make and who it is for. What did it look like at first, when they started making it? The knitter can show the ball of wool and needles, and do a couple of stitches. Hold up the needles with these stitches and point out that it doesn't look much like a jumper/scarf yet! But the knitter went on working at it, knowing that one day it would be ready.

God knew that one day everything would be ready for Jesus to come into the world, but he, too, took a long time making things ready. He started by calling one person, Abraham. (Show the folded garment, but don't refer to it – it is there to be visual reinforcement of what you are saying.) Over the years God went on to prepare all Abraham's family. (More of the garment is revealed.) Until over more years that family became one nation. (Reveal some more of the garment.) But God's plan still wasn't finished. He went on to include not one nation but all the nations and everyone in them. (Shake the whole garment out and display it.) Today is called the Epiphany because the word 'epiphany' means 'showing' or 'revealing' or 'manifesting', and when those wise men arrived at Bethlehem with their presents, God was showing or revealing himself not just to Abraham or his family, not just to the whole nation of Israel, but to all the rest of us in the world as well.

Whatever country you come from, whatever you look like and whatever language you speak, God is saying to us today that he is there for you and no one is left out. You don't have to have the right ancestors to know God. You don't have to pass any exams to know God.

We sometimes get so interested in the presents the wise men were bringing to Jesus that we forget what brought them there in the first place. It was God who called these wise men from other nations to be there when Jesus was still a baby, so he could welcome them as well. They were there representing all the nations, so when God welcomed them he was welcoming each of us.

The Baptism of Christ

Thought for the day

As Jesus is baptised, the Spirit of God rests visibly on him, marking him out as the One who will save his people.

Reflection on the readings

Isaiah 42:1-9
Psalm 29
Acts 10:34-43
Matthew 3:13-17

In this season of Epiphany it is as if the mystery of the Incarnation is gradually being unfolded like a richly patterned carpet. Not that it will ever become totally understood this side of death, but even so, as year by year we examine it and marvel at it, truths of God's working and God's nature will gradually become apparent, and enable us increasingly to understand ourselves and our world. The knowledge of God is the beginning of wisdom.

Gestalt psychology talks of the 'Aha!' moment when fragments of knowledge suddenly form a pattern of fresh understanding in our minds. Peter's experience at Joppa led him to a sudden, new level of realisation about God's purposes: it was all so much bigger and wider than he had understood before. God was not the privately owned treasure of a few, but the glory and hope of the whole of humanity, in all places and all ages.

It must have been a similar 'Aha!' experience for Matthew, when, with his spiritual eyes open, he suddenly linked the moment of Jesus' Baptism with the prophecy from Isaiah. Perhaps you can remember an experience which has been marked with significance for you particularly in the light of subsequent developments? For those who have lived through the subsequent events of Christ's ministry, his death and resurrection, the Baptism of Jesus marks the taking on of the role of that servant described in the book of Isaiah.

It is no mistake that the words of God, heard by Jesus as he comes up out of the water, closely echo the opening words of Isaiah 42. Anyone with a working knowledge of the Isaiah passage would immediately call to mind the rest of the passage, with its hope and its tenderness.

All-age talk

Ask various children if they know what job they would like to do when they grow up. Ask various adults what they wanted to be when they were children, and whether they did it or not. Ask some of the children if they have seen pictures of their mums and dads when they were babies and toddlers. Do they look anything like that now? Ask some of the mums and dads if they can imagine what their children will be like in twenty years' time.

A week or two ago we were thinking about when Jesus was a baby. Now, suddenly, we're looking at what he was like when he grew up. Here he is at about thirty years old. He's a carpenter, so he's probably quite strongly built. He's heard that his cousin, John (do they remember John?), is washing people in the River Jordan as a sign that God has forgiven their sins. We wash to get our bodies clean. John baptised people to show they were getting their souls clean. They were all getting ready for the Messiah, or Christ.

And now here comes Jesus, wading into the river, and wanting John to baptise him as well! (We know that Jesus is the Christ they were waiting for, but the people didn't know that yet.) John realises who Jesus is, and is shocked that he wants to be baptised. 'It ought to be the other way round!' says John. '*You* ought to be baptising *me*!'

Jesus insists. 'No, it's right for you to baptise me. God's work of putting things right all through the centuries is coming together now in this Baptism.' So John agrees to baptise Jesus. He pushes Jesus down under the water in the river, and when Jesus comes up out of the water, something amazing happens.

It's as if the heavens are opened up, and Jesus sees the Spirit of God coming to him and resting on him. Matthew tells us it looked something like a dove flying down to him. Jesus hears God his Father speaking to him deep into his being. God is saying that Jesus is indeed his well-loved Son, chosen and marked out for a special life that will save the world.

So that tiny baby, born in the stable, visited by shepherds and wise men, looked after by Joseph and Mary all through his childhood, is now at the start of his important work on earth. His job is to show the world God's love.

Epiphany 2

Thought for the day

Jesus is recognised and pointed out by John to be God's chosen one.

Reflection on the readings

Isaiah 49:1-7
Psalm 40:1-11
1 Corinthians 1:1-9
John 1:29-42

Today, as we continue to think of Christ being shown, or revealed, to the world, there is another of the 'servant' readings from Isaiah. Set apart before birth, the servant has been brought into being to gather up Israel and bring her back into a right relationship with God, not through a dynamically successful campaign which the world might recognise and expect, but actually through worldly foolishness – failure, suffering and rejection.

Not only that, but as the plan unfolds it spills out of its original boundaries to include the possibility of salvation for the entire world. Gradually the prophet is starting to understand the scale of God's intended action.

We pick up echoes of the Gospel pictures of Jesus in that reading from Isaiah: the pre-natal cherishing, the light for the world, the redeemer, the homage paid by kings and important people. They are echoes that the people of Israel would have noticed, and they reveal Jesus as the One who fulfils the Old Testament writings in a most remarkable way.

John wants to tell everyone about it. It says a lot about John that he was able to direct his own disciples to Jesus. Probably with hindsight, the Gospel writer has John describing Jesus as 'God's Passover Lamb', with all the significance of sacrifice and the way to freedom which that suggests. Though he had been preparing them for this, it could still have been a moment to indulge the human instinct to be possessive, critical and defensive, yet in John we rather sense excitement and great enthusiasm.

In John's Gospel the emphasis is not so much on Jesus going out to find his disciples as them going to find him, and bringing one another along. We are aware of the attraction of this itinerant teacher and holy man, with his remarkable gift of discernment and wisdom. Can this really be the promised and long-awaited Messiah? It will only be time spent in Jesus' company that will enable these followers to decide about the truth of Jesus' identity.

And, as Paul writes in his letter to the church in Corinth, the same is true for all those who seek Jesus, whatever time or place they live in. As we spend time in Jesus' company we will find that it shows, and then others, spending time with us, may recognise the truth that Christ is living in us.

All-age talk

Start by hiding some treasure while a volunteer 'seeker' covers their eyes. Everyone else needs to know where it is hidden. Now set the treasure-seeker off to search, with everyone else guiding them by calling out whether they are colder or hotter. With all this help it shouldn't take too long for the seeker to find.

Lots of people are truth-seekers. They want to find out the truth about life and about God and about the reason we are here. These are the deep questions that humans have always asked, and it is important that we ask them. Questions are good things; never stop asking them, just because you're grown up. Grown-ups need to learn from the children here – children are very good at asking important questions!

When we are seeking for the truth about God, it helps if there are people who have already found him, who are happy to tell us when we're getting nearer or drifting further away. John the Baptist is one of those who is calling out to us, 'Warmer! You're getting warmer . . . you're boiling hot!' That's what he was doing to his disciples when Jesus came by. 'Look!' he said. 'That's the one I was telling you about – this is the one you've been waiting for! This is the Son of God!' And the two disciples took John's advice and started following Jesus.

One of those disciples was Peter's brother, Andrew. Peter was probably a truth-seeker as well, and his brother Andrew helped guide him to the truth. He told Peter they had found the Messiah, took hold of his brother and led him to Jesus. (Get two brothers to walk this through as you say it.)

Think about whether you ever help other people find the truth about God. Think about whether other people help you, and how they do it. And if you don't think you've been doing much helping, today's readings are giving you some ideas as to how to start:

- telling people what you have noticed and found out about God;
- mentioning that he's worth spending time with;
- suggesting that they come with you to find out more;
- and introducing them to God by the way you live.

Epiphany 3

Thought for the day

The prophecies of Isaiah are fulfilled in a new and lasting way in Jesus of Nazareth.

Reflection on the readings

Isaiah 9:1-4
Psalm 27:1, 4-9
1 Corinthians 1:10-18
Matthew 4:12-23

At the time when Isaiah of Jerusalem spoke of the great light of hope appearing in the darkness, and the yoke of oppression finally being shattered to bring people freedom, the people of Israel were threatened with a takeover bid and exile by Assyria, if they did not sort their values and reconcile themselves to their God. All their dreams as a nation could be wiped away if they were taken captive, under the yokes of their conquerors, away from their own beloved land, their city and their temple. (And eventually, through the Babylonians, this did happen.)

Any of us who have watched our hopes and dreams crash in pieces around us will have some idea of how such an experience takes us on a journey through questioning, self-doubt, anger, guilt, reassessment and eventually, hopefully, into a new maturity born of acceptance, greater self-knowledge, forgiveness and the value of encountering human suffering.

In their collective experience, the people are given hope, both in the short term (Jerusalem was indeed saved from the Assyrian threat) and, as we now can see, in the long term, since Jesus startlingly clearly fulfils the prophet's words as he treads the ground of Galilee, preaching, teaching and healing. The liberation he proclaims is not tied to one generation whose threatened oppression is averted, but, as Paul emphasises in his letter to the church in Corinth, it also applies to every person sensing the liberating power of God's forgiving love which can set them free to live life to the full.

All-age talk

Out of strong card (or a wooden broom handle) make a demonstration yoke to show, on a brave volunteer, how conquerors used to subdue their captives. When you release the volunteer captive, talk to them about how good it feels to be free of the yoke.

Explain how in our first reading today we heard from a man called Isaiah. He was a prophet – someone who clearly speaks out God's words to the people. At the time, the people he was speaking to were being threatened by another country. It looked as if Assyria might well come and yoke the people up as captives, and take them far away from their own homes and their temple and their country, to live in exile in the country of their conquerors.

Isaiah showed the people that if they went on turning away from him by treating the poor unfairly, and spoiling themselves while others starved, then God would not save them from this attack. They were already 'yoked' up as slaves to their greed and selfishness, and their worries about the Assyrians.

Through Isaiah the prophet, God spoke to his people. He told them that he loved them, and that he longed for them to sort their lives out and trust him again. God would then be able to look after them and keep them and their holy city of Jerusalem safe. It would be like their yokes being broken in pieces, so they would be completely free.

Show the demonstration yoke again on another volunteer. Do any of us wear invisible yokes and need to be set free? We may be wearing yokes of selfishness, or resentment; we may be always wishing for things we can't have. We may still feel guilty about something we did. We may need healing of some emotional damage which is holding us back from living freely.

41

Jesus came so that we could be set free from all these yokes. He's an expert 'yoke shatterer'! He's the kind of light that makes all the darkness in our lives and minds and hearts disappear. If we let him in to walk around our own lives, as well as the lake of Galilee, he will set us free from all those yokes that hold us captive. And then we'll be able to walk through life with a new spring in our step, full of hope.

Epiphany 4

Thought for the day

Jesus shows us in action the loving provision of the God who made us.

Reflection on the readings

1 Kings 17:8-16
Psalm 36:5-10
1 Corinthians 1:18-31
John 2:1-11

Elijah went to Zarephath at God's instruction. He was used to listening to God prompting him, and was willing to go along with what he sensed God was asking him to do. The widow, too, shows remarkable hospitality and obedience, recognising Elijah as a holy man and generously sharing her last meal with this stranger. In a similar way, the servants at the wedding recognise that Jesus is speaking with an unusual authority, so they go along with his strange instructions and risk the embarrassment of pouring water into the cup of the master of the banquet. In the event their faith is rewarded, as is the widow's, and people's ordinary needs are met with finest quality provision.

John uses the 'water to wine' story as a sign to teach us a bit more about who Jesus really is. The point of the water turning into wine is not a magic trick, but a clue to help us see that in Jesus the invisible, creative God is made visible in human form and behaviour. Here we can see God's sensitive understanding of our needs and daily difficulties, his delight in working co-operatively with us in the provision, and his courteous manner of leaving us the space to choose for ourselves whether to work with him or not. God never forces our hand, but always respects our God-given capacity for free will.

Our calling as the Church – being members of the Body of Christ – is to carry on that work of showing the compassion and love of our God in the situations we live in, to the people we meet in our ordinary lives every day. We need no letters after our names in order to do this, and there are no lower or upper age brackets. We simply need to be filled with the inner life of Christ so that the work of 'epiphany', or 'revealing', can continue in every place and in every generation.

All-age talk

Ask a volunteer to stand at the front, holding a large piece of card in front of them so that no one can see their face. Point out that we can't be certain whether the person is looking happy, sad or angry, because we can't see for ourselves. Ask the volunteer to make one of those expressions behind the card. We can talk to them and listen to them, but we can't see them. It was a little like that for the people of Israel. Sometimes the prophets would speak out God's word to them, and they prayed to God, but it wasn't until Jesus came that people could see what God was like.

(Take the card from the volunteer's face.) We can now see clearly whether the person is happy, sad or angry, and we can see how s/he behaves, and what s/he thinks is important. When Jesus came to live as a human being on our earth, walking about in the actual place of Galilee and in the actual time of Roman-occupied Palestine, people could see exactly what God thought was important, and how much he loved them.

They saw that God really is interested in our everyday worries such as having enough food, or enough time or energy to get our work done. (In the story we heard today, Jesus was interested in the problem of a wine shortage at a wedding.)

They saw that God goes on loving us right to the very limit and still carries on loving! (Jesus went on loving and forgiving right through being put to death on a cross.)

They saw that God likes to work with us in solving some of our problems, and, if we are happy to work with him, amazing things can happen. (The servants went ahead and filled the water pots with water, as Jesus had told them, and started pouring it out *before* they had seen it was now wine.)

There will be lots of times this week when we can choose to do 'exactly what Jesus tells us' and, if we agree, God will be able to use us in providing lovingly for someone's needs. Perhaps we will be giving our complete attention to someone when they talk to us, or providing financial help or emotional support. Perhaps our smile will cheer someone up, or our help will give someone a well-needed rest. Perhaps by letting someone play we will be making them feel less lonely and happier. Perhaps the spare curtains we remember to take into the charity shop will be exactly what someone is hoping to find as they struggle to furnish a home with very little money.

Let's make sure that this week we listen out for the ways God asks for our help, and then do what he whispers in our hearts, so that the people in this town can actually see God's love in action.

Epiphany 5

Sunday between 3 and 9 February (if earlier than 2 before Lent)

Thought for the day

We are commissioned to live so that we shine like lights which direct others on to God, the source of Light.

Reflection on the readings

Isaiah 58:1-9a (9b-12)
Psalm 112:1-9 (10)
1 Corinthians 2:1-12 (13-16)
Matthew 5:13-20

Salt and light can both make a great difference. Apart from its wonderful preserving and disinfecting qualities, a pinch of salt brings out the full flavour of other ingredients; light allows everyone in the room to see the shape and texture of all kinds of different objects which were hidden by darkness. And we as Christians are called to be salt and light to the world. We are called to live so that our way of living brings out in other people their full flavour, or potential; we are called to live in a way that helps people see where they are going, in the room, or context, of eternity.

We have all met people whose attitude and behaviour towards us makes us shrivel up inside, and others in whose company we feel accepted and acceptable, and therefore free to be our true selves. It is loving reverence for one another that makes the difference, and the Gospels are full of incidents where people noticed this in their encounters with Jesus.

If we behave as the salt of the earth, we will be content to make ourselves available so that others feel free to become more truly themselves, and we shall recognise the need to be there, but not to overwhelm! Too heavy a dose of salt kills off the flavour. If we behave as the light of the world we shall once again be in the role of enablers: we are at the service of the world, quietly enabling it to see more clearly. And again, we recognise the need to provide illumination, but not to blind or dazzle. Dazzling performances of ostentatious 'religion', such as those we heard about in the Isaiah reading, are not at all what God has in mind for his people, either then or now. What God wants is for the people in our world to be so impressed with the light we shine around that they want to find out where we get it from. Our shining is to set others off on their way to discover God for themselves.

Of course, we can only behave as salt and light if we are the genuine article, and are prepared to work co-operatively with God. That is where it is so helpful to have our faith 'earthed' in practical living. As Christians we all need to have our feet on the ground; we need to be engaged in the messy, hard work of caring, challenging injustice and offering practical help and support. Only then will our praises mean something, and our worship glorify God.

All-age talk

You will need a large saucepan, a pack of spaghetti, a jar of Italian sauce and a large carton of salt, a jug, a teacup and a tablespoon. You will also need a table lamp and a bright spotlight.

Produce the first set of items, setting them out and talking about cooking pasta. Invite a good cook from the congregation to supervise! Explain that the best cookery books say that pasta can't be seasoned after it's cooked, so we need to add the salt to the cooking water. Pick up the salt, and wonder aloud how much salt to use. A jugful? Get the cook to explain what would happen if you put in that much salt. A teacupful? Still too much! A tablespoonful? Still too much. If we use that much all we will taste will be the salt, and the whole idea of salt is that it isn't really noticed but brings out the flavour of the other ingredients.

That's what we are called to do as Christians: not to take over and dominate or possess people, or want to control them, but in humility to make ourselves available and useful in helping to give other people the freedom and the confidence to be themselves. That may mean more listening and less speaking; it may mean being less concerned about being thought important and more concerned about other people's needs being recognised. It is the way of quiet, loving service.

Now flash the spotlight around so that it goes in people's eyes (but don't overdo this!). Explain that Jesus also calls us to be light. That doesn't mean trying to blind people with our natural brilliance, or trying subtly to impress others, so that we're more like disco lights, designed for a flashy effect. The kind of light we are called to be is a much more practical sort, rather like a table lamp, perhaps, which simply helps people to see better, so they don't bump into things and hurt themselves, and so they can get on with living more effectively.

Salt and light are just simple things, but they are things which can make a great difference. As Christians we are called to be like that – just our ordinary selves, but through our faith in God, able to make a difference.

Epiphany 6

Sunday between 10 and 16 February (if earlier than 2 before Lent)

Thought for the day

To live God's way is to choose the way of life.

Reflection on the readings

Deuteronomy 30:15-20 or Ecclesiasticus 15:15-20
Psalm 119:1-8
1 Corinthians 3:1-9
Matthew 5:21-37

Jesus always insisted that he had not come to abolish the Law but to fulfil it. One of the challenging ways he does this is to take the ten commandments and work through them, pointing out not just the letter but the spirit of the law. Today we have an excerpt from this teaching in the Gospel reading, and by the time Jesus has finished preaching it is clear that the way of love is a demanding commitment, involving one's whole attitude and outlook as well as one's actual behaviour. The ten commandments are a kind of shorthand for this; they are the broad brush-strokes or guidelines, but not the whole picture. The danger is that people can feel they have completely fulfilled the law when they have simply taken care about the 'brush-stroke' examples; they can feel virtuous about not committing murder, for example, while their attitude to others continues to be destructive and patronising. With the law of love, expounded by Jesus, these attitudes are also considered 'murderous'.

Life is full of choices. Many times each day we have to decide whether to choose the way of life or the way of death, and unless we have taken time to decide what main direction we want to walk in, we can become hopelessly confused. That is why it is good to use today and the reading from the Old Testament as a challenge: what direction do we really want to face?

If we make such a decision calmly and in our right mind, rather than waiting until we are in the grip of some temptation, then we are far more likely to have the courage to stand up for what we know in our hearts to be right.

As the community of Christ, we all need to be facing the 'Godwards' direction of life, using godly love as the compass. Then all the greater and lesser decisions to be made in our individual lives, and in our society and in the Church itself, can be worked out in line with these principles. Recognised mistakes are far healthier and easier to put right than unrecognised hypocrisy.

All-age talk

Begin by drawing attention to the direction everyone is facing in church. Obviously this will vary according to your architecture and the age of the building. The architecture reflects a focus and a general direction which the planners thought of most importance. Perhaps if you were all about to start planning from scratch, you might arrange things slightly differently!

Once you have established the general seating focus, move to another part of the church, such as the baptistry. If people are going to continue facing you, they will all have to turn round. That is because at the moment the important thing going on is you speaking, and that takes over in importance from the general focus of the building.

Now move somewhere else so that everyone has to turn round again. Today we heard Jesus teaching about the Law, which is summed up in the ten commandments. Have these displayed on card, or on an OHP, or walk to the part of the church where they are written on the wall. They are good rules to live by and our whole law system is still based on them. But with all rules there is a problem. Jesus wanted his followers (and that includes us) to remember that the really important thing is to stay focused on God in everything we do.

Perhaps you haven't ever killed someone. But the spirit of the law means more than that, just as our focus is more than just sitting facing the front. It also means making sure we haven't got unkind or destructive thoughts about people, that we're not making people feel stupid or useless, that we aren't putting other people down or running them down behind their backs, because those things are in the destructive spirit of hate, which is the opposite of God's law of love. As you mention each of these, move around the building so people have to move their 'attitudes' to see you.

What we need to do is keep our eyes fixed on Jesus, and whatever we are doing we can think to ourselves, 'Does this thing I'm doing or saying or thinking make Jesus happy? Is it a loving thing to do or think or say?'

And if it is, carry on. If it isn't, stop and change direction.

Epiphany 7

Sunday between 17 and 23 February (if earlier than 2 before Lent)

Thought for the day

We are called to be holy; to be perfect in our generous loving, because that is what God our Father is like.

Reflection on the readings

Leviticus 19:1-2, 9-18
Psalm 119:33-40
1 Corinthians 3:10-11, 16-23
Matthew 5:38-48

When those who were adopted as young children meet up with their birth parents, it is often startling and amusing to find that they share some mannerism which must have been inherited but had seemed more like a personal habit. When Jesus talks about our calling to be perfect in such things as generous loving, he gives as his reason the fact that God our Father is perfect. We, as God's children, need to share his characteristics – his 'mannerisms' – an example of which is a tendency to generosity of spirit which is lavish to the point of extravagance.

We are to be like 'chips off the old block', so that the way we live and behave demonstrates to everyone our spiritual parentage. This is not so much learned behaviour, in the way that one might act out a part in a drama production, but more like the natural result of being God's children. When we wake up each morning allowing that to happen, and giving the living God access to our minds, emotions and bodies, then God's natural characteristic of generous loving will start to show through without our having to contort ourselves to achieve it.

Jesus is trying to get us to examine not only our actions but also our motives and our attitudes. We are to think at all times not 'What can I gain out of this?' but 'What can I give away and how can I serve here?' The worldly perception of perfection is measured by a completely different set of success criteria. The ever-present danger is that even Christians soak up the worldly values of success and start applying them to spiritual matters. That leads into the legalistic and judgemental zones which Jesus so deplored. God's way is as happy to use our failures as our strengths, our muddles and mistakes as much as our slick, poised control.

God's way has us viewing cancelled trains and traffic jams, undeserved criticism and demanding phone calls as unscheduled opportunities for learning and possibly serving. It is our God-filled attitude to them that unclenches the tight jaw and relaxes the facial muscles! It may also be what enables us to express our concerns calmly and sort out a workable alternative without being churned up inside with resentment and hidden rage. God's way of generous loving is not only the best way to live; it is also the way God designed us to be, and the way in which we are most fulfilled and most effective.

All-age talk

Bring along a rubber stamp and inkpad, making sure it isn't permanent ink. Begin by putting the stamp on a number of volunteers. Talk about the way we sometimes get stamped at theme parks or discos to show that we have a right to be there because we have paid our entrance fee.

When we are baptised we have the sign of Jesus Christ marked on our foreheads. (What is that sign? It's the cross.) It's as if we've got God's stamp on us. (You could get everyone to trace a cross on their foreheads with their thumb to feel it freshly.) We are marked out as his children, whether we are one-day-old children, twenty-three-year-old children or ninety-seven-year-old children, and we have been freely given the right to belong in God's kingdom, which is a kingdom full of love and peace and joy, patience and kindness, goodness, gentleness and self-control.

As well as us belonging in God's kingdom, God's kingdom now belongs in us! As we've got God's stamp on us we will want to behave like him, and he will help us to do that. Our behaviour will then be a visible sign to other people that we really do belong to God as his children. When they see us being honest and kind and patient and joyful, loving and working for peace and justice, they will be able to say, 'That must be a child of God – look how generous he is, even when he isn't going to gain anything by it!' And, 'That must be a child of God – look how loving she is with those difficult people!'

The whole point is this: we don't work to behave nicely so that God will love us. We don't need to do that, and we can't ever earn his love anyway. God simply loves us! He thinks we're really special, and he always wants the best for us.

When we love him back, and let him work in us, we will find we are beginning to behave more like our God. The closer we get to God, the more generous loving we will find ourselves doing. Instead of looking out for what we can get all the time, we'll find we're looking out eagerly for ways we can give instead! Instead of making sure we are doing whatever *we* want, we'll find we are looking to check if other people are OK. And that is actually a much happier and more fulfilling way to live.

Second Sunday before Lent

Thought for the day

God is creative and good; seeking his rule, as our priority, will mean that everything else falls into place.

Reflection on the readings

Genesis 1:1-2:3
Psalm 136 or 136:1-9, 23-26
Romans 8:18-25
Matthew 6:25-34

As soon as we become aware of the fact that we are individuals, living in somewhere called 'place', the natural human reaction is to start wondering about it. Why are we here? Who are we? How are we here? These are universal, important questions, and enable us to become fully ourselves.

This later version of the creation of the world in Genesis 1 is a glorious poem exploring the deep human wondering, and recognising that in some way God is at the very centre and source of it all, calling creation into being through the creative power of his love. In some sense the parental longing for children and the creative urge of the artistic are the human reflection of the divine love which fashioned us.

Today's readings celebrate the overarching and undergirding love and care of our God. Jesus shows a wonderfully childlike and relaxed assurance about this, which he longs for us to know and share. So much of our time is spent anxiously worrying about things over which we have no control, and it is not God's will that we should go through life harassed and agitated like this. We can learn much from young children here. Toddlers are so good at accepting the way they drop off to sleep in one place and wake up somewhere completely different, while we in the meantime have vacuumed and washed up, fixed them into the car seats, driven through the roadworks and emerged at the supermarket. The sleeping child trusts that the parent will be looking after them. Humans take time to learn to distrust.

Jesus is recommending that we relearn that trust in our Parent God as soon as possible, so we can live freely, basking in the faithful love that will never let us down. It is this security which enables us to meet and cope with all the inevitable stresses and strains of living, because our roots are firmly fixed in what is greater and more profound than anything else.

If that is in place, the rest becomes manageable and less threatening. And once we are feeling our survival unthreatened, we are able and willing to take risks, and accept disappointments and pain without being overwhelmed by them. Eventually, as Paul suggests, all things will be accomplished and transformed.

All-age talk

Beforehand prepare some large speech bubbles from thin card, with the typical worries of those in the congregation written clearly on them. Here are some suggestions:

- My hair's going grey / thin on top!
- What can I wear?
- Weetabix or Coco Pops or toast?
- Suppose they don't like me?
- Brut or Denim – and how much of it?
- I'm the wrong shape!

Ask some volunteers to hold these worries up high. They're the kind of things we all waste our time and energy worrying about. Jesus was sad to see people worrying their lives away, and he wanted them to be free of this constant worrying. Point out that the volunteers will start to get aching arms if they have to go on holding the worries up for too long.

In our Gospel reading today Matthew tells us that Jesus says to us, 'Put all those worries down – they're heavy to carry and are making your arms ache.' Let the volunteers put the worries down, and talk about what a relief it is to have our worries sorted out.

Jesus wants us to know that although life is bound to be full of difficult and uncomfortable times as well as easy and happy times, we don't need to worry about it as well as live through it! That makes it twice as bad for us. The way to be free of worry is not to be massively rich or refuse to grow up, or bury your head in the sand and pretend not to see the problems. The way to be free of worrying yourself sick is to trust that your Parent God loves you, likes you, and is well able to help you cope with everything you'll face in your life.

Jesus suggests we live one day at a time, instead of worrying about things that might never happen, or which are bound to happen, and God will bring us safely through it all to heaven, where we will be safe with God for ever.

Sunday next before Lent

Thought for the day

In Jesus the full glory of God is revealed and encountered.

Reflection on the readings

Exodus 24:12-18
Psalm 2 or Psalm 99
2 Peter 1:16-21
Matthew 17:1-9

Today's Old Testament reading is full of the mystery and awe of God's majesty, symbolised by the devouring fire at the top of the holy mountain of Sinai, and the cloud into which only Moses, the one set apart by God, is allowed to enter. All the people are left down at the bottom of the mountain, gazing up at its distant holiness and the spectacle of almighty God's transcendent power. Chapter 25 goes on to relate the commission God gave Moses on this occasion, to make preparations for building a special sanctuary – a tabernacle – where God will dwell among his people in what became known as the Ark of the Covenant.

The Gospel takes us to another mountain made holy by God's presence there. Matthew tells us that Jesus has taken three of his disciples with him, and as he is praying, communicating directly with his Father, he becomes transfigured, so that Peter, James and John witness the glory of God shining in the human body of Jesus. And into that intimate conversation walk Moses and Elijah, representing the Law and the prophets. To the disciples and to Matthew's original readers, well acquainted with the scriptures, the echoes of Moses' experience on Mount Sinai will have been obvious. It must have seemed almost like a time warp, and perhaps, in a sense, it is, since at such moments of eternity we are as much present with Moses in the holy cloud and Elijah listening to the still small voice as we are with God speaking through Jesus and drawing together past and future at a moment of intense reality and depth of love.

No wonder, then, that Simon Peter refers to the subsequent conversation of God and Moses, and wants to build tabernacles so that God's transcendence can become immanent among his people. But Peter has not yet grasped the extraordinary extent of God's immanence which has now gone far beyond tabernacles. In the person of Jesus, as the transfigured glory shows, God is now personally and intimately among his people in a way never possible before, and the approaching act of self-giving love on the cross, and triumph over death, are going to mean that the personal closeness will be possible far and wide in all places and in all generations, including ours. It is vital that these followers of Jesus understand something of this, and there is urgency in God's voice heard by them encouraging them to trust the amazing identity of his Son and to hang on his words. They have been shown God's glory on the top of the mountain so that they will be better able to recognise God's immanence at the bottom, when the cloud has faded.

All-age talk

Bring along a family photograph album with snaps of holidays or celebrations in it, and if possible a camera which takes instant pictures. Also have two cards to hold up, one with a large plus sign on and the other a large minus sign.

If you have an instant camera, begin by taking a picture of some people or the day's flower arrangement. Show the album and talk about the way we all like to snap away to capture the moments when we are on holiday or at a special celebration, or when our children and grandchildren are growing up. We want to hang on to the moment and cherish it for years to come, because we know the moment itself won't last. The children will soon grow up, and we may never have the chance to visit the Eiffel Tower or Southend illuminations ever again!

The 'plus' side of taking pictures like this (encourage everyone's suggestions) may be that we will remember better if we look back at the picture – it may help us see the importance of the occasion, it helps us pass on the family tradition to the next generation, and it lets us enjoy more at our leisure later than we were able to take in at the time.

The 'minus' side may be that we're so busy taking pictures at the time that we aren't able to concentrate properly on the actual moment.

In the Gospel we heard about something amazing which happened on a mountain in Galilee. Three of Jesus' friends – Peter, James and John – saw Jesus shining with God's glory as he prayed. It was one of those times when Peter wanted to reach for the camera (except that cameras hadn't been invented then) so they could hold on to the wonderful moment for ever. Perhaps they had never before felt God quite so close to them! They even heard God's voice. He wasn't saying, 'I hope you're watching carefully and I'm sorry cameras haven't been invented yet or you could have got a pretty dramatic picture here today!' He was helping them understand the real, actual experience they were in, assuring them that Jesus really was God's Son, and wanting them to listen to Jesus in a way they had never listened before.

God doesn't just want Peter, James and John to know – he wants St Peter's church and St James's and St John's and all the other churches to know. He wants all the people in all the world to know who Jesus is, and he wants us all to pay attention to what Jesus says, and really listen to him with our hearts and minds as well as our ears.

Lent 1

Thought for the day

Jesus knows all about temptation; and he can deal with our sin.

Reflection on the readings

Genesis 2:15-17; 3:1-7
Psalm 32
Romans 5:12-19
Matthew 4:1-11

Temptation always has that element of good sense which makes the sin seem appealing and plausible. We can imagine that Eve could be praised for wanting to stretch the limits of her and Adam's potential; wisdom for the human race was arguably a sensible step in promotion terms. The darker side of temptation is that the illusory good sense masks the basic clear fact that doing or saying or thinking this particular thing is simply wrong. In Adam and Eve's case the serpent's suggestion went against God's instructions, and resulted in them choosing to be disobedient. Typically, what initially looks so attractive turns out to cause misery and confusion. The pattern of temptation and sin is a depressing one, and one for which we can all bring regretful and painful examples to mind.

At which point, God's plan for mending and healing springs thankfully into action in the person of Jesus, who is tempted in exactly the same way we are. First, Satan goes for personal well-being and comfort: making stones into bread. When Jesus stands firm on what is really important, rather than self-centred needs, Satan goes for another favourite: self-doubt. He suggests a good and foolproof way for Jesus to test whether or not he really is God's Son. But, if we look at Jesus' answer, we find he is remembering that putting God to the test like this, as the people of

Israel had done at Massah in the wilderness, is an insult to God's love and faithfulness.

So Satan, homing in on Jesus' loyalty to his Father and his respect and love for him, suggests a clever and speedy way to please God by claiming all the people and presenting them to the Father, just as he is genuinely hoping to do. There's a big catch here, though. Jesus will need to pay for the privilege by worshipping Satan. Satan has overstepped the mark here, and made it plain who he is, and how evil the plan is, so the battle is over, at least for the moment.

If we can copy Jesus in clinging on to the real underlying truths during our temptations, they will eventually emerge to be seen as obviously wrong. The danger in temptation is the point when we are being won over by the persuasive attraction and plausibility, so that our hold on what is right and good is temporarily loosened. It is as if we are temporarily 'off balance' and therefore easy to knock down.

Thankfully, Jesus did much more than wade through terrible temptation without sinning. He went on to take on freely the punishing cursed death which results from sin, and so opened the way back into the garden of hope and promise. As we hold on to Jesus in faith, he enables us to exchange lasting death for full and everlasting life.

All-age talk

Talk about some of the rules we are given, such as 'Wear your seatbelt', 'Don't lean out of the window of a moving train', 'Don't play on the railway line' or 'Don't keep poisons in old lemonade bottles'. Gather ideas about why they are good, sensible rules which are worth keeping. Point out that they are good rules whether we actually know the reasons or not.

Now ask for some volunteers to stand around as trees in the garden of the story from Genesis. Give the volunteers real or paper fruits to hold. God's rule for Adam and Eve was 'Don't eat fruit from this tree'. Hang this rule round the tree in the centre of the garden. Now God has very good reasons for making this rule, based on his love for Adam and Eve and his concern for them. And since God is God, that rule is the most important thing for Adam and Eve to remember. However tasty the fruit looks, whatever they may be told it will do to help them, they are always to keep hold of God's rule (what was it?), and stick to keeping that. Anything that cuts across God's rule must be wrong.

Ask two people who think they will be able to keep to God's rule without disobeying it. These two are going to be Adam and Eve. Show them how tasty the fruit looks and try to persuade them to try it. Tell them that it will do wonderful things for them, and make them wise like God. When they (hopefully) manage to resist the temptation to do what God's rule told them not to, praise them, and then point out that they managed it this time, but we are always being tempted to be disobedient to God's rule of love, and when it next happens we need to stick close to God, and remember his rule: 'Love God and love one another'.

Adam and Eve in the story stand for all of us who are human. And humans tend not to be very good at resisting temptation. God loves us and understands what it is like to be humans being tempted. We know that because Jesus was tempted during his life on earth. He will give us the strength we need to resist those pressures of temptation, but that doesn't mean it's going to be easy. Resisting temptation is *very hard*, and that's why Jesus told us to pray about it every day of our life: 'Lead us not into temptation but deliver us from evil.' Let's use the strength God offers; we need all the help we can get!

Lent 2

Thought for the day

Anyone who believes in Jesus can know his power to save and set us free.

Reflection on the readings

Genesis 12:1-4a
Psalm 121
Romans 4:1-5, 13-17
John 3:1-17

If you want to join the local fitness centre or golf club, it's quite clear what you do – you pay your membership subscription and agree to abide by the rules so that you can enjoy the privileges. Anyone expecting to enjoy the privileges without being fully paid-up members would be shown the door. This is rather how the Jewish people in the early church community felt about the new Gentile believers. They felt they ought to become full members of the Jewish religion in order to take advantage of Jesus' saving work.

Paul is anxious to point out that the real heritage is not through genetics or traditional customs like circumcision. It comes instead through faith. Abraham received God's promise that he would become the father of many nations when he took God at his word and uprooted his whole life. Anyone who has that kind of faith in God is, in effect, a descendant of Abraham.

Nicodemus was struggling with God's broad-mindedness as shown in the way Jesus is living, welcoming the marginalised and the sinners. Can he really be the Messiah? When he came to talk things over with Jesus one night Jesus explained to him that understanding God's ways requires being born into a new dimension. The pragmatic Nicodemus is still puzzled as he is used to taking everything literally and knows people can't scrunch up into womb shapes when they are grown up. But Jesus is trying to help him think spiritually, rather than literally. He tells him that living by faith in God – living 'in the Spirit' – is rather like being blown along in a strong wind, and it's no good trying to cling on to stationary objects to anchor ourselves or we won't be able to allow ourselves to be moved along in God's direction and at God's speed.

That is very difficult because we all tend to want to retain our independent control in life, and allow God access to some areas but not to others. We can thank Nicodemus for being honest about his narrowness and preconceived ideas, thereby giving us the courage to talk over with Jesus the things which puzzle and disturb us about our faith. This is far more healthy and far more likely to promote eventual spiritual growth than denying such feelings to ourselves or feeling guilty about them. Questions are a tried and tested route to understanding, and do in themselves require of us a certain trust, because through our questions we are moving out into uncharted territory.

We can be reassured that wherever God leads us, however strange or disturbing the journey, however our assumptions are challenged, moving in God is an ultimately safe and good place to be, and we will be fully alive both in this age and in eternity.

All-age talk

You will need a hand-held hairdryer (and possibly an extension lead).

Begin by talking about the wind, and how we can tell it is windy, even though the wind itself is invisible. Collect examples of the signs from the congregation. Draw together the signs with the principle that wind makes things move.

Now ask some volunteers to scatter some cut-out paper people on the ground, fixing some firmly to the ground with sticky tack or paperweights. In the Gospel today we overheard a conversation between Jesus and a man called Nicodemus. We know Nicodemus was a Pharisee, and knew lots of clever things.

But Jesus puzzled him. He could see that the miracles Jesus was doing made it look as if Jesus really was God's promised Messiah who they were all waiting for. The problem was, Jesus didn't seem to be sticking rigidly to the rules Nicodemus and the other Pharisees felt he ought to be. He seemed far too broad-minded. He was spending time with sinners.

The good thing about Nicodemus was that he didn't keep his worries to himself, or pretend they weren't there, or reject Jesus because he was making him think about things in a new way. He went to find Jesus one night and talked to him about it all. And that's what we need to do with all our doubts and puzzles and questions.

Jesus gave him some funny answers, and one of the answers was about the wind. He said that living in the Spirit is rather like being blown by the wind. God wants to move us along and he can do that so long as we don't fix ourselves down. Watch how the wind from the hairdryer can move these people. (Switch on the hairdryer and blow the people along.)

Look at these people who were stuck down to the floor. The wind blew but they haven't moved anywhere. And sometimes we are like that. We might sing on Sundays about wanting to live in God's Spirit, but when that means being ready to move or change in our life or our attitudes or ideas, we start fixing ourselves to the floor where we feel safer, and can enjoy moving a little to the breath of God, but not enough to be actually moved along.

This Lent let's work at being brave enough to come to Jesus with the deep worries and puzzles of life, knowing that God is quite able to cope with them and won't suddenly disappear or be offended. And let's work at being brave enough to stand out in the wind of God's Spirit, without fixing ourselves to the spot, but willing for him to move us as a parish and as individuals wherever he wants to move us.

Lent 3

Thought for the day

God both knows us completely and loves us completely; meeting us where we are, he provides us with living water, to satisfy all our needs.

Reflection on the readings

Exodus 17:1-7
Psalm 95
Romans 5:1-11
John 4:5-42

Whether it's a blind date, a job interview or meeting the future in-laws for the first time, we are likely to take extra care with how we look and behave, wanting to show our best selves in order to give a good impression. That is a kind of game we all play. If we really thought about it we'd realise that it has to do with not trusting these strangers to notice our good qualities unless we underline them a bit with some visuals. We may suspect that if they really knew our ordinary messy selves, before they had got to know and enjoy us better, they may well disapprove or dislike us.

With God it's different. We can't 'dress to impress' because God knows us inside out already. When Jesus had that conversation with the woman at Jacob's well in Samaria she was stunned by the sudden realisation that Jesus knew her; he understood where she was coming from and what was important to her, where she was weak and where she was strong. He understood her potential as well as her mistakes. So it did not feel like invaded privacy because, along with the full knowledge, she sensed full acceptance.

Perhaps you have felt yourself shrivel up in the company of those who seem to judge and condemn, and open out and blossom in the company of those who love and delight in you. In the level, direct gaze of the loving God we can all be reassured that we are both known and accepted. That accepting love is like living water which our spirits need to survive and thrive and grow.

Out in the wilderness the people of Israel were well aware of their needs, but they were looking backwards nostalgically, rather than trustingly at the living God to supply them. And that too is a very human reaction. We tend to try all kinds of inferior, stagnant or temporary water supplies rather than going directly to the source of living water which never runs dry, is guaranteed pure and wholesome for us, and is exactly what we need at every changing moment of our journey through life.

All-age talk

You will need some paper cups, one with holes poked in it, a washing-up bowl or bucket and a jug of water.

Remind everyone of the way the people in the desert were very thirsty, and Moses asked God how their thirst could be quenched. He also told God how grumpy everyone was getting – they were so grumpy that Moses began to think they might take their anger out on him physically! God answered by providing water tumbling out of a rock, fresh and pure and delicious. There's nothing more wonderful when you're thirsty than the refreshing sound and taste of water. Now pour some water out and enjoy the sound of it. Invite some thirsty person to drink some from the proper cup. The people wanted to be back in the past, but God wanted to lead them on into the future.

We heard about two more water supplies today. Did anyone notice what they were? One was a well, where a woman had come to collect water, and where Jesus was sitting, feeling thirsty. Perhaps his own thirst reminded him of the people getting grumpy with Moses in the desert, and the way God had given them the flowing, living water they needed.

The other water supply is a bit unusual. Jesus told the woman about some water which would quench her thirst completely, and become a spring of water inside her welling up to give her life that lasts for ever. At first the woman thought this sounded too good to be true! What Jesus was doing was explaining the way God fills our lives, and leads us into the future, satisfying us all the way along, and refreshing us when we are sad and longing for good and right and fair and helpful things to happen in our world. The more we go to God to be filled with his living water of life and love, the more we shall find that we too are becoming sources of love and comfort and fairness and truthfulness for other people.

Let's see what happens when we pour some water into this cup with holes in it. (Station some people around with proper cups.) Pretend this hol(e)y cup is a Christian drinking the living water of life and love from the living, loving God. Can you see how the Christian then pours out that love to other people he or she meets? There's no problem that God will suddenly dry up, because God is living, flowing, for ever. And the other people may well want to become hol(e)y themselves, drinking that eternal supply which they can see is changing us for the better.

So if your life feels rather dry or thirsty or stuck in the past, go to Jesus; keep going to Jesus; and let him fill you up with the living spiritual water that really satisfies. And don't keep it all to yourself – pass it on!

Lent 4

Mothering Sunday

Thought for the day

Thanking God for our earthly opportunities for mothering and being mothered, we also remember the mothering parenthood of God.

Reflection on the readings

Exodus 2:1-10 or 1 Samuel 1:20-28
Psalm 34:11-20 or Psalm 127:1-4
2 Corinthians 1:3-7 or Colossians 3:12-17
Luke 2:33-35 or John 19:25-27

Both Moses and Samuel have touching mother-and-baby stories related in the Old Testament. Samuel was the result of Hannah's answered prayer; she did not forget this once the better times came but kept faith with God, which meant that the whole people of Israel benefited from a spiritual leader and adviser of remarkable integrity and wisdom. Moses inherited the resourcefulness and perseverance in the face of threats shown by his mother as she hid her son among the bulrushes where Pharaoh's daughter was bound to be enchanted by the baby's vulnerability and disarming innocence.

And then we have the words of Simeon, spoken to Mary, when, as a young mother, she and Joseph take the baby Jesus into the temple. Or we stand with the heartbroken Mary at the foot of the cross where her promising son hangs dying a cursed death inflicted by the army of occupation and demanded by the religious leaders and teachers.

In all these mothering stories there is no attempt to sugar or sentimentalise what mothering involves – the pain and aching, the bewildered confusion and times of misunderstanding and grief, as well as all the joy and affection, shared laughter and the delight in watching a human being develop and mature. The Bible tells about the real human condition, and in all this mothering and being mothered we sense something of God's mothering, or parenting, of us. When on the cross Jesus commits his grieving mother into the care of the disciple he loves, we are seeing a wonderful example of the way we are all given to one another to care for and look after.

That is a two-way process: we need to cultivate the art of receiving the mothering as well as giving it. We need to recognise that it may well involve both times of great joy and deep sorrow as we increasingly bear one another's burdens and suffering, and watch one another developing spiritually. Mothering of this sort is rooted in God's parenting of us, and will break our hearts of stone and give us tender hearts of flesh that are willing to give one another both support and space.

All-age talk

Begin by interviewing a couple of mothers, one young and one older, using such questions as: What do you like best about being a mum? What do you find hardest? How has being a mum helped you grow as a person? What advice would you give to a young Christian couple about to become parents?

Talk about the way we all need to look after each other in this unselfish, loving way which we think of as mothering, and how that is the way our loving God treats us. He doesn't smother us or stop us exploring our world and trying everything out, but he encourages us and guides us so we know where to walk safely. If we fall over and hurt ourselves in life, he's there to comfort us and make us better, and if we go off and get ourselves lost in bad or stupid behaviour, he comes to search for us until he finds us, calling our name again and again until we hear him and shout out, asking to be rescued.

When we are little, our parents have to dress us, because we can't do our buttons up or tie our laces on our own. A good way to remember that we are all called to look after one another in a loving, caring way, is to think about it as dressing ourselves in clothes of kindness, forgiveness and patience, compassion, humility and gentleness. As you say this, dress a volunteer or a rag doll in various garments. Finally, to bind everything together, we need love (a belt is tied around the other clothes).

So tomorrow, and every morning when you get dressed, think of yourself also putting on the clothes of kindness, forgiveness and patience, compassion, humility and gentleness, and tie everything together with love. That way we'll be learning to look after one another the way our God looks after us.

Lent 5

Thought for the day

Jesus is the resurrection and the life. He can transform death and despair, in any form, into life and hope.

Reflection on the readings

Ezekiel 37:1-14
Psalm 130
Romans 8:6-11
John 11:1-45

Things don't come much deader than dry scattered bones. It is a powerful image of the totally hopeless, without even a whispered memory of life. Ezekiel the prophet speaks God's unlikely hope to a dislocated and despairing people. In the hands of God there is no abandonment but promise of restoration, bone by bone, sinew by sinew, inbreathed by the Creator's breath.

Psalm 130 echoes the dazed amazement at the way God proves again and again that with the Lord there is mercy and fullness of redemption. In Romans we find the same realisation worked out in a more cerebral way, celebrating the profound truth, born of real experience, that Spirit-filled life is a completely new and fulfilling life, in comparison with which other life seems like a kind of deadness.

And in today's Gospel reading we hear the whole narrative of Lazarus and his sisters, living through his dying and death, while the Lord of life is elsewhere. It is an evocative story, with Jesus portrayed at his most human, and many layers of meaning packed into the event. Why did Jesus delay? What about those conversations, first with Martha and then with Mary?

John is wanting to tell us deep truths about Jesus' total humanity and divinity; if ever a story revealed the nature of

Emmanuel – 'God-with-us' – then this is it. The practical, less emotional Martha is better able to grasp the logic of what it means for the Lord of life to be present, whereas Mary is simply devastated and feels wounded by Jesus' absence which doesn't make sense to her.

We may recognise this terrible sense of loss and distance when in our own lives we feel God ought to be there yet he seems not to be; and Jesus himself knew it on the cross: 'My God, why have you forsaken me?' But it is this raw grief in all its honesty and candour which tears Jesus' heart and shakes him with agonised weeping. With us, too, he is there at such times of raw pain, sharing our searing pain and grief and weeping with us.

Jesus, as the Lord of life, is God's voice speaking right into the darkness of death and drawing out life.

All-age talk

You will need an inflatable ball or a balloon, and, if possible, a dummy used for teaching mouth-to-mouth resuscitation. Otherwise, bring along a large baby doll.

Begin by asking everyone to breathe in deeply, hold their breath while you count to twenty and then let their breath out. They will all have noticed how much we need that air. By the end of just twenty seconds we're getting desperate! Most of the time we breathe in and out without even thinking about it. Although it's such a vitally important thing to do, we're designed so that the breathing mostly goes on automatically so we can do lots of other things at the same time. Yet without that breathing we wouldn't be able to do any of those other things because we would be dead. That's how important breath is – it's a matter of life and death.

Ask a volunteer to demonstrate what we have to do if we come across someone whose breathing has stopped. Point out that what is happening when we are doing mouth-to-mouth resuscitation is that we actually do the breathing for the other person. With our living breath we can save someone's life.

Today in the Gospel we have heard an amazing story of Jesus actually bringing someone back to life. It was his friend Lazarus, and when Jesus' voice, as the Lord of life, broke into the place of death, Lazarus heard his name being called and walked out into life again towards that voice.

Jesus calls each of us by name. He calls into the place we are, even if that place is full of darkness and sadness, or if the noise of unimportant things we like wasting our time on nearly drowns his voice, or if we're running as fast as we can away from God's way of living. Wherever we are, Jesus keeps calling because he wants to bring us out into new life. He knows his breath in us will transform our time in this life, and beyond that into the time after our physical death. As Jesus breathes his life into us it will make such a difference to us that we'll wish we'd gone for it ages ago!

Ask someone to blow up the ball or balloon, and as they do so point out what a difference it is making to have that breath inside. Once they are filled with our breath they have a whole new dimension – they're much more useful and they're much more their true selves. It's the same with us. When we let God breathe his life into us every minute of every day, we become much more our true selves, our life has a whole new dimension, and we are of more use to God in caring for the world he loves.

Palm Sunday

Thought for the day

Jesus rides into Jerusalem cheered by the crowds. Days later crowds will be clamouring for his death.

Reflection on the readings

Liturgy of the Palms:
Matthew 21:1-11
Psalm 118:1-2, 19-29

Liturgy of the Passion:
Isaiah 50:4-9a
Psalm 31:9-16
Philippians 2:5-11
Matthew 26:14–27:66 or Matthew 27:11-54

Today we begin the heightened drama of the walk through a week known as holy. Since Christmas we have traced the life of Jesus through his birth, childhood, Baptism and preparation in the wilderness, and touched on the main areas of his ministry; and now we come to that final week of his earthly life. All the Gospel writers move into noticeably greater detail in their narratives, with these events taking up a sizeable proportion of each Gospel. The words and events are carefully and thoroughly recorded, in keeping with the intense significance of these days which focus all of life before them and all that has happened since.

Quite deliberately, the readings and liturgy take us on a roller-coaster of spiritual experience. We stand with the ecstatic crowds waving palm branches and celebrating the entry into Jerusalem, the holy city, by Jesus the Messiah. There is great hope and expectation that final things are drawing to accomplishment. We are poignantly aware that Jesus is both acknowledging the crowd's excitement at his kingship and also trying to show them something of the true nature of his kingship which has nothing to do with temporal power and wealth or narrow nationalism.

And then we are gripped by the detailed seriousness of all that led up to the crucifixion, like a profound family memory indelibly written on hearts and handed down with great care and reverence from generation to generation. We both cry out against what is happening and also know it to be necessary and inevitable. We both balk at the way people could treat Jesus, the Lord of life, and also know that we do it ourselves every day. We recognise the utter failure and futility of it all and also know it to be the strangest and most complete victory for the entire world.

All-age talk

Have the London underground map printed out on the weekly sheet, or have some larger versions available to show everyone.

Look at the plan and talk about the way it is simple sign language to help us make sense of a huge complicated network of rails and tunnels criss-crossing under the streets. The whole thing is so enormous to understand that we need this simple map.

But when we travel on the underground it only works because, as well as the simple map in our hand or on the station wall, the real massive tracks are laid in all those dark tunnels, and the electrical power is surging through all the thick cables, and the tilers have been busy fixing tiles on the station walls, and the computers are busy checking where each train is so that they don't bump into one another, and those moving stairs, the escalators, are well oiled and running smoothly. Although all this doesn't show up on our plan of coloured lines and blobs, we only have to look at it and we know that all the real stuff is right there.

In a way the cross shape is like one of those plans. Draw people's attention to the crosses they can see around them in church. It is only a simple shape, and we can all make it ourselves by placing one index finger across the other. (Do that now.) When people say 'fingers crossed' what do they do? (Ask some people to show this.) Today it usually means hoping we'll be lucky, but a long time ago it was people making the sign of the cross as they prayed about something they were worried about. (We could go back to using the sign that way!)

Now if the shape of the cross is like the underground train plan, what is all the real, deep stuff that the cross reminds us of? Ask everyone to find or make a cross and look at it, as you tell them about the deeper meaning: God loves the world so much that he was willing to give up everything, and come and live with us in person as Jesus. That loving led him to a cross where he gave up his life for us, taking all the selfishness and sin on himself, and stretching out his arms in welcome and forgiveness, because he so longs for us to be free.

Easter Day

Thought for the day

It is true. Jesus is alive for all time. The Lord of life cannot be held by death. God's victory over sin and death means that new life for us is a reality.

Reflection on the readings

Acts 10:34-43 or Jeremiah 31:1-6
Psalm 118:1-2, 14-24
Colossians 3:1-4 or Acts 10:34-43
John 20:1-18 or Matthew 28:1-10

Just as in the story of creation, God rests on the Sabbath, when his great, creative work is complete, so now there has been a Sabbath of rest following the completion of this great re-creative work of salvation. In Jesus' last cry on the cross, 'It is finished!', there was the sense of accomplishment and completion, and now, in the dark of early morning on Sunday, the tomb is no place to stay and linger.

It is wonderfully human that all the accounts of the resurrection are slightly different; just as in any life-changing, dynamic event, people's accounts of the details are fused with their attempts to interpret and grasp the significance of what has happened. What is clear beyond all doubt is that somehow they began to understand the extraordinary truth – that Jesus had died but was no longer dead, in the human sense of the word. He was totally alive, but not in the merely human way – like Lazarus, for instance – where it would only be a matter of time before death came again.

Jesus, having gone into death with the power of life, and with his selfless love untarnished, could not be held there, but broke out into a new kind of life which is never going to end. Compared with this life, death is shadowy and powerless; it is temporary suffering and a journey of darkness which leads into unending daylight.

Peter and the other disciples can tell it from first-hand experience. They have actually seen Jesus fully alive, and have even eaten and drunk with him. Not that they were any different from the rest of us in finding it all impossible at first to imagine and believe; Jesus had been preparing them for this, but they still didn't really expect it to happen. After all, full life like this, after that very definite and horrific death through crucifixion, is simply impossible. Isn't it?

Like a catapult that has been pulled and stretched right back in one direction, the force of a sudden change of direction is very vigorous. Having been through the bewildered acceptance of Jesus' death and having lived a couple of days with numbing absence, the truth shoots them into a passion for telling everyone the amazing news, once they are equipped with the Holy Spirit's anointing. It is those who are witnesses to what God has done in their lives who tell the good news of the Gospel for real. And that is what convinces others of a truth which has the power to transform their entire life, both in time and after death.

All-age talk

Bring along a few fresh eggs in a carton, and a chocolate egg.

Begin by reminding everyone that we are here for an exciting celebration. Draw attention to all the flowers, and the cleaning that has been going on, and any banners or other special Easter decorations and symbols. What is it we're celebrating? That Jesus had died on the cross and is now alive – alive for ever!

Introduce the chocolate egg. For some reason we've been seeing a lot of these at Easter. No doubt some people gave some away. No doubt some ate one before breakfast! What have they got to do with Jesus? Why do we all like to give one another eggs at Easter time?

One reason is that people were giving one another eggs around the time of Easter long before they had heard about Jesus. This is springtime, and eggs are all part of the spring, with its promise of new life.

New life! That's interesting – we've been hearing about the new life that Jesus gives us. When people came to our country and told us about Jesus, they thought the egg was a very good way of explaining the Gospel, so they kept it.

How does an egg help us to understand the Easter story? Show everyone the carton of ordinary eggs, and hold one up on its own. What is it? (An egg.) What comes out of a fertilised egg like this? (A chicken.) Yes, it's a new life – in this case a chicken. An egg is the way new creatures come into being. And Easter is about Jesus being alive in a new way and making it possible for all of us to be given new life.

What does the inside of an egg look like? (It's got yellow yolk and some thick runny stuff which is white when it's cooked.) What are some favourite ways of eating an egg? (Gather suggestions.) So what is inside the shell turns into something quite different. Jesus' life now, as from the first Easter Day, is different. For a start, he's never going to die again; his new life isn't a life that runs out. Even though Jesus has now been alive again for nearly two thousand years, he is outside time, so he hasn't got old. And he isn't tied to space like us, so he can come and go without having to catch a bus or open doors. He doesn't have to be seen to be real.

Now break one of the eggs. When we enjoy eating an egg the shell needs to be broken; otherwise we wouldn't be able to get at the white and the yolk. When a chick is ready to live in the big wide world it has to crack the eggshell before it can climb out. What does that tell us? Sometimes we want to hang on to things just as they are. We don't always want to change, even if change in our lives is for the best.

Will we let our shells be broken ready for the new life Jesus wants us to have? God is calling us out of our shells into a whole new, different way of living. It is the loving way of living, trusting in God with our heart and soul and mind and strength, and loving one another. That may mean that some of our habits and fears may, like shells, have to be broken before we can live freely in the loving way. The good news of Easter is that Jesus has already broken through death and sin, so if we hold on to him, he can bring us through the shell breaking and out into the light and space of day – a daylight which lasts for ever.

Easter 2

Thought for the day

Through the risen Jesus we have a living hope which will never spoil or fade.

Reflection on the readings

Acts 2:14a, 22-32
Psalm 16
1 Peter 1:3-9
John 20:19-31

In these Easter readings we have a rather intriguing perspective, since we hear first from the post-Holy Spirit days and then go back to the events close to the Resurrection in the Gospel reading. It has the effect of sharpening our senses, making us more aware of the changes in this group of disciples. Peter is confident and speaks out in authority to the listening crowd. He seems to have got his act together, and has obviously been reflecting deeply on the way in which Jesus has fulfilled the prophecies of Scripture in a quite extraordinary and largely unexpected way. He has been able to see how his Jewish heritage is wonderfully enriched and given fresh meaning, and he cannot wait to share these insights with his fellow Israelites, so that they, too, can experience the liberation of living the new life.

His enthusiasm and confidence continue in the reading from 1 Peter, where he encourages those having to endure very real and terrifying suffering for their faith. Only someone who had also suffered would be able to make such assertions with any credibility, and Peter speaks from the heart. He knows what it feels like to be scared of standing up for what you believe in; he knows what it feels like to fail miserably after good intentions, when you try to do things in your own strength. And he also knows that even the most timid of us can cope with anything when we are living the risen life in the power of Jesus Christ.

The Gospel shoots us back to a very anxious group of people, terrified of the Jewish authorities even though they are (apart from Thomas at this stage) actually convinced that Jesus is alive. Although they know he is risen, they have not yet accessed the power of that risen life, and have at present the boldness of mashed potato.

What Jesus does is to reassure them by his visible and tangible presence. There is a wonderful sense of normality in his greeting. When someone we love has died, and our life seems thrown up in the air and is falling slowly in pieces around us, what we crave is for things to be back to normal again. Jesus understands this, and provides his friends with the reassuring presence they need. Then he breathes into them, as Adam was breathed into at the creation. This breath is what gives the disciples the power of new life, and with it comes the conferring of authority, whose hidden side is responsibility. Like Jesus they are sent out, as the word 'apostle' proclaims, to tell the good news with confidence in the living spirit of Jesus.

Thomas was also scared. He was scared, like many of us, of being taken for a ride – of belief being only wish-fulfilment. Thomas was going to stick to an honest recognition of where he stood until he had definite proof. When he is offered it, he finds he no longer needs it; the sight of Jesus is quite enough. Suddenly prophetic, Jesus acknowledges the faith of all those, including us, who do not have the benefit of visual and tactile sightings of Jesus, and yet are still able to believe in him and share his risen life.

All-age talk

Ask for one volunteer who is brave and one who is more scared and timid. Tell the timid one that you are asking them to fall backwards. You promise them they won't come to any harm (but you don't say you will catch them). Suggest that they watch the brave volunteer to try it first, so they can see what happens. Now ask the brave volunteer to fall backwards, and make sure you catch them, or arrange to have someone strong to catch them.

Now ask if the timid person is able to try it, now that they have seen that it is safe. If they are, let them try it, making certain they are safely caught!

Sometimes it is very hard to know whether we can trust something or not unless we have seen it in action. Perhaps we have bought a tape recorder, or a jigsaw puzzle at a boot sale or a jumble sale, and it looks fine, and we are assured that it's in good working order. But when we get home we find the tape recorder chews up our favourite tape, and the jigsaw puzzle has two or three pieces missing.

It's all very disappointing to be let down like that. And the longer we live, and the more we are let down by things or by people, the more disappointed we get, and the more determined we are not to trust anyone or anything in case we are let down again. Thomas was a bit like that. He had probably been badly let down by people during his life. Like lots of us, it made him scared to trust good news. We and Thomas would love good news to be true, but we'd rather not trust it at all than trust it and risk being let down.

Now Jesus himself knows that he is alive, and will stay alive for ever. He knows it would be quite safe for us to believe this, because he knows it's true! He hopes very much that we will be able to believe, because he knows it will make such a wonderful difference to our lives – we'll be able to live in a new kind of freedom, and become more and more our real selves.

So what does he do about it? In our Gospel reading today we heard how Jesus came into the room, joining his friends as they were praying, so that they knew he was there. And Jesus still does that, nearly two thousand years later. He is here now, with us, his friends. Whenever we gather in Jesus' name, he joins us. When we live on the lookout for him, we'll find we start noticing him more and more. We won't see him with our eyes, but we'll feel his love and peace, and suddenly know he is there.

Easter 3

Thought for the day

Jesus explains the scriptures and is recognised in the breaking of bread.

Reflection on the readings

Acts 2:14a, 36-41
Psalm 116:1-4, 12-19
1 Peter 1:17-23
Luke 24:13-35

Once again our first reading takes us into the middle of a crowd of people who are listening, devastated, to Peter, as he speaks powerfully about who Jesus is, and the terrible truth begins to dawn on them that they have all been instrumental in annihilating the Messiah, the hope of the nations. Yet Peter is not proclaiming God's imminent judgement but his fulsome mercy and offer of forgiveness. Somehow this God of limitless love is able to take anything and transform it; we can know this for certain because in Jesus he has taken death itself – and a cursed death – and turned it into Resurrection, with new and lasting life.

The Psalm for today celebrates that wonderful sense of release as God frees us from our chains, whatever they are; and in his letter, Peter writes of the cost of our freeing, which points to such an extraordinary love that it draws out love in us both towards God and towards one another.

We are then taken back to that period of numb misery after the crucifixion, when all hope seemed dead for ever. We are on a road, with two grieving and confused disciples of Jesus, walking away from Jerusalem towards the town of Emmaus where they lived. Why was it that Jesus drew alongside these particular people, we may wonder. Perhaps his heart went out to them as a shepherd might look at his sheep who are in pain and lost and don't understand. Certainly Cleophas, who presumably shared this detailed account with Luke, recognises the low point their faith had reached and doesn't try to hide that.

Jesus walks along in the same direction they are going, leading them patiently and carefully to see the hints and clues in the scriptures which point to the necessity for the Messiah to suffer and die before being glorified. When they near their home, Jesus gives them the option of taking his words thus far and no further. He never forces his company on us. But the disciples can't bear to part from him now, and as he breaks bread they suddenly realise who he is, at which moment he no longer needs to be visible to them. They rush straight back, seven or eight miles, to Jerusalem, in their utter joy and excitement.

With us, too, Jesus draws alongside and helps us understand the words of scripture. He gives us the option of walking with him no further. And whenever we invite him to stay, he comes in and shares bread with us. Whenever we meet together and break bread in Jesus' name, Jesus is there in person among us, and very often that presence is almost tangible as we sense his love and his peace.

All-age talk

Bring in some kind of game or piece of equipment which needs putting together and setting up properly before it can be used. This could be anything from a computer to a folding bed – it all depends on what is available and the interest area of the congregation. It needs to have a set of instructions to go with it.

Begin by introducing your item of equipment. We are continuing to look at the resurrection stories, when one person after another is astonished by amazing events. The congregation may well be astonished to see one of these brought into church for the sermon! Pretend that you are having a real problem with this thing because you don't understand it at all. You don't understand how to get it to work.

Have a primed helper who comes up at this stage and shows you the instruction leaflet. They tell you that if you read that it will tell you how the thing works and how to use it. Be surprised, but set to reading some of the instructions, without relating them to the equipment. They don't make much sense to you, and you get fed up. It's no good – you don't understand and it doesn't make sense.

Explain that this is rather like the way the two disciples felt as they walked sadly back home on the very first Easter Day. They didn't understand anything any more. They had great hopes about Jesus, but now he was dead, so their hopes were dead as well. They had heard about the women saying they had seen Jesus alive early that morning, but that didn't make any sense to them either. How on earth could someone be dead as dead and now be alive? It couldn't possibly be true!

Just then, as we heard in the Gospel just now, someone joined them and asked what they were so sad about. And when they told him, he started to show them how it actually did make a lot of sense. (Break off as the helper comes and offers to take you through the instructions and sort the equipment out. Accept their help and marvel as gradually, step by step, it starts to come together, and eventually works. Be excited about this and thank the helper. Then come back to the Emmaus story.)

Well, it certainly helps to have someone who really understands to help you when you are in a muddle! That's how those disciples felt when the stranger explained that it was all there in the scriptures (pick up a Bible) about the promised Messiah having to suffer and die before there could be new life. When they reached their home they invited the helpful stranger in to stay with them, and when their guest took the bread and blessed and broke it (mime this) . . . what do you think they suddenly realised?

It was Jesus!

And that is still what Jesus does. He walks along with us where we are walking. He helps us understand about God through the words of scripture (pick up the Bible again), he helps us make sense of life and its problems (stand beside the working piece of equipment), and (move to the altar) he makes himself known to us in the breaking of bread.

Easter 4

Thought for the day

Jesus, the Good Shepherd, has come so that we may have life in rich abundance.

Reflection on the readings

Acts 2:42-47
Psalm 23
1 Peter 2:19-25
John 10:1-10

Reading today's passage from Acts 2 is rather like being given a photo album of the Early Church to look through. There are snapshots of the community which give us some idea, in a few sentences, of how it all worked and what made it hum. We see the people at worship, making their financial commitments and decisions, working in loving service wherever there are needs, and simply enjoying themselves together. We can imagine similar snapshots with the familiar faces of our own church communities. Permeating all the worship and all the action is a fresh amazement at the power of God; the Resurrection plugs the Church into the reality of God's dynamic immanence. In God's frame of reference, it is still only like yesterday that the Resurrection happened; every Sunday we can 're-member it' – in other words, 'put it all together again' in our minds so that we never lose the freshness.

This freshness will affect the way we live out our faith, as the passage from 1 Peter reminds us. It is so easy to get back into the old habits and mind-sets where we are entitled to moan and protest about any hardship or punitive treatment we don't consider we deserve. But Peter takes issue with that way of thinking. Suppose we turned it on its head, taking Christ as our example? Suppose we were able to consider all those unjustified sufferings not simply as painful (which they certainly are, of course) but also as a kind of privilege to be taken to God for transforming, rather like raw diamonds which we might take to be expertly cut and polished.

Could we then treat those insults and unkindnesses towards us with more grace and reverence – as raw hope in the making, perhaps? And as we wrestled to live out God's foolishness like this, could it be that we would actually be involved in a huge and vital strengthening of the whole body of Christ, worked out in each of our individual battles, whenever joyful self-giving triumphed over self, and unlimited loving over presumed rights?

The possibility sets alarm bells ringing in us, as we recognise the risk of exposure and vulnerability involved in such complete self-giving. Are we prepared to trust God that much? Isn't it all too much to expect?

Today's Gospel shows us a God who is not out to get us, to steal from us or put us down. He is not in the business of destructive behaviour; he is not wanting to wear us down with guilt or demand of us more than we can possibly give. Sadly the Church has sometimes given this impression, and sent the sheep racing away in understandable alarm. But the image Jesus chooses is of a shepherd whom the sheep sense they can trust, and who will only use his power to provide wisely and faithfully for those in his care. In that care they are free to come and go, living out their lives doing what sheep do without panic or confusion.

What does that mean for us? We too are like sheep in the way we tend to panic and scatter, the way we are so vulnerable to following wrong values, empty and unsatisfying lifestyles, and unprincipled and irresponsible leaders. We desperately need the Good Shepherd, but need so much coaxing before we realise it. I sometimes wonder if the angels of heaven are standing around like the spectators at sheepdog trials, willing those sheep to go where they need to and cheering when they finally get the message!

Yet in the keeping of the Good Shepherd we are set free to live out our lives more truly as ourselves than ever before.

All-age talk

Using chairs, build a circular sheepfold, with a gap for the entrance. Ask for some volunteer sheep to go inside. Explain that this is what a sheepfold was like in Jesus' day, except that it was made of stones, not chairs. Is there a door? No, there isn't. That's because the shepherd himself was the door. Ask a volunteer shepherd to come and be the door of the sheepfold. (You could even give the shepherd a stick or crook from the Nativity costumes, and a shepherd's sling.) Why is this living door likely to be a good safe one for the sheep? Because the shepherd would hear any dangers, such as wolves, or bears, or sheep stealers, and take action to protect the sheep, using his staff or sling. (The shepherd can pretend to frighten off a dangerous wolf.)

Another thing about sheep is that they get very frightened by lots of things, but when they hear the voice of the shepherd at the door they know they can trust him, and they feel safe. They will even follow him when he calls them and leads them off to some good juicy grass. (The sheep can try this.) And then they will follow the shepherd back home at the end of the day. (They do this.)

Now why are we getting a lesson in sheep farming this morning? What has all this got to do with Jesus? Or us?

In the Gospel today we heard Jesus telling the people that he is the sheep-door. (And you know what that means, now.) He told them all about the sheep being safe when the shepherd is the door, and the sheep knowing the shepherd's voice and following him. (You know about that too.) But the people didn't have a clue why Jesus was talking to them about sheep and shepherds. So they asked him to explain.

Jesus said he was trying to tell them something important about God. (Can anyone think what it was?) He was telling the people that they were a bit like sheep and Jesus was like the good shepherd who lies down in the doorway to keep the sheep safe. He was saying that God looks after us and defends us with his life because he loves us so much. He hates the thought of us coming to harm, and fights off evil. We can trust God's voice when he calls us, and follow him without any fear because we know God is always faithful and good and loving.

So whenever you are scared to face a bad problem, or bad ideas and temptations keep coming at you, stand there in the sheepfold behind Jesus, the sheep-door, and you will be safe. And whenever you are muddled about whether to do something or not, or whether to be selfish or not, listen out for the quiet calling of the Good Shepherd (you won't hear it with your ears, but you will know it in yourself) and follow him into the way that is right and good and kind and loving.

Easter 5

Thought for the day

Jesus is the Way, the Truth and the Life, through whom we can come into the presence of God for ever.

Reflection on the readings

Acts 7:55-60
Psalm 31:1-5, 15-16
1 Peter 2:2-10
John 14:1-14

Rocks are solid things, which makes them very strong as foundations but exceedingly painful and obstinate to kick. They do not give. This makes the rocky image given to us by Peter, himself nicknamed 'the rock', such a splendid one for helping us visualise the utter faithfulness and solid assurance of Jesus. Being built up on such a foundation is an exciting prospect for the household of faith. And the building depends on those living stones in every generation which continue to be added to the great living temple of worship and praise. Like stones we are to be strong in our faith, a faith that is not merely existing but fully and dynamically alive. What a Church it can be, when it is firmly set on the foundation of Christ and built through his power alone with the offered lives and gifts and sufferings and struggles of millions and millions of ordinary human beings!

We have a wonderful example of just one of those living stones to inspire us today. As we watch the young man, Stephen, standing gazing into heaven as stones of hatred, misunderstanding, misplaced zeal and righteous indignation are hurled at him, we can see how his faith fixes him securely, even as he is being put to death. His loving forgiveness of his enemies proclaims the reality of his faith – it stands the worst testing and still holds.

How does he do it, we may ask? Perhaps we find ourselves feeling not so much inspired as dampened by people who seem to have such great faith when we are trying to muddle along and are woefully aware of how inadequately we witness to Christ most of the time. Perhaps we feel more in common with Philip, as he tries so hard to understand what Jesus is saying, but is thinking on a completely different plane, unable to put the signs and clues together and come up with a meaningful answer. It took the death and resurrection of Jesus for things to suddenly start making sense to the disciples, and that is still true for us today. Still it is the death and resurrection of Jesus which enables everything else to make sense.

In the light of Jesus' death and resurrection we can grasp that he really is the Way, the Truth and the Life. It is through believing in this Jesus, who gave up his life in total self-giving love for us, and lived out for us in human terms the loving nature of almighty God, that we too can die to sin and be brought into a new life relationship with God which is valid both in time and eternity. So the Way is not a code of behaviour but a relationship with a person. And that is as basic to our human experience and need as the child/parent bonding which is also present from birth, rather than the codes of behaviour which are only later acquired.

It is a living, personal relationship that Jesus offers and hopes for us to accept. The relationship will never end, but will continue getting deeper and more satisfying, and continue developing and strengthening us in our faith, throughout our entire life.

All-age talk

Ask two or three experts to come and explain the way they do whatever it is they are good at. (The actual areas of expertise depend on the interests of your congregation, but try and choose people from representative age and interest groups. The skill should be capable of being demonstrated in front of everyone, so it could be ironing, juggling, dribbling a football, doing a cartwheel or skipping, for example.)

First ask each one to explain it to you, placing them out of sight of everyone as they do so. Share with the congregation how it all sounds incredibly complicated, and difficult to follow, even though it is obviously expert advice. That's rather how it is with the Old Testament Law – everyone respects it highly and it's very good advice for living, but somehow we never seem to manage to follow the instructions or get the hang of them. They help us to know how to live a good life, but they don't change us so that we are able to do it. Some of the prophets had told everyone that one day it would be different. People wouldn't need those instructions any more, because they would already know, in their hearts, how to behave properly.

Let's find out if we can understand our experts any better if we can actually see them doing these clever things. (Invite them to demonstrate, one by one.) Ah, that's much clearer! We may not be able to do it ourselves, yet, but at least we have their example in front of us, to learn from and copy. (Someone might like to try copying one of the skills.)

When Jesus came, it was like being able to see God's way of living – in person. 'So that's what it means to love God and love one another!' people thought. 'So that's what God's love for us is like!' And even though we may not yet be able to do it very well, at least we have a wonderful example to learn from and copy.

If we're still full of bitterness about something that happened to us long ago, we can look at Jesus and copy his forgiving. If we're looking down on someone because they aren't as clever or rich as us, we can look at Jesus and copy his way of enjoying people and accepting them for what they are. If we are always worrying about clothes and possessions, we can look at Jesus and copy his simple way of living, and spend our energy cultivating the treasures that we can take with us to heaven. So Jesus is like a living 'Way' – he's a walking, talking Way to live.

In fact that's what Jesus called himself in our Gospel today; he said, 'I am the Way, the Truth and the Life'. With Jesus we go one better than having his example to copy – since the Resurrection we can have his life living in us! That would be rather like our experts being able to fill us with all that makes them able to do those clever things. Imagine what a skilled parish we would be if that were possible! We'd all be expert ironers, football dribblers, jugglers and cartwheelers! Well, I have to tell you that we can't do that. As humans we have to pass on our skills the hard way, by teaching and learning. But with Jesus it's different. He really can live in our lives, enabling us to love God and one another. All we need to do is invite him into our personal lives and our church, and be prepared to be gradually transformed.

Easter 6

Thought for the day

The Spirit of truth, given to us, enables us to discern the living, risen Christ.

Reflection on the readings

Acts 17:22-31
Psalm 66:8-20
1 Peter 3:13-22
John 14:15-21

It wasn't just that the Greek people were hedging their bets by building an altar to the unknown god. It was also part of their spirituality that in all their deities they were seeking to get in touch with the unknowable – the ultimate reality – which defies human knowing. That hit a chord with Paul, because he could see how Jesus was not only fulfilling the Judaic law, but also all the other genuine human attempts to grasp the mysteries of God's truth. They were right; if it weren't for Jesus, the essence of ultimate reality would continue to be hidden from our sight and understanding.

What God chose to do through the Incarnation was to draw close to his beloved people in such a way that they could see what this mystery we call God was like, in human terms of reference. That had to include a demonstration of what love means even in the face of total cursing and rejection, and God went ahead and showed that, too, in the death of Jesus. It had to include a demonstration of how this power of creative life is even stronger than death – which is, in human terms, annihilation and destruction. So God went ahead and did it. It's called the Resurrection.

In our continued reading of Peter's letter, we are advised to hold on, literally for dear life, to this Christ, who is God's dependable love, and brings us through all suffering with the dynamism of resurrection life. Peter likens our Baptism into faith, using the dramatic symbol of drowning and washing, to the way Noah and his family were brought through the destructive flood waters to a new life experience and a fresh start. And we know we are in that new life by the experience of being alive in Christ.

The reading from John's Gospel unpacks that for us a bit. What do people look like who are living Christ's risen life? How would we know one if we saw one? John states Jesus' words with a straightforward bluntness that does not let us hide behind high-sounding and noble ideals: it is the way we live obediently to the commands of love that sets us apart and proves that we are followers of the way of Christ. Well-intentioned, but never getting round to it, is not part of the deal. Neither are excuses, cop-out clauses or allowable exceptions. It is quite clear from today's Gospel reading that if we really love, we will live that love out, not in a fair-weather friendship, but in a sacrificial way that often chafes and hurts, and leads us in ways we may not have taken by the comfort choice.

And what is the point of choosing such a path? What is in it for us? Jesus promises that, through the gift of the Spirit of Truth, we will become intimate friends with the almighty and merciful God, and will increasingly be honoured with discerning his presence, not as a memory or a hope, but as a real experience of the living person who brought us into being, redeemed us and loves us for ever.

All-age talk

Start by displaying a fairly simple equation, such as $2x+3=x+10$, or $y(5+2)=21$, or $x+4=6$ (difficulty depends on your congregation), perhaps on a blackboard. Provide chalk, and ask someone mathematical to take us through the stages of solving the mystery of this unknown value of x or y.

When Paul was in Athens he saw an altar to 'the unknown god', and set about explaining to the people who this God was. It was as if the people had been calling God 'x'. Now when we tried to solve our *x* mystery, we worked it out, step by step, gradually getting a clearer idea of what *x* meant, until, in the end, it was quite clear to us (or some of us!).

That's rather like the way we can look at the beauty and order of our world, and all the physics and chemistry of it, and all the variety and colour and shape in it, and begin to work our way towards discovering what God is like. We can work out that he must be clever and thoughtful, and imaginative and faithful, for instance.

But with Jesus coming, and showing us exactly what God is like, it's more like this.

Set up the same equation as before, using solid shapes, like building blocks. Each *x* is a bag, filled with the correct number of blocks. We could still work out what *x* is, but if the bag is opened, we can actually see what it is. (Do this.)

With Jesus' life there in front of us through reading the Gospels, and through living in his company every day, we can have a very clear idea of what God is like. We can see that he is forgiving and totally honest and good, that he is responsible and stands up for what is right, whatever happens to him and however much people sneer. We can see that he looks for the good in people and doesn't condemn them or give up on them. We can see that his love has been proved stronger than death.

If we put our faith in that God, whom Jesus has revealed to us in a new and clear way, and if we claim to love him, then we will have to start doing what he says. Who finds it easy to be obedient? Most of us find it very hard. We don't want to do what we are told; we want to do what we like!

Jesus says that the way you can tell if someone really does believe in him and love him, is by whether they are obedient to him, and obey what he says. That means listening to God and saying yes to him, whether it's what we want to do or not.

That is a *very hard* thing to learn, but it's worth learning, because being friends with Jesus is the best and happiest thing that could ever happen to us.

Ascension Day

Thought for the day

Having bought back our freedom with the giving of his life, Jesus enters into the full glory to which he is entitled.

Reflection on the readings

Acts 1:1-11 or Daniel 7:9-14
Psalm 47 or Psalm 93
Ephesians 1:15-23 or Acts 1:1-11
Luke 24:44-53

The Ascension marks the end of Jesus' appearances on earth and his physical, historical ministry. It is also a beginning, because this moving away from the confining qualities of time and place means that Jesus will be present always and everywhere. It also means that the humanity of Jesus is now within the nature of the wholeness of God. Our God has scarred hands and feet, and knows what it is like to be severely tempted, acclaimed and despised.

In a way, it is at the Ascension that the value of all the risk and suffering involved in the Incarnation becomes apparent. The saving victim takes his rightful place in the glory of heaven, and only that can enable God's Holy Spirit to be poured out in wave upon wave of loving power that stretches to all peoples in all generations.

Amazingly our own parish, our own congregation, is part of this glorious celebration with its far-reaching effects. Each of us, living squashed into a particular time frame lasting merely a lifetime, can be drenched in the power of that Spirit, and caught up in the energising nature of it.

As we celebrate the Ascension we, like the disciples, are expectant with joy at the prospect of the gifts God has in store, and yet still mulling over the breathtaking events of Easter. It is like being in the still centre, in the eye of the storm.

All-age talk

Begin by staging a Mexican wave, which runs through the whole church or assembly. Point out how it only worked so well because all of us as individuals were working together as a unit of energy.

Remind everyone of the events leading up to today, giving them a whistle-stop tour of Jesus' life, death, Resurrection and post-Resurrection appearances. Explain how the disciples needed that time to get used to Jesus being alive and around, though not always visible or physically present.

Now they were ready for the next stage in the plan. Jesus leads them out of the city and he gives them his blessing, telling them to hang around Jerusalem without rushing off to do their own bit of mission work. (Enthusiasm is wonderful but it can sometimes make us race off to start before we've got everything we need.) The disciples have got to wait because God is going to send the Holy Spirit to empower them and equip them for the work they will be doing. It will make it possible for the news of God's love to spread out through the world like our Mexican wave.

When Jesus had finished giving the disciples their instructions and his encouragement, we are told that the disciples watched him being taken into heaven, until a cloud hid him from their sight. Those are the only practical details we have, so we don't know exactly how it happened. But we do know that the disciples were in no doubt about where Jesus had gone, and they were full of joy and excitement as they made their way back to the city to wait for the Holy Spirit, as Jesus had told them to.

A lot of years have gone by since Jesus ascended into heaven – nearly two thousand years. But that isn't much if you aren't stuck in time as we are, and God isn't stuck in time. He's prepared to wait to give us humans the chance to turn to him in our lives, and we don't know the date when Jesus will return. We do know that in God's good time he will come back, and everyone will see his glory together, both the living and those who have finished the earthly part of their life.

In the meantime, we have been given the Holy Spirit, so that God can be with us in person every moment of our life, helping us and guiding our choices, steering us safely through temptations, and teaching us more and more about our amazing God. All he waits for is to be invited.

Easter 7

Thought for the day

God's glory is often revealed in the context of suffering and failure in the world's eyes.

Reflection on the readings

Acts 1:6-14
Psalm 68:1-10, 32-35
1 Peter 4:12-14; 5:6-11
John 17:1-11

When Jesus prays to be glorified he is looking straight into the face of a cursed death. At first it shakes us that this imminent time of suffering and apparent failure, of disappointed rejection and dashed hopes should be what God deems glory. But of course it speaks of what is at the very heart of our faith, that our God is a Servant King, and his kingdom is one of humility and love, rather than success and popularity. Power and glory are emotive words which often conjure up images of military strength and empire-building, but God's power and glory are of a very different kind.

In today's Gospel we see Jesus at prayer, his will and total direction aligned with that of the Father, ready to be the human person in whom God's glory will be perfectly shown through the outpouring of love on the cross. In an extraordinary paradox, the nails of rejection and ultimate insult are allowed to fasten his body into the classic position of welcome and acceptance, arms outstretched. His written accusation means that he is even given his authentic title to die under, mocked and despised. And this is glory. This is what shows the length to which perfect loving goes, for the innocent One to take on all the sins of the world, accept their pain without complaint or retaliation, and offer them for transforming into freedom and new life at the cost of everything.

In the light of this it begins to make sense that Peter can encourage the early Christians, undergoing severe persecution for their faith, with the thought that to suffer in this way, in Christ's way, is the earth where glory flowers. To undergo suffering beautifully, by the grace of God, is to have the Spirit of God in all his glory resting upon us, and the privilege of witnessing to God's strength and capacity to transform and redeem anything.

We are nearing the end of this season of Easter, as the disciples were nearing the end of their earthly understanding of who Jesus was. Having gone through death and accomplished his work on earth, Jesus' risen life will take him out of the world, in one sense, but only in order to be right in the centre of faithful lives across the world and the centuries. Just as the angels at the tomb had asked the disciples why they were looking for Jesus in the place of death, when he was alive, so now, as Jesus is hidden from their sight and returns to heaven, the angels ask why the disciples are peering up into heaven.

We can all get far too bogged down in the technical details, which don't actually matter that much. What does matter is that Jesus hasn't gone away and left us, but is going to be with us and in us as we make ourselves increasingly available for his loving service.

All-age talk

Begin by talking about saying goodbye. The kind of goodbye it is depends on how well we know each other, whether we love or hate each other, and whether we are saying goodbye for a short time, a long time or for ever. Today in our first reading we were with the disciples as Jesus said goodbye to them. Since Easter we have been looking at various times when he had been meeting up with them after the Resurrection. Sometimes he had met them when they were all together, sometimes on their own. They would suddenly recognise him, or he would suddenly be there among them, and the disciples had begun to get used to Jesus being with them even when they couldn't see him with their eyes.

Now, here they are, all together with Jesus, and this is going to be their last goodbye to him as a person whom they see with their eyes, because he is going back to heaven. He tells them two things: (show a picture of rushing wind and flames) that they are going to be given power when the Holy Spirit comes upon them, and (show a picture of an empty speech bubble) that they are going to tell lots of people all over the world about the Jesus they know and love so well.

Then we are told that he was lifted up, while they watched, and a cloud took him from their sight so that they couldn't see him any more. So they stood there, peering up into the sky, rather like you do when you've just let a balloon go, and you watch and watch until you can't see it any more. What happened next?

They realised that two people, dressed in white, were standing next to them. 'Why are you standing here looking up into the sky?' they asked. They told the disciples that one day Jesus would come in the same way they had seen him go. But what they wanted them to know was that there wasn't any point in hanging around in that one place for a glimpse of Jesus, because he had gone on to the next phase, where he would be with all his friends, including us, all the time, not in a way that we can see, but in new ways. Just as real, just as much alive, but in a form which makes him free to be in all kinds of different countries and places and dates and times all at once!

What he said to the disciples that day, he says to us as well: we will be given power when the Holy Spirit comes upon us (show the first picture again) and we are going to tell lots of people about the Jesus we know and love (show the second picture).

Pentecost

(Whit Sunday)

Thought for the day

With great power the Spirit of God is poured out on the expectant disciples.

Reflection on the readings

Acts 2:1-21 or Numbers 11:24-30
Psalm 104:24-34, 35b
1 Corinthians 12:3b-13 or Acts 2:1-21
John 20:19-23 or John 7:37-39

Even if the passage from Numbers is not chosen for today, it is well worth reading as part of the Pentecost reflection because it expresses such a wonderful delighted longing in Moses for the Spirit of God to be poured out on every single person, if only that were possible. The amazing truth is that Jesus has made it possible. The coming of the Holy Spirit on God's people at Pentecost is directly the result of the victory won over sin and death on Good Friday, which became obvious with the Resurrection on Easter Day.

Since Easter we have been tracing the growing understanding of what all that meant, and where it might lead, rather like a potential smouldering fire that has suddenly burst into flames. The disciples had already experienced the risen Christ appearing among them and filling them with peace and happiness, reassurance and enlightenment. Now, on the day which celebrated the giving of the ancient law, the new, fulfilled law is seeringly burnt into their hearts; Jesus comes not so much among them as right within them, in a breathtaking way which is, in answer to his prayer, allowing them to be truly at one with him as he is one with the Father. From now on, the group of followers are collectively the Body of Christ, breathing the breath of his life, which is the life of God.

That power is immediately noticeable. The Jewish tradition was familiar with spirit-filled ecstatic prophecy, and many recognised that these people were proclaiming the wonderful works of God which had just been revealed to them with a new vitality and heightened perception. But it was even more than that.

Peter sees it as the fulfilment of Joel's prophecy, and quotes those words to the listening and curious crowd with the excitement of one who is aware that this very day they are present at history in the making. It is an extraordinary occasion for the whole nation of Israel, if they will only recognise it. In a sense it is the day when the new Israel is born. For from now on the bright revelation of God's reality, power and mercy, sown in the promise to Abraham and his family and spreading to the chosen nation who were called to be God's light, will be available to the whole world; all believers will be part of that holy nation, filled with the life of the living God.

Pentecost was only the beginning. It was not only to those first disciples that God came intimately and completely in the Holy Spirit. There is plenty of it left for us! Freshly and vigorously in our times, too, God is prepared to make his dwelling with expectant believers of any tradition and any age, culture or personality. It is a terrible myth that the Holy Spirit is only for some, that any are shut off from that inner God-given life. The truth is simple: anyone at all who prays expectantly and longingly for the real, living God to come upon them in power will receive the gift that God longs to give. Let's not get too worked up about the 'how'; that is God's agenda, and we can trust that it will always be in the time and way which is best for each asking person.

What we do need to return to is deep, passionate longing for God, more than anything or anyone else. And God will come and breathe his life into us all, and the effects will show.

All-age talk

Bring along an electrical appliance and, if necessary, an extension lead. Alternatively, have a torch or game powered by batteries, and keep the batteries separate at first.

Refresh everyone's memory of today's dynamic event, with the disciples praying and waiting on God, and the early morning experience of his power coming to them like a rushing wind, or flames, searching out each one of them and touching them with the touch of God.

It quite overwhelmed them, and left them fired up with excitement at what God is capable of doing in people. They were bursting to tell everyone else about it, and wanted everyone to share this sense of God actually living in them. It was quite different from knowing about God; it was even different from walking about in the company of Jesus. This was like being flowed through with new life that set them living, talking and working in a new way.

Show the electrical appliance you have brought. Explain what this thing is capable of doing, but point out that at the moment it can't do any of those things. It has everything in place to work in that lively way, but something is missing at the moment – it isn't linked up to the power supply. Would it help if the appliance knew exactly how electricity works? Not really. However much is known about electrical circuits and the power grid, that won't bring this appliance to life. What it needs is this. (Plug the appliance into the power supply and switch on.)

Now the thing springs into life, and all kinds of potential are activated. That's what it's like having God's Spirit living in us and flowing through us. It makes that much difference! Just think what our world could be like if we were all full of the power of God's Spirit. Just think what a difference it would make in the world if all those in churches today all over the world asked God, seriously and openly, for a fresh outpouring of the Holy Spirit!

So often we are like well-finished appliances or games, knowing all about God's power, but not wanting to have the power switched on in us, just in case. Just in case what? Our God is the true, living God of love and compassion and mercy. Which means that any power he sends to touch us and affect us, will be only and entirely good for us. God is longing for his Church to be 'live' with the active power of his Spirit; we may be in good working order, but we also need to have the power, so that we actually 'work'!

Trinity Sunday

Thought for the day

The mystery of God – Creator, Redeemer and Sanctifier all at once – is beyond our human understanding, yet closer to us than breathing.

Reflection on the readings

    Isaiah 40:12-17, 27-31
    Psalm 8
    2 Corinthians 13:11-13
    Matthew 28:16-20

There are some things which we sense, but which start slithering out of our grasp as we try to pin them down in words. Some deep relationships are like this, and some intense experiences. It is also true of the nature of God. Whenever we attempt to explain what we mean by the Trinity we are bound to end up falling short of the truth, and inadequately picturing what is simply so deep and vast that it is beyond the power of human understanding.

Isaiah tries to give some idea of the huge scale of God in relation to familiar countries, resources and natural cycles, and the psalmist marvels at the God who is maker of stars. What both Isaiah and the psalmist stress is what that vastness *doesn't* mean. It doesn't mean that the God we fail to understand is therefore somehow remote and aloof from us; so transcendent that he can have no grasp of us or our situation. His very omniscience, or all-knowingness, means that both the smallest details and the widest sweeps of space are intimately known by the loving God; he not only knows about us in our smallness, he cares and is interested in everything we do and think and dream.

If we take the image of a young baby being suckled, we can see that here the baby has a wonderful sense of what being loved, cared for and nurtured is all about. Yet all it can do is gurgle its understanding, and is probably more likely to express that knowledge by falling asleep, trusting and satisfied.

That is rather how it is with us. To understand the nature of God, and what the Trinity really means, is in one sense always beyond our scope as humans. God is never going to be quantifiable in human terms because he far surpasses what it means to be human. But in another sense we are able to understand his nature as we experience relationship with him and feel his love, nurturing and committed care. All our attempts to express that are rather like a baby's gurglings, or a contented and trusting tranquillity which shows in our lives.

The great commission, which Matthew records, sends the disciples out into the whole world to baptise people in the name of the Father, the Son and the Holy Spirit – the one God is all his completeness and community. It is the relationship with this God which transforms his people, rather than an impossible definitive explanation of it. That is expressed in the other part of the great commission: 'I will be with you always, to the end of time.'

All-age talk

Produce a jacket or sweater of a young child's size, and invite a much larger volunteer to get into it. (It should be obvious that they won't be able to, even though they try.) Agree that it is impossible to get Ben into Justin's jacket – he's simply too big to fit!

Sometimes we expect God to be able to fit into our human-sized minds. We start to think about God, and say things like, 'But how can he possibly be able to hear us all praying at once?' when what we really mean is that we know humans couldn't do that, so it must be impossible for God as well. Or we say, 'God *must* have had a beginning sometime, because *everything* does!'

When we do this we are holding out a small human shape (hold out the little jacket) and expecting God to climb into it. And of course he doesn't fit, because being God is much bigger and deeper and wider than being a human being. God is so great that he is always going to be full of wonderful mystery for us, however much we learn about him. As humans we cannot hold his nature and understand it, any more than this small jacket will hold a big boy like Ben.

So does that mean that we can't really know God? Not at all! Invite Ben and Justin to come up and shake hands, and say hello to each other. You could have Ben asking Justin some questions, so that everyone can see that both boys are able to have a conversation.

Just because God is God and you are human doesn't mean you can't be good friends. There are lots of people here today who talk with God every day (it's called praying) and know that he is the person they love and trust best in their whole life.

We have been given a lifetime to get to know God really well and live as his friends. Sometimes we waste that time, and sometimes we suddenly realise that nothing else is quite so important. Sometimes we don't bother to tell other people about our loving God, or we let our behaviour tell them that we don't think he is worth very much at all. And other times we feel such love for our God that we can't wait to let other people know about him. And then our loving behaviour tells them as well as our words.

Our God is wonderful and all-knowing. He is the maker of our universe and of us all, he is the one who came as Jesus to die for love of us and save us, and he is present with his people, living in us as the Holy Spirit. How could we possibly ever expect to completely understand a God as amazing as that!

God being so great that he is full of holy mystery should make us excited, not frustrated. Let's enjoy being friends with the God who is so amazing that no human can ever explain what he is really like! And let's lavish our worship on him; any god smaller, or knowable, wouldn't be worth worshipping anyway.

Sunday between 29 May and 4 June

(if after Trinity Sunday)

Proper 4

Thought for the day

Wise listeners build their lives up on the strong rock of the word of God.

Reflection on the readings

Deuteronomy 11:18-21, 26-28
Psalm 31:1-5, 19-24
Romans 1:16-17; 3:22b-28 (29-31)
Matthew 7:21-29

Those whose homes are built in an area of clay or sand will be familiar with the extra insurance required. Prolonged dry spells following heavy rain are notorious for causing ominous cracks. In such areas underpinning is a common sight – manufactured rock foundations out of reinforced concrete. Jesus' example still holds today: lives built on rock foundations last without ending in ruin.

There was plenty of rock in the landscape of the psalmists, who would often use the reassuring security and permanence of it to describe God and, by extension, God's law – the words of God. Rather as we might stick revision facts to the bathroom mirror, or leave scribbled notes about swimming kit by the front door, the hearers of Deuteronomy are advised to strap reminders of the Law everywhere, so that it becomes really soaked into their everyday life. It is all aimed at turning hearers into doers, at getting that Law turned into a holy people.

Of course, it was no easier for the people of Israel to keep up their practice of God's Law than it is for us to keep up our violin or German-speaking practice without a weekly lesson. We all need the constant nagging nudge which the strapped-on law boxes were designed to provide. But besides being strapped on to the outside of us, they really need strapping to our hearts. And that is what the Holy Spirit can do for us, setting our hearts on fire with such love for our God that we long to spend ourselves in pleasing him and working for the coming of the kingdom. Yes, it is certainly wise to build on the words of God, but wisdom is itself one of the gifts that grows out of love – love for the One who has freely given us the freedom we could never achieve by ourselves.

All-age talk

Set up some young children and an adult or two to build with building blocks or a variety of cartons in the aisle during the talk. Draw attention to the building they are involved with and explain that today we have heard Jesus advising us on a wise building policy in our lives. We are also concerned that we do as much as possible to ensure that our faith is passed on faithfully to our young children, and their children yet to come. Having them building here in front of us will serve as a memory jogger to remind us both of our life building, and our responsibility to the young ones entrusted to our care.

Let's look again at that verse from Deuteronomy about passing on our faith. We are not to expect our children to pick up the faith all by themselves – we are to talk to them about it in all kinds of situations, so that they get to realise that it is relevant and valuable, of great importance for the whole of life. What does that mean in practice?

- It means that our children will not see God as the firm, secure rock he is unless they see the adults around them trusting that rock and building their lives on it. They need to see adults living their faith, every day of the week.

- It means that if our children see the adults in their Christian community saying they believe in God, coming to church and behaving in ways which are selfish, prejudiced, unforgiving or without loving respect for everyone, they may get the impression that God is not strong rock at all, but sand; that he is not to be taken seriously. Heaven forbid that we should lead any of our little ones astray by the inconsistency of our life.

- It means that we need to get over our embarrassment in talking about God, and chat about him with our children as we would talk about all the other things that are important and excite us.

- It means that we need to start praying aloud with our children, and praying daily with them, so they learn what it is to talk over everything with the loving God, sharing both the lovely times and the sad ones with him. We need to get back the habit of thanking God – aloud – for our food before we eat. Our homes need to become places where it is natural to pray. How else will our children learn to pray naturally?

Of course, this is not going to be easy, especially if we live in a community where only part of the family are believers. But that makes our church community particularly important. Children can cope with the fact that one of their parents believes and one doesn't. It is the hypocrisy of conflicting words and behaviour that confuses them. All our families need the support of the whole Christian community in the precious work of parenting. We are all part of that, whether we have young children ourselves or not.

So let us watch how we build. When we hear Jesus' words, let's really start acting on them, changing our behaviour and our habits to sing out those words in all we do. And then we shall be taking seriously our charge to nurture our little ones, and pass on to them faithfully the Gospel that sets us free to live abundantly, even through storms and floods.

Sunday between 5 and 11 June

(if after Trinity Sunday)

Proper 5

Thought for the day

Jesus' life of healing and compassion acts out God's desire for mercy rather than empty sacrifice.

Reflection on the readings

Hosea 5:15–6:6
Psalm 50:7-15
Romans 4:13-25
Matthew 9:9-13, 18-26

Last week we were looking at the dangers of giving empty lip-service to Christ, yet not being prepared to put his teaching into practice in our lives. Today we look at another danger – of going through the motions of following God, but without our hearts being in it, and without any real acknowledgement of the sacrificial cost involved.

What was basically wrong in the story of Matthew's calling? At one level we can accept that the religious leaders are justified in pointing out to Jesus that he is associating with those whose lives appear to have deliberately rejected God's values. Surely these people are a disgrace to the name of the chosen nation of Israel? How are they a light to the rest of the world? The speakers know that they themselves have deliberately chosen to keep the sacred law, and follow all the teachings to the letter. They know they are doing their bit to uphold the values of a chosen people set apart for God. So far, so understandable. If we are honest, how would we feel if Jesus came and spent more time with the gang smashing into our church and spray-painting it, than with us in our specially prepared Bible studies?

The crunch comes with the attitude of the religious leaders to what Jesus is doing with these 'sinners'. Had they been genuinely seeking to uphold God's values of mercy and justice, they would have had an openness which looked curiously at what Jesus was doing and tried to understand it. They would have noticed the gradual change in the 'sinners' and suddenly realised with excitement and delight that, although Jesus was acting unexpectedly, he was actually helping these people to healing and wholeness. They would then have been there rejoicing with Matthew and the others, and nothing could have given Jesus greater joy.

As it is, they disassociate themselves from the healing work of God; they are, in a sense, selling their true birthright for a bowl of broth. Jesus listens to their complaints, and we can imagine his heart aching at their blindness. He gives them a clue as to what he is doing, by talking about sick people and doctors. They must have reacted to that, not with sudden insight and joy but with supercilious self-righteousness which told Jesus they knew better; these people were evil, not sick, and if he was really a religious teacher he would know they should be avoided and rejected for the purity of the nation. Such an attitude was an appalling insult to the God of mercy and compassion, and brought out Jesus' passionate response: 'Go and learn what this text means . . . and start getting your priorities right!' The whole point of Jesus coming was to do this work of loving sinners into a right relationship with the God of their making.

The story is a sobering one. What had begun as well-intentioned ways of lavishing true worship on the living God had become distorted into worship of empty systems and rituals, to the extent that, when faced with the genuine active presence of God, it was not even recognised. We need to come back, constantly, to the heart of worship, to the feet of God, and listen intently to what he is saying, so that our worship expresses our loving service to the loving God.

All-age talk

Beforehand work with one or two people who don't mind acting in front of the congregation. They are going to say 'Hello' to one another in various different ways that mean:

- I was really hoping I wouldn't meet this person here.
- I have no respect for this person whatsoever.
- This person is of no interest to me at all.
- This person has a swimming pool and I'd like to be invited round, so I'll suck up to them.
- I'm really glad to see this person.
- I respect and love this person very much.

Begin the talk by getting the actors to say 'Hello' to one another in each different way, and each time follow their greeting with the interpretation, read like a label.

We all show what we think of each other by the greeting we offer one another. (Incidentally, does the way we offer the Peace tell the other person that they are really valued, or are we looking at someone more our type or more interesting while we greet some people?)

Today we have come to meet together as Christians for a reason. Why have we come here? We haven't come just to see our family or friends (though that is always nice to do!) and we haven't come just to play with the Noah's ark, or to get out of mowing the grass. We have come to greet our God in worship and to greet one another in his name. What kind of 'Hello' are we giving to God by our worship?

Perhaps we are hoping that we won't actually meet God here, in case he asks of us something we don't want to give. We glance in his direction, but don't want to make eye contact, so to speak. Today we are reminded that to worship God beautifully we need to COME TO GOD HONESTLY, JUST AS WE ARE. (Display this.)

Perhaps we nod in his direction, but have really got our thoughts on the people coming for dinner and whether the bathroom should be white or pale green. Or we are thinking more of the piece of chewing gum under the seat in front of us, or the behaviour of the young, or the middle-aged or the elderly, or how many candles need replacing. Today we are reminded that to worship God beautifully we need to GIVE GOD OUR FULL ATTENTION. (Have that written up.)

Perhaps we are here thinking God will notice and tick off our names for good attendance, so that when we die we will have a pre-booked place in heaven. We intend to join in with all the hymns and prayers in church, but for the rest of the week we plan to carry on with the real life in the real world, where Christian values are not actually practical. Today we are reminded that to worship God beautifully we need to KNOW THAT GOD IS NOT FOOLED, and MATCH UP OUR WORDS WITH OUR LIFE (or WALK THE TALK).

Our God is the God of compassion and healing. He does not want our empty words, dry habit worship or closed-up prejudice. He does not want pretence or hypocrisy. God loves us and delights in his people coming to meet with him in worship, Sunday by Sunday. Wherever we are in our spiritual journey he can work with us, and he will never turn anyone away who is genuinely seeking. But whether we greet him in worship with our faces scratched and bruised, as we lie sprawled in the dust of life, or whether we greet him as we stop for breath from running away from him, or whether we greet him timidly but bravely, what we must do is greet him honestly, openly and expectantly.

Suggest that, not out loud but in the silence of their hearts, everyone says their own 'Hello' to God, honestly, openly and expectantly.

Sunday between 12 and 18 June

(if after Trinity Sunday)

Proper 6

Thought for the day

Jesus sends his ambassadors out to proclaim God's kingdom and bring hope and peace of mind to the harassed and lost in every age.

Reflection on the readings

Exodus 19:2-8a
Psalm 100
Romans 5:1-8
Matthew 9:35–10:8 (9-23)

Stand on any railway station at rush hour and you see the harassed and tense faces all around. Perhaps that is an unfair place to pick, but it is noticeable that the stress and conflicting demands and expectations, and the relativism of our society, which places huge pressures on individual choice of action, combine to make 'peace of mind' a yearned-for impossibility for many. Today's readings speak quite a lot about hope, and being at peace with God and oneself.

In the passage from Exodus we find the people of Israel being given the hope of becoming the treasured possession of God, of being a kingdom of priests and a holy nation, if they are prepared, as a whole community, to work with their God rather than against him. We hear their confident response: 'We will do everything the Lord has commanded.' What poignant reading this must have made for those in exile, with the scattered trail of sin and rebellion behind them. What poignant reading it makes for us as we think back to promises confidently made and subsequent failures!

The wonderful thing about Christianity is that it speaks hope, not to a non-existent strong people who can save themselves, but to the reality of a well-intentioned and blundering race who know that saving themselves is not one of the things that humans can do.

In the reading from Matthew we feel Jesus' fondness and longing for the people, whom he describes as harassed and disturbed, agitated and without peace. He urges his disciples to join him in praying earnestly for more workers in the harvest, knowing that God will be dependent on human co-operation and availability to accomplish the healing and gathering in. That is just as true for us today as it was then, and we need to take Jesus' urgency to heart. True religion is being at peace with God, and the absence of that peace is obvious in our society.

Immediately after this, the twelve are sent out, in the role of ambassadors, to proclaim the kingdom of God and accompany the news with signs of healing. All the detailed instructions they are given point to a loving commitment which is total and without ambition, personal gain or personal comforts. That still needs to be our attitude, as the Church, so that our motives are transparent and uncluttered by sub-agendas or empire-building. We are called simply to love people into the kingdom, where they can know the joy and hope of being at peace with God.

Hope is an intriguing word. It is a mixture of desire for something and expectation of getting it. If either of those is missing, it isn't hope, and if either is overbalanced, there is no peace. But when you have both in balance, hope makes you very happy and contented in the present, as well as in the fulfilment. Paul addresses this phenomenon in his letter to the Romans. We are justified by faith, or provided with an 'honorary pass' to God's presence through Jesus' self-giving death, rather than trying hopelessly to earn it. It is this which gives us freely the illusive peace we all crave.

This is not just for the good times but for the grim ones as well. The kind of love that was ready to die for us when we were God's enemies, in effect, is hardly going to let us down now that we have been reconciled to God. We can be assured that our loving God will provide everything we need in the way of support and comfort during the worst sufferings life may throw at us. In fact, it is his love in us that enables us to grow and develop through such times.

All-age talk

Ask everyone to place their hand flat on their tummy. This is often the place where we can tell if we are anxious or stressed, because it feels 'uptight'. When we are at peace, and not tensed-up, this place is where we feel calm and relaxed, and contented. (In fact, one way of calming yourself down is to do what you are doing now, and breathe slowly in and out a few times.)

Recently we have been looking at what religion *isn't*. We've found that it isn't telling God he is Lord of our life and then behaving as if he is not important. And it isn't going through the motions of worshipping him without showing his love and compassion to other people.

Today we are looking at what religion *is*. It is all about being at peace with God. Ask for two people who are really good friends to come to the front, and talk to them about what it feels like to be with each other. How does being together make them feel? Do they feel worried about how the other friend will treat them? Would they trust their friend with a secret?

Best friends are good news. You are contented and happy to be with them, and are not worried all the time that you might say the wrong thing and offend them, or that they may start being nasty to you, so you need to be ready to hit them back if necessary. You know you can trust them with your secrets, and they won't laugh at you or think you are stupid. Even going through bad experiences isn't as bad if you are both in it together, because you know you will help one another along.

Well, that's what being at peace with God is like, and it has the spin-off effect of making us deeply happy and calm inside – a feeling that, whatever happens, all will be well. We heard today how Jesus wanted everyone to know this sense of calm assurance and peace and joy in their lives. He knew there were lots and lots of people going around worried and lost, with no peace inside them because they were not at peace with God. And he sent his disciples off to tell them that the kingdom of God was coming very soon, and soon they would be able to have that closeness with God which would give them peace.

Between the two 'best friends' put up a very large piece of cardboard with the word 'Sin' on it. Sin shuts us off from God and from one another. It makes us think of God as our enemy instead of our friend.

We know that Jesus went on to die for love of us all, which knocked that block of sin away between us and God. (Knock the cardboard away.) So now we can all know that lovely closeness to God which gives us real peace and hope, not just when everything is going well for us, but also through the times of suffering.

Sunday between 19 and 25 June

(if after Trinity Sunday)

Proper 7

Thought for the day

When we are willing to take up our cross with Jesus we will also know his risen life.

Reflection on the readings

Jeremiah 20:7-13
Psalm 69:7-10 (11-15) 16-18
Romans 6:1b-11
Matthew 10:24-39

There is a fundamental paradox in the Christian faith which sounds like nonsense and yet turns out to be true when you try it. Today's readings paste it up large so that we cannot avoid it, however much we might like to. It is the claim that through death you gain life. In fact, it goes even further: unless you take on death you cannot know life. How on earth can this really be true?

We all know that our strong life-force, or libido, works constantly for our survival. Our brains use vast quantities of energy in supporting life systems and keeping us alive. There are all kinds of emergency strategies that kick in when anything threatens our survival, and the body is so good at managing these that it all goes on without us noticing, most of the time, and while we are occupied in other ways. Had it not been so, the human race could not have continued for as long as it has, nor succeeded in a fraction of its remarkable achievements. How does 'taking up our cross' and 'losing our life for his sake' fit in with this?

There is much value today placed on self-confidence and self-assurance, in an effort to help people become their true selves without being so vulnerable to abuse or pressure from others. Self-assertiveness is the quality to prize, and any deliberate giving-up of one's rights is viewed with suspicion and often considered weak and wrong. How does this fit in with Jesus' teaching that whoever gains his life will lose it, and whoever loses his life for Christ's sake will gain it?

We cannot get away from the fact that this is a hard teaching to accept. It requires a drastic and complete change of values and direction in life. It can hurt. It is very costly. Jesus wants his potential followers to understand the full implications of commitment. So why would any normal person want to 'lose' their life like this by choice?

Jesus' answer has been experienced and found to be true by many people in each generation. Just as the result of Jesus' total self-giving in death was new, resurrection life, so the result of us giving up our natural self-centredness is a new sense of life in which we find we are more free to be ourselves than if we had slaved over it. It is the answer of a God who loves and cherishes us.

It is like the difference between a tissue-paper flower and an alpine meadow in spring. The kind of fulfilling life we think we are going to gain by accumulating wealth and prestige at other people's expense, over-indulging our tastes, and feverishly totting up as many experiences as possible in case we lose out on anything, turns out to be disappointing and never as satisfying as we had hoped; there is always something else we really must have or try. In comparison, the way of Jesus gives an inner sense of rightness, calm and integrity, which is very richly fulfilling and enables others to become their true selves as well.

All-age talk

Today we have heard in the reading from Romans that we are to think of ourselves as dead to sin and alive to God through Christ Jesus. What does that mean?

Well, perhaps a few sleeping lions can help. Ask for a few volunteers to play 'sleeping lions' in the aisle, while you and some others try to get them to move. They have to remain as still as they possibly can. Point out that they have to think of themselves as 'asleep' to all those temptations to move which are going on around them. That is rather like us thinking of ourselves being dead to sin. We have to remind ourselves that sin is something which no longer concerns us or has any hold on us.

Ask a few people to say what noises there are in their home at night – any creaks or tickings or chimes. Then draw people's attention to the way we have no difficulty sleeping through these noises, because we know we don't have to worry about them. Some parents will have found that if it isn't your turn to get up and feed the baby you're quite likely to sleep through the crying. You are 'dead' to that sound because you know it isn't anything to do with you. And we are told that we are to think of ourselves as dead to sin.

But it isn't just being dead to sin – it's also being alive to God. What does that mean? Perhaps some people who like chocolate can help us here. Choose a few volunteers and tell them to stand with their backs to you and the congregation. When they think they can detect the presence of chocolate, tell them to raise their hand. Now, as you talk about the way we can always hear what we want to hear, start to open a bar of chocolate, and even though there isn't much sound, and they have their backs to you, it probably won't be very long before they notice, either by hearing or smelling, or both.

That's like us being 'alive' to God. We are going to live as dead to sin, but expectant and interested as far as God is concerned. We will be so tuned in to God that we notice his still, small voice, recognise him in all we see and in those we meet, and live with our hearts and ears and wills turned in his direction all through every day, whatever is going on around us.

Sunday between 26 June and 2 July

Proper 8

Thought for the day

As Christ's people we are no longer slaves to sin, but available for righteousness.

Reflection on the readings

Jeremiah 28:5-9
Psalm 89:1-4, 15-18
Romans 6:12-23
Matthew 10:40-42

Some people are unfortunate enough to suffer from vertigo, and find that when they are perched anywhere high there is a terrible urge to throw themselves off into that space beneath them. They have to back away from the edge for fear of plunging to their death. It is as if the space commands them and they have to fight against it. Sin is like that. It pulls us strongly towards our death, and we have a real battle to fight against that urge to go along with its pressurising command. Even while we know that sin is bound to be damaging to us, to those we love, and to our world, our wills and emotions can still drag us over the edge into behaviour which leads to death. As Paul says, it is like being a slave to a tyrannical master, obeying its commands and feeling 'owned' by it. It can seem impossibly difficult to imagine how we could ever break free.

Holding on to Christ, through the cross where that grip of sin has been broken for us, leads us into a completely different place. Sin will still attempt to pull us over, but the power of Christ living in us enables us to back away from the edge as free agents, rather than slaves. It is as if, rather than being drawn to look down into the strangely enticing death-fall all the time, we can enjoy the loftiness of the breathtaking view without fear.

It is interesting that Paul talks of sin earning death, which implies hard, wearying work. That is true: living enslaved to sin drains us of energy and wears us down. In contrast, righteous living is not a heavy duty, but a loving, happy response to a personal free gift.

In today's Gospel we are reminded that anyone responding to one of God's people will actually be responding to their God. This suggests that our behaviour as freed slaves will be obvious to those around us, since we will be behaving differently. Our attitude and outlook will be open and available to good, rather than knotted up with fear and self-absorbed in our own wants and demands. We will be more ready to speak out God's words rather than pandering to what we think people will want to hear, so that we are popular. But it is important to realise that this change is a natural result of responding to God's love, and not an unhealed determined effort in which we remain slaves.

All-age talk

Bring along a kitchen knife, a pen or pencil, a can of paint spray and a £10 or £20 note. You will also need two signs, one saying 'Good' and the other 'Evil'.

Begin by observing that lots of things we handle every day can be used either for good or for evil. Ask for two volunteers to hold the signs, some distance apart, and go through each of the objects in turn, gathering from different people how each can be used. Take the objects to the appropriate notice for each suggestion.

Now ask a person to stand up. It's not only *things* which can be used for good or for evil; it's people as well. Stand the person beside the 'Evil' sign. In what ways can a person use themselves for evil? (Collect suggestions from people of all ages.) Stand the person by the 'Good' sign. In what ways can a person use themselves for good? (Collect suggestions.)

In our readings today we heard about how the false prophet Hananiah used his voice to encourage God's people to believe lies, and how Jeremiah wanted to use his voice differently – to build up God's people. We need to try and use our voices to encourage one another and help one another. We need to use our voices to tell out the truth, and not use the voices God has given to spread unkind gossip, or lies, or to be rude and unkind.

We heard Paul writing in his letter to the Romans that all the different parts of our bodies can either be offered to sin as instruments of evil, or offered to God as instruments of good. We've looked at our voices. What about our hands? Our minds? Our maleness or our femaleness? Our feet? Our ears? Suggest that during this week they make a point of checking how they are using all the parts of their body, and seeing if they offer all those parts of themselves to God for good.

Sunday between 3 and 9 July

Proper 9

Thought for the day

To all who are weary with carrying heavy burdens in life, Jesus offers rest for our souls and unthreatening relief.

Reflection on the readings

Zechariah 9:9-12
Psalm 145:8-14
Romans 7:15-25a
Matthew 11:16-19, 25-30

The first of today's readings, from Zechariah, gives us a clear image of peace and humility, as we hear of a king entering in triumph, but on a donkey. It is an image which Jesus made his own, and it speaks of a king totally in touch with the ordinary people and their needs, an unpretentious king who is unimpressed by the worldly idea of wealth and power, and is not in the business of domination and threat, but openness and integrity.

The psalmist pours out a whole list of God's wonderfully supportive and gracious qualities, in the knowledge that this God-king's kingdom is not like the earthly temporary and fickle ones, but everlasting in its goodness.

So when we meet with Jesus in today's Gospel, what we find is completely in keeping with the discernment of those Old Testament writers who had waited on God and trusted him. Jesus' heart goes out to all who are weighed down in their lives, and his welcoming offer is not to do with domination, or strict rules which terrify with their potential for failure. Instead, Jesus shows himself open and unarmed, offering relief and rest for our souls, through becoming joined, or yoked, with his life in the living God.

It is all so simple in contrast with the complexities we struggle to handle when we are not at peace with God. And this very simplicity, while welcomed with joy by anyone ready to hear it, conscious of their failure to achieve it on their own, is also what brings out the childishness in those who petulantly reject God's help, manufacturing one reason after another to justify their rejection. Sadly, it is often those who pride themselves on their learning or mature, independent thinking, who continue to see Jesus' offer of rescue as a threat and an insult to their maturity and success.

With sorrow Jesus sees the religious leaders of his own people behaving like a bunch of quarrelsome children: they complain, but there is no pleasing them! While they are behaving in this childish way, unable to take advantage of what God is doing in their lifetime, it is largely the ordinary, uneducated crowds who are responding with childlike openness and spiritual maturity.

The same is true in every generation, including ours. While we are never meant to leave our brains at the church door, it is also true that sophisticated cynicism or intellectual smugness can blind us to the true value of our great, saving God coming to us meekly on a donkey.

All-age talk

Bring along four bags or cases, labelled 'Worries', 'Guilt', 'Duty' and 'Wants'. Inside each wrap up heavy bundles, labelled appropriately. Here are some ideas:

Worries

- What if it rains?
- They might crash.
- She hasn't got enough money for that bill.
- He's in with a bad lot of friends.
- I might get it wrong and look silly.
- What if we get broken into?

Guilt

- I'm so ashamed.
- God can never forgive me for that.
- I'll never be able to put that right.
- It haunts me every day.
- I'll never forgive myself.

Duty

- I should drive myself even harder.
- I just grit my teeth and wait for life to be over.
- I'll do my duty even if it kills me.
- Day off? That would be lazy!

Wants

- They've got one – I want it too.
- I wish I was rich and could buy whatever I liked.
- I want more freedom.
- I want to look like Leonardo DiCaprio.
- I'd be happy if only I had a . . .

Talk about how hard it is to struggle along carrying heavy shopping bags, or loads of kit and books for school, or a delivery of newspapers, or a supposedly portable laptop computer and printer. Who has ever found their load after school too heavy and given it to someone else (like Mum or Dad!) to carry home, so they can be free to run and play? We all find that carrying heavy loads makes our arms ache, and slows us down. We all enjoy it when we can put that heavy load down, and our arms start lifting up into the air, because they suddenly feel so light!

Today we heard Jesus giving us a wonderful offer. He said, 'Come to me all you who carry heavy loads and I will refresh you. Take my yoke upon you and learn from me, for I am gentle and humble in heart, and you will find rest for your souls. For my yoke is easy and my burden is light.' They are such lovely words to hear for any one of you who feels that you are lugging along heavy loads in your life. Let's look at some of the heavy loads we carry.

Struggle along with the four bags, and read their labels. These are some of the most common heavy loads we carry. What is inside them to make them so heavy? With the help of some volunteers open up each bag in turn. Different people can read out the kind of things that weigh us down so much. It's strange that even wanting things can weigh us down, but it's true. Whenever we are not at peace, we are carrying heavy loads. The good news is that Jesus says we can give those loads to him, so that we are free to play; free to live at peace; free to enjoy life again. (If there is space by a cross, or by the altar, have the bags placed there as you speak.)

When we are yoked, or joined up with Jesus, it is going to be much easier to carry the loads we need, and unnecessary to carry the ones that weigh us down so much.

Sunday between 10 and 16 July

Proper 10

Thought for the day

Seed of God's word, sown in good soil, watered by his rain and warmed by his sunlight, produces a good crop of spiritual fruit.

Reflection on the readings

Isaiah 55:10-13
Psalm 65:(1-8) 9-13
Romans 8:1-11
Matthew 13:1-9, 18-23

We have a wonderful picture of God's faithfulness given to us every year in the round of the seasons, as the bare earth receives the winter weathering before the seed is sown and the growing begins, leading through the warmth of summer to the gathering-in of the harvest in autumn. It is still relatively recently that all this was basic to our everyday lives, and we still get nostalgic about it, even if we have lived all our lives in the centre of a city.

It is not surprising that many biblical images are to do with this annual round and the desperately important blessing of rain. Today's passages from Isaiah and Psalm 65 give us an ancient lesson on the water cycle, beautifully and wonderingly observed. Isaiah uses it to illustrate the way God's word has a habit of being accomplished, working its way down into the human condition and providing all that is necessary for what has been spoken to come about. It may sometimes look unpromising, but, then, so do bare earth furrows unless you have lived through a previous summer. We sometimes need to trust Isaiah's words during our darker, barer seasons of life.

In today's Gospel we are aware that Jesus has been out walking this same earth we inhabit, watching the yearly sowing of seed and hearing the squabbling birds. It speaks to him vividly of the different ways we all respond to the word of God, and, prophet that he is, he tells it out straight as it is. Leaving people to puzzle over his story is an important part of the process of sowing the seed. It gives that seed a good start, wriggling it well down into the hearer's being as curiosity rolls it around before sleep or in conversation in the firelight. What is this seed which takes root and grows fruit in good soil? What was he really telling us? Growing opposition to Jesus' ministry also makes the parable a safer method of teaching. Perhaps it will serve to soften up the ground of defensive hearts in a less threatening way.

The disciples are surprised to hear Jesus using such a learned method of teaching for them and the crowds. Unlike the crowds, they are at least able to ask him to spell it all out clearly for them. Inevitably, they and we are bound to ask ourselves serious questions about where we are, and how we are responding to the word of God. Presumably the ideal is for the Church to be filled with seed growing in good soil, for all that requires is to be open and receptive, nourished and developed in the watering and warming of God's love. And those of us who prepare the ground need to check that we are providing the very best environment for the seed of God's word to grow strong.

All-age talk

You will need a seed tray filled with seed compost, some large-sized seeds, a dibber (to poke holes for the seeds) and a cloth bag of pearl barley. You will also need to arrange for a broom to sweep up the scattered barley after the talk. Lay down in the aisle one large piece of paper to represent a rocky patch, and a few footsteps to represent a stony path.

You might like to play a snatch of the *Gardeners' World* theme tune at the beginning, as you set out the seed tray and compost on a table and invite a couple of keen gardeners in the congregation to demonstrate planting. As the gardeners work, talk with them about why the seed planted like this is more likely to be successful than if we just shake the seeds outside.

Today we heard a story, or parable, that Jesus told, which was all about seeds being sown, and the best growing conditions. Of course, it wasn't just about seeds being planted and growing. Parables are stories with secrets inside, and the secret of this story is that it was really all about us, and how we respond to God's word when we hear it. This is how it works.

Where Jesus lived, it was very rocky, and the farmers had fields with bare rock showing here and there (put down the paper), and stony roads that went right through the middle (put down the footprints). They ploughed the earth in long furrows, like we did here in the seed tray, only much bigger of course, and then the person sowing the seed walked up and down the furrows sowing the seed like this. (Demonstrate with your bag of pearl barley, scattering the seed to left and right.) The problem is that not all the seed goes in the nice soil you have prepared. When God's word is spoken, we are not always ready to accept it. Let's look at where some of those seeds have landed.

Involve a volunteer to look at the stony path and stand over any seeds they find there. Sometimes we read or hear God's teaching and we're more like a stony path than good soil. It just goes in one ear and out of the other, and we hardly notice what we've heard. We might sit here for the readings and our thoughts fly in, like birds, and take away God's message so we don't even remember what was said.

What about the rocky ground? (Send a volunteer there.) Sometimes we hear God's message and get really keen, and take on far too much far too early, so, like plants growing up on rocky soil, we haven't got good roots. We burn ourselves out and drop away.

What about the soil next to the rock? (Send a volunteer there.) Lots of weeds grow here, so there's a lot of competition for the seeds. Sometimes we hear God's message, but there are so many other things going on in our lives, which we consider important, that the really important message of God gets choked and crowded out.

But all the rest is in good soil. We are like good soil when we listen to God's teaching carefully, think about it and what it means, and then live with it. That way we shall certainly grow and produce a good harvest. Let's check this week that we are taking good notice of God's words to us, and giving him proper space and time, so that we grow in his love.

Sunday between 17 and 23 July
Proper 11

Thought for the day

God's justice is always blended with mercy and loving kindness, so that we have real hope.

Reflection on the readings

Wisdom of Solomon 12:13, 16-19 or Isaiah 44:6-8
Psalm 86:11-17
Romans 8:12-25
Matthew 13:24-30, 36-43

We are usually quick to complain if something is unfair, provided we or our loved ones happen to be on the losing end. Most shoppers will more readily point out short-changing than over-changing. We watch our children's developing sense of fairness with wry sympathy as they experiment with changing the rules in their favour whenever they start to sense things going against them. It takes maturity to accept fairness whether we gain from it or not. Also, the more complex the situation, the less clear it is to see what is actually fair. Our whole lengthy judicial system is built on the recognition of this.

The Old Testament writers, contemplating God's nature and open to his truth, could discern that in the eternal Being of all truth, justice by itself would be insufficient, and was in fact softened with the compassionate quality of mercy. Mercy can only come from one who has the power, right and authority to punish, since it involves waiving one's right, or even the absolute justice of deserved punishment, in the light of loving concern for the wrongdoer. It is this blend of justice and merciful loving kindness which is a hallmark of the nature of our God.

For a race of beings who know all too well their capacity for making stupid mistakes and deliberate wrong choices, this is all very good news which makes us able to have hope. If we are brave enough to look candidly at our lives we can easily see that justice alone would leave us in a pretty poor state. We would all be poked to death by accusing fingers of absolute fairness accumulated over a good few years of blundering and sin. There would be no hope for us at all.

We catch a glimpse of this inevitable condemnation when we think of the way we are often particularly harsh and critical ourselves about other people's failings which are similar to our own, or about faults we feel we have managed to overcome. What causes this is a large helping of self-righteousness, fuelled by a sense of fairness but lacking in mercy. Thankfully, God holds his love for us as paramount in all his dealings with us, as the life and death of Jesus clearly shows.

In the passage from Romans, Paul's whole argument is grounded in the certainty that we are ultimately safe in the hands of our God, and in Jesus' parable of the wheat and darnel we have a tender picture of God's loving forbearance tempering his justice. How can we, who claim to love such a God, do other than follow this example in our own dealings? Revenge of any sort must be out for us, as must a rigidity of fairness which refuses to look at each individual situation through the eyes of compassion. It is not for us to take God's judgement into our own incapable hands, but to recognise with humility that we all stand condemned, were it not for the amazing merciful love of God, which has dropped the charges and set us free.

All-age talk

Borrow and bring along one of those toys (Polly Pocket or Mighty Max) which look like a plain box and hold inside a whole miniature world.

Show everyone the toy, and explain that today we heard another of those parables which Jesus told. Parables are a bit like these toys, because they are stories which have secret meanings inside. You need to open up the story to find the meaning. (Open the toy.) First of all, let's look at the story Jesus told.

If you have an OHP you can illustrate the story using cut-outs of weeds and wheat, and the evil enemy based on the pictures below, as these will show up in silhouette on the screen.

Remind everyone of the story, using volunteers to be the farmer sowing his seed (accompanied by music from *The Archers*), and the evil enemy creeping into the field at night to sow the weeds (accompanied by everyone doing a pantomime hiss). When the farmer finds that his field is sprouting loads of weeds as well as wheat, he is faced with a choice (hold a question mark in a thought bubble over his head).

All the servants say, 'Shall we pull the weeds out for you?' (Have this written on a speech bubble so everyone, or a small group, can say it together.)

The farmer shakes his head. (He does.) He knows that if he pulls all the weeds up now he might pull out some of the wheat as well, and he certainly doesn't want to lose any of his wheat. So instead he decides to let both the wheat and the weeds grow together until harvest time, when the weeds can be gathered up and burnt, and the wheat harvested and put in the barn.

That's the parable Jesus told. What's the secret meaning of it? Here's a clue. The field is the world, and we can all see that in our world there is a lot of good, but also a lot of evil. Why doesn't God burst out of heaven and stop all the evil in the world straight away, and punish the people who get away with doing cruel and terrible things? The parable gives us the answer.

If he did that while life is still going on – while the wheat and weeds are still growing – some good might get lost or damaged. It is because God cares about us so much that he won't risk anything that would cause us lasting harm. There's time enough for punishment when the world comes to an end. Then all that is good and honest and kind and thoughtful will be gathered up safely forever. All that is mean and selfish, cruel and greedy will be completely destroyed forever. We can trust our God to know the right time to punish and the right time to hold back, because he always acts with love and mercy as well as justice.

Sunday between 24 and 30 July

Proper 12

Thought for the day

Jesus, the teacher, enables the ordinary, unlearned people to understand God's wisdom – the eternal laws of his Father's kingdom.

Reflection on the readings

> 1 Kings 3:5-12
> Psalm 119:129-136
> Romans 8:26-39
> Matthew 13:31-33, 44-52

It is with disarming and endearing humility that Solomon prays, as he stands at the starting line of his reign, overwhelmed by the impossibility of the task ahead and very conscious of his lack of experience and the heaviness of responsibility. It is typically at those times when we are acutely aware of our dependence on God, that God can act with power in our lives. The wisdom which Solomon requests is to do with having a heart which is skilled in listening, so that good can be distinguished from evil. In a world where every situation has many facets and interrelated issues, the gift of wise discernment is desperately needed by all with decision-making authority. And, as God's reply makes clear, to desire such a gift is entirely in keeping with his will.

It is a gift which is increasingly recognised and valued by those in management training, so that look-alike versions are marketed to reproduce the actions while bypassing the more costly genuine listening heart.

In Romans, Paul establishes the reality of the situation: we, like the young Solomon, find ourselves having to admit that we are very weak in many ways, and do not even know how to pray adequately. Yet God recognises our groans and mutterings of prayer as beautiful in intent, and the Spirit in us pleads through that, aligning our prayer to what is in harmony with God's will. God is on our side. That means he is in no way going to condemn or reject us, and there is nothing at all that can ever separate us from his love.

This knowledge, which is heart knowledge, turns lives upside down and remakes them, alters long-held priorities, and opens up all kinds of possibilities for life-spending. We cannot grasp this truth about God's loving personal relationship with us and remain unchanged. In today's Gospel Jesus gives a whole series of images to help us understand what it is like to glimpse the kingdom of God and enter it.

We are told about the excitement and often the surprise of discovering it, upon which everything we presently value seems so insignificant and temporary in comparison that as a matter of urgency we want to give up all that keeps us from owning such a possession. We are told of the way it grows and spreads with astounding effect, so that not only our own lives but the lives of many others are affected for great and lasting good. We are urged to take this teaching seriously to heart, because the consequences of how we lead our lives here are not insignificant or temporary or a matter of personal taste. It is all much bigger than that, and Jesus does not want his hearers, whom he loves, to reach the end of their earthly lives and find they are totally unprepared for the next phase of life and the consequences of living habitually tied to selfish wants.

He hopes for us to cherish both the ancient wisdom of God's guidance through the law and the prophets, and also the new, heady joy of having God's Spirit breathing through our being with the power and forgiveness that makes living good lives an outpouring of thankfulness to a God whose grace alone makes it possible.

All-age talk

Bring along something that is precious and old, and something that is precious and new. Choose items which your congregation are likely to relate to. (It could be a well-worn teddy and a new Teletubby for a baby, for instance, or an old stained-glass window in the church and someone's new engagement ring.)

First introduce everyone to the old thing, pointing out why it is so treasured and important and valuable. In our faith there are also ancient things which we as Christians value and treasure, such as the stories in the Old Testament which teach us about our God (for example, creation, Noah's flood, the great escape from Egypt, and the teaching of the prophets), and God's law, the ten commandments given through Moses to the people to help them live well and in line with God's will. Although these are old, ancient things, they are precious to us because they help us get to know God and live as his friends. We don't just throw them out because Jesus has come. Jesus valued them himself, and told his followers to go on valuing them.

Now introduce the new thing, explaining why it is treasured, important and valuable. In our faith there are also new things which we as Christians value and treasure. With the coming of Jesus, we are able to have a completely new kind of friendship with God that had never before been possible. Through Jesus dying, rising and returning to heaven, we are able to have the gift of God's life breathed into our own lives. That means that every new morning of our lives there are new possibilities in our daily friendship with the living God!

Not only are we looking forward to the coming of God's kingdom at the end of all time – we can also enjoy living in it now. In our Gospel today Jesus gave us some ideas of what the kingdom of God is like. Here is just one of them.

It's like some treasure you might find in a field. (You could have an exciting-looking treasure box there.) You're so excited about this precious treasure that you go and sell everything else you have, just so you can buy the field and own the treasure. Let's think about that. If you found a diamond ring, would you go and sell your house and car and World Cup coin collection to get hold of it? Probably not. You'd only bother to sell your house and car and cherished possessions if the treasure you had found was worth far, far more than all the things you already had. Jesus is saying that knowing God in a loving friendship and living in him each day is actually worth far, far more than anything else you own.

I don't think many of us realise that yet. It's as if we dig up a treasure box, look at it and think, 'Oh, that's interesting – a box of treasure. I'll pop over and look at it sometimes.' Then we bury it again and go home to carry on living in the same old way without realising what we're missing out on. Next time you catch a glimpse of what God is really like, and how incredibly wonderful he really is, commit yourself to doing something about it, so you can enjoy that treasure of living in peace and love with him every day of the rest of your life.

Sunday between 31 July and 6 August
Proper 13

Thought for the day

God feeds all who come to him hungry, and we, as the Church, are expected to share in that work.

Reflection on the readings

Isaiah 55:1-5
Psalm 145:8-9, 14-21
Romans 9:1-5
Matthew 14:13-21

Supermarkets are very good at placing 'useless' but attractive things right next to the checkout, so that all the children, wheeled past in their trolleys and bored to distraction as the shopping is loaded, crave what is on display at a time when pressurised parents are most likely to give in! Our whole society is skilled at creating inviting displays of things we could well do without, and which encourage us in all kinds of wrong directions. Whether it is the lure to unnecessary spending in an affluent society, to oblivion or happiness and well-being through drugs or alcohol, or the lure to join guerrilla rebellions in areas of instability and poverty, what we are all after is some gratification which is immediate, and we are prepared to ignore the long-term consequences in order to achieve this.

In today's passage from Isaiah, the prophet speaks out God's yearning for something better for his beloved people. All these short cuts to satisfaction and fulfilment are going to leave us unfed at the deepest level of our humanity, dissatisfied and craving, but too disillusioned to try the only truly satisfying food for our souls – God himself. Psalm 145 marvels at the qualities of this God and the individualised provision he gives us all.

Paul, in his letter to the Romans, lets us catch a glimpse of God's heartache for all humanity, as Paul's own national and family ties heighten his sadness for those in this particular group. They could so easily be with him, revelling in the fulfilment of the scriptures in Jesus, and yet have missed out on what should have been their own heritage.

The Gospel for today describes the feeding of five thousand people. It is a clear picture for us of God's delight in feeding all who have come to wait on him and listen to him. These people had deliberately set out into the open country to find Jesus. They sensed that he had things to say which they needed to hear. They sensed that he cared about their welfare and their lasting happiness and peace of mind. Jesus was himself in need of refreshment and comfort when he arrived, in the wake of the tragic death of John the Baptist, but still his compassion reached out to a crowd of people who knew their need of him.

As always, in every situation, Jesus takes whatever is made available to him and uses it for great good which far outstrips our expectations. As always, he involves his followers in the work of preparation and distribution. In this act of bodily feeding Jesus teaches the people in a living, three-dimensional parable, about the real, satisfying feeding for the soul which can be theirs, and which is the Father's delight to provide. In order to receive, we have to know our need enough to go out of our way to seek God and listen to him.

All-age talk

Begin by asking people how they like to spend their pocket money. Invite representatives of all ages to join in this. Has anyone ever spent their money on something which has let them down, or been disappointing, so that they end up wishing they had saved their money? Ask a few people to share their experiences.

It may be that you have had to watch as someone you are fond of wastes their money. You can see that it's all going to end in disappointment, or even tragedy, but they won't listen to you, and all you can do is stand by and wait to pick up the pieces when it all goes wrong, without saying, 'I told you so'! It's our love for the other person that makes us ache to see them wasting their money like that; because we love them we want better for them than to be sad and disappointed by things that aren't worth buying.

That's how it is with our parent God, who loves us to bits, and aches as he watches as we spend not just our money but our time and our love on things which are not going to be good for us, or satisfying or rewarding. He wants better for us than that. God wants us to be aware of our need for his love and power in our lives, and to come to him for it, because he is happy to give it to us free.

Look at all those people in the Gospel story today. Why had they bothered to leave their towns and villages and walk miles out into the country? They bothered because they knew their need of Jesus and were prepared to 'spend' their whole day looking for him and listening to him, hanging on his words. What did Jesus do? Did he let them down or disappoint them? No! He was there for them, ready to heal the sick friends and relations they had brought, ready to reassure them that God loved them, and teach them about how they could best please God in their lives.

And when their tummies started rumbling, and they knew physical hunger as well as spiritual hunger, what did Jesus do? He fed them! All he used was what they had. That's what he always uses. Are you a three- or four-year-old, ready for Jesus to use your life? Then that's what he'll use to make lots of other people really happy. Are you a seventy- or eighty-year-old, ready for Jesus to use your life? Then that's what he'll use to bring blessing and hope to lots of other people. And it's the same with all the rest of us in between.

What about our church? Is St Martin's ready to be used by Jesus? If we are, he will use us, and lots of people in this area will be blessed and given hope; if we aren't, and can't be bothered to go and spend time seeking Jesus out and listening to him, then he won't be using us and the people in our area will lose out.

Let's make sure that doesn't happen. Our job is to make ourselves available, and help give out to the people the gifts of God, so that all are properly fed.

Sunday between 7 and 13 August

Proper 14

Thought for the day

God is faithful to us through all the storms of life, yet our faith in God is so very small.

Reflection on the readings

1 Kings 19:9-18
Psalm 85:8-13
Romans 10:5-15
Matthew 14:22-33

In a sense both Elijah and Peter are sinking, and both are given firm-handed rescue by the loving God. In today's passage from 1 Kings, Elijah is exhausted and worn down, and therefore vulnerable to those nagging negatives which whisper the futility and hopelessness and unfairness of it all. It is a place that many of us will recognise well, and there is rich comfort in the way God responds. First, he has provided Elijah with the basic practical needs of sleep and food, and now comes the spiritual feeding – the teaching that will gather up Elijah and show him new direction and new insights. In contrast to all the turbulence in Elijah's mind and heart, God is noticeable by his absence in the violence of wind, earthquake and fire. The presence of God gradually becomes recognisable in the peace, the intimacy of shared tranquillity.

Still Elijah states his case from his place of misery; God's presence is never kept at bay by such honest aching. But Elijah is now ready to cope with being led out, provided with the new direction and clear instructions he needs. God does not attempt to dissuade Elijah from how he feels, but offers him instead the way forward to view it differently, or as less overpowering and crippling. He does the same with us, taking us through at a pace we can cope with, using where we are as a starting point and gently offering a route of hope.

Peter, too, is suddenly overwhelmed by the sense of his vulnerability, as it dawns on him that he is out in the middle of a huge stretch of dark and angry water, buffeted by the violent wind, and with nothing under his feet except fathoms of cold water. It would be hard to imagine a less secure environment! So how had he got into this precarious and vulnerable place? By responding to Jesus' calling. How vividly this matches the experience of many Christians, responding in joy and enthusiasm to the call of Jesus to trust him and come to him, only to be thrown completely at the realisation of where this places them.

It is all very well to say that, like Peter, we need only to fix our gaze and concentration on Jesus for everything to be fine. But the truth we are shown in today's readings is that there will be moments when we are made desperately aware of our vulnerability. When we take that decision to climb out of our neatly constructed lives and follow Jesus, we open ourselves up to an environment where Christ is our only and total security; the truth of our existence is that we are out on deep water without a boat, and it is only at the moment of this realisation that we begin to learn what faith is all about.

Thankfully, Jesus is always there to grasp us firmly, in our lack of faith, and bring us back to where we feel safe. It is a learning process, and we progress at a pace God knows we can manage. If we compare Peter's performance here with the Peter who boldly proclaims the Gospel in spite of being insulted and thrown into prison, we can see dramatic growth in faith. The environment is no less stormy or insecure, but it is matched by the working knowledge that dependence on the faithful God is all the security we need.

All-age talk

If you know a juggler, invite them to come and juggle as part of today's talk. Failing this, give out some balloons to a group of older children and ask them to keep them in the air, in as controlled a way as possible, using hands, head, knees and feet.

As the juggler or children perform, draw attention to the way they need to concentrate and keep their eyes on the balls or balloons if they are to be sure of catching them under control. Notice how the moment they lose concentration, or lose balance, things go wrong.

Today we heard in the Gospel about some people in a boat, weathering a terrible storm. It was the disciples, and Jesus had sent them off home while he himself went off to pray on his own after he had fed all those five thousand people. He needed to be alone with his heavenly Father to talk that over, and give special thanks for all that had happened. The waves were churning, and the boat was rocking and the disciples were frightened – especially when they saw Jesus walking across to them. This was water, and you can't walk on that! We are told they thought Jesus must be a ghost, and they got more scared than ever.

Let's look at what Peter did next. He called out to Jesus, 'If it really is you, then tell me to come to you over the water.' Why did he say that? What was he doing? It sounds as if he was testing whether Jesus was real or not, like us saying to a friend, 'If you've really been up in space, show me a photograph to prove it', or 'If you really love me, how about helping with this washing-up'.

Jesus knows he isn't a ghost, and he takes Peter up on what he's asked. 'Come on, then!' he says. There's no way out now! Peter concentrates on Jesus, like the juggler concentrated on the balls. He gets as far as climbing out of the boat, and he starts to walk towards Jesus, still concentrating on him, and then suddenly it all hits him. 'This is crazy! This is impossible! The water can't possibly be holding my weight! Rationally I know I ought to be sinking!' And as those doubts make him panic and lose his sight of Jesus, he does just that – he starts to sink and has to shout out in terror to Jesus to save him. And, of course, Jesus reaches out to him and gets him to safety straight away.

Trusting Jesus is keeping ourselves concentrating on him and his love, underneath everything else that we do. Suppose you're buying some sweets. At the same time you're aware of Jesus and his love. What difference does that make? You will probably buy without being greedy, and you'll probably end up sharing what you get. Suppose you are travelling to work, and you've also got your eyes on Jesus. That will affect the way you drive, and the way you treat other commuters.

Today Jesus is saying to each of us, 'Yes, it is OK for you to put your total trust in me. Just keep that in mind and all the things which make you feel frightened and insecure will not let you sink – you can walk straight over them, confident in my love and power.'

Sunday between 14 and 20 August
Proper 15

Thought for the day

The good news of salvation is not limited to a particular group or nation but available for the whole world.

Reflection on the readings

Isaiah 56:1, 6-8
Psalm 67
Romans 11:1-2a, 29-32
Matthew 15:(10-20) 21-28

The idea of God's salvation being for all nations did not emerge as a new concept of the Early Church. It had been there, intrinsic to that first promise to Abraham, and today's reading from Isaiah is representative of what all the prophets proclaim. In fact, the whole reason for Israel being called as a nation of light is so that other nations can see their way to the true and living God. Zechariah's song at the birth of his son, John the Baptist, sets it all out clearly.

Paul, with a passion for spreading the good news to the Gentile world, is equally strong in proclaiming hope for his own people of promise. God is never fickle, and if his promise has been made, it will, in good time, be fulfilled. He can even see how God can bring blessing out of their rejection of Jesus, the source of hope. What that does is to place even the chosen people of promise in the position of receiving God's mercy, spelling out to them his amazing forbearing love.

In today's Gospel we are given an example, a foretaste, of those putting their faith in God who are Gentiles. Not only the centurion (who was obviously closely involved with the Jewish people, since he had built their synagogue) but also this Canaanite woman (belonging to a country which was the traditional enemy to God's ways) is recommended by Jesus for her remarkable faith, which touches his heart and impresses him. It is seen in sharp contrast to the 'experts' – the Pharisees who are able to see Jesus at work and hear his teaching with all their background of promise behind them, and are still blinded to the truth of fulfilment.

Such tunnel vision not only makes it unlikely that they will relate to anything Jesus says, but also creates terrible obstacles for other people coming to faith, and that is what disturbs Jesus so much. Self-righteousness, self-sufficiency and cynicism are excellent for stubbing out flickering flames of faith. On the other hand, as we see in the tenacity of the Canaanite mother, perseverance, trust and hope, even in the face of opposition and difficulty, is excellent for building up faith in others.

Exactly how much faith we really have in the true God will be shown not by what we say or claim but by the way we respond and act.

All-age talk

Ask everyone who is a Brownie to stand up. That means that everyone left sitting down is a non-Brownie. Do the same with various other groupings, such as Scouts, servers, the short-sighted or Coco Pops-eaters. Each time we become a member of a group, there are lots of others who are not included.

Remind everyone of the promise God first made to his friend Abraham, whose family the Bible traces right back to Noah. What was it that God promised to Abraham? God promised that (1) he would make his family into a great nation, and (2) all the people on earth would be blessed by this nation which was starting with Abraham. That's quite a promise! And because God always keeps his promises, it came true. Abraham's grandchildren and great-grandchildren and great-great-great-grandchildren did grow into a great nation of God's chosen people.

The people of Israel (as the nation came to be called) were rightly proud of being God's chosen people. Like the groups we had standing up, they thought of themselves as God's chosen, and everyone else was outside and not included. They called all the outsiders 'Gentiles'. Probably most of us here are Gentiles.

So much for the first part of that promise to Abraham: 'I will make you into a great nation.' But there was a second part, wasn't there? What was that? It was that *all the people on earth* would be blessed by the nation which God had started with Abraham. All through the Old Testament there were prophets like Isaiah who reminded the people of this bit of the promise. 'This is not just for you, remember,' they'd say. 'We are called to bring blessing to all the other people on earth eventually!'

It was true. Starting with the chosen nation, God wanted all the people on earth to have that special friendship with God which Abraham had. It isn't just for a few people, or for one particular nation, but for people of every age, country and time. It's for all the Brownies and the Scouts and the short-sighted and the servers and everybody else, because with God not one person is left 'on the outside'. God's loving is for everybody, everywhere, every time.

If that's how it is for God, then that's how it must be for us as well. We must make sure that in all our loving we don't leave people out. Think about that when you are playing or working in a team, or chatting in a group. Check whether there are people we deliberately avoid. Do we assume some people are not worth telling about Jesus? Would we rather some types of people didn't come to our church?

If God had thought that about us, most of us wouldn't be here. It's his love for us that brought us, and he has love for lots of others who need us to show it to them, and love them into the kingdom.

Sunday between 21 and 27 August

Proper 16

Thought for the day

The Church is the Body of Christ, built on strong rock of faith and energised by the living Breath of God.

Reflection on the readings

Isaiah 51:1-6
Psalm 138
Romans 12:1-8
Matthew 16:13-20

It is part of being human to ask questions. As soon as children can speak they badger their parents with the constant 'Why?' questions, and that is the way we all learn to make sense of the world we live in. The deep, spiritual questions are searching for the meaning of identity and the meaning of life itself, and it is these questions which are at the heart of all faiths and systems of belief. They surface particularly at times when a people has its sense of identity shaken, and today's Isaiah passage comes from the time of exile, when the people of Israel were having to think through the seriousness of their situation and the meaning of it all.

Speaking through the prophet to his beloved people, God reminds them to look back to their roots and take heart from the great faith of Abraham, their father, which marked the beginning of their identity as the chosen nation. This is where they have sprung from, and God's promise still stands, in spite of all their wayward stubbornness, their blindness and sin. As they recognise the need to get themselves right with God, the door is once again opened for progress, and that spells hope not just for them but for the rest of the world.

For us as the Church, standing at the start of a new millennium, there are bound to be questions about our identity and our calling. We cannot look back over all the terrible costly mistakes without regret and sadness, nor at the divisions and lingering anachronisms which still cripple the spread of the liberating Gospel today. But today's readings are full of practical help and real hope for the Church.

In Romans, Paul encourages us to catch hold again of the joy of sacrificial giving, in every area of life, which he says will actually help us cultivate valuable discernment. We are beginning to recapture the truth that costly giving, in financial terms, is not really about usefulness for a Church short of money, but has deep, spiritual value, and is in fact extremely necessary for us. The cheerful giving nature has spin-offs in all kinds of other areas, including the way we see ourselves as the Church – members, or organs, of a living, working body. No empire-building here, no false humility or boasting, but a loving harmony of people with a commonly held life and purpose.

And the Gospel reminds us to look back to our roots for further encouragement. We, too, share the faith ancestry of Abraham, and all the prophets, and Jesus talks of the Church which he will build on the rock of discerned faith in the revealed God, as spoken out by Simon. Symbolically, he is given the name of 'Rock' to mark the importance of this recognition. The Church is to last, through all kinds of attacks and dangers, cosmically safe in the keeping of the eternal love of God, constantly renewed and equipped for its work in every age.

All-age talk

Beforehand, ask a few people of different ages to provide you with a photograph of them when they were very young, and have these pictures duplicated, or shown on an OHP. Don't identify them, but say they are all members of the church community. When people have had a go at guessing the identities, ask the people to come to the front. This narrows the choice, and makes it easier to see who's who. We might have a hunch about someone, and can ask them directly. They will tell us whether or not we are right, and then we'll know for certain. (Invite people to do this.) Once we know the true identity, it's often easier to see the likeness!

In today's Gospel, Jesus knew that people had all sorts of ideas about who he was. Some ideas were close to the truth, some were wide of the mark, and Jesus always wanted his followers to make the discovery for themselves. Discovering something for ourselves means that we always remember it far better than when we have simply been told things. (People may remember discovering for themselves that fire burns, for instance, that cement hardens into a solid lump, or that overloading a computer can cause it to crash.)

No doubt Jesus sensed that the disciples had almost got to the point of discovering that he was not just their friend and teacher, but also the promised Messiah, the Son of God. This conversation, starting with what other people think, will help them tip over into that 'Aha!' of learning, that point when you suddenly know something and everything falls clearly into place.

It is Simon, the fisherman, who comes out with it for the first time. 'You are the Christ,' he says, 'the Son of the living God.' It must have been a bit like when you first say the words 'I love you' or 'I'm three'. It's the first time you have ever said it and as you say it, you know it is really true, and your life will never be quite the same again.

Sunday between 28 August and 3 September

Proper 17

Thought for the day

As Jesus prepares for the necessary suffering of the cross, he is tempted, through well-meaning friendship, to avoid it.

Reflection on the readings

Jeremiah 15:15-21
Psalm 26:1-8
Romans 12:9-21
Matthew 16:21-28

The harder we hit against God's will for us, the harder that will appears to be. Today's readings prepare us for the serious business of committed following, and we need to listen very carefully if we are not to be thrown by what can seem impossible demands while we are in the wrong place, and yet which suddenly turn into blessing as soon as we approach them differently.

Jeremiah is thoroughly fed-up with his impossible position. He knows God's hand is on him to be a prophet and speak his word to the people, and he feels that he has made a very good job of sacrificing the pleasures of life in order to be obedient. Yet what has he got in return? Only misery and loneliness, rejection and insult. He complains bitterly, full of self-pity (which always comes from self-righteousness) that it simply isn't fair. God is not that sympathetic, suggesting that he gets himself back to the right place and starts speaking some sense instead of all the moaning, so that God can use his mouth once again to proclaim what needs proclaiming. But he does assure Jeremiah, very tenderly, that he is going to stay with him and keep him ultimately safe through everything he will have to suffer.

It is so easy to get into the worldly habit of trading where spiritual matters are concerned; so easy to start totting up the noble sacrifices we have made, and the time or money we spend for God, expecting tangible returns of our own choosing. Even our intercessory prayer can so easily turn into a kind of bullying of God, or bribery, and, of course, as soon as this happens, we have actually swung round with our backs to the Lord we claim to love.

There is another danger, too. Peter has genuine love for Jesus, and his horrified denial of the necessary suffering is so very understandable. Would we not all react in the same way at the prospect of a loved friend having to go through that? Yet Satan has hijacked this human friendship to tempt Jesus as powerfully as he possibly can: 'Avoid the cross and gain the crown without having to go through all that agony of body and spirit. How will you or your dear friends cope?' Jesus' reply shows us how sharply the temptation has stabbed him, and how deeply he must have yearned, in his humanness, for Peter to be right. But he recognises in it Satan's cunning, and shows Peter that he is, in this instance, not a rock of God's strength but a rock for Jesus to trip over, with all the terrible consequences of that for the whole world.

The suffering has to be. There is no other way. Jesus braces himself for the way ahead, in the certainty that it is for great and permanent good, and that is also the message he needs us to hear and understand. Any cross laid on us will be heavy, and it will hurt, but the loving God lays it on us with such tenderness and as gently as he can. Any cross laid on us is not to do with us only, but has far-reaching effects which we will never realise until we reach heaven and see there the value of the painful journey we have lovingly travelled in God's company.

All-age talk

You will need two lengths of bramble, and gardening gloves to handle them. If you can get hold of a length of chain as well, this would be excellent; otherwise, rope, or a paper chain will do fine.

Lay the two lengths of bramble to form a cross on the floor, explaining what you are doing for the benefit of those who will not be able to see this. Make the point that you are wearing protective gloves as the brambles are painful. Explain that the brambles represent all the suffering and pain of the cross. Ask for a volunteer to stand at the top end of the cross. This person represents all of us humans, chained up in all the sin and selfishness that stops us from living freely. (Chain their hands together.) Ask another volunteer to stand at the foot end of the cross, some distance from it. This person represents Jesus at the point of today's Gospel.

Last week we heard how Simon Peter was ready to speak out the truth he had realised about Jesus – that Jesus was the Christ, the Son of the living God. Jesus knew his friends had to be sure of this before they could cope with the next stage of the plan. Now that was in place, and it was time for Jesus to get his friends ready for what had to happen next.

Jesus couldn't just go on working in one part of our world, because he had come into the world to save all of us. That would mean walking a very painful road – the way of the cross. The pain of giving his life on the cross was the only way for Jesus to be able to reach us and set us free. He couldn't get round it; he had to go through with it, even though he knew it would hurt.

Ask the person who is representing Jesus to take their shoes off and start walking towards the cross. Before they get there, stop them as you remind people how Simon Peter couldn't bear to think of his friend going through all that pain, and said, 'Never, Lord! This shall not happen to you!' But if Jesus had listened to him (walk round to the representative human in chains), we would never have been set free from the sin that imprisons us. Never. There would have been no hope for us any more.

(Go back to 'Jesus'.) The good and wonderful news is that Jesus loved us far too much to let his own suffering stop him from saving us. Today we won't make (Lawrence) walk barefoot over those brambles, but as we think of Jesus gladly stepping out to Jerusalem, where he knew he would meet terrible pain and suffering, let's thank him in our hearts for loving us so much that he was prepared to do it anyway (walk round to the human in chains) so that we could all be set free. (Set the person free.)

Sunday between 4 and 10 September

Proper 18

Thought for the day

It is our responsibility to encourage and uphold one another in living by the standard of real love.

Reflection on the readings

Ezekiel 33:7-11
Psalm 119:33-40
Romans 13:8-14
Matthew 18:15-20

It is never easy to tell someone you think their behaviour is out of order. It is particularly unpleasant to do this to a loved one, or to a member of your Christian fellowship. At the mere thought of it, we are bombarded by fears of judgementalism and hypocrisy, and the possibility that picking someone up on their behaviour runs counter to the Christian principles of compassion and accepting love. It is a difficult path to tread, but that is no reason for dismissing it, and for too long we have been content to do so.

Obviously, we are to love one another with God's love, and that will guide us to approach anyone with respect and honour, regardless of what they have done or failed to do. But we do one another no kindness by turning a blind eye to behaviour which is clearly contrary to God's way of living, or excusing and accepting standards of behaviour which are against his law of love. There are many cases of people who, having waded through great suffering as a result of their sin, have heartily wished that someone had been courageous enough to challenge them about their behaviour at the outset. Through Ezekiel we are warned that any of us who opt out of such challenging, however difficult it might be for us, are actually held partly responsible for any evil that results.

Today's Gospel has some practical advice for us in this delicate area. Matthew places it in the teaching Jesus gives his followers about the kingdom. He has just been telling the story of great love and compassion about the way a shepherd searches for one lost sheep until he finds it. It is in the context of this total concern for each individual, and God's loving commitment to the idea of rescue, that we are told to take one another discreetly aside and talk over the problem with them. This is no judgemental confrontation, then, but it is a recognition of our concern, the concern of the Church, and, most importantly, God's concern for the well-being of a loved sheep.

This meeting may be enough, especially if it happens early enough, to bring about a change of heart, or a realisation of the dangers, and a change of direction before the situation gets totally out of control. So often, this is the stage we miss out on, with serious and often tragic consequences for all concerned.

We are given a graded list of courses of action, which, in principle, allow as much opportunity as possible for the matter to be treated discreetly and calmly, so as to avoid the damaging public humiliation and self-righteous hysteria which the media revel in and which is so alien to the concept of Christian love. In the event of all approaches being deliberately rejected, there is the need to recognise where the person is. It is both pointless and dangerous to pretend that what is sinful is acceptable and right. Someone who is deliberately placing themselves outside God's care is doing just that. What they then need is our honest acceptance of where they are, and our continued love and prayer.

All-age talk

Ask a number of volunteers to get themselves into a line in order of size. When they have achieved it they can be applauded. Draw attention to the way they helped each other in the task, and showed one another if they were in the wrong place, whenever that was noticed. Because they were working on the task as a team, no one got terribly upset by seeing they were in the wrong place – they just moved into the right place.

Today's Gospel gives us all some teaching about helping one another to keep in order as we live as Christians. The good thing about being a Church is that we are all in the same team, God's team, and we can help one another along. But we're not always very happy to do this. The truth is that we are all going to make mistakes and be in the wrong place with God sometimes, so we need to get used to reminding one another and being reminded without getting too upset about it.

Let's look at what we mean by being in the wrong place with God. (Ask some volunteers to stand facing the cross.) Explain that when we are facing God we are living in his love, and whenever we don't live lovingly, we are turning our backs on God. (Ask the volunteers to turn and face the cross when you say something which is loving, or turn their backs on it when you say something which is unloving.) Here are some suggestions: telling lies, telling the truth, looking after someone, being friendly, grumbling about everything, making sure you get your own way, being generous in your giving, telling dirty or unkind jokes, being bossy and pompous, listening carefully, cheering someone up.

And this is the way we want to be as the Church, with all of us facing God's way. It's our job to help one another keep facing that way, and to help them turn round if they are facing the wrong way.

Supposing we are behaving in an unloving way, then, turning our backs on God? (Turn one of the volunteers around and make up the wrong behaviour they are involved in.) How can the rest of the church help?

In today's Gospel we heard what Jesus said: 'Go and take him to one side and talk it over with him.' (Let one of the volunteers tap him on the shoulder and lead him off a short way from the others, pretending to talk with him.) The point is that we don't always realise that we're in the wrong place, and it is kind to let one another know, so that we can do something about it.

We actually ought to be grateful if someone takes us aside and says, 'Look, I've noticed that you've got really snappy lately. Is anything the matter?' We may have thought we were hiding our worry very nobly, and it will help us to talk it over and recognise that we've been taking our problems out on other people. Or perhaps someone is kind enough to take us aside and say, 'I don't suppose you realise, but you never actually look at people when you are saying hello, and it makes them think you aren't interested in them.' Or 'Have you noticed that every time I say anything at all you contradict me? Have I offended you in some way?' Or 'I've noticed you are always nasty to Paul whenever Steven and you are playing, and that's not very kind. What do you think you could do to stop that happening?'

It may not be a wonderful feeling to know that our faults and failings are noticed, but if it's going to help us put things right, then let's practise being thankful instead of offended, and be ready to help one another up whenever we fall down.

Sunday between 11 and 17 September

Proper 19

Thought for the day

Forgiving is a natural result of loving, so it is not an option for us but a command.

Reflection on the readings

Genesis 50:15-21
Psalm 103:(1-7) 8-13
Romans 14:1-12
Matthew 18:21-35

Today's Genesis reading is one of the tenderest passages in the Old Testament. We feel Joseph's affection for these brothers of his, who even now are too scared to be honest. We sense his wise, gentle discerning of the real fears under their naive scheming, and can learn so much from the way he reacts to these genuine fears rather than to the behaviour they present. Out of such wise loving pours forgiveness. There is no question of it being refused, and through the whole experience Joseph can help them to see God's redeeming and transforming.

Psalm 103 celebrates the wonder of God's forgiveness, extending naturally from his loving and compassionate nature and his genuine longing for us to be set free from the hold of sin. In today's section from Romans, Paul is dealing with a question the churches were finding difficult. Judgementalism was creeping in as Christians vied with one another in the holiness stakes, assuming that their way was the only right way of going on. Paul suggests that in matters which are not central to the faith there are bound to be differences, and the last thing we should be doing is condemning what another finds helpful. He points out that God is the one to whom we are all answerable in the end, and since Jesus is Lord of both life and death, there is nowhere that he isn't, or that his mercy isn't, so we should stop bothering with what is really not our concern.

In today's Gospel, it's Peter again as spokesman, voicing the thoughts of the disciples about forgiveness, and a fair slice of self-righteousness colouring their thinking. Peter would have been considering himself generous to be suggesting forgiveness that stretches to the seventh offence, but, as ever, Jesus shocks him, and us, with a glimpse of God's ideas about things. Suddenly we are in a whole new dimension, placed in the position of the one on the receiving end of mercy, rather than thinking of ourselves as the noble one dishing it out to those inferior to us.

Rather like Nathan the prophet, when he used a story to show King David the reality of his sin, Jesus tells a story which begins by making us identify with the servant who owes millions of pounds and has had that whole debt cancelled. Peter, who had fallen to his knees when he first met Jesus and said, 'Go away from me, Lord, I am a sinful man!' would realise immediately that he was like the servant in the story, owing so much and yet totally forgiven. If we imagine Jesus looking into our eyes as this part of the story is told, we are similarly shown what God has let us off.

From this place, the concept of forgiveness is very different. How can we dare to treat others without forgiveness in view of what God has done in us? It isn't a question of totting up scores against us any more, but simply a natural effect of loving.

All-age talk

First ask anyone who has never done anything wrong, *ever*, to raise their hand. Make it quite clear that doing wrong doesn't stop when you grow up, and it's a problem that we all have to deal with. In which case there's going to be another problem we need to deal with. What about when people do things wrong which hurt and upset us? It's bound to happen, and today we are given some very useful teaching from our Lord Jesus to help us with it.

Suppose someone lets you down, cheats on you, loses their temper with you and says some cruel unkind things, lets you down again, steals from you, makes you look stupid, and breaks something you've let them borrow. (Count on your fingers seven typical offences.) Peter goes to Jesus and says, 'Is seven times about the limit for forgiving someone? It seems fairly generous to me. You might as well give up on them after that, don't you agree? Or am I being a bit over-generous – more forgiving than is good for me?'

Jesus says, 'Actually, seven times isn't nearly enough! You need to keep on forgiving until you've lost count and just do it anyway.' And then he tells one of his stories to explain what he means.

Give a volunteer a sign to hold which says 'IOU millions'. The story is about a servant who owes loads and loads of money. He has a wife and children, and he's borrowed so much and has been using his plastic money facility so much that he's stacked up a huge debt to his master, which he can't pay off. The master calls for him (use another volunteer and give him a mobile phone or a smart jacket) and demands the money. The servant kneels down and begs (he does this) to be given more time to pay. The master feels sorry for the servant and lets him off the whole debt! Just like that! (Master draws a thick black line through the IOU.) How do you think the servant feels? (Collect ideas.)

Now that is what God has done for each of us. Ask them to think of all the things they've done wrong, perhaps which no one else knows about except them and God. Think of all the meanness, selfishness, pride, hypocrisy and so on that we have been forgiven completely by God. It's just as if we owed God millions of pounds (hold up the IOU) and God has drawn that line through it, setting us free from the debt.

So here is this happy, free servant, who finds a fellow servant owes him a few pounds. (Give another volunteer a sign with 'IOU a few pounds' on it.) And the same thing happens. The servant goes on his knees and begs (he does this) to be allowed more time to pay. But what does the servant do? He grabs him by the neck and shakes him (not too realistically) and has him thrown into prison until he pays up. What Jesus wants us to ask ourselves is this: Is it fair or right for the servant to behave like this? What do we think?

Next time we are not wanting to forgive someone, let's remember how God has treated us, and pass on loving forgiveness time and time and time again.

Sunday between 18 and 24 September
Proper 20

Thought for the day

We have no right to be envious at the generosity and mercy God shows to others.

Reflection on the readings

Jonah 3:10–4:11
Psalm 145:1-8
Philippians 1:21-30
Matthew 20:1-16

There is a wonderful candour in the way the Bible records people's relationships with God, warts and all. In today's reading from Jonah we find the prophet sulking, angry and resentful that the enemies of his own people should be let off the total annihilation he considers they deserve. He almost spits the words out to God, quoting from the psalms he knows, and finding God's qualities of compassion and gracious understanding, in present circumstances, exceedingly irritating!

We have all done it, we have all been there. We all know how righteous indignation makes us boil, and we take it out on someone whom we know, deep down, we can trust. God doesn't come rushing out defending himself against Jonah's attack because he can see where his prophet is coming from and he loves this angry ball of resentment just as much as ever. He gives him time, a little comfort, and a little experience which enables him to see things from God's perspective. That is quite typical of the way God treats us, so it's worth looking out for it next time.

The point that Jonah had completely missed, and that we so often also forget, is that God does not only love and care for those we think he ought to. He doesn't share our lines of demarcation, which label some (usually including ourselves) who are 'deserving' and others who are decidedly not. This has always brought anger God's way, and, of course, it happened when Jesus started living it out in practice, much to the disgust of the religious leaders, who thought they knew better how a prophet ought to behave and with whom he should spend his time.

Time and again in his teaching, Jesus tries to help us grasp something of the nature of God's loving, which is so much wider and more far-reaching than we seem to understand. Today's parable of the hired workmen is a case in point. The first lot are happy to agree a day's wage, but they cannot cope with the employer being generous to those who started work near the end of the day. Naturally it is not those paid first who complain, but those who see the arrangement as a raw deal for themselves and resent it. If our basis for reckoning in life is simply what we're worth on an hourly rate, then the longest working labourers have a point.

But the owner is looking at it quite differently, and sees the holistic needs of all the men in the market place, just as God sees all people with their needs and is concerned to provide for them all. Whenever we see God's generosity in evidence, however much of a surprise it is in view of our perceived suitability of the recipient, we have no right to question or quibble, but should be rejoicing with the angels at the amazing love of our God.

All-age talk

Today we are given some useful teaching on being grumpy and sulking, something most of us do from time to time. (Have one or two volunteers to give a really sulky, grumpy face.) Did they notice how sulky and cross Jonah was in our first reading? Perhaps some of them do the same in rows – remembering things that were said at other times and throwing them back at the person we want to upset, and saying, 'I *knew* it would end up like this! If you'd listened to what I said, this would never have happened!' We feel quite at home here! And if we're a loving parent on the receiving end of all the anger and resentment, which we know comes from a lack of understanding or experience, perhaps we can sense something of how God feels, loving this very hot-headed, angry person shouting at us, and knowing that our job is to stay calm, stay loving, and pick up the pieces once they've got over it.

What is it that makes us sulk, usually? (Collect answers.) Usually it's when we feel hard done by, as if we have been unfairly treated and been given a raw deal. That's how Jonah felt. He didn't think his enemies should have been let off being smashed to pieces. Why on earth would God want to take pity on that lot! He'd even got Jonah to tell them to sort their lives out, and the annoying thing was that they had listened, and changed the way they were living. But forgiveness for them was the last thing Jonah wanted. So he sulked. (Have the sulky faces.)

Jesus told a story about some sulking workmen, which we heard today. The ones who worked all day agreed their wage, and at the end of the day they got it in full. Why were they sulking? Because some other workmen, taken on much later in the day, were paid the same wage. So they sulked. And we often behave in the same way. (Sulky faces.)

God helps Jonah understand with the help of a nice olive plant which grows up to shade him one day and dies away the next. Of course, Jonah is fond of this plant and sad when it is destroyed. So then God can talk to him about the people of Nineveh. Just like Jonah and his olive plant (only more so), God loves the people of Nineveh and doesn't want them destroyed, so, of course, he tried to save them, with Jonah's help. And in Jesus' story the owner helps the workmen to understand why they are sulking. He asks them, 'Are you jealous because I am good to these people as well?'

We all need to understand that God doesn't split us up into some who are OK to be saved and some who aren't worth bothering with. We shouldn't get jealous or angry if Christians of another church or tradition seem to be having God's blessing as well as us, or if people who have made bad mistakes in the past are allowed to be part of our fellowship. If we are loving, like God loves, this will make us not sulky (sulky faces) but happy (happy faces).

Sunday between 25 September and 1 October

Proper 21

Thought for the day

God longs for us to die to sin and live, but it has to be our choice, too.

Reflection on the readings

Ezekiel 18:1-4, 25-32
Psalm 25:1-9
Philippians 2:1-13
Matthew 21:23-32

However much we may long for our loved ones to go to the doctor, do their homework or take a holiday, we all know from experience that, unless they share our concern, they won't get round to doing what, to us, seems so sensible and good for them. We may nag or drop hints, threaten or cajole, but in the end it is up to them and we can do nothing about that.

It must be rather like that for God, as he sees what would be such lasting good for the children he loves, and yet must watch us all making disastrous choices, never getting round to tackling our habitual sins, wasting opportunities, and taking no notice of all his hints and teaching, his examples and offers of help.

We can sense that longing for our good and grief at our turning away from it, all through the Bible, in both the Old and the New Testaments. Ezekiel is just one example of the way God keeps speaking to his people through the voice of the prophets, to urge them to look seriously at the consequences of wrong choices and the joyful hope of right ones. Time after time he explains that he is not out to shoot them down, or to condemn; no way does God find pleasure in anyone perishing as a result of leading a life of evil and wrong choices. At the same time, being of nature ultimate truth, goodness, love and justice, it is impossible for God to have deep life companionship with evil, deceit, hypocrisy, corruption or impurity.

We are each of us only responsible for the choices we ourselves make. It is very important to understand that God will never hold us to blame for any evil committed by our parents or ancestors, and any guilt we may be carrying as a result of another's abuse of us is guilt that belongs to them, not us. It is God's will that we should be freed of such unjust burdens.

The truth is that God promises to teach us how to make good choices, and through Jesus he is working within us, inspiring both the will to do good and the act of carrying it out. What the religious leaders in today's Gospel needed to see was that talking about it is not enough; a good choice is completed in the action. It is the son who gets round to doing the work who is recommended, rather than the one who airily talks about it but does nothing.

So we are involved in the kind of caring, encouraging relationship with God which really does enable us to tackle those wrong areas in our life. We are never too old, too set in our ways or too busy to take God up on his offer of live-in help.

All-age talk

Bring along the details of a children's colouring competition, and also one of those junk mail promotional letters which tell you that you have already been selected as a winner.

Begin by sharing this exciting letter with everyone, reading out some of the blurb, and getting a volunteer to scratch any secret messages included. No doubt many of us receive these kinds of letters. When we do so, we have a choice: are we going to bin it (or preferably recycle it), or will we take them up on their wonderful offer and claim our prize? What we decide will depend on all kinds of factors, such as how busy we are, how desperate for winnings we are, how many previous disappointments we have experienced, and whether we actually believe them.

But one thing is certain. Unless we decide to return our reply slip, we have no chance of winning anything at all. It's the same with colouring competitions. A prize is offered and anyone has a chance of winning. But if you don't get your felt-tips or paints out and do the colouring, and send it off in time, you will have no chance of winning a prize, however good you are at colouring.

Today we are being reminded by God that he has great prizes and gifts for us, which he longs for us to enjoy. He wants to see us all as winners, happily receiving the gift that has been reserved specially for us. But. . . and it is a big 'but'. . . unless we choose to turn to God and take him up on his offer, we will have no chance at all of winning. If we choose wrong instead of right, evil instead of good, and self instead of God, we cannot have the joy and peace and life that God longs to give us. We don't just get it anyway, however we live. Lots of people think that is what happens, but it isn't because God isn't like that. He is a God of goodness and love, truth and kindness. Do we want to go along with that? We have to choose it, then, and start doing something about it.

As soon as we choose it, God can give us all the help we need, and he will, because all he wants is for us to know complete and lasting happiness with him.

Sunday between 2 and 8 October
Proper 22

Thought for the day

God does everything possible for our spiritual growth and well-being, but still we can choose hostility and rejection.

Reflection on the readings

Isaiah 5:1-7
Psalm 80:7-15
Philippians 3:4b-14
Matthew 21:33-46

Following on from last week, we hear today how Jesus responds to the challenge of the religious leaders to name his authority and qualifications. First he had met their confrontation with a return question, which directed them both to the answer and to their unwillingness to accept it. Now he follows this up with a parable drawn directly from their own familiar tradition. As soon as they hear the beginning of it, they are bound to tune in to the passage from Isaiah, which is also our Old Testament reading for today. There is a good chance, therefore, that they will already be looking out for God's loving exasperation with his people, in whom he has invested so much and whose fruit is so disappointing that exile and suffering are inevitable.

However, although the two parables begin in a similar way, Jesus' story suddenly changes direction. If the religious leaders are going to hear anything, this is surely the time their ears should prick up and their hearts be challenged. Before, God had found bad fruit instead of good, and the tenderly planted vineyard was abandoned to the encroaching wilderness. In this story the owner does not come in person but sends his servants, who meet an appalling reception of hostility and rejection. Anyone already familiar with identifying God as the vineyard owner would perceive that his servants must be God's prophets. So when the story goes on to talk about the owner sending his own son, and the vineyard managers choosing to plot his death, Jesus is telling them in as clear a way as he can about his own identity and authority.

Yet what do we find? The smug reply of the Pharisees shows that they are not yet willing to take on board the implications of this parable for themselves, even though Jesus has brought them to the very brink of understanding. Yes, they can see what a terrible thing it would be to treat God like that, but, no, it can't have anything to do with them, for they are bastions of the faith, are they not?

It is a warning for all of us. We cannot assume that just because we were born into a church-going family, have been to church for years, are on the PCC, or live in a so-called Christian country, that we are immune from the responsibility of making a personal choice to follow Christ each day of our lives. As Paul says in Philippians, he has more reason for such assumptions than anyone, but would cheerfully throw the lot away since finding new life, freedom and joy in Jesus Christ.

One of the reasons we reject God is because he will insist on telling us the truth, and we prefer the flattery and indulgence of self-deception. Yet if we can be courageous enough to allow ourselves to hear him, we gain so much.

All-age talk

Bring along a watering can, secateurs, a gardening fork and some slug pellets. Show everyone these things and ask the gardeners in the congregation (both young and old) to explain to you what they are all for. Ask if anyone has been using these this year, and what has been grown and eaten by the congregation.

All gardeners can feel in good company, because one of the often-used pictures of our God is as a gardener. In our reading from Isaiah, God is imagined as a gardener planting vines in a vineyard – digging the ground, and getting it all ready, planting carefully, weeding and watering regularly, supporting the branches and pruning, and really caring for this vine so that it may bear a wonderful juicy crop of grapes. Gardeners are always fond of what they grow – that's why they'll go to any lengths to protect their plants from things like slugs and greenfly. We can imagine God caring like that (only more so) for his people, and wanting desperately to protect them from evil and sin.

But when this gardener comes to pick the crop of grapes which he has grown so carefully, he finds they are not delicious and sweet but bad and sour, and the lovely vineyard ends up all overgrown and wild. Like a gardener, God has looked for the good fruit of justice in his people but found only bloodshed; he has looked for the good fruit of righteousness and found only the cries of those who are treated badly. What kind of fruit does God the gardener find in us, in his Church, or in our society? Does what he finds in this church and this world put a smile on his face, or does he find instead sour fruit which makes him sad?

We all know the kind of thing that delights God. He loves to find such fruits as love, joy, peace, patience, kindness, goodness, gentleness and self-control. He loves to see justice, mercy, right living, purity and honesty. May this garden grow a bumper crop of such fruits, that will gladden the heart of God and bring blessing and healing to our town.

Sunday between 9 and 15 October

Proper 23

Thought for the day

We are all invited to God's wedding banquet; in accepting we must allow the rags of our old life to be exchanged for the freely given robes of holiness and right living.

Reflection on the readings

Isaiah 25:1-9
Psalm 23
Philippians 4:1-9
Matthew 22:1-14

There is a lot of rejoicing in today's readings, the kind of rejoicing which is born of relief and victory, such as was experienced when peace was declared after the Second World War. The images used in the passage from Isaiah emphasise protection and safety in the middle of turmoil, as, for instance, 'shelter from the storm' and 'shade from the heat'. The well-loved Psalm 23 echoes this sense of all being well in God's company, even if we are walking through the valley of the shadow of death, and in both these readings the banquet is prepared by God for his loved ones as a feast of celebration in full view of those who mean harm, emphasising their powerlessness and God's complete victory over evil.

In Philippians, Paul is able to talk about rejoicing in the same breath as suffering. He has trusted God as you might trust ice you have tested, and has found with relief and joy that God does not let us down. In that case, all our time spent worrying anxiously about what might happen is rather a waste of time. Paul suggests that instead of filling our heads with such anxious thoughts we would do better to spend our time contemplating the wonderful things which lift our spirits and make us rejoice, simply hearing them in a list: whatever is noble, right, pure, admirable, excellent and praiseworthy.

We so often slip into the habit of worrying and complaining, rather than rejoicing. At those moments of joy and relief after a difficult or dark patch, we may say to ourselves that we'll never grumble or worry again, because we are at present full of thankfulness; but it doesn't take long before we're back into our old habits. Yet what a lot we miss by failing to rejoice, whatever the circumstances. Rejoicing is a result of trusting God to be the shelter in the storm, and really knowing that he will not let us come to ultimate harm, so that we have, ultimately, nothing to fear.

The parable Jesus tells about the wedding feast once again features the rejoicing and celebration with God which happen even in the face of violent opposition and rejection. All of us can count ourselves among the guests who have accepted the invitation once it is thrown open to those walking in any direction and with a good or bad past life. And it is quite a celebration, stretched over all time and space, heaven and earth. We can afford to savour that rejoicing, rather than rushing on immediately to the next section of the story.

Wedding garments would have been provided, free of charge, so there is deliberate insult in the guest who has decided not to wear his, but remain in the filthy rags of his old life. Jesus wants his hearers (and Matthew his readers) to be under no illusion. Accepting the honour of a place at the banquet obliges us to accept also the grace to be renewed and transformed. Living with our former outlook, attitudes and behaviour is not on, and places us alongside those who have chosen to reject the invitation.

All-age talk

As people come into church make sure that everyone is given a small picture or cut-out paper shape of a robe of righteousness, with this title on it:

ROBE
OF
RIGHTEOUSNESS

Probably we have sometimes looked into our wardrobes before a party and decided that we have nothing suitable to wear. However jam-packed the wardrobe is, with all that extra junk stuffed in to keep it out of sight, we can't find anything we want to wear! Prepare to be impressed: the wardrobe space of today's teaching is quite something.

Mention the piece of paper they were all given when they came in, checking for any who have been missed and providing for them now. Everyone has been given a beautiful wedding garment! That's what used to happen when guests were invited to palaces. It was the practice for kings to provide thousands of guests with a suitable robe each from their vast wardrobes in which thousands of garments were kept ready specially for such occasions. (Dress a volunteer up in a clean white robe – a surplice is fine.) They had special servants to be in charge of those huge wardrobes.

In Jesus' parable of the wedding feast we can imagine all the poor and the dirty straggling along to the palace in their smelly rags, and the people in charge of the king's wardrobes fitting up everyone with a clean, beautiful robe to wear, before ushering them into the grand dining hall. No doubt they felt different dressed like this – perhaps they even walked taller and were more polite to each other than usual! Then the king comes in to inspect his guests. (Perhaps everyone sits up straighter, like you do when someone important walks into assembly.) He is glad to see the palace full of guests who have accepted his invitation, because the original guests had refused to come. Everything is light and warm and happy.

Suddenly the king finds a guest who has accepted his invitation but rudely refused to wear the proper clothes provided. He's still in the filthy rags he came in, and the king has him put outside in the darkness with those who had chosen to turn down his invitation.

What is Jesus teaching us in this parable? One thing is that God is very happy to invite all of us to the Church of Christ and feed us here with love and rejoicing. So we can be happy together in God's company and enjoy ourselves in our worship. The other thing is that if we say yes to God, we do need to let him reclothe us, and not expect to go on wearing the rags of bickering and fighting, lying and cheating, self-indulgence and lack of self-control which we came in. That's why we always start our worship by saying sorry to God, and hearing his forgiveness, letting him clothe us with robes of righteousness.

Sunday between 16 and 22 October
Proper 24

Thought for the day

All leaders and rulers are subject to the ultimate authority and power of God, the living truth.

Reflection on the readings

Isaiah 45:1-7
Psalm 96:1-9 (10-13)
1 Thessalonians 1:1-10
Matthew 22:15-22

One of the difficulties students have is when there are exaggerated expectations of emotional returns on money contributed by parents towards their keep and education. But, of course, they are dealing with different currencies here, and the confusion is what causes the frustrations and disappointments. Today we are looking at another such clash of currency; our duty and responsibility towards God and to 'Caesar'.

The Pharisees had simply contrived the question in order to catch Jesus out, picking one of those 'Catch 22' situations where you can't win. If Jesus said they should give their taxes to Caesar, it would be an insult to the national pride of his followers, and if he said they shouldn't, the Roman authorities would be able to sort him out for them. We can imagine the quantities of midnight oil spent planning the scheme.

Jesus sees exactly what they are planning, and deftly counters the attack by means of stating the truth. He points out that in fact the two are different currencies. This challenges his hearers to check their balance and commitment both to earthly and heavenly citizenship. It completely avoids the confrontation hoped for, and alienates neither the people nor the authorities, so the Pharisees, impressed but no doubt furious, can only withdraw and leave Jesus alone.

It conveniently allows us to learn from Jesus about authority and those in charge. Both the Isaiah reading and Psalm 96 are grand and glorious, proclaiming the total and ultimate authority of God over all creation and all peoples, including their rulers, and in Thessalonians there is the same sense of God's authority as the living truth. These are concepts of cosmic proportion, and remind us of the transcendence of the God we worship. Human authority and empires shrink as we contemplate the reality of God's glory and power. Yet the Son of God, breaking into our human system of life, chooses to walk among the ordinary people in the squalor of their need, and enter the holy city on a donkey.

What does this tell us about giving to God what is God's? Certainly it burns into our consciousness that the great almighty God, source of everything we have, including life itself, is not to be 'paid off' with our small change, either in money or time. He is worth nothing less than everything – all that we are, our past, present and future, freely given back in gratitude and love to the one who has given us so much.

Immediately it becomes clear that our commitment to 'Caesar' is a completely different type of giving. However much earthly rulers may like to think of themselves as close to divine, we are in fact all equal in human status before the majesty of God, and our governmental structures are matters of convenience and useful order to be respected and upheld where they express God's will, and challenged wherever they do not.

All-age talk

Unless the size of your congregation makes it far too expensive, give everyone a penny. Invite everyone to look at their coin. On one side there is a picture of someone's head. Whose head is it? It belongs to Queen Elizabeth II. She is there, just as Caesar's picture was on the coin Jesus looked at, because she is the Head of State and we are her subjects. In our country there are taxes to pay to make sure that everyone, both rich and poor, can have schools, roads and hospitals. There are laws to keep, so that we can all live safely and peacefully, and there are police to check that we keep the laws. Those who break them are sent to prison or charged a fine.

Each country works out its own way of organising all this, and some are fairer than others. Each country has leaders – people who are in charge – and the country Jesus lived in was ruled by the Romans.

Now invite everyone to hold their coin in the palm of one hand. This penny is not very big. It won't buy very much. It sits here in your hand, and your hand is here in this church building. It's only a very little part of all the space in here. As you hold your penny, your hand is surrounded not just by the space of this building but by the whole universe. Now God is greater than the universe, because he is the One who thought and loved our universe into being.

There's a huge, huge difference between the kind of power and authority human leaders have, and the kind of power and authority God has. We are to give to God what is God's. What is God's? Is there anything God doesn't know? No. Is there anywhere God can't reach? No. Is there anything or anyone God doesn't care about? No. God is much greater and more wonderful than we can imagine, and he holds all creation in the palm of his hand, like you are holding the little penny in the palm of your hand.

No wonder we've all chosen to come and spend some time praising him this morning! God is worth everything we can ever give him. Of course, we are to respect our leaders, and keep the laws. We are to be good citizens, just as our Christian rule of love tells us. But we also need to remember who is ultimately in charge, and put God first. We need to be prepared to make a fuss if any laws are passed which are against God's law, and we need to do what we can to help our leaders uphold the authority of the God who made us all.

Sunday between 23 and 29 October
Proper 25

Thought for the day

We are to love God with our whole being, and love others as much as we love ourselves.

Reflection on the readings

Leviticus 19:1-2, 15-18
Psalm 1
1 Thessalonians 2:1-8
Matthew 22:34-46

If any proof were needed that Jesus had come not to condemn but to save, it is here in today's Gospel. Jesus' response to the Sadducees, putting them right in an area of understanding, had the effect of making some of the Pharisees much more open to Jesus, and this time they come not to trick him but examine him, to sound out more of his teaching on the law, in which they considered themselves expert. They ask Jesus what kind of commandment is the greatest, and this would have arisen from the debates they were used to having with the Sadducees about emphasis. From the Gospels and Letters we can see that current debate must have centred on such matters as right observation of the Sabbath, right giving and tithing, and the question of purification and circumcision. Where did Jesus stand?

Typically, Jesus takes them back to the heart of the matter, quoting a specific commandment, the first, which they would have been assuming intellectually, but which in their lives was being crowded out by all the detailed laws and rules. Jesus was willing to stand alongside the Pharisees as soon as there was the faintest hint of openness, and he shows respect for what they have got right: the law's importance. From the fairly obscure book written for the Levite priesthood, and revered by the Pharisees, Jesus draws out the summary of the law: love given to God first and, by extension, to our neighbour, using the measuring stick of self-love to help us understand its meaning. At least the Pharisees have it in their heads, even if not yet in their hearts.

Answering their agenda of detailed differences with this broad sweep of general principle, taken from writings they cherished, opened up the possibility of truth dawning on these over-conscientious law-keepers. As with old paintings, the years of familiar yellowed varnish needed removing so that the original vibrant colours could once again shine. Jesus patiently chips away, flake by flake. He asks them to look again at the Messianic promises, looking deeper than the traditional snap responses towards a curious questioning which might lead them to look at wider possibilities of fulfilment than they have previously dared.

With Jesus we are always being drawn forwards, deeper into the love and meaning of God, and he will use all our doubts and experiences of life to help us. We need not be afraid to question where God is concerned, for that is how we learn.

All-age talk

Hold a large edition of the Bible, and tell everyone that today we are all going to read the whole lot as part of our talk!

Explain that today we heard Jesus giving us a summary of the whole of the Bible, in a couple of sentences. (Reader's Digest can eat their heart out!) He was saying that everything in all the law and the prophets was an exploring and working out of this. (Have Matthew 22:37-39 written out large, and invite everyone to join you in reading it out.) There – we've read the Bible! Or, to be more precise, we have read the subject matter of the whole Bible, because everything in it is to do with what we just read – people learning to love God with their whole being, and their neighbours as themselves. It's the story of their learning, their mistakes and failures, and of God's great love helping us make the impossible possible. (Well worth reading the full-length version!)

Let's look at what it means to love others as we love ourselves. How do we love ourselves? Invite a couple of friends to come and help show us. Get one to stand behind the other, with the front person putting their hands behind their back, and the back person providing them with substitute arms by pushing their own arms through the front person's. Have someone offering them a wrapped chocolate which they eat, and give them a brush so they can do their hair.

All day long we look after ourselves like this, feeding and washing and scratching ourselves whenever the needs arise. Even if we don't admit to loving ourselves our actions show that we do. If we start getting too hot, our body kindly makes us sweat to cool us down. If we're threatened by the cold, our helpful body sets us shivering and raises our hairs to warm us up again. And if there's a real emergency (the children can make an ambulance siren sound), the body shuts down some systems and kicks in with others to keep us alive as long as possible. That's love for you!

So if we are to love others like that, we'll be attentive, looking out for one another's well-being and ready to help when we see someone in need. We'll be doing what we can to feed the hungry and look after those with problems. We'll scratch where it itches but not where it doesn't. We'll be ready to drop everything and be there for people if there's an emergency and they need us. We'll do everything we can to help them feel better and get through the difficult times.

And where does all this love come from? From our wonderful God, who made us all in the first place, and loves to see all his children caring for one another like this.

All Saints' Sunday

Sunday between 30 October and 5 November

Thought for the day

Lives that have shone with God's love on earth are filled with joy as they see their Lord face to face.

Reflection on the readings

Revelation 7:9-17
Psalm 34:1-10
1 John 3:1-3
Matthew 5:1-12

Saints are not a special breed or caste. They do not possess a certain prescribed blend of skills, and emerge out of particular sets of circumstances. There is really only one thing which marks out a saint from the rest: they are the ones who know, without doubt, that they need God, so they do something about it, and go to him, just as they are and open to receive from him.

Psalm 34 obviously comes from experience when the psalmist reflects that those who go to the Lord for help will have every good thing, and the saints would agree. In the vision of heaven in Revelation we find them utterly filled with joy and peace as they lose themselves in worship and praise. Describing heavenly things in earthly language is naturally difficult, but this passage gets close to touching the heavenly in us, and draws us into a sense of heaven's fulfilment, where there is no more pain or hunger and all tears are wiped away forever.

Here is the reward promised in the Beatitudes – reward in the sense that it is the natural outcome of living so knowingly dependent on God's goodness, love and guiding. We are all called to be saints, and become so in direct proportion to the extent we desire God. That is linked with the way we perceive him. There are so many who reject a god they wrongly assume to be the God of living truth, and if only they were introduced to the real person would have a very different response. There are others who lavish attention and time on false images they think are true, so that desire for the real Person of the true and powerful, living God is treated with suspicion and renounced.

The wonderful thing about our God is that he searches for us, wherever we are, listening for our bleating, lifting us on his shoulders and carrying us safely home. It doesn't matter where we have been, how bedraggled and smelly we are, or how long we have been lost. As we bleat in our brokenness and long for our Shepherd-God to give us all we need, we begin the path to sanctity, and only lose our way again if we start to lose sight of the truth of our dependence on God's grace, and his unwavering provision.

As John writes in today's reading, to be really Christlike is to see things as they really are, with our perception healed. And that takes us back to the saints in heaven, gazing on the Lord they have been drawing close to throughout their lives, and whom they now recognise clearly. That integrity of perception drenches them in the beauty of holiness, and their eternity is filled with worship and praise.

All-age talk

Today we are celebrating the festival of all the saints of God. Saints are God's close friends, and there are lots of them around, as well as all the famous ones like Mary and Joseph, Peter and the other disciples, Francis, Benedict, Clare and Catherine.

What makes a saint?

Suppose your car breaks down on the motorway, and, as you drive skilfully on to the hard shoulder, smoke pours out of the bonnet. At this moment there is no doubt in your mind about it – you know that you need the AA or the RAC to sort you out. Suppose you've fallen down in the playground and find you can't move your ankle without terrible pain. At that moment you know without doubt that you need some help from the teacher on duty and the first aid people in the school office.

Show everyone a large arrow on which is written 'We know our need'. As soon as we know our need that points us towards getting it sorted. (Have 'Get help' written on a large piece of paper or card.) But what if we don't know or realise our need?

Suppose you have got some spaghetti sauce on your chin and you are just going out to meet an important client, or a new boyfriend or girlfriend. If we realise we have the sauce on our chin (show the arrow), then we'll probably go and wipe it off. (Show the 'Get help' sign.) But if we aren't aware of the sauce on our chin (show a sign without an arrow which says, 'Don't know our need') then we won't do anything about wiping it off. (Turn the 'Get help' sign over so it's a blank sign.)

If we don't realise our need of God (show 'Don't know our need') then we won't go to him for the help we urgently and desperately need. (Keep the blank sign up.) But if we *do* realise how much we need God (show the arrow) then that will lead us to seeking God's help in our lives. (Turn over the 'Get help' sign so it shows.)

Saints are ordinary people like us who realise their need of God (show the arrow) and spend their lives close to him so that he can help them in all they do. (Show the 'Get help' sign.)

Fourth Sunday before Advent

(For use if the Feast of All Saints was celebrated on 1 November)

Proper 26

Thought for the day

With God's light and truth to guide us, we shall be brought safely through to the end of time.

Reflection on the readings

> Micah 3:5-12
> Psalm 43
> 1 Thessalonians 2:9-13
> Matthew 24:1-14

Today marks a change in direction and mood in the Church's yearly cycle. We embark on our preparation for the great seasons of Advent and Christmas, when we shall once again be celebrating the first and anticipating the second coming of Jesus Christ. We start with a reading from the prophet Micah, deeply disturbed by the corruption and injustice around him, and able to discern the inevitable suffering and pain that is bound to result.

Jesus shares this grief for the holy city. He has been voicing his sorrow and love for Jerusalem, and realises that Micah's prophecy of the city becoming a pile of rubble is tragically true, and not that far off. The disciples are stunned by Jesus' words, and we can imagine them thinking it through in silence on their way across the Kidron valley, before plucking up the courage to broach the subject with Jesus again. They need to know more.

Jesus sees the waves of destructive forces sweeping through the next forty years and culminating in the sacking of the city of God. It is an inevitable and natural result of the coming of the Messiah to a chosen people who mainly fail to recognise and choose to reject him. And so it proved to be. The earthquake recorded on Good Friday began a series of tremors in the area which Seneca, writing in AD 58, describes as spreading devastation over Asia, Achaia, Syria and Macedonia. There were famines and plagues in the reign of Claudius in Syria and Rome, and many wars involving the Jewish people. The letters of John, Peter and Paul warn of the rash of false prophets, and Acts records the Church facing opposition and the beginnings of persecution. Jerusalem fell in AD 70, when the Romans tore it apart so that, quite literally, not one stone was left on another.

Hearing today's Gospel is like witnessing an accelerated film of these terrible events over the space of a generation and throughout much of the Roman empire; we are very conscious of the aching sadness of it all – and the inevitability. Yet it was also the sacking of Jerusalem which scattered Christians far and wide, so that the Gospel was spread rapidly over the known world; it was like the birth pangs as the Christ brought in the new life of the Church.

The reading from Thessalonians is a refreshing glimpse of careful witnessing and teaching, with the good of others and their rescue at heart. It links with the lovely words of Psalm 43: 'Send forth your light and your truth; let them guide me; let them bring me to your holy mountain, to the place where you dwell.' We are left with the conviction that through all the terrible, tragic places we may have to walk on our journey, we shall be kept ultimately safe, through faith in Jesus, and we will have with us the light of his guiding and the yardstick of his truth which will enable us to persevere to the end.

All-age talk

Place around the church such warning signs as, 'Wet paint' on a chair, and 'Wet floor' next to a bucket and mop. Ask a couple of volunteers to go round the church to find the signs and bring them to you. Warnings are very useful! What would we do if we saw the 'Wet paint' sign? Avoid sitting on the chair. That's useful because it means our clothes don't get spoiled. What would we do if we saw the 'Wet floor' sign? We'd make a point of walking carefully, instead of running, so that we didn't slip on the wet floor and hurt ourselves.

It's quite normal for prophets to speak out God's warnings to his people, and Micah is doing that in today's reading. He doesn't mind that his message is going to be unpopular, any more than Jesus minds speaking out the truth. That's because he knows that warnings from God may help people sort out what is wrong in their life, say sorry to God for it, and ask his help to put things right as best they can. He tells his hearers the things they need to sort out and change. If they listen, and really start to repent, or turn their lives around, they will be able to work with God to put things right. Otherwise, they will end up with their holy city being destroyed.

In our Gospel today we heard Jesus warning his disciples that Jerusalem was going to be completely destroyed, even before some of them had died, because people had taken no notice of all the warnings they had been given. Jesus was talking in about AD 32, and over the next forty years all those earthquakes, wars and plagues happened in the area. In AD 70 the Romans stormed the city of Jerusalem and destroyed it completely, just as Jesus had foretold.

Warnings are useful, and we need to take notice of them. Some of us have been shown films to warn us about the dangers of smoking and drugs and AIDS, and we are warned each summer to protect our skin from sunburn. The captain on the *Titanic* was warned that too much speed could be dangerous. These warnings are there to help us, but we do need to listen to them and act on them if they are going to work.

It's just the same with our spiritual health and well-being. Show a torch and a ruler. God gives us his light to see by, and his truth to measure our lives by. If we become aware of God warning us about our attitudes or behaviour or our relationships, we need to take it on board and do something about it before it's too late.

Third Sunday before Advent
Proper 27

Thought for the day

We need to keep ourselves awake and prepared so that the Day of the Lord does not come to us as darkness rather than light.

Reflection on the readings

> Amos 5:18-24 or Wisdom of Solomon 6:12-16
> Psalm 70 or Wisdom of Solomon 6:17-20
> 1 Thessalonians 4:13-18
> Matthew 25:1-13

Today we continue to look at the potentially terrifying future. The prophet Amos proclaims to the people God's warning. It is all very well for them to think cheerfully about the Day of Judgement, assuming that the judgement will be in their favour since they are the chosen nation, but if the society they live in is filled with corruption and injustice, they will have a very nasty shock waiting for them. It will be, he suggests, like when you reach your home, where you assume you are safe, and casually put your hand on the wall, only to be bitten by a snake. The horror is even worse for being unexpected and supposedly undeserved.

Blindness to reality is a theme which surfaces again and again throughout the Bible. As Jesus said to the Pharisees after healing the blind man, if they recognised that they were blind there wouldn't be a problem; it was because they thought they could see that there was no hope of healing. The first and most important stage of healing for all addicts is to recognise their addiction. That opens up the route to freedom.

Most of us see in ourselves what we want to see, and have blind spots about areas we do not wish to change. The human brain is immensely good at self-deception, packing in layers of psychological wadding to protect us from truths we do not wish to hear. This is why, if someone trespasses anywhere near the truth we are avoiding, we tend to react with what seems like irrational anger and irritability. In fact, it is exceedingly rational, since we are protecting ourselves from discovering that hidden core.

The risks of living without self-knowledge, however, far outweigh the attractions. The less we live a lie, the more integrity we have as people, and that has benefits for the society in which we live, and for our local church community. A whole group of people with self-knowledge can bring about great good and widespread healing.

The unprepared bridesmaids in today's parable alert us to the terrible possibility of being shut out of the kingdom by default. As we consider the tragic, eternal consequences of living in denial of God's law of love and truth, we need to be brave about those areas we may have hidden from ourselves, perhaps for many years, and ask for God to reveal them to us, so that we can have them healed before it is too late.

All-age talk

Beforehand prepare some sticks with red paper flames stuck on the end.

Begin by asking who has ever been a bridesmaid or a page-boy at a wedding. Were any of them late for the wedding? Today we heard a parable Jesus told about some bridesmaids. Some were ready when they were needed, but some weren't.

Show the 'torches' which were used at that time. Material was soaked in oil and tied on to the end of sticks. When you set light to them they would burn well, so the bride and bridegroom, coming from the bridegroom's house in the evening of the wedding, could have their way lit by the bridesmaids' torches. (Have a bride and groom and some bridesmaids to show this, holding their torch sticks.) At least, they could if the bridesmaids had their oil with them.

The problem in Jesus' story was that half the bridesmaids hadn't checked their oil supplies, so when the bridegroom needed their torchlight, they were rushing off to buy more oil, and ended up being shut out of the wedding feast.

What is the hidden message in this parable? What is Jesus wanting us to understand?

He wants us to be ready, and have our oil supplies topped up, so that whenever the bridegroom returns, even if he takes longer to arrive than we were expecting, we will be there waiting, shining brightly in the darkness. Then the bridegroom can lead us all into the celebrations and the feast.

Fill the oil lamp and light it. God's Spirit is like the oil we need to keep us burning brightly with God's love. If we stop keeping ourselves 'topped up' by forgetting to pray and read the Bible each day, our lives will stop shining, just as the girls' torches went out. Then, if Jesus suddenly returns, unexpectedly, either at the end of time or in a situation where our bright Christian love is badly needed, we won't be able to help.

So Jesus is telling us to keep praying, keep listening and keep loving. That way, we'll be all ready whenever he needs us.

Second Sunday before Advent

Proper 28

Thought for the day

The Day of the Lord will hold terror for the wicked and unprepared, but rejoicing for those living in God's light.

Reflection on the readings

Zephaniah 1:7, 12-18
Psalm 90:1-8 (9-11), 12
1 Thessalonians 5:1-11
Matthew 25:14-30

People speak sometimes of being petrified by fear; they are so terrified that the fear paralyses their bodies, and they are, momentarily, 'turned to stone'. There is much in the reading from Zephaniah to petrify. The prophet pours out horrifying descriptions of the Day of the Lord, full of wrath and anguish, trouble and ruin. It is like the shock tactics used in documentaries to terrify us out of speeding, and it pronounces unrelieved condemnation, justly deserved. Zephaniah is a particularly gloomy prophet; the times he lived in were grim in terms of both religious and social corruption, and he still remembered better times to compare them with. Total annihilation seemed inevitable.

But we are not to let such warnings petrify us to the point of preventing change and action. It is good that our Old Testament reading is tempered with the positive, though still serious, words of the letter to the Thessalonians. Certainly the Day of Judgement will come 'like a thief in the night', at a time we are not expecting, but that need not make us over-fearful if we are people of daylight. Christ's coming and his saving work has given us access to the necessary protection against evil, and, provided we make use of it, we do not need to live in terror. We are reminded that it is certainly not God's will that any should perish, and what he longs for is that we should all be saved

Accordingly, we need to spend our energies as the Church more in encouraging one another, and loving sinners to repentance, than coming in heavy with scare-mongering and condemnation. We should not behave as 'daylight dwellers' through terror of eternal punishment, but through a natural thankfulness as the extent of God's love dawns on us, and his ways of love and truth become increasingly attractive to us.

This carries with it not terror but peace and joy, together with the maturity of responsibility. The kingdom of God is not about people terrorised into submission; part of salvation is being given the grace to grow up. Today's parable of the talents reminds us of this expectation in our new life. God expects us to make the most of all we have been given, rather than hiding our gifts away, either out of a mock modesty or a fear which insults the loving justice of God. All these gifts we have been provided with can be used and enjoyed, both for the encouragement and building-up of the Church and in the service we are called to give in the world.

All-age talk

Beforehand place three boxes of different colours around the church. In the red box put five one-pound coins (cardboard ones are fine!), in the blue box put two one-pound coins and leave the yellow box empty.

We know that one day the world as we know it will come to an end. We know that life as we know it will finish. All the prophets and Jesus teach us in the Bible that there is going to be a Day of the Lord, when we will see Jesus in all God's glory, and all that is evil will not survive. That includes people. How we live now in our lives will affect what happens to us that day. We do need to know that.

When will it happen? We don't know the time or date; in fact, what we do know is that it will happen suddenly, without us having loads of time to change. That's why we need to live every day as if it were our last.

But God doesn't want us so scared of the last day that we can't enjoy life here. Jesus came to set us free from that fear, and, if we are walking through life as Jesus' friends, there is nothing to be frightened of, because it's only the evil and bad and selfish that will be destroyed; everything that is good and loving and honest will be gathered up safely for ever.

Jesus told one of his stories with secrets – parables – about making the most of all the gifts God has given us, and we need three people to help us with it. (Make sure that the third servant chosen has been warned beforehand that she will be told off in the story, and is confident enough to cope with that.)

In Jesus' story, a man is going on a long journey and, before he goes, he gathers his servants together and entrusts his property to them to look after. (Give five coins to one servant and send her off to find the red box. Give two coins to another servant and send him off to find the blue box. Give one coin to the last servant, and send her off to find the yellow box.) The man went off on his travels, and after a long time came back home. He called the servants to him to settle accounts with them. (Call the volunteers together with the boxes.) Let's see how the first servant has got on. (She opens the box and counts out to the owner ten coins. Be very pleased. Everyone can clap.) What about the second servant? (He opens the box and counts out four coins. Praise and applause.) What about the third servant? Tell everyone how this servant told the owner she was too scared to do anything with her gift, so she just hid it as it was. (She gives it back.) The owner was not pleased at all because the servant had not made good use of the gift she had been given. (Tell the servant off, and thank all the actors for their help.)

We all have gifts God has enjoyed giving us. Some of us are good at being friendly and welcoming, some good at looking after animals, working out money, ironing, or thinking out solutions to difficult problems. Whatever our gift is, we need to enjoy using it and making the most of it for the good of everyone.

Christ the King

Thought for the day

In total humility, at one with the least of his people, Jesus, the Messiah or Christ, reigns as King, with full authority and honour for eternity.

Reflection on the readings

Ezekiel 34:11-16, 20-24
Psalm 95:1-7a
Ephesians 1:15-23
Matthew 25:31-46

There is a glorious contrast between the high office, power and authority given to the Messiah and the tender humility in which he acts with his people. This high office is not of the worldly kind, which tends to take promising people away from the practical caring and isolate them in managerial offices where they can easily lose the common touch.

The Messiah finds his true identity in searching for the lost, bringing back the strays, binding up the injured and strengthening the weak. Ezekiel the prophet proclaims the humility of this Servant King, whose mercy and loving kindness soothes aching souls and reassures us all. It is not that sin is excused or ignored, but that God longs to mend whatever is broken in us, and to gather us up, even after our own foolishness has caused our scattering. Psalm 95 echoes the image of us belonging to God and his kingdom as sheep belong to the shepherd and his pasture.

In the reading from Ephesians, Paul talks of the great power at work in raising Jesus from the dead, which places him in the position of eminence, King of earth and heaven, and which is also the cause of our hope. In becoming one with Christ through faith in him, we are brought into the everlasting kingdom where he reigns, and can rejoice that it is so, since it is not earned by works but freely given through grace.

In the Gospel we reach the end of the series of parables in Matthew dealing with the Day of Judgement. We have seen it from the viewpoint of the Church (the bridesmaids), the leaders with responsibilities (the talents), and now those who live and die without knowing the revealed truth. As all these people of other faiths and none are gathered before the throne of God, it is shown to them how, in their human goodness and thoughtful service to others, they have unknowingly been serving the God of love, and therefore belong to his kingdom, whatever name they may have given it before.

Of course, the reverse is also true, and it is not simply doing harm to others which marks out our rejection of God's ways. It is the goodness we fail to do, the needs we do not notice and ignore. Such blindness works in opposition to the law of love and places us outside the kingdom. The separation of sheep from goats is not so much judgement and punishment as sorting out those already shown to belong to the kingdom of God by their life's intent from those who are already shown to belong to the kingdom of darkness.

All-age talk

Bring along a crown and robe, some pretend bags of money, a dish of fruit and two fans on sticks, as shown below. Drape some cloth over a chair.

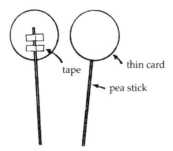

Tell everyone that today we are celebrating that Jesus Christ is King for ever. Ask a volunteer to come out and dress them up in the grand robe of very costly material, hand-embroidered by expert craftsmen, and the solid gold crown, studded with real diamonds and rubies. Sit the king on a grand throne covered in pure silk and made from finest marble, and provide him with some servants to stand around and wave him with fans, bowing before him. Give him bags of money on a table nearby, and provide a dish of fresh fruits for him to snack on between banquets.

Is this right? Is this what King Jesus is really like? No, it's all wrong! Although Jesus has been given all power and majesty and honour, and is King of all time and space, he is a very different sort of king. He lays aside his majesty (help the king up from his throne), lays aside his robe and his crown (take them from him), lays aside all wealth and comfort (the servants move the table), so that he can be one with us (he shakes hands with the servants) and live among us, caring for us, searching for the lost, and binding up the injured. (Thank the servant and the king for their help.)

Now if that's how our king behaves, then that's how we are to behave as well. If we worship and honour a Servant King, who doesn't greedily look after his own needs all the time but makes a point of looking after other people's needs, then that's what we have to do! Our wealth and treasure will be in loving service, wherever we're needed. That's how Jesus will recognise us as his people, when we get to the gate of heaven.

YEAR B

Advent 1

Thought for the day

Be alert and watchful; keep yourselves ready.

Reflection on the readings

Isaiah 64:1-9
Psalm 80:1-7, 17-19
1 Corinthians 1:3-9
Mark 13:24-37

There is a sense, in the reading from Isaiah, that, but for God's mercy, we are in a hopeless situation. Even as we beg for God's help, recognising that he has proved himself to be the one and only real God, we know that our behaviour has been a rejection of all God is and values. So what point can there be in asking for help from the One we spend so much time ignoring, rejecting and dismissing?

Yet there is hope; the prophet clings on to the fact that we are of God's making. Perhaps his love and affection for us will, even now, move God to show mercy to his wayward creation of humankind. Psalm 80 echoes this pleading for rescue and restoration, undeserved as it is. Both these readings from the Old Testament give us a flavour of the generations of longing and yearning for a saviour, often from the pit of human experience and in a very candid recognition of the human condition.

In contrast, the reading from Paul's letter to the Christians in Corinth is written after the coming of Jesus, the promised Saviour. It is full of the confidence which comes from knowing that, though we cannot save ourselves and our weaknesses are as weak as ever, the life of Jesus in us has power to keep us strong to the end and uphold us in what is right and good. God has indeed acted with an outpouring of unearned and undeserved love and generosity, simply because it is God's nature to act with grace and mercy. Since God is utterly faithful, we can trust him even with the worst of ourselves; his power in us is always going to be sufficient.

Today's Gospel is Jesus speaking to us of real and serious things. Never does Jesus pretend to us; never does he gloss over costs or dangers. Treating us with respect, he warns us so as to prepare us, and we need to take notice of what he is saying. He is speaking of great cosmic turmoil, and disturbing self-appointed leaders with power to attract and lead many astray. We are warned against gullibility and fashion-chasing where truth is concerned. Even Jesus is not in possession of the exact times and dates, but he is concerned to pass on to his followers, with considerable urgency, the need to be alert and watchful, so that whatever time the end comes we will be ready and prepared.

All-age talk

Beforehand prepare a large sun shape from yellow paper and a large cloud from grey paper.

First show everyone the sun. If this is showing in the sky during the summer, what can we tell about the best clothes to wear? Now slide the large grey cloud over the sun, so that the sun is hidden. What might it be wise to take with us if we are going out in this weather? We are very good at reading the signs in the weather to help us keep comfortable.

We read lots of other signs as well. At traffic lights, or at the top of scary water chutes, we know that red means stop and green means go. We know by the special music when *The Simpsons* or the news is about to come on. We know by the smell of cooking that dinner is nearly ready.

In today's Gospel, Jesus tells us to keep alert and check the signs which will tell us when he is going to come to earth again. This time he won't be coming as a tiny baby, but full of God's glory and in great power, riding on the clouds of heaven. It will be such an amazing event that it will rock the whole cosmos – the whole of nature will be shaken. Jesus tells us that the sun will be darkened, and the moon will lose its light, and stars will fall from heaven. This is something that every being will notice, both those who are alive on earth at the time and those who will have already died. Jesus tells us that even he doesn't know exactly when it will happen, but it certainly will take place, and we will all need to be ready for it, whether we are still alive here or already dead.

So how can we make sure we are ready? How can we read the signs?

The best way of making sure we stay ready is by keeping our eyes open – our spiritual eyes. That means keeping in touch with God on a daily basis. We need to get into a habit of praying, not just once a week on Sundays, but all times of every day. A good way of remembering, and getting ourselves into such a habit, is to get in touch with God every time we check our watches, or every time we put something to eat in our mouths.

Sensible sailors or hill walkers will check the weather forecast every time before they set out, so they are prepared. We need to check with God his will and guidance every time before we make decisions or spend money. Then our faith will be living and active, growing as we grow, and keeping us alert and available, so that whenever Jesus comes again in glory we shall be ready to welcome him with joy.

Advent 2

Thought for the day

John the Baptist prepares the way for the coming of the Messiah by helping the people to realign their lives.

Reflection on the readings

Isaiah 40:1-11
Psalm 85:1-2, 8-13
2 Peter 3:8-15a
Mark 1:1-8

Mark's Gospel bursts straight in with the dynamic claim that we are hearing about nothing less than the Messiah, the Son of God, entering into the realm of ordinary human life. Just as the prophet Isaiah had foretold, this event would require some drastic preparation work, and here is John (we are given no other introductory details about him) suddenly fulfilling the old prophecy and urging people to get their lives and attitudes sorted out and cleaned up. He is using the effective symbolism of baptismal washing as a sign of washed lives. If you are willing to step into the river, publicly, confess your sins and be pushed down under the water as a sign of your repentance, you are quite likely to mean what you say, and emerge from the experience full of new, fresh enthusiasm for walking God's way.

This is exactly the thorough kind of repentance we all need regularly. Perhaps we should use every shower and bath time as an opportunity for such spiritual washing. Then we would experience daily the fresh start and openness provided by God's forgiveness of acknowledged and confessed sin.

Along with John's call to thorough repentance and baptismal washing was the message he preached, directing his followers to look for the powerful person of great honour who would be coming shortly and whose baptism would be not with water but the Holy Spirit of God. Just imagine standing dripping and cleansed by the Jordan as you hear about someone who will drench and immerse you in the holiness of the Spirit of God. It must have triggered in many the deep longing and expectant thirsting for God which allows lives to be shaken, hearts to be softened and the kingdom to come.

The same is true now. It is as an expectant people, thirsty for God and longing for a total immersing in his life, that we prepare during the season of Advent for the festival of Christmas. The extent to which we respond to John's call across the centuries will determine how open and receptive we are to welcoming Jesus and allowing him into our lives. The life which Peter describes – of harmony, repaying even evil with blessing, and doing good regardless of the consequences – is a direct result of living immersed in the Holy Spirit of God.

All-age talk

Bring in a washing-up bowl with some water in it and a mop. Produce a mug or two which you were using earlier and explain how these are dirty and need washing up. You hope the mugs won't be too embarrassed by being shown dirty like this in full view of everyone. They are very particular mugs and prefer people to see them clean.

We are often a bit like that. We like people to see us when we're proud of what we are like and what we are doing. We don't like it much if someone catches us screaming at the dog, telling or living a lie, or being lazy or greedy. Usually we try to cover up the things we do which we aren't proud of. Perhaps we'll make out it's someone else's fault that we're late or grumpy; perhaps we'll think up good excuses for wrong behaviour. We get so good at this that often we believe our cover-up stories and stop noticing that instead of pretending we're clean-living Christians, what we actually need is a good, thorough wash.

The people who came to hear John the Baptist were just like us. There were things in their lives which were wrong and selfish, and they had become used to making excuses for themselves till they were quite content to live with their bad habits and carefully groomed images. But John got them thinking. And as they thought about their real selves and what they were really like, they suddenly started to realise that they were like dirty mugs which needed a good wash. If they were washed clean, they could be free from all the pretending and cover-ups, and just be themselves again.

John told them it was quite easy to do – they just needed to name all those big and little sins aloud to God without hiding them, and choose to turn their back on that way of living. He said he would dip them right under the water in the river as a sign that their lives were being washed clean.

(Ask for a volunteer to come and wash up the mugs.) For some of them it must have felt very humiliating to do that in public, especially if they had groomed their images so well that they had kept their sins well hidden. And it must have been such a relief for others, who had worried about their sin for years and years, to have it washed away at last.

When they were all washed clean, like our mugs, without any need to hide from God or each other any more, John told them something very important. This washing was just the beginning; soon someone was coming who would be able to plunge them deep into the depths of the Holy Spirit, so they would be completely surrounded and filled with the loving God. And the person who would make that possible was coming very soon.

During Advent we can get ourselves ready for Jesus' coming to us, just as they did. We can look at what we are really like; how we really behave with others; recognise the parts of us that are real enough but we hope others won't see. Anything we find which needs washing away we need to confess to God, tell him how sorry we are about it, and the way we have made excuses, and choose to turn our backs on that way of living. You can talk to God on your own or go to your priest or minister and pray with them, especially if you feel you need some help with changing. But however we do it, we all need to come to God regularly for thorough washing, and he is the only one who can make us clean and free.

Advent 3

Thought for the day

In Jesus, God will be fulfilling the Messianic prophecies about the promised Saviour.

Reflection on the readings

Isaiah 61:1-4, 8-11
Psalm 126 or Canticle: Magnificat
1 Thessalonians 5:16-24
John 1:6-8, 19-28

Advent almost engulfs us with its spirit of urgent preparation. Everyone writes lists and tries to organise food, apt presents and thematic decorations; the store cupboard fills with things no one is allowed to touch yet, and tops of wardrobes become hiding places for bulky secrets. The Church's season of Advent is a kind of spiritual equivalent of all this, not just because we are rehearsing Christmas carols and Nativity plays, but because we are standing alongside the people of Israel in their period of waiting and preparation for the coming of the promised Saviour. In these four weeks we can sense something of their generations of waiting and longing.

It is the Messiah's Advent that we journey through at this time of year, and here too we find checklists and plans, secrets and mysteries, half-seen puzzles, and truths which have yet to be unpacked and savoured. The Isaiah reading for today is a case in point. We are given a kind of checklist of pointers to look out for in the promised Saviour, which will ensure that we recognise him when he comes. It is a wonderful checklist, full of hope and freshness, the overturning of negatives and the victory of good over evil.

Hearing either Psalm 126 or the Magnificat from the standpoint of the Isaiah passage is like having a peep into the wrapped future, and sensing that on Christmas morning we shall not be disappointed. And, of course, the Incarnation of Christmas morning is indeed the unwrapping of that promised secret. Even as John the Baptist was teaching by the river Jordan, he knew that the Christ was already there among them, though still hidden, since his public ministry had not yet begun. It would not be long before those qualities on Isaiah's list could be checked out and validated by the people, provided they had eyes open to recognise in Jesus all that the prophets had foretold.

But at the moment we are still in the waiting place, and all that is in the future. For now, we sense the expectancy of the faithful people of Israel, and also recognise our own place of waiting for that final coming of total accomplishment at the end of time. We live with our hopes and our questions, our puzzles and our trust in the faithful God. We know that in God's way all the checklists of qualities and characteristics both for the first and the second coming will hold good.

John the Baptist finds the authorities trying to do a full story on him, mistakenly homing in on the messenger instead of the coming King. He describes himself, in the words of the prophet, as simply a voice – not to be curiously interviewed, but heard, with the heart as well as the ears. We can make this Advent such a time of listening to the real message, rather than being sidetracked by all the less important things. The reading from Thessalonians gives us sound, practical ideas for this.

All-age talk

Talk about the buying of Christmas presents and take out a list you've been making of all the Christmas jobs and how far you have all got with them. At this stage of Advent some people have probably got all their presents bought, wrapped and hidden, while others have hardly begun.

Before Jesus had been born, the people of Israel had been waiting ages and ages for God's Saviour to come and save them.

Every young woman would pray that her baby might be the Messiah, just as her grandmother had done before her. Through all the terrible crises of national life, the prophets had kept alive in the people of Israel their calling to be God's people. One day, the prophets all said, God would actually come in some way to be really 'with them' personally. They were to keep themselves ready and watchful for when that happened.

(Take out another 'list', and unroll it. On this are written the checkpoints from today's Isaiah reading.) The prophets even gave them a kind of 'Christmas' or 'Messiah' list of things to look out for in God's chosen one, the Messiah, or Christ. They would be able to recognise the Messiah when he came because these are the things he would do:

- tell the good news to the poor
- comfort the broken-hearted
- set free those feeling imprisoned
- announce the time when God would show his merciful judgement
- give people clothes of praise and joy to replace their sadness
- be fair to everyone
- make what is right grow strong
- put wrong things right

Now who do we know who did come and do those things, and is still doing them now? Jesus! And when was it that Jesus came into our world? At Christmas. So all their waiting and hoping was worth it. And anyone who wasn't sure could check with the Christmas (or 'Messiahmas') list and see for themselves. And so can we.

Advent 4

Thought for the day

God's promised kingdom, announced both to King David in ancient times and to Mary by the angel Gabriel, will go on for ever.

Reflection on the readings

2 Samuel 7, 1-11, 16
Canticle: Magnificat or Psalm 89:1-4, 19-26
Romans 16:25-27
Luke 1:26-38

When King David is filled with enthusiasm for building a great and holy temple to house the ark of the covenant, his offer is turned down, but the graciousness of his attitude very much accepted by God. Through the prophet Nathan, God points out to David that the seeming permanence of a grand building is nothing to be compared with the real permanence of the eternally present God. With such a nature there is no problem with flexibility; eternal Presence can move wherever the people go, untied by structural foundations.

Having assured King David that the building idea will be taken up by his son, God reveals his own blueprint for an everlasting kingdom, and the coming of a reign within the royal House of David which will eventually spread throughout the whole world. It was out of this promise that the hope of God's Messiah was born, particularly in the dark years following the collapse of the monarchy. Gradually the understanding of this Messiah became less tied in people's minds with temporal ruling power and more with a priestly kind of kingship which would bring worldwide blessing and hope.

So when we find Gabriel visiting Mary with a message that her son will reign on the throne of his ancestor, David, and his kingdom will never end, we are listening in on a gathering together of all the hopes and longings of generations, right back to King David himself. By this time, the overtones of a Messianic, priestly kingship will be there, and through Mary those hopes and plans can be accomplished for the saving of the whole world.

The passage from Romans gives us a glorious sense of a crescendo as the full spread of God's kingdom builds to completion. John Ellerton's well-loved hymn *The day thou gavest, Lord, is ended* puts it like this:

So be it, Lord; thy throne shall never,
like earth's proud empires, pass away;
thy kingdom stands and grows for ever
till all thy creatures own thy sway.

Our amazing privilege is to be part of the building.

All-age talk

Bring in something to show which you thought would last you a long time, but hasn't (like a pair of shoes or a felt-tip pen), and something else which you didn't think would last at all and it has (like a paper bookmark or a jar of Marmite).

Talk about these and the way some things, like great cathedrals, are built to last for hundreds and hundreds of years, while other things, like newspapers or toilet paper, are not designed to last very long at all.

King David was wanting to build a temple for the glory of God which was a strong, permanent structure, rather than a temporary tent. And God told David that his ideas for the kingdom were far more long-lasting even than a strong building; God's idea was for a kingdom of love and peace that lasts not just for a long time but for ever and ever and ever. And Jesus would be the king.

The angel Gabriel was sent to Mary to tell her all about it. 'You are going to have a child, Mary,' said Gabriel, 'and he's going to be the king of a kingdom that will last for ever.' The angel even told Mary what to call her child when he was born. (Show a large notice with the word 'Jesus' on one side of it.) He was to be called Jesus.

Names are important, and they often have a special meaning. Pick out some of the names in the congregation and look up what they mean in one of those 'your baby's name' books. The name Jesus has a meaning as well. It means 'Saviour: the one who saves' (show this written on the other side of the Jesus sign). Through King Jesus, God was coming to save his people.

When Jesus, the Saviour King, was born at the first Christmas, that was just the beginning! God's kingdom is still here today, and it's still growing.

Christmas Day

(Set 2)

Thought for the day

Jesus Christ, the world's Saviour, is here with us, born as a human baby.

Reflection on the readings

Isaiah 62:6-12
Psalm 97
Titus 3:4-7
Luke 2:(1-7) 8-20

Dogs and cats will never let you forget that it's feeding time. They go on and on reminding you loudly until you do something about that empty bowl. At the same time they are voicing (and wagging) their excitement that you will definitely be feeding them because you always do.

Today's reading from the book of Isaiah has a lovely sense of God's watchmen being posted where they can see what is going on, and given clear instructions to keep shouting both their need for God to send the promised Saviour, and their faith that he will, until he acts. Christmas is the great celebration of that action – of God breaking into his creation in a new and extraordinary way in order to save us.

Like the shepherds, we have been getting on with our daily and nightly lives, and on this night we remember the splash of God's glory across the sky, and the cry of a newborn child on a heap of straw. The ordinary and the extraordinary are shaken together, the hopes and promises become fused in practical reality, and the whole world is closer to salvation than ever before.

The Incarnation – with all its risk, its glory laid aside, its daring love – speaks as clearly to us, two thousand years on, as it did to those shepherds marvelling at the angels' message as they discovered the baby in the stable. Marvelling is filled with questions as well as wonder, and most of us find that God's presence in our world as a human baby raises many questions. Such questions are to be valued, as they can lead us forward into deeper understanding.

We are told that Mary kept all these questions and pondered them in her heart. Christmas is a time for such pondering, as well as the more usual feasting and celebrating. Wrapped up in those swaddling bands is God's answer to our longing for inner peace, our need for healing and wholeness, and our recognition that we cannot save ourselves no matter what effort we put into it. The baby in Mary's arms is God hearing our hidden fears and tears, and coming in person to save us and set us free.

All-age talk

Ask a few volunteers to take the microphone (or shout) and wish everyone a happy Christmas. We've all spent the last month preparing everything – the food and drink, the surprises, the gifts, the decorations – so that we can make a good job of wishing our loved ones a really happy Christmas.

What are we wishing them when we say 'Happy Christmas!' to them? Collect some ideas of what we want for them. They will probably include lots of good wishes directly linked with partying and family celebration. We choose this particular day to wish people those good things we might want for them every day of the year.

Why is the festival of Christmas such a good time to wish people wonderful things in their life? (Arrange for someone to be given a lighted candle at the back of the church at this point, which they carry up to you.) All those things we wish those we love are to do with wanting their lives to be bright and shining, well lit and beautiful in every way. And today, Christmas Day, we are celebrating a life shining with God's glory, which has come right among us. Jesus, the promised Christ, has been born.

So we are right to wish everyone a happy Christmas. What better way to celebrate God's great love for us all than by wishing everyone we meet the light of loving in their lives! Don't let it stop at the ones in your family or circle of friends. Wish it (and mean it) even to those you don't always get on with; wish it to those you hardly know, like the bus conductor, the toll collector at the road tunnel, the other people walking their dogs this afternoon and anyone else you should meet. Pray for them and wish them the light of God's blessing in their lives as you spread the message – Happy Christmas!

Christmas 1

Thought for the day

Just as the angels said, a Saviour has been born for us.

Reflection on the readings

Isaiah 61:10–62:3
Psalm 148
Galatians 4:4-7
Luke 2:15-21

Right from the very beginning of his life on earth Jesus is revolutionary in his mission. Born as the bringer of God's saving power and justice, Mary gives birth to him on the straw of a stable, far from home and family support. Those who came hotfooting it along the streets in the middle of the night to welcome him were neither familiar neighbours nor religious leaders but shepherds, who were considered unclean and unrighteous due to the nature of their job. Yet it was to them that Luke reports the angels coming, a sign that this Saviour is linked both with David the shepherd boy turned king, and also the marginalised and the powerless. It is not dutiful legalism affirmed here, but the grace of God's wide, unconditional love.

Christmas is often known as the season of goodwill, taken up from the angels' message, and many push the boat out at Christmas in trying to live as people of goodwill, at least over the bank holiday! Sadly the effort and the expectations of goodwill-living are a great strain, with the result that Christmas is also the season when fragile relationships in families explode or implode, and suicide rates are higher than usual. Duty is a terrible burden and weighs our living down.

That's why this baby we welcome into the world at Christmas is such good news. There is a shift of emphasis away from the hopeless struggle most of us know of honestly living up to what we feel we are supposed to be: the heavy duty routine. In contrast, this child is already spreading different news, which really is good to hear. Our calling is simply to be ourselves, human beings with a particular, unique set of genes, in the image and likeness of the God who created us.

This means that the more we allow ourselves to be the unmerited recipients of God's giving, and stop trying to impress him, ourselves and one another with what we are not, the more our real selves we will become, and the more Godlike we shall grow in the process. That is occasion for cosmic rejoicing!

All-age talk

Bring along a pot of jam, some toffee or fudge, a skipping rope and a camera. Talk about the importance of getting the timing right when you are making jam or toffee, skipping or taking a photo. Invite experts from the congregation to describe that 'right moment' and how you know when it's there and don't miss it. Sometimes we do miss the right moment and end up with solid stuff that won't spread and tastes of burnt saucepan, our legs tangled up in the rope or a photo of a giraffe's bottom.

Saint Paul talks about Jesus being born 'when the time was right'. That particular date in history – whenever it actually was – fitted in perfectly with God's rescue plan. And so he acted, and what we call Christmas happened: a baby was born who was God's own Son, and would grow up to show everyone what God is really like, in the language of being human, which we can all understand.

God is very good at knowing the right time to act. We can always trust him with that. Often he will bring things together in a way and at a time which brings blessing to many people rather than only one. Those who are older can look back over their lives and see how this has been true. We might have prayed for something to happen and got fed up with God not seeming to answer for ages. But later on we can see that the time of waiting perhaps helped us, or allowed something else important to happen, and God's timing turned out to be for the best.

Sometimes we don't understand God's sense of timing and would much prefer him to take our advice! Perhaps we are still feeling let down by God over something which we so wanted and has never happened. We need to remember that it is the God of all eternity that we worship, and it may be that we shall only understand when we get to heaven. We are a bit like bewildered pets at the vets who find their owners bringing them along to have a stranger poke needles into them; we don't understand and just know that it hurts.

Jesus himself was not born into a comfortable home with an efficient maternity hospital just down the road. The family had to escape to another country before he was two years old, because King Herod wanted him killed. But still the time of his birth was right.

What God did was provide his Son with a human family to love him and look after him. When couples who love one another take on that commitment of marriage, and raise their children together, through all the inevitable strains and stresses, they are giving newborn children a wonderful, Godly gift. And as the Christian family here, we are all given one another to look after and be looked after by. Whatever our age, sex or marital state, we are all children together, born into God's family and enjoying God's own parenting, which is one thing in life we can really trust.

Christmas 2

Thought for the day

The Word made flesh at Christmas was always with God, always expressing his creative love.

Reflection on the readings

Jeremiah 31:7-14 or Ecclesiasticus 24:1-12
Psalm 147:12-20 or Canticle: Wisdom of Solomon 10:15-21
Ephesians 1:3-14
John 1:(1-9) 10-18

Sympathy cards will often bear messages like 'A word of comfort . . .', and the whole idea of sending cards of sympathy to those who are distressed or grieving is the knowledge that the expressed sympathy of another human, sharing the anguish, can be so supportive and comforting.

The supreme Word of comfort and hope to all of us in any age and every circumstance is the Word of God's loving wisdom, lying here among us as a human baby in the hay. All the nakedness, vulnerability and self-giving, which assure us of real, trustworthy love, are here, spelt out to us in the Christmas season as we marvel at the intimacy of God with his people, the Creator with the created.

All through the process of creation, this expressive Word of love has drawn life and hope into tangible form. All through the developing discernment of spiritual things, the expressive Word has spoken eternal truth and mystery, Godliness and the way of love.

So Christmas does not spring on to our consciousness a raw, untried and untested phenomenon, out of nowhere. The Incarnation tenderly affirms and shows in person all that the human spirit had sensed through the ages, and the created world from the first calling of light into darkness and order into chaos.

All-age talk

Start by giving everyone one minute to find out from and share with someone else something that went really well, or was really funny, or was a complete disaster over this Christmas. One thing all humans have always loved doing is talking together! Toddlers, children, young people, middle-aged and old people all love a chat. Even babies talk, in their own way. What would we do without the telephone, especially if we can't get out like we used to. With e-mail we can chat to people all over the world, and with television, radio, magazines and newspapers people can chat to us about anything and everything. Ground control can direct astronauts in space, pilots can be talked down to a safe landing, and surgeons can talk their students through complicated heart operations. Politicians can shout their ideas to crowds of people, and friends can whisper their secrets. All of this is the magic of words.

Why do we talk about Jesus as the Word of God? Whenever we use words we express ourselves. Jesus expresses God, not in a speech bubble but as a human being like us, so that we can understand God in a better way than ever. God has always expressed himself, of course, so the Word of God has been there as long as God has . . . for ever. God *said*, 'Let there be light!' God *said*, 'Let there be stars and plants and animals, fish and birds.' God *said*, 'Let there be people in our likeness to look after the earth.' So it was the Word of God which spoke those things into being through love.

Then, at Christmas, the Word of God actually took shape itself – human shape. And his name was Jesus, which means 'the one who saves us'.

Epiphany

Thought for the day

Jesus, the promised Messiah, is shown to the Gentile world.

Reflection on the readings

Isaiah 60:1-6
Psalm 72:(1-9) 10-15
Ephesians 3:1-12
Matthew 2:1-12

We are well used to thinking of the Church's call as outreach. Partly this is because of the empty chairs we have got used to seeing around us each Sunday and on weekdays. Partly it is a growing awareness of the deep spiritual hunger of many who have not been brought up to go to church and do not see it as a viable answer to their need. So there is almost a daydream quality for us, as well as the dispirited people of Israel, when we are asked to imagine crowds and crowds of people from all walks of life, actively seeking us out, in order to find God and spiritual fulfilment.

I wonder how the Church would cope with such a situation? Would we be able to help them with their search? Would we understand their questions? Would we be overjoyed to see them pouring through the doors, or would they pose a threat to our traditional way of doing things?

When we recognise that being 'a light to lighten the Gentiles' can actually be quite disturbing, we can start to understand something of the hesitation the Jewish people had about welcoming the early Christians, many of them totally 'unsynagogued'. We can also thrill to the hope of a new direction – of a Church on the grow at last. The signs are there, and the tide is turning.

Epiphany has therefore particular significance for us at the moment. The light of the world is for everyone – all groups and nations, all cultures and ages, not just those we are familiar with or approve of, or who know 'how we do it' in our own church. Since most of us are Gentiles ourselves, the significance of Christ being shown to the Gentile 'outsiders' tends to pass us by unnoticed, unless we ask ourselves another question. Which 'outsiders' might those wise men represent today? To enter into the spirit of Epiphany we need to alter our vision until we understand that God has no outsiders, and no person or group is excluded. It was God's delight to reveal his baby Son to searching pagan foreigners.

As we hear once again the story of these outsiders, travelling many miles over difficult terrain in order to find for themselves the world's enlightenment, we could do well to bear in mind all those in our own times who are spiritually awake and searching, many travelling over difficult terrain, and make sure that we light the lamps, ready to welcome them.

All-age talk

Have a number of masks, based on the pictures below, to put on some volunteers, which alter the way we see them and act towards them.

Vicky

Sidney

With the first volunteer, explain that Vicky is feeling really fed up because her Christmas tokens were stolen before she got round to spending them. (Aah!) Have everyone making a 'ding dong' doorbell noise. It's the football-squad coach! Quick, Vicky chooses to put on the bright, happy mask! (Help her on with it.)

With the second volunteer, explain that Sidney's feeling really fed up because his Christmas tokens went through the wash by mistake and are now a hard crusty blob. (Aah!) The doorbell rings again. (Ding dong.) It's someone Sidney doesn't know, and they're wearing the colours of a team Sidney doesn't support! Quick, where's that angry 'What on earth do you think you're doing here?' mask? (Help him on with it.)

We all have lots of masks which we keep by the door. Sometimes it's right to wear them, and they help us get out of a bad mood faster. But sometimes we forget what is mask and what is real, and that's not so good.

For some people we are always on our best behaviour, showing them how kind and friendly we are, how ready to help and forgive them. With others we want to show them that although we're doing our grudging best to be polite, it's a real effort and we'd far rather we didn't have to have anything to do with them. Some people we're happy to welcome to church, some we hope will never come, at least to the same church as us! Sometimes we're not very good at welcoming people who look different, wear different clothes or speak with a different accent from ours. We make it quite clear to them that they are outsiders.

But today we hear that God led these strangers all the way to Bethlehem, specially to show them his baby Son! We hear that King Herod pretended to make them welcome. And we hear that at Jesus' home they really were made welcome. God wanted these 'outsiders' to be among the first to meet his Son because Jesus had come into the world for everybody, and not just for the Jewish people.

As Christians, we need to remember that the good news of the gospel is for everyone, and not just those like us. So today we ask God to turn us into people who are happy to welcome outsiders, without needing any masks to pretend.

The Baptism of Christ

Thought for the day

Through the Holy Spirit, Jesus is affirmed at his Baptism as God's beloved Son and we too are given the Spirit of God which affirms us as God's adopted daughters and sons.

Reflection on the readings

Genesis 1:1-5
Psalm 29
Acts 19:1-7
Mark 1:4-11

The believers Paul found at Ephesus had never heard of the Holy Spirit. They had made the decision to repent of their sins and change the way they lived, but had not realised that God's Spirit could actually live in them to make this change a reality. There are still many people today who value Jesus' ethical teaching, and use his guidelines as ideals to strive for, but have not taken on board as a real possibility that God's life can live in them, changing them from the inside out.

We have to acknowledge that it is indeed an odd concept. All the time we are making decisions of the will – about which potatoes to buy for baking, which make of car to go for, whether to stop smoking or carry on, whether to give money to an appeal or not. We also make decisions about life direction – we decide to marry, or to complete the tax return honestly, to campaign for justice or to eat no meat. All this reinforces that we are in control of our own lives, as mature, independent people.

The Holy Spirit can sound like a takeover bid, and many are suspicious of this, and find it all rather far-fetched; Yes, we can choose to live God's way, as rational human beings, but aren't we kidding ourselves to talk about God's life and Spirit actually taking up residence?

All today's readings give us evidence of the real living Spirit of God at work. The Spirit broods over the chaos and breathes God's creative life into it. As Jesus is baptised God's Spirit settles on him, affirming his identity and his mission. And in Acts we hear how a random group of representative new Christians breaks into a whole new dimension of living faith as they are baptised with both water and the Holy Spirit. God breaks into our human confines with his divine nature, and that opens up possibilities of full life which could never otherwise happen. Rather than a takeover bid, it is a setting free; rather than kidding ourselves, it is truth in all its fullness.

All-age talk

Bring along a pair of wellington boots which fit you, or arrange beforehand for a volunteer to bring their boots and do the actions as you talk.

Stand the boots together where they can be seen, and explain that these boots (being very keen, conscientious boots) want to walk wherever you go. (Walk about and watch the boots, still sitting there and not moving.) They are trying very hard, but they don't seem to be getting anywhere, do they? Perhaps they need a bit of encouragement. (Some of the children can encourage the boots from a distance!)

Poor old boots – they'd love to be walking where you walk, but they just can't manage it. Why not? Because they haven't got you inside them!

Climb into the boots and see the difference. Suddenly they are able to walk around wherever you walk. They can even jump with you, run with you and dance with you! And all because they have you in them.

Now what has a keen pair of boots got to do with our Bible readings for today? In the reading from Genesis nothing happened, nothing was drawn into life, until God's Spirit made creation happen. And in the Acts of the Apostles we heard about some people whose lives were changed when they received the Holy Spirit, just as our lives can. We can know lots about Jesus and what he did on earth and what he said, and that can make us very keen to live like him – in a loving, generous, honest way. But unless we ask God to be in us, getting to know him as a person, rather than a set of facts, or a bit of a history lesson, we'll be like the boots on their own, wanting to move with God, but not able to do it on their own. (As you say this, take off the boots and put them on their own while you move around.)

As soon as we ask God into our life, his Spirit comes and moves in us (put the boots on again), and that makes it possible for us to go wherever God wants us to go, and act as God wants us to act. The Spirit of God which was seen settling on Jesus when John baptised him in the river Jordan, settles on all of God's children as they put their faith and trust in him.

So let's not waste our time trying hard to do good things *for* God like a pair of boots without any living feet in them. Instead, let's invite the Spirit of God every day to come and fill us, so God's life is *in* us, and can let us dance through life with praise, walk beside those who need our help, and stick to the right path all the way to heaven.

Epiphany 2

Thought for the day

Jesus, the Christ, unlocks the mysteries of God.

Reflection on the readings

1 Samuel 3:1-10 (11-20)
Psalm 139:1-6, 13-18
Revelation 5:1-10
John 1:43-51

Generally it makes us uncomfortable if someone claims to be able to 'read us like a book'. Are we that simplistic? Is there no unique mystery about us which is hardly fathomable to ourselves, let alone another person? If we know this to be true for individual human mysteries, how much more so is it true of God. None of us, and no particular group, can realistically claim to 'know' God fully and discern his nature; we are simply provided with a lifetime each, to travel a little deeper into the mystery that is God.

The season of Epiphany is all about God being revealed, and it is to the young child, Samuel, that God reveals something of his thoughts; to one who is still innocent of life's ethical complications which so often cloud our spiritual vision as adults. Samuel becomes an intermediary between God and Eli, whose short sight is not only physical.

Psalm 139 celebrates the intimate knowing which God has of us, having been totally involved with us from conception to birth and beyond. Simply the thought of God knowing us so well is something the psalmist finds mind-blowing, since it emphasises the extensiveness of God which surpasses all we can imagine.

In the reading from Revelation we have that terrible picture of all God's thoughts locked up for ever, since no one can be found who is worthy to break the seals on the scroll. John weeps at the hopelessness of it, until the figure of the Christ appears who has become human, has given up his life and triumphed through love, so that the secrets of God can be revealed through him.

We need to grasp the urgency and immediacy of this vision, and the life of Jesus in the Gospels. Do we, as we plead for the world and its people, weep for the places where God is not being made known, and weep for the souls to whom the truth of God's love is not being revealed? We, who are privileged to have met with Jesus, are the only ones who can spread news of who the true God is, as revealed in Jesus Christ. We are the ones in this generation who can speak it in language our contemporaries understand. And if we don't, the thoughts of God, which the world desperately needs, will remain effectively closed and inaccessible.

All-age talk

Bring along one of those locked secret diaries, or a locked briefcase or file.

Who usually has the key to the secret thoughts and ideas inside here? Only the one who wrote them. To use e-mail, or a hole-in-the-wall cash dispenser we need a special password or number to make sure that our secrets are safe and no one else can get at them unless we give permission. Only we ourselves have the key, and the authority.

Only God has access to God's own secret thoughts. He chooses to make some things known to some people, but there's no way his thoughts are all left wide open for anyone to see and understand at a glance. Is there any human person you can think of whom you really know completely? We can't even fully understand another human person, let alone the mind of the all-powerful living God!

The only person who could have the key and be authorised to open God's thoughts up to us would have to be someone who was both human and God. But *is* there anyone who fits that description? Who is it? It's Jesus! Jesus is authorised and worthy to open up God's heart to us because he is both God and human. And he spent his life doing just that.

Epiphany 3

Thought for the day

Signs of glory lead us to believe in Jesus as Lord and Saviour.

Reflection on the readings

Genesis 14:17-20
Psalm 128
Revelation 19:6-10
John 2:1-11

Melchizedek is a strange, shadowy figure, who emerges briefly in the Book of Genesis as an ancient priest-king bearing gifts of bread and wine and a blessing from the great God of heaven for Abram. He is almost more sign than character, a bringer of God's gifts and perhaps the reassurance of God's blessing which Abram badly needed at the time. God will use all kinds of unexpected people and situations to speak his love to us, often just when we most need to be reassured of it.

The changing of water into wine at the wedding party in Cana is described by John as being a sign of glory in Jesus, which led his disciples to believe in him. This, too, is a strange, mysterious sign, quite unlike many of the other Gospel stories. It is recorded as being the first of the signs Jesus did, and takes place immediately after the disciples are called. Since Mary is aware of the wine shortage she is presumably a close friend or relative of the family, and she is convinced that her Son will be able to help them out of a difficult situation. But unlike many other Gospel events, this isn't a healing, it isn't a matter of great importance, and the family hasn't asked Jesus for help. The water is not spoken to (as in the calming of the waves) and the disciples are not being asked to act in faith but are merely onlookers.

Certainly the servants show great faith in serving water as wine to the chief guest; the tone of Mary's instructions had obviously convinced them that it would be worth their while doing exactly what the young man said, no matter how odd it sounded. Mary herself is a sign in this episode, directing the servants, and all of us, to 'do whatever he tells you'. But we are left wondering why Jesus' power was used in this 'parochial' way at this stage in his ministry at Mary's insistent request, and whether the chief guest was ever allowed into the secret so he, too, could marvel. What is clear is that Jesus Christ is named here as having authority over the created world. Water into wine is a natural process, but a long one in terms of time. In this miracle, we glimpse life in terms of eternity, rather than being trapped in time. We and the disciples are led to see Jesus himself in terms of eternity and authority.

The reading from Revelation reinforces this, as with John we hear the great thunder of voices lifted in praise and worship, honouring the one in whom the victory of goodness and truth is accomplished for ever. However tempted we are to give worship to the bearers of God's good news, we are reminded here that all worship is to be directed only to the true and living God.

All-age talk

Prepare beforehand a teddy with an envelope containing a picture of a married couple (from the congregation) tied to its arm; a plastic jug of water with a picture of a Bible stuck on to the outside; and a Bible with a red bookmark, on which is written 'John, chapter 2, verse 11'. (The married couple need to be provided with empty wine glasses.)

Explain that in this Epiphany season we are following signs, just as the wise men followed the sign of the star, and today we are all going on a journey.

Take everyone on a sign-by-sign journey, starting by inviting a couple of very young people to go to the children's corner and find a teddy with a message round his arm. (Have someone primed to place teddy with his message in the right place just before you start the talk.) When they return, they can open the envelope and find a picture of a married couple in the congregation. (These people are primed, of course.)

Another child can take the picture and match it up with the actual married couple, who are led by the child to the front. They are each holding an empty wine glass. Greet the couple and remind everyone that we've been hearing in the Gospel today about a wedding that Jesus went to in a place called Cana. Why are their glasses empty? Because in our story the wine had run out! Send another child to look for a jug of water (which should be placed somewhere fairly obvious). While the child pours water into the wine glasses, remind everyone of how Jesus had changed the water at Cana into the very best quality wine. (Let the couple take a sip and check that our water is still water. It probably is!)

No wonder people were amazed at what had happened. It pointed them to look at Jesus in a new way; he had authority over things like water! Look again at the jug and point out that it has a picture stuck on the side – another sign for us. Ask a couple of older children to see what it is. The picture is of a Bible with a red bookmark in it. Invite these children to find a Bible with a bookmark. (It has been placed somewhere fairly obvious, such as on the lectern.) When they bring it back they can read out the verse indicated on the bookmark: John 2:11.

The miracles that Jesus did when he was walking this planet about two thousand years ago were signs that led people to realise that he was not just a good human being, or a clever preacher: he was none other than the Son of God.

There are signs of God's love all over the place today as well – in answered prayers, in the courage we get to do what we know is right, even though we're scared, in the peace and reassurance we are given sometimes; and in the grace which enables us to do impossible things, like forgiving our enemies, or giving up an addiction. What all the signs point to is a very real, very powerful God of love.

Epiphany 4

Thought for the day

Jesus displays all the signs that mark him out to be God's chosen One.

Reflection on the readings

Deuteronomy 18:15-20
Psalm 111
Revelation 12:1-5a
Mark 1:21-28

When Moses had approached God on the holy mountain, the people had watched all the signs of God's power and mystery and been so terrified of such a close encounter with the almighty One that they had trembled and begged Moses to act as intermediary for them. God's holiness threw their sinfulness into terrible focus and they knew they couldn't cope with such purity.

We find a similar reaction in today's Gospel, when a man in the congregation breaks the awed hush following Jesus' teaching, to scream out in the quiet synagogue. We can imagine the panic and horror expressed in that uncontrolled outburst. What could have set it off? Was the man merely a familiar local madman, used to disrupting the orderly services?

Mark suggests that this was something startlingly different from a mad heckler. Something has thrown the man into a frenzy of fear, and it seems to be linked with the way Jesus has been behaving. So what has Jesus been doing? We are told he has been teaching, and his teaching, unlike the usual preachers, has the distinct ring of authority.

Presumably so much of God's glory shone through Jesus' words and manner that it was highly challenging, and therefore offensive, to whatever in the man was evil, and in opposition to

God's nature. He could not face the light of God's goodness shining into his soul and showing it up for what it really was. That carried with it a sense of horror at the destruction bound to come to that evil, if God were to get too close. So he screams out, seeing the loving God only in terms of cauterising purity.

And in one sense the man was right. Whatever we are – both the evil and the good – cannot be hidden from God, and as we allow him close, the evil cannot survive the power of his love. In Jesus, God's transcendent glory becomes immanent, in the only way this can happen without our destruction: in the complete self-giving of the cross.

All-age talk

Strike a match and light a candle. Talk about how useful fire is to heat up food and cook it, to keep us warm, melt steel and make steam to generate power. But fire is very powerful, and so it can be very dangerous. Show a picture or a model of a fire engine, and enlist the children's help in talking about what happens when fires get out of control, and how the firemen fight the dangers. We need to have a healthy fear of fire to keep us safe.

God is very powerful. When you think of the power needed to create fire and oceans, ranges of mountains and galaxies of stars, you can't help but be a bit fearful at the thought of getting in touch with such a powerful person.

We are sensible to stand in awe of this great Being, on whom we depend for everything, including life itself. We are right to respect the Lord of life, and think carefully before we speak to him, and give him our full attention whenever we pray. We are right to humble ourselves in his presence and behave well during church services. God sees everything we do and knows everything we think, both the things we are pleased about and the things we are secretly rather ashamed of. Sometimes we behave as if God is more of an easy-going pet than the Lord of the entire universe. We need to take God seriously and recognise that he is very powerful indeed.

(Pick up the candle again.) But that great power of God is only part of the story. Just as a candle is a person-sized fire, which we can hold and which gives us light, but doesn't frighten us like a house on fire, so Jesus is the way we can approach the great creative God in person.

Epiphany 5

Sunday between 3 and 9 February (if earlier than 2 before Lent)

Thought for the day

The good news about God is far too good to keep to ourselves.

Reflection on the readings

> Isaiah 40:12-31
> Psalm 147:1-11, 20c
> 1 Corinthians 9:16-23
> Mark 1:29-39

In the Isaiah reading for today we find a valiant effort to get us thinking, and imagining the unimaginable. The prophet is trying to help us glimpse something of the vast and limitless essence of the Being we know as God, whose creation we inhabit. We are taken on a quick guided tour of the universe, marvelling at the God who made it all and whose creative loving holds it all and sustains it. From time to time the prophet gives up on the descriptions as totally inadequate for the amazing reality, and simply points out how crazy it is even to attempt any comparisons with the living God. The wonder of God beats everything, and leaves us open-mouthed and speechless when we get anywhere near the truth of his nature.

The Psalm echoes these thoughts, and then we find Paul, in his letter to the Christians in Corinth, so excited at spreading the good news about God that he is quite happy to devote his whole life and energy to it. There is utter dedication to the cause in the way he does his research and fits his language and teaching programme to the diverse needs and backgrounds of his hearers.

Why is he so willing to adapt himself and put himself out? Because his encounter with the living God has revolutionised his own life; the God he has met personally through Jesus is simply so wonderful that he can't bear anyone to get through the rest of their life without knowing about him.

In today's Gospel we hear about Jesus' enthusiasm for spreading the good news. He has set Peter's mother-in-law free of her fever, and liberated all kinds of other visitors to the house from their mental, physical and spiritual suffering. We know that following this concentration of healing ministry, Jesus rises before it's light, in order to spend time in prayer, and when his friends find him, wanting to take him back to the community who are asking for him, he is instead concerned to move on. Having seen the look of liberation in the eyes of those set free in Capernaum, he cannot wait to spread the good news of God's freeing love far and wide.

It is whenever we get a fresh and breathtaking experience of who God is and what he is like, that we find ourselves longing for others to share what we have discovered, and cannot wait to pass the good news on.

All-age talk

Prepare beforehand a made-up description of a favourite food or drink, something that doesn't actually exist. Give it a spectacular name and explain how it's virtually impossible to find in the shops – only one particular specialist store ever stocks it. It's very expensive but worth every penny of the extra cost because it's so special and unique.

Then attempt to describe your imaginary food/drink in great detail. Pile on the adjectives when talking about the wonderful aroma that fills the air when you remove the wrapping/take off the lid. Explain what it does to your taste buds, the feel of it on your lips, the texture and its incomparable taste. Talk about how it makes you feel so full of joy and well-being when you eat/drink it and how you enjoy the experience so much – there's nothing to compare with it.

Go on to choose a well-known food/drink and briefly explain what that is like, in terms of taste, aroma, texture and so on, but add that your imaginary favourite food/drink is far better. Nothing they've ever tasted could possibly be as good. Say that you love it so much that you want everyone else to know about it and enjoy it too. It's far too good to keep to yourself.

Conclude by talking about how hard it is to describe something so wonderful that it's impossible to imagine. The only way other people are really going to find out how special your invented food/drink is, is to experience it for themselves.

Today's reading from the prophet Isaiah is a bit like this. The prophet is doing his best to describe to us how wonderful God is, but God is simply so incredibly amazing that we find it almost impossible to imagine. There's only one way to find out, and that is to experience God for ourselves. If you ask anyone who has become aware of the great, loving God working in their life, they'll agree that there really aren't any words to describe how wonderful and amazing he is. They just know because they've experienced him in action.

In the Gospel we heard how Jesus had been busy healing lots and lots of people at the house of Peter and Andrew, where he was staying. It started with Peter's mother-in-law, who had a bad fever and was very ill, and Jesus made her better. After she'd made them all supper, full of new energy, no doubt, crowds of visitors came, all wanting Jesus to heal them as well. So he did. Through Jesus, God was working right there in those people's lives, and making them more free and happy than they had ever felt before. It was so exciting to see! We can imagine how happy it made Jesus to see these people suddenly realising at last how wonderful God was! He couldn't wait for everyone else to find out.

Well, people are still finding out that our amazing God can set us free to live happy and joyful lives doing good and standing up for what is right and true. And how are they going to discover God? Only if those of us who have found out already how wonderful he is are prepared to tell them about him, and introduce them to him!

Epiphany 6

Sunday between 10 and 16 February (if earlier than 2 before Lent)

Thought for the day

Jesus wants to heal us to wholeness, and to him no one is untouchable.

Reflection on the readings

2 Kings 5:1-14
Psalm 30
1 Corinthians 9:24-27
Mark 1:40-45

To be considered untouchable is a terrible thing. To have people shrink away from you, either openly or more subtly, and to watch them draw their children out of your contaminating danger, inflicts deep wounds on the psyche, almost worse than the illness itself. It is not only leprosy; AIDS sufferers can meet the same kind of rejection, the Dalits of India are stamped with it from birth, and political regimes can concoct it legally and devastatingly, as, for example, in Apartheid. Any who live under tyranny and oppression, whether in police states or in dysfunctional family homes, are familiar with the erosive wearing-down of it. To some extent all minorities experience it, and only those who have been on the receiving end can have any idea of the effect it has on self-esteem and the capacity to relate positively with others.

Our readings today show us God's attitude to untouchability in all its forms. We read of Naaman's wife's servant girl from Israel, who instinctively knows that God would like to restore her master to wholeness. Through Elisha the prophet, Naaman is offered God's healing. It is deceptively simple, being based on humility and obedience, both of which are bound to cause an angry reaction in a highly respected, wealthy army commander. As far as God is concerned, Naaman is no special case because of his position or wealth; he is a special case because he is a child of God, created and loved into being, as are we all. That is what makes God eager to bring people to wholeness, whoever they are.

In the Gospel we meet another leper, in whom the years of untouchability have taken their toll. He can hardly believe that anyone would want to be bothered with him. He has come to see himself as others have treated him. Yet he senses that with Jesus there may be a spark of hope and, illegally, the man approaches him, doubting not his power but his desire to help. And how does Jesus react?

With anger. This comes as a shock, and some manuscripts have Jesus being moved with compassion, which is perhaps more what we might expect. But it is worth looking at the stern, strong words Jesus uses in reply. Emphatically he insists that of course he wants to heal the man. It may well be that he wants things done properly in keeping with the law, and that is why he directs the man to do what the law requires, going to show himself to the priest. But surely the overriding impression we are left with is of Jesus willingly touching what is considered untouchable, and making him whole, not only physically but holistically.

If this is God's nature, then it also needs to be ours. We cannot claim to be followers of Christ and live comfortably with any kind of marginalising, or any system which makes human beings out to be untouchable for any reason. If untouchability makes us angry, and urges us to do what we can to bring about change, then we shall be offering the touch of our healing God.

All-age talk

Invite a volunteer to run up the aisle as if they really want to win a race. Then ask them (or another) to run as if they aren't much bothered whether they win or not. Everyone can pick out the differences in the two performances.

Paul tells us to think of our lives as Christians being like running in a race we are determined to win. What will that mean? We'll be taking our following of Jesus very seriously, and trying very hard at it, practising it every day and building up our stamina. We'll be like 'professionals' instead of wishy-washy drifters. And we'll be getting better and stronger as we practise. If we don't bother, and don't take it seriously, we won't make much progress.

Today in the Gospel we are given another example of what it means to be a follower of Jesus. Let's look at how Jesus behaves with the man who has leprosy. Then we can practise living like that, as we try to follow Jesus.

But first, what does it mean to be a leper? (Lepers and leopards both have spots, but there the similarity ends, so make this clear!) Leprosy is a skin disease. When people get leprosy, they first find they lose the feeling in a finger, or a bit of the foot, and gradually the skin turns very white in patches. It is a bad illness, and people die of it if they don't get the medicines which can cure it. In Jesus' time, lepers were sent off to live on their own because they were thought of as 'unclean'. No one else was allowed to touch them. If they did, the law said they would become unclean as well.

So what did Jesus do? There was the leper, knowing Jesus had the power to heal him, but not sure that Jesus would want to have anything to do with someone as unclean as he was. And there was Jesus, so much wanting the man to be healed that he did something very shocking. He reached out . . . and *touched* the leper! Jesus wasn't afraid of the law saying he would be unclean; he just knew that this man, who had been untouchable for years, more than anything needed to feel touchable again. We know what happened – the man's skin was made better straight away, so he could go and show the priest and have it all made official; he was no longer unclean.

As Christians, we are followers of Jesus, so now we know a bit more about how we must try to live. We must try wanting the best for people, and we must try not to shut people off or have nothing to do with them just because they are poorer than us, or richer than us, ill, smelly or just different. Even if other people avoid them, as Christians we must never think of anyone as unclean or untouchable, because God made and loves every one of us.

Epiphany 7

Sunday between 17 and 23 February (if earlier than 2 before Lent)

Thought for the day

The Son of Man has authority on earth to forgive sins.

Reflection on the readings

Isaiah 43:18-25
Psalm 41
2 Corinthians 1:18-22
Mark 2:1-12

Most of us have at some point in life got stuck in a guilt zone. Whatever it was that we did or failed to do keeps washing around in our head and refuses to disappear. It alters our outlook and our attitude to the present, it distorts our capacity for walking freely into the future, and can, if we let it, actually drive us further into guilt-ridden places! The prophet speaking in today's passage from Isaiah obviously understands what it feels like to be trapped by guilt about the past. And so, of course, does the God who made us.

The passage is like a breath of fresh air: God is saying to us that we can stop thinking about all those past things, and put them behind us once and for all, because he is about to do something completely new. It is described in images of hope taken from the natural world – water in the wilderness and rivers in the desert. And why is God embarking on such a comprehensive forgiveness programme, erasing the guilt of the past in this way?

It is not because of anything his people have done to earn it, but simply because it is God's very nature to set people free like this. Since he is God he can't help doing it! And it is therefore not surprising that we find Jesus exercising authority over sin in the same way. The scribes, knowing their scripture, are quite right in observing that only God can forgive sins. They know that he alone has the authority over evil to erase it and render it powerless, thereby setting people free of its effects in the rest of their lives.

So when Jesus picks up on their thoughts and asks whether they think it is harder to forgive sins or make a paralysed body mobile again, he is leading them to the point where they will have proof of Jesus' identity. They are about to see, in the outward body, what only God is able to do in the realm of the human spirit. Just as the forgiveness has unlocked and liberated the man's spirit, so now his limbs are unlocked, setting him free also physically. Surely the authenticity of the one will convince them of the authenticity of the other? Only if they have eyes open to see.

In the passage from 2 Corinthians, Paul spells out the great truth which the scribes could not cope with: that all the promises of God have their 'Yes' in Christ. The liberating power of God's forgiveness is physically shown in the person of Jesus, and its vitalising effects continue to liberate prisoners two thousand years on.

All-age talk

Start by explaining that you have a list of hard things to do, and you are going to ask everyone which they think is the easier of two options. They can have a moment to think or confer, and then a show of hands should indicate their communal decision.

Here are the options:

1. Learning to ride a bike, or learning to talk.
2. Earning money, or saving your money up without spending any.
3. Doing something brave, or doing something thoughtful.
4. Talking non-stop for an hour, or being completely quiet for an hour.

In today's Gospel we heard Jesus ask a similar question. Remind them of the circumstances – the crowds, the paralysed man let down through the roof, Jesus telling him his sins are forgiven, and the scribes, knowing that only God can forgive sins, horrified that

Jesus has done what only God can do. This was his question – which is it easier to say to the paralysed man: 'Your sins are forgiven you' or 'Stand up, take your bed and walk'?

Let's try and work out an answer. First we need to make a few things clear. Who is the only one who can forgive sins? It's God. And what about a paralysed man suddenly being able to get up and walk home – who's the only one able to do that? Once again, it's God. So in a way, Jesus is saying to the scribes, 'Is it easier for me to act like God, or to act like God?' And what would be the answer to that? There'd be no difference; both are a natural way for God to behave.

The man's body was paralysed – that meant he couldn't make it move freely. When Jesus healed him he was free to move about again. It's like that when our lives are jammed by sin and guilt about bad things we've done in the past. When God forgives us completely, he unjams us, so we are free to live happily again.

Second Sunday before Lent

Thought for the day

Christ is the image of the unseen God.

Reflection on the readings

Proverbs 8:1, 22-31
Psalm 104:24-35
Colossians 1:15-20
John 1:1-14

Last week we were reflecting on the forgiving nature of God, and today, with the reading from Proverbs to help us, it is as if we are savouring the extraordinary creative energy of God's wisdom, holding it and marvelling at it, personalised for accessibility. What is God's wisdom like? With a poet's vision it is described as a creative woman, sensitive, delighting in all the unfolding wonders, appreciating and valuing with a childlike innocence which is playful, yet candid and pure.

It is a lovely if unexpected image, and helps us to understand more of God's nature. There is a lightness and gentleness of touch here which acts as a balance to our more usual serious-minded image of a God of power and responsibility. We sense a wonderful harmony of what we, from our separate-gendered perspective, might see as the masculine and feminine attributes of God.

Coming to the introduction of John's Gospel from such an approach road tunes us in to appreciate the mystery of the eternal Word. In one sense, it is so much an intrinsic part of the nature of God that it cannot be seen as separate from him, any more than his wisdom can. In another sense, Jesus the Christ is that Word separately enfleshed, visible to us when God remains hidden from our sight. There is clearly a link between personified Wisdom, of the Hebrew tradition, and the personified eternal Word, which resonated with Greek thinking. The One who draws all this together is Christ, living out, in human person terms, the creative loving of God.

As Paul explains in his letter to the Christians at Colossae, God was dwelling in all his fullness in the person of Jesus, so that he alone was able to reconcile all to himself, healing the creative harmony which sin had ripped apart. The wisdom Christ displays, then, is of complete integrity and vulnerable love.

All-age talk

Bring with you a few Mr Men books – *Mr Muddle, Mr Bump* and *Mr Chatterbox*, for instance – and invite the children to help you explain to the adults why they are called those names. Point out how they look just like their names and their characters. In those stories we put shapes to ways of behaving. Meeting the characters helps us understand what it's really like to be muddled, accident-prone or extra chatty.

Our readings today look at the same kind of idea. To help us understand more about what God is like, we meet aspects of his nature as characters – we are introduced to Miss Wisdom and Mr Word.

Miss Wisdom shows us how wise God is. It isn't just a question of knowing lots of clever things (though God is all-knowing). Miss Wisdom is described as being beautiful, happy, and excited by all the loveliness of creation, enjoying it almost like a good friendship. So we now know that God's nature is like that.

Then, in the Gospel reading, written by John, we meet Mr Word. We are told he's been around as long as God has. From his name we would expect Mr Word to be telling us something, as that's what words do. And we'd be right, because that's exactly what Mr Word does. Mr Word is a person whose life tells us exactly what God is like. (Show a large version of the picture on the following page.)

He's a bit like a human speech bubble – which God himself is speaking. And although we may not usually call him by his name of Word, we do actually know him already quite well. He is Jesus,

God's Mr Word, who was born as a baby at Christmas, and lived on earth loving, healing and teaching, very wisely.

Sunday next before Lent

Thought for the day

God's glory shows.

Reflection on the readings

2 Kings 2:1-12
Psalm 50:1-6
2 Corinthians 4:3-6
Mark 9:2-9

It is easy to understand why, since ancient times, people have worshipped the sun. Quite apart from its dazzling beauty, and its faithfulness in appearing each morning, all living things seem to sense that they depend on the sun for survival. Plants grow their first tentative shoots towards it, and adjust their flowering according to the length of daylight. Many flowers turn their heads to follow the sun's progress through the day, and all the complexities of animal and plant activity are locked into their relationship with our nearest star. Earth and the other planets in the solar system owe their very development to it.

So it is not surprising that sun-like images of fire and light are frequently used to describe the presence of the living God – images which speak of power, essence of life, sustaining support, faithfulness and beauty that hurts when we look at it directly. Or we can look at it from the other direction and see how God inevitably displays his nature in his creation, and it says a lot about him that the very first word of creation was 'Let there be light!' Creating the sunlight, and a teeming planet's life depending on it, was providing us with clues about the energising Creator, and our dependence on him.

It certainly feels entirely appropriate that God's glory, being seen in Jesus as he is transfigured, shows him being lit up, bright and seemingly pure. The people of Israel had in their communal history many stories of fiery encounters with God, such as Moses' burning bush, the pillar of fire guiding and protecting them on their escape from Egypt, the extra person seen in the burning fiery furnace, and the heavenly chariots of fire as Elijah is taken from Elisha's sight. Today's Psalm is one of many expressing God as a consuming fire.

Mark's account of the transfiguration comes immediately after Jesus has been telling his disciples about his necessary suffering and death before he comes into glory. To help them cope with what is ahead they are allowed a fleeting glimpse of the holistic truth, where the glory is evident, so that when it is hidden in the horror of the cross, they may begin to understand what real glory involves.

All-age talk

Bring along something that gets transformed when the light in it is switched on, such as an illuminated globe, table lamp or OHP with a picture on acetate. Or people can look at the church's stained glass windows.

First show it without being lit up, and then switch on to show the difference. When it is lit up we can see patterns and colours that we may not have seen before. Today we heard in our Gospel reading about a time when three of Jesus' friends saw him 'lit up', and it really did help them to see him in a new light.

We're none of us used to that kind of thing happening, so it all sounds rather strange to us. Let's imagine ourselves that morning, climbing up a steep, rocky mountain path with Jesus leading the way, and Peter, James and John struggling to keep up behind him. We're all panting a bit, and sometimes pieces of stone and grit get stuck in our sandals. We might see a lizard or two sitting in the early sun, and hear the wind in the grass.

When we reach the very top, we can see all around us, with the lake and the little villages far below. It's like being on top of the world. Jesus has come up here to pray. He knows that he needs to get away from the crowds sometimes to spend time quietly with his Father in heaven. We all need that, too.

Peter, James and John suddenly realise that Jesus is looking different. He seems to be shining – Mark says 'dazzling' which is like when you look into the sun and have to screw up your eyes because it's just too bright to look at comfortably. It's as if they're looking at the presence of God himself, here on the mountain. And Jesus isn't alone, either. As if he's in heaven, rather than standing on the mountain grass, two other people are talking with him, and we recognise them from history. One is Moses, who led the people out of slavery in Egypt and gave the people God's ten commandments, and the other is a prophet from long ago called Elijah; both very holy people.

It's actually very frightening – all so holy and full of glory, and so unusual. It's then that the cloud comes over, and I think Peter, James and John have shielded their eyes from all the brightness. They hear a voice speaking out of the cloud, and they somehow know that it is God speaking. What is it he's saying? 'This is my beloved Son: listen to him.'

That's Jesus he's talking about! And we've just seen with our own eyes that Jesus wears God's glory – we just haven't been allowed to notice it before.

When the disciples look up again the brightness has passed, and their friend Jesus is standing there on his own, looking quite normal. On the way down the mountain path he tells them not to say anything about what they have seen and shared until he has risen from the dead. Peter, James and John don't really understand yet that Jesus will have to suffer death before he is glorified.

But we know what happened, don't we? And perhaps it helped Jesus' friends, when the first Easter Day came, and they met Jesus alive again.

Lent 1

Thought for the day

After his Baptism Jesus is led by the Spirit into the wilderness before returning to proclaim God's kingdom.

Reflection on the readings

Genesis 9:8-17
Psalm 25:1-10
1 Peter 3:18-22
Mark 1:9-15

Today we begin the season of Lent, committing the next six weeks to preparing ourselves for the festival of Resurrection by looking seriously at the implications of turning to God at our baptism. So it is appropriate to start at the point of Jesus' baptism filling him with God's Spirit and promptly driving him into a six-week ordeal of vocational testing and spiritual battling.

Jesus' ministry did not begin with warm glowing feelings but rigorous self-discipline, painful soul-searching and cost-counting. When he later spoke about our need to count the cost of discipleship he was talking from personal experience. Committing ourselves wholeheartedly to God's service is indeed a costly business, and one it is quite natural to back away from as we start to realise the full implications. Are we really willing to say to God, 'Thy will be done; thy kingdom come'? Wouldn't we far prefer it to be our will and kingdom with God's blessing! Most of us feel fine about obedience until it differs from what we want in life; at which point we start jumping up and down complaining about the unfairness of it all.

One of the precious, valuable things we can learn from Jesus' example is to recognise the conflicts as a valid part of the process. Jesus knew he had some difficult things to face, and he knew he would not be ready for his ministry until he had taken time out to face them squarely, however unpleasant that might be. All too often our reaction is to deny our fears and questions, or edit them before approaching God with them, as we consider them inappropriate prayer material.

But the truth is that God wants our real, honest selves, and can't start working in earnest with us until we are willing to share with him everything – and that includes misgivings, things which embarrass us to mention to anyone, recognition of things we had hoped for and dreamed about and which we dislike the idea of giving up. If there is anything we feel ashamed to mention to God, then that's probably the most important thing he wants us to say.

Of course, we are not going to come to any of this lightly or easily. We are wonderfully inventive when it comes to rewriting agendas we find threatening to us or prefer to ignore. That is why we all need a wilderness, and time to be alone with God, without distraction. The wilderness is honesty, and we need to get used to its bare and uncompromising landscape, where conflicts are bound to confront us, but from which we will emerge stronger and more integrated as people, ready to go out in God's power.

Noah and his family are at that point as the rainbow of God's saving promise marks the end of the storms and floods, and they can walk as new people into a new landscape.

All-age talk

Bring with you a compass, and a chart showing that there are six weeks before Easter Day.

Explain that in six weeks' time it will be Good Friday and Easter Day, when we will all be celebrating Jesus rising to new life that lasts for ever, after being put to death on the cross. That's such a very special, important thing to celebrate that the Church decided we all need a few weeks to get ourselves ready for it. Time to think carefully about what it means to be a follower of Jesus. Time to sort our lives out a bit. Draw attention to the change of colour in church – purple is quite a serious, thoughtful colour, to match our serious, thoughtful mood in these next six weeks, which are called Lent.

Why *six* weeks? We are told that when Jesus had gone to the river Jordan and been baptised by John, he went straight off into the desert hills, to spend forty days, getting ready to tell everyone the good news of God's kingdom. He didn't get ready by reading lots of books and doing lots of homework, or talking to lots of people. He got ready by living very simply, even going without food, and letting God lead him into the areas he needed to think about. He wanted to spend time finding out what God really wanted him to do with his life.

So, as the Church, we're going to do the same. Today is the day we all set off into the desert for six weeks. What do you think we'll need to take with us?

Produce various items of combat gear, and mountain-walking clothing and equipment. Then kick it all away. We're not going to need any of this. All we need is one thing – a compass. What does a compass do? It helps you walk in the right direction. We need a special compass that always points us in God's direction.

Explain that you happen to have just the compass we need, and produce a cross – a wall-hanging one is about the right size so that people can see it easily. This is a special compass for us to take into the desert of Lent with us. Hold the cross flat. It points us always towards God's love, and at the same time it points back at ourselves. We can't pretend in this desert. We've got to be honest to God about who we are and how we are thinking and feeling. That's the only way the compass will point us in the right direction. Are we ready for the desert of Lent?

The first step on our journey is to agree to live more simply for a while, and go wherever God takes us. We can spend this week doing that, remembering to use our compass every day.

Lent 2

Thought for the day

A commitment of faith has far-reaching implications.

Reflection on the readings

Genesis 17:1-7, 15-16
Psalm 22:23-31
Romans 4:13-25
Mark 8:31-38

The desert experience of Lent continues today with Jesus determined that his disciples should be fully aware of the implications of his true identity. Mark tells us that, immediately following their recognition of him as God's Messiah, he starts spelling out to them what this means, and how it differs from their dreams.

The God of truth insists on our knowing the truth, even if it might turn us against him or temporarily hurt us or upset our plans; never will he pander to our misguided longings – he has too much respect for us. Gently, but firmly and openly, Jesus outlines the real Messiah's role – a role in which suffering, rejection and death are inevitable.

Such apparent failure, though clearly explored in the scriptures, had been conveniently overwritten by the popular dream of a resistance fighter who would lead the victorious struggle against Roman oppression and occupation.

From Jesus' response to Peter's protests, it is clear that the horror of such a future can still tempt him to sidestep what he is called to go through. The temptations Jesus had been facing in the desert are here flaring up again through the misguided well-wishing of his friend. Impressed by personal experience of the power of such temptations, Jesus gathers not only his disciples but all his followers in the area together, to prepare them as thoroughly and honestly as he can for such temptations in their own lives to sidestep the will of God.

It is quite true – we shall be tempted, time and again, to take the easier route and thus avoid the conflicts which are bound to accompany committed discipleship. But if we go along with such temptations, where do we end up? Without any 'life' (in the fullest sense of the word) left to live. And, as Jesus suggests, isn't it better to have the wicked ashamed of us, rather than Jesus and the holy angels of God?

But how on earth do we manage to be strong enough to resist the pull of the world of comfort, personal safety and self-gratification? We are given the example of Abraham, whose faith kept him walking and thinking God's way, even when it did not look exactly promising. He trusted God so firmly that he stuck with it through thick and thin, and that is what delighted God.

Anyone is a child of Abraham who is a child of faith; and in no circumstance whatsoever will God ever let them down.

All-age talk

Bring along some advertisements which proclaim special offers which look absolutely wonderful bargains, and completely good news, but when you read the small print you find all sorts of extra bad news which makes the bargain not quite so fantastic as it first sounded. (For example: '£50 OFF! – when you spend £300'; 'Children go free! – but only if you travel after 10 o'clock and buy two full adult fares'.)

Of course, those who designed the advertisement hope that by the time you've read the small print you are so keen to take them up on the offer that you will be prepared to go along with the extra requirements.

Jesus is never like that with us; he is always completely open and honest. Jesus always gives us both the good and the bad news gently but firmly because he loves and respects us. That's why we know that we can trust him absolutely. If someone is always saying how wonderful we are, even when we know very well that we have not been at all wonderful, we can't really trust that they are telling us the truth. But if someone tells us the bad news when it's bad and the good news when it's good, then we know we *can* trust them to be honest with us.

In today's reading from Mark's Gospel, we find the disciples expecting something that can't happen. They are thinking that, as Jesus is the Messiah, he is one day going to lead an army to drive out the Romans from their country. Jesus takes the risk of them rejecting him, and being angry and disappointed, rather than lead them into false hopes. In effect he's saying, 'OK, so you know I'm the Messiah, but I'm afraid I'm not going to be the kind of Messiah you're all expecting. It's not going to look like a great victory at first – it's going to look like complete failure.' Jesus tells them he's going to be killed, all as part of his work as Messiah.

And Peter can't bear to hear this 'bad news'. He tries to shut it out, and persuade Jesus that he must be mistaken. Sometimes we do the same. Perhaps Jesus nudges us to give something up, or change something in our lives or make friends with someone we don't want to, and we spend a lot of time and energy pretending not to hear, or pretending that God must be mistaken. He isn't mistaken; he's just being lovingly honest with us, and we take it as bad news because we don't want to hear it as the truth.

We've reached the second week of Lent, our thoughtful time in the desert. Let's use the coming week to take notice when Jesus nudges us, and go along, with what he suggests, even if it means giving up something we like doing.

Lent 3

Thought for the day

God's wisdom may shock us. Jesus, obedient to God's Law and fulfilling it, dies a death which, according to the Law, makes him cursed.

Reflection on the readings

Exodus 20:1-17
Psalm 19
1 Corinthians 1:18-25
John 2:13-22

Probably no one was more surprised at Jesus' behaviour in the temple than those sitting buying and selling there. It had become normal practice – a tradition even – for the marketing side of worship to flourish, and the petty corruption involved was something everyone had come to expect and live with. We all get used to our own dirt and scruffiness and stop noticing it after a while. But Jesus finds it highly offensive. Why?

One of the hallmarks of Jesus' life is obedience, born of attentive listening to his heavenly Father. Understanding the Father's longing and will urges him to work for its accomplishment on earth. Lack of obedience, on the other hand, is closely linked with the desire to act independently of God. Throughout the desert time of testing, Jesus drew great strength for resistance from his mature obedience to the words of God in scripture. He found, like the writer of Psalm 19, that 'the Law of the Lord is perfect, reviving the soul. Jesus knew that he had come to fulfil the scriptures, and that full obedience, even when severely challenging, was the only way for this to happen.

In our own society there is very little of an obedience ethic, and a rather distorted image of obedience as being something mature people can grow out of as they achieve rational independence. So we find the whole idea of commandments rather heavy, and might even feel that the rights of those temple sellers need to be upheld against Jesus' action.

Jesus knows that our holiness will only develop in line with our obedience to God, and, if we casually break God's Law as if it doesn't matter, we will find ourselves weak and unable to withstand temptations when they come. For our own survival spiritually we have to be rigorous with ourselves. One of the benefits of this desert time of discipline in Lent is that we are strengthened.

What Jesus finds offensive is that God's temple, set apart to be a place of holiness and prayer, is filled instead with buying and selling, profit-making and cheating. Our bodies are temples of the Holy Spirit. Are they also filled with buying and selling, profit-making and cheating? And, if so, do we care that we are therefore being disobedient to God's Law? Does it occur to us that we would be stronger and better enabled to resist temptation if we were rather 'houses of prayer'?

All-age talk

Begin by asking for some volunteers to read the following conversations.

1. Mum: David, it's time to stop playing and go to bed now.

   David: Oh, but Mum, I'm much too busy!

2. Dad: Turn that music down, Gary!!

   Gary: But I like it, and it needs to be loud!!

3. Hilda: George, it's time you gave up smoking.

   George: But, Hilda, it's my decision, and none of your business.

4. Fred: Now, Mother, you need to wear a hearing aid.

   Mother: What's that, Fred?

   Fred: A HEARING AID! YOU NEED TO WEAR ONE, MOTHER.

Mother: No, I don't – I can hear perfectly when people
bother to speak up properly!

All through our lives we're supposed to be obedient, and all
through our lives we prefer to do as we like!

Today we're on the third week of our desert journey together
through Lent. And we're going to look at what it means to be
obedient, and why it's a good thing to work at, even though we all
find it so very difficult to do what we're told.

Scatter the ten commandments, written on pieces of card, over
the aisle, or stick them with sticky tack on to pillars.

In our first reading we heard the ten commandments – ten
useful rules to help us live God's way. These rules were given to
the people through Moses, the great leader who had led the
people out of slavery in Egypt. They've all been in the desert for
quite a long time, learning to be God's people, like we are through
Lent. And then God gives them the Law, which they are told to
obey. They are still good rules, and when Jesus came he didn't
say, 'Listen, everyone, now I've come you don't need to bother
with all those commandments any more!' Jesus insisted that he
had come not to destroy the Law but to fulfil it, to fill it full of
God's love.

So Jesus summed all the rules up in two parcels. Produce one
bag labelled 'Love God' and another one labelled 'Love one
another', and sort out the first four commandments into the first
bag and the second six into the second bag. That makes them
easier for us to carry around in our heads (hold a bag in each
hand), but we need to remember what's inside each bag, and take
them out to look at from time to time, like we've done today.

So Jesus thought it was good to be obedient. He was obedient to
his heavenly Father, even when that turned out to mean he had to
die on the cross! The reason he was obedient was because he
really understood why it was important.

If we understand the reason for being obedient, we're much
more likely to try and do what we're told. If Fred's mother really
understood how difficult it was becoming for the family to talk to
her without her hearing aid, she'd *want* to wear it. If Gary really

understood how hard it was for his Dad to concentrate on his work with the music so loud, he'd *want* to turn it down a bit.

In other words, obedience is all to do with acting out of love. As we get to understand and love God better, we shall find we are more and more keen to do what he wants us to.

Lent 4

Mothering Sunday

Thought for the day

God provides comfort in all our troubles and sufferings.

Reflection on the readings

Exodus 2:1-10 or 1 Samuel 1:20-28
Psalm 34:11-20 or Psalm 127:1-4
2 Corinthians 1:3-7 or Colossians 3:12-17
Luke 2:33-35 or John 19:25-27

Television advertisements would have us believe in a normal family life of immaculate mums smiling as their families appear with their best clothes filthy; of inept dads being shown up by their perfect wife-and-mother partners, and hideous children who rule the whole family by their tyrannical demands. It is not many years since we were fed normal families of laughing togetherness, combined with perfect fashion sense and model good looks, where dad ruled and everyone was happy.

The styles may change but what stays the same is the pressure of image. All the media brandish the latest image instructions, and the pressure is on to conform, with the implied carrot that living the image will lead to success. Strewn along the wayside are all the casualties – those who have struggled to achieve the impossible in an illusory competition.

Refreshingly, our readings for Mothering Sunday place us fairly and squarely in the real world. Here family life is the wonderful patchwork of bright and dark colours, glowing sections and dull areas that we all recognise. It includes troubles and tragedies that hit us between the eyes and send us reeling, and also those moments of tender comforting which have such power to heal and enable us to carry on.

What we are being reminded of is God's parenting, which is no false, demanding image, but the real thing – the parenting we all need for our survival, and crave, sensing its importance. Not that we always remember to come to God for it; all too often we search for it instead among fallible humanity, and find ourselves let down and abandoned as a result. As humans we do bear a resemblance to God's parenting, but we are bound to let one another down sometimes. God's arms are the ones that embrace all of us, holding us all in those loving arms, mopping all our tears and setting us on our feet again.

We hear of terrible, tragic situations of heartache in today's readings, which are redeemed by God's parenting love. As Paul says, God is the one who comforts us in all our troubles. We don't have to pretend with God that there aren't any troubles, or that we're managing very nicely, thank you. God knows what family life is about – and single life. He knows the heartaches and the conflicts. He knows that loving makes us vulnerable.

That's why God is so well able to comfort us within our real situations, and enable us to cope with the ordinary troubles of life without being overwhelmed by them; he has the resources we need available and his arms are outstretched in welcome.

All-age talk

If you have stained glass windows, direct people to look at these during the talk. If not, bring a picture or poster which is full of contrasting colours, or have such a picture or photograph made into an OHP acetate and project it.

Draw everyone's attention to the different colours that are used, asking them to pick out their favourites, to pick out some of the darks and some of the lights. Perhaps there are also different textures involved.

Explain that family life is rather like this – a whole picture made up of bright and dark colours, of happy and sad times, angry and contented times, worrying and relaxed times. Ask for examples of these from everyone, so that our own colourful picture starts to take shape.

It isn't just us on our own who are making these family works of art – it's us and God together, and we go on making them all through our lives. Whenever there is a whole lot of dark, sad colour, God will brighten it for us with the rich, warm colours of his comforting love.

Lent 5

Thought for the day

Through Christ's death, full life would come to people of all nations and generations.

Reflection on the readings

Jeremiah 31:31-34
Psalm 51:1-12 or Psalm 119:9-16
Hebrews 5:5-10
John 12:20-33

The people of Israel had been advised to strap the Law to their foreheads and around their doorposts in order to try and keep God's rules always in mind, but Jeremiah looks forward to a time when people will have God's Law deep within them in a new and dynamic way. And it is with the coming of Jesus that the prophecy can be fulfilled. With Jesus Christ there in person, people can see and understand what God is like, and with God's Spirit poured into their hearts, after Jesus' Ascension, the new and intimate relationship with God becomes a reality for those in every age and place.

In today's Gospel we are told by John that some Gentile Greeks are actually seeking Jesus out. He had just finished cleansing the temple so that it could be restored as a house of prayer for all nations, and now here are representatives of those other nations asking for him. With their coming, it is as if Jesus suddenly catches sight of that future, rolling out into the distance of time and space, with people of all nations giving God glory and worshipping him in Spirit and in truth. At the same time he recognises that his own finger is poised on the button that will make it possible. He is acutely aware of the necessary agony he must suffer for it to happen, and, in his humanness, shrinks from that. He battles with what we all know so well – the powerful human instinct to preserve ourselves and avoid pain and conflict. Being the Son of God did not immunise Jesus against the struggle of sacrifice. Gloriously, love triumphs, and Jesus relinquishes everything to the will and glory of God; it must be done, and willingly done.

Immediately and powerfully the Father's love affirms what he has chosen, and all in the crowd who have ears to hear, whether Jew or Gentile, hear that unity of loving will for the good of the whole world.

All-age talk

Bring with you a box of assorted sweets or chocolates, and invite a couple of volunteers to choose one. Ask them why they chose it (there may be no reason at all) and whether they are happy with the choice they made.

All our life long we are faced with making choices. Sometimes the choice isn't that important; if you make a mistake and choose a chocolate which isn't a favourite, you haven't lost out much. But sometimes the choices are more important. Invite a couple of car owners to talk about their choice of car and whether they are happy with their decision. Ask a student which A levels they have chosen to take, or which degree course, and a child what they have chosen to do for a birthday treat.

Sometimes we have to choose even more important things than that! Let's look at a very hard choice Jesus had to make, which we heard about in today's Gospel. Jesus knew that he was alive on earth for a very important mission – he was here to save the world, and he really wanted to do that, because he loved the people. But there was a problem. He also knew that saving the world was bound to land him in terrible pain and danger, more pain and agony than anyone has ever faced before or since. It would involve taking on himself all the sin and evil of the world, and going on loving right through it.

So he had the choice – to go ahead with saving the world, taking on the suffering as part of the deal, or to avoid all that appalling suffering by opting out, in which case the world would have no hope of being saved.

And it wasn't an easy thing to choose. Everything human in him screamed out against going through the pain of it all; but everything divine in him pleaded for love and compassion, and selfless giving whatever the cost.

We know what Jesus chose. Love won, and he chose to go through hell, giving up everything, including his life, just so that we could be set free to live.

Palm Sunday

Thought for the day

As the Messiah, Jesus enters Jerusalem, knowing that he rides towards rejection and death in order to save his people.

Reflection on the readings

Liturgy of the Palms:
Mark 11:1-11 or John 12:12-16
Psalm 118:1-2, 19-24

Liturgy of the Passion:
Isaiah 50:4-9a
Psalm 31:9-16
Philippians 2:5-11
Mark 14:1–15:47 or Mark 15:1-39 (40-47)

Palm Sunday takes us through the great drama of what it means for Jesus to be the Messiah. This week, often named 'Holy Week', is the culmination and accomplishment of all the Law, prophets and history of the Bible. It's here that the promises make good, that the secrets of the kingdom are displayed, and that the truth of God's saving love is acted out. Just as at moments of crisis our brains click into a kind of slow motion where the events are crowded in, so the Gospels report this last week of Jesus' earthly life with all the detail and heightened perception of people witnessing to the most significant and important week ever.

As he comes into Jerusalem riding on a donkey, Jesus is choosing to act out, three dimensionally, what he is. He does what the prophecies had said the Messiah would do, spelling out to everyone both his authority and his style of leadership. Donkeys are humble beasts of burden, and Jesus, son of King David both as family and as the anointed One, is proclaiming that God's Messiah comes to his people as a servant King.

The only way we have any hope of grasping what this means is by going on to hear, as fully as possible, the extent to which the humility and obedience of this servanthood is taken. This enables us to see the waving palms and shouts of victory through the racking torture of the cross; and the seeming cursed failure of the cross through the waving palms and shouts of victory. Both are victory and both are sacrifice.

Mark's account of the Passion shows us a poignantly human Jesus, fully integrated with the frailty of human nature we are so familiar with ourselves. How he longs for it to be possible to avoid what he dreads, and how he needs support from his heavy-eyed and terrified disciples, who abandon him. Perhaps the most terrible part of the whole ordeal of the arrest, trial, torture and crucifixion, is that acute sense of utter abandonment, blocking him off even from his heavenly Father.

The liturgy of today shakes us and prepares us to travel with Jesus through this week of most costly loving.

All-age talk

Beforehand make two large, clear signs, one saying, 'Hosanna! Blessed is he who comes in the name of the Lord!' and the other, 'Crucify him!'

First remind everyone of the way the crowds had welcomed Jesus as he rode into Jerusalem on a donkey. They were all giving him the red carpet welcome, throwing down greenery and their coats for the donkey to walk on, and waving palm branches as flags, cheering and singing. One of the things they shouted was from one of their traditional songs, which we know as Psalms: 'Hosanna! Blessed is he who comes in the name of the Lord!' (Everyone can shout this as loudly as possible.) It meant they were welcoming Jesus as the new King David; they were really excited, expecting Jesus to become their king and throw out all the Romans so they would be free again. They thought they really wanted God's kingdom.

Sometimes we are like the people in this crowd. We get all excited by Jesus, and promise to work with him, and feel ready to do anything to help the kingdom come. 'Let your kingdom come! Let *your* will be done!' we pray, and we really mean it. We work hard at our praying, and do our best to be loving and honest in the way we live. We give God the worship we know he deserves, and we give of ourselves simply because we are filled with love for him.

In today's Gospel we heard what happened to Jesus on Good Friday. It makes us very sad to hear what happened to our friend, and we might find ourselves thinking that we wouldn't have left him alone like his friends did; we would have been there for him; we would at least have prayed with him and not fallen asleep in the garden.

But the crowd remind us of something rather nasty. They weren't singing 'Hosanna!' any more. They were shouting, 'Crucify him!' (All shout this.) And although we wish it wasn't true, we all know there are times when we do that as well. Those times when we know very well what is the right and loving thing to do or say, and we want Jesus out of the way so we can be as unkind and dishonest as we like. It's hard work having Jesus there when we don't want to be loving, or humble, or obedient. At those times we don't much like his kingdom. Every time that happens we are joining the crowd which shouted, 'Crucify him!'

Let's remember that, and pull ourselves together when it next happens so that, instead, we shout with our lives, 'Hosanna! Blessed is he who comes in the name of the Lord!'

Easter Day

Thought for the day

Jesus is alive; Love has won the victory over sin and death.

Reflection on the readings

Acts 10:34-43 or Isaiah 25:6-9
Psalm 118:1-2, 14-24
1 Corinthians 15:1-11 or Acts 10:34-43
John 20:1-18 or Mark 16:1-8

So the unavoidable, total sacrifice was given, along with all its pain and suffering which Jesus had dreaded. Through rejection, brutal torture and utter abandonment, Love held strong and refused to be conquered by the worst that evil and sin could throw at it. It took the Lord of life deep into the darkness of death, so that even that journey, which we must all make alone, is graced forever with his presence. Left behind, stirred and shaken, the followers and friends of Jesus don't know what to think about anything any more.

And now, on the third day after his death, the impossible happens, and Jesus returns to life. It isn't the same kind of life, of course – how could it be with that journey behind him? Death has taken him beyond ordinary human life. God's loving power has drawn him out of death into the 'eternal life' which is completely full and has no limits either of time or space.

In the Gospel accounts of the Resurrection we are constantly aware of the struggle people had with accepting that Jesus was really with them again. Whenever we are faced with amazing good news, we find it almost 'too good to be true', and these first fragmentary meetings with the risen Jesus are often as much filled with terror and confusion as joy.

Jesus lets them take their time to grasp the reality of what has happened. Patiently he explains the scriptures, eats with them and loves them, until it dawns on them that, although it is so extraordinary and so wonderful, they can believe it – because it's true.

All-age talk

Bring along a hot cross bun, a chocolate Easter egg, an ordinary hen's egg, and one of those fluffy Easter chickens.

Ask a volunteer to take the first object (the hot cross bun) around the church so everyone can see what it is. As they go, explain that these buns remind us that because God loves us so much he was prepared to live among us in person, and go on loving us even when he was arrested, tortured and killed on a cross. It's in Jesus' life, and in his experience on the cross that we can 'taste and see that God is good'.

Now for the next object (another volunteer does the rounds) which is a hen's egg. The egg looks as dead as a smooth oval stone, but we know better. We know that if the egg is fertilised, and kept warm by the mother hen, that hard shell will start to crack, and into the world will climb . . . (a volunteer takes the chick around) a fluffy yellow chick, full of life! So the egg reminds us that what looked dead and hopeless on Good Friday (when Jesus' dead body was taken down from the cross, and it seemed he had failed as a Saviour) was actually full of new life, because on the third day after that, Jesus broke out of death to be alive for ever!

And so our last object (a volunteer walks the chocolate Easter egg around) is what we all enjoy having on Easter Day – chocolate Easter eggs. They're always bright and colourful, fun and delicious, and that's because Easter Day is party time for Christians!

Today we celebrate the fantastic truth that Jesus Christ is Lord – Love has won the victory over evil and death for ever!

Easter 2

Thought for the day

Our faith in the risen Christ is bound to affect the way we live.

Reflection on the readings

Acts 4:32-35
Psalm 133
1 John 1:1-2:2
John 20:19-31

If we are travelling along dark roads at night and trust the road surface, we probably drive quite quickly and confidently, whereas driving along a road we know to be full of potholes is a matter of gingerly approaching and peering, so as to avoid damaging us or the car. What we believe affects the way we behave.

On this second Sunday of Easter the readings lead us to recognise that belief in a risen crucified Christ is bound to change things. With the Resurrection we know, more completely than ever before, that God is to be trusted, God is light without any darkness at all, and, what is more, we can share in that companionship of light and freedom with the living God.

In the reading from Acts we are shown a few snapshots of how this was worked out in practice for the early believers. We find them united in a common purpose, without in-house arguments, and free of possessiveness; individual belongings no longer seem important to them as their concern for one another's needs has taken over. Central to all this is the fact that they are still excited and amazed by the Resurrection; they are conscious of the risen Jesus living among them in person.

Do we, as a Christian community, live in that conviction, or has the Resurrection, over the years, turned into history for us? As we reflect on these Easter readings, they can light up our faith again;

rather like turning up the thermostat on the heating, so that instead of just the quiet, steady pilot light burning away, the whole boiler flames into action. The risen Jesus walks into any gathering in any age, even those who have locked themselves in. And the meeting with Thomas, a week after the others have met with Jesus, shows us clearly that he is quite prepared to start with us where we are, addressing our particular fears, doubts and misgivings and leading us at a pace we can cope with, into the fullness of faith.

All-age talk

Bring with you some items of clothing which alter the way you move when wearing them, such as a pair of flippers, a pair of very heavy boots, a pair of binoculars and a pair of very high-heeled shoes.

Invite volunteers to demonstrate that when they are wearing (or looking through) these, it changes the way they walk. The changed way of moving is all part of wearing them.

It isn't only clothes and footwear which change our way of going about; it's our thoughts and feelings as well. If we've just won a match, if the person we love has just realised they love us as well, if the mortgage rate has gone down, or if we've just been fed and changed, then the whole day looks rosy and happy, and we'll pass on our feel-good factor in the way we react to those we meet. On the other hand, if the cat's been sick on the new sofa, you've lost your spelling list and know you haven't learnt the words, if the 7:27 is half an hour late, or you're hungry and your bottom feels damp and sore, then those feelings will probably make you less friendly and forgiving, and far more grumpy!

When we look at today's picture of life in the early Church, we're struck by how much love there seems to be in the community. Something is making these people happy to look after one another instead of fighting and arguing, and happy to share everything instead of looking after number one all the time. So what is making them like this? It must be something very good and very powerful!

It's all to do with them knowing something. They *know* that Jesus is alive and among them, so they are living in Jesus' company all the time. Jesus being there changes the way they live.

Now for a big question we all need to ask ourselves. Would anyone guess, just from looking at how we think and speak and behave, that we *knew* Jesus was living here among us? He is, so it should show!

Easter 3

Thought for the day

Having redeemed us by his death, Jesus can offer us the forgiveness of our sin, which sets us free to live.

Reflection on the readings

Acts 3:12-19
Psalm 4
1 John 3:1-7
Luke 24:36b-48

The Gospel for today recounts the events of that first Sunday evening after the crucifixion, when Jesus was suddenly there in person among his terrified disciples, putting their fears to rest, directing them to tell people they can be forgiven, and forgiving them in the name of the risen Christ. Of all the things Jesus might have said to his disciples on these brief encounters from life beyond death, why does he focus on repentance and forgiveness?

Surely because something had happened during those hours of agony on the cross, and at the moment of dying, which changed things for ever. We are told that the curtain of the temple ripped from top to bottom, a symbolic tearing down of the barrier of sin between God and his people; and now, from the perspective of the Resurrection, Jesus passes on to his disciples the urgent work of tearing down that barrier wherever it exists, in every person of all time.

In the reading from Acts we see Peter doing exactly what Jesus had said. Using every opportunity – in this case the people's amazement at the healing of the man unable to walk – he directs their attention to the real power and the powerful reality. It is through Jesus that the man is healed. This leads them straight on to the spiritual 'setting free' of repentance and forgiveness which is now available.

John, too, speaks from the viewpoint of one who knows what a difference it makes to be set free like this; the extent of God's love which makes such an enriched life possible still amazes him. It isn't a one-off operation, this forgiveness, though it often starts with a dramatic change of life direction. But we need to come regularly before the throne of God with humility to voice our sin, and our longing to be forgiven, and to experience that cleansing and refreshing which come from God's acceptance and forgiveness.

In fact, as our relationship with the living Jesus deepens, we shall find it increasingly uncomfortable to carry on in a state of sin without going to God to have it lifted from us, so as to restore us once again to that marvellous freedom we have experienced before. It is God's longing that all his humanity should be able to share the liberating joy of repenting and being forgiven. Knowing what we are all missing out on by lugging our sin around, and living only the 'till death' kind of life, Jesus sees repentance and forgiveness as urgent priorities for us – the stuff of a new order; the stuff of God's kingdom.

All-age talk

Bring along a dry stick and a growing plant with fresh shoots.

Easter is all about a different, richer sort of life which we can now have, thanks to Jesus going through death for us. It's a bit like the difference between this dry stick (show it) and this one which is full of life and growing (show it).

In today's Gospel we heard that Jesus comes into the locked room where his frightened disciples have met (display a number 1), and puts their minds at rest, so they aren't terrified, even though they are open-mouthed at God's power. Then (display a number 2) Jesus explains things to them so that they begin to understand that Jesus had to die and rise again, and lastly (display a number 3) he commissions them, sending them out to set everyone free to live this way (the shooting plant) instead of that (the dry stick).

We may not have noticed, but there are lots and lots of dry sticks like this walking around. Dry-stick people are often disguised. Because they are only interested in money, possessions or following their own wants, they often look attractive, with the latest everything to wear, smear on their face, drive or play. But a look into their eyes will show you that they are hard and dry as people, without any real joy, and may well be full of worries and anxieties, guilt and fear. Many of these dry sticks really know that this way of living is 'second best' but don't know how to get fully alive, or are frightened that God would say they were beyond his help.

Today is great news for all dry sticks! In going through evil and death without love slipping, even for a split second, Jesus has won for us all the victory over the sin and evil which dries us up and stops us living God's full life. All any dry stick needs is God's forgiveness; as they admit to themselves and to God what they are really like, and how they are cut off from him, his forgiveness starts to work on them, turning them into vibrant, warm, joy-filled people, happy to be living God's full life, and no longer bullied and caged by things that don't matter.

Easter 4

Thought for the day

'I am the Good Shepherd and I lay down my life for the sheep.'

Reflection on the readings

Acts 4:5-12
Psalm 23
1 John 3:16-24
John 10:11-18

Being imprisoned for the night may not look much like an opportunity, but in fact it provides the perfect opening for Peter and John to speak out about the power of Jesus who, though crucified, is now alive for ever. We heard last week how they had already been able to use healing to preach the good news to the crowds, bringing the number of believers to about five thousand. Just as Jesus had said would happen, they are given the words to say when asked to bear witness to the truth.

It is quite easy, of course, to make a point of not talking much to God about being given opportunities (in case he takes us up on it!) and to ignore or side-step such opportunities when they do happen. All too glibly do we persuade ourselves that we are not meant to force-feed people, or put them off by actually talking about God's involvement with lives and events. Certainly ramming God down people's throats is both unloving and counter-productive. But there is a great danger of using this as an excuse for avoiding the work we are commissioned to do, in many situations where people lose out on the blessings of forgiveness God longs for them to enjoy, simply because we chicken out of passing on the good news.

In today's Gospel, we hear the well-loved and treasured words of Jesus, describing himself as the Good Shepherd, the one who gathers the flock and tends the sheep, looking after their needs and leading them safely. In contrast to the hired worker, the authentic shepherd is even prepared to lay down his own life for the protection of the sheep. And that is good news worth passing on, at whatever cost to us. John reflects on what it means, and how it expresses incredible love – the willingness to lay down one's life for one's friends.

Quite importantly, it makes clear that Jesus was not forced into dying; it would have been possible to avoid it, right up to the very last breath. There had been the temptation to do so at intervals throughout his ministry, and even as he hung dying he was goaded to 'show his power' by coming down from the cross. It was, then, at the moments of greatest weakness that Jesus actually showed his greatest strength of love.

And that is often true for us as well. Weakness feels just that; without glamour or nobility or anything other than the recognition that we have no strength of ourselves to do any more; yet it is in living through such times in God's strength that others turn out to be blessed and God's name to be glorified. If only we will trust God at such times, who knows what sheep will be rescued?

All-age talk

Gather all the young children in the aisle and get them doing sheepy things like eating grass, drinking from a stream, sitting and chewing, and bleating. Place a few older children around the edges of the building to be wolves and bears, sheep-watching and hoping for a chance to eat one of the lambs. They can howl sadly as they wait, or growl.

One person is a good shepherd, keeping an eye on the flock, and watching out for any signs of wolves and bears.

The wild animals are waiting for the shepherd to go for a break, or doze off, because that's when they might get a chance to grab a lamb or sheep. But this shepherd loves his sheep, and that means he isn't going to give the wild animals any opportunity to attack the flock. He's ready to defend them with his life, if necessary.

Now swap the shepherd for a hired hand. Here's a different flock, with a different shepherd, further up the valley. The wild animals have gathered here now, and they're still waiting. (Howls and growls.) A couple of wolves start to come closer, but this shepherd doesn't frighten them away – he just runs away! The wolves get more confident. They're getting dangerously close, and the sheep are all huddled together, when that good shepherd walks up, with stones in his catapult, and the wolves back off quickly!

Thank the sheep and wild animals for their help, and explain that Jesus is like a good shepherd, who cares for us and looks after us, protecting us from evil. He loves us, so he isn't going to let us down, and is even ready to lay down his life for his sheep. In fact, as we know, Jesus did just that – he was ready to lay down his life to set us free.

Easter 5

Thought for the day

To produce fruit we need to be joined on to the true vine.

Reflection on the readings

Acts 8:26-40
Psalm 22:25–31
1 John 4:7-21
John 15:1-8

This week the reading from Acts continues the Spirit-led proclaiming of the good news, once again following the same pattern given by the risen Jesus during his encounters with the disciples. Philip arrives at the right place at the right time, because he has been closely in touch with God's leading. He tunes into the Ethiopian official's questions and seeking after truth, and explains who Jesus is and why he died, using the scriptures and interpreting them in the light of the Resurrection. It is all to do with working co-operatively with God, and allowing respect and love for one another to sensitise us to people's real needs, even if these are confused and unvoiced.

What happened to the Ethiopian as a result of this encounter? We only know that he went on his way rejoicing; probably he carried on the broadcasting of the good news, so that many others were also set free to live rejoicing lives.

The elderly John is still marvelling at the way God loves us, and is anxious to make it quite clear that double standards on our part will not do. Faced with the beauty of God's perfect love, it is no good claiming to love him if we are full of hate for another human being. Real love of God is bound to lead us on to love one another in the same tender, unselfish way that he loves us.

This is why the image of the vine and branches is such a vivid and useful one; being joined on to the vine makes all the difference, and we cannot expect to produce spiritual fruit unless we are well attached, with the life sap flowing through us. Jesus places himself in the role of vine and his Father as the gardener. Why does a gardener plant a vine and tend it? For the fruit! What a thought it is to imagine wine made from the fruit of love, joy, peace, patience, kindness, goodness, faithfulness, gentleness and self-control, all possible because of the life of Jesus flowing through our living and growing. Wine of the kingdom of God.

All-age talk

Cut six long strips of green crepe paper, or lengths of green string. Also prepare ten cut-out bunches of grapes from coloured paper.

Begin by suggesting that if you came in and said you were a pair of curtains, everyone would probably tell you to pull yourself together. But in our Gospel today we find Jesus saying, 'I am a grape vine.' Obviously he wasn't really a grape vine, was he? So what on earth did he mean?

To help us understand, we're going to make a kind of grape vine. Ask one volunteer to hold a green string in each hand, and two others to tie the strings round their waists. They can now hold four strings between them, and four others can tie these round their waists. Now for the fruit. Each of the last four people can hold a bunch of grapes in each hand (eight altogether) and the other two bunches can be stuck with a loop of sticky tape to the fronts of the second two volunteers.

In just a short time, and with just a few people, we've grown quite a big vine and ten bunches of fruit! Just imagine how much fruit there would be if everyone here were joined on the vine.

Jesus said he was the true vine and his Father was the gardener, looking after the growing and helping the vine branches to produce as much fruit as possible. Obviously these branches are only able to produce their fruit if they're joined on to the vine, because all the life-giving sap feeds them and if they're cut off they don't get anything to keep them alive.

Jesus was really saying that if we want our lives to produce fruit like love, joy, peace, patience, kindness, goodness, faithfulness, gentleness and self-control (stick these labels on the grapes), then we have to make really sure that we're joined up to Jesus and in touch with him. We need his life in us all the time. We need to keep in touch with him every day!

Easter 6

Thought for the day

We are to love one another as Jesus loves us.

Reflection on the readings

Acts 10:44-48
Psalm 98
1 John 5:1-6
John 15:9-17

In the reading from Acts we witness an extraordinary outpouring of the Holy Spirit, which doesn't even wait for Peter to finish speaking. Not surprisingly, when you look back to what he had just been saying, you find once again that powerful truth about forgiveness, which Jesus had commissioned his disciples to tell everyone about. 'Tell them they can be forgiven,' he had said straight after the Resurrection. As Peter proclaims this, the little crowd of people in Cornelius' house, who are searching single-mindedly for God's truth, suddenly experience the rush of God's forgiving love, and the freedom it brings.

And this is the kind of love we are given as an example to follow – the kind of forgiving, accepting love that wants people to be free. So much of what we name as love is actually to do with self-gratification and possession. It is tied up with our own need for fulfilment. But the love that Jesus talks of in today's Gospel is about obedience, willing co-operation, and sacrifice which produces joy.

There is a danger of mishearing what Jesus means here. He is not saying that in order to be his beloved friends we have to obey his commands. That would be fine if we could earn God's love by clocking up the points, and many people conscientiously live like this. But it does not set them free. It was because we can't earn

God's blessing that we needed a Saviour to give us freely the forgiveness which liberates us to live; and it is because God has treated us with such love and respect and generosity that, as his friends, we take delight in obeying his commands and living the loving way.

Jesus doesn't want to have us as servants, who obey because it's their job but know nothing of their employer's business. He has gone out of his way to involve us at every stage, pointing out the policies and plans, and the 'mission statement'. That makes us more like friends and colleagues with the God of creation, which is a heady prospect and also quite a responsibility.

All-age talk

Begin by pointing out that Jesus said he was no longer thinking of us as servants but as friends. That means we are people he is happy to talk things over with, co-operate with and involve in the work. There is going to be companionship and perhaps some good-natured teasing. Above all is the sense that we are in this together, and enjoying one another's company.

Another thing Jesus said is that we are to love one another in the way he loves us. So how is that? How does Jesus love us? Collect people's ideas; here are some that occurred to me:

- as friends
- with affection
- treating us seriously
- understanding us
- with honesty
- with forgiveness
- ready to put himself out for us
- with faithfulness
- consistently

Is this how we are treating other people? Or is it how we treat the people we like? As Christians we don't have the option to choose certain people to treat with God's love, while behaving how we feel with all the rest. We can't claim to love God and then decide that some people aren't worth treating with respect or understanding.

Of course it isn't easy to love one another like this. Lots of people are difficult to love in God's way – perhaps we are, ourselves! But when we look at how amazingly God treats us, copying his way of loving is the very least we can do. And the often surprising thing is that putting ourselves out and making the effort to live God's way is very rewarding, and makes us feel much happier inside.

Ascension Day

Thought for the day

Having bought back our freedom with the giving of his life, Jesus enters into the full glory to which he is entitled.

Reflection on the readings

Acts 1:1-11 or Daniel 7:9-14
Psalm 47 or Psalm 93
Ephesians 1:15-23 or Acts 1:1-11
Luke 24:44-53

The disciples have walked with Jesus on his journey to the cross, watched his suffering there and known the darkness of that time, then met him full of Resurrection life on various recorded occasions since Easter. During these encounters they have gradually begun to understand God's purposes and are getting used to knowing Jesus' constant presence, whether they can actually see him with them or not. And Jesus has accomplished all that he set out from heaven to do.

So the time has come for Jesus to move into the full glory of heaven, united with his Father and given his rightful place. In a sense the Ascension is like the completion of the Resurrection. Those post-Resurrection meetings were an essential part of the mission, preparation for the spread of the good news which could only be done after the victory over death.

When Jesus had met Mary of Magdala in the garden on that Sunday morning, he had told her not to hold him as he was not yet ascended to his Father. After his death, Jesus had preached to the dead, and now he was walking about among the living on earth. But this was not to be his permanent home. With the Ascension, Jesus is finally 'resurrected' into the glory of heaven forever. He is also fully available to touch every life in a way never possible before.

No one witnessed the Resurrection, but now, with the promise of power to be sent on the disciples, they see Jesus taken up into heaven. We are reminded of Elisha, promised Elijah's power only if he was allowed to witness his master's parting from earth. And from now on until the Day of Pentecost, they wait in expectant obedience for the empowering of the Holy Spirit.

Today is one of those festivals which look in both directions at once. We look back over all that led up to Christ's coming, and over that earthly human sharing from the manger to the empty tomb; and we look forward to the spreading of the kingdom far and wide through space and time, empowered by the Spirit. As Emmanuel, 'God-with-us', bridges earth and heaven at the Ascension, the human is caught up in the divine forever.

All-age talk

Prepare a large cardboard arrow pointer, and have the following things ready to use as signs: a Nativity play manger or a doll wrapped in swaddling clothes; a pair of sandals; a cross, a lit candle.

Explain that today is called Ascension Day (which means 'going up' day). Why is it called that? Because we are remembering the day when Jesus went out to a hill with his disciples this time after Easter, and they watched him returning to heaven. We are told that it looked as if Jesus was going upwards, not so much up into the sky as out of their sight. It was the last time Jesus was seen on the earth.

In a way, today is like being with the disciples on the top of a hill. If we look down one way (point the arrow backwards) we can look back to when Jesus first came to earth, as a newborn baby.

(A volunteer takes the baby or crib to stand as far as possible behind the arrow, but where they are still visible.) We're not just looking back to last Christmas (which does seem quite a long time ago!) but right to when Jesus was actually born. From our Ascension hilltop we look back to Jesus' life, and all the travelling around he did.

(The sandals are taken behind the arrow, but closer than the crib.) Jesus walked from town to village, healing the sick, teaching and loving the people. We can look back to the cross (the cross is brought behind the arrow, closer than the sandals) which Jesus' love brought him to, and we can remember what a great victory over evil was won there.

And we can look back to that first Easter morning (the lit candle is brought close behind the arrow) when death couldn't hold the Lord of life any longer, and Jesus burst into fuller life than ever.

(Turn the arrow to point upwards.) So today marks the end of Jesus' time on earth, tied to a time and a place, and we are celebrating his triumphant return to heaven, having won the victory and defeated the power of evil for us.

(Turn the arrow to face forwards.) From today's Ascension hill we are also looking forward into the future. And what do we find in the future? Among other things, all of us, sitting in this church in this year, with our lives transformed and filled with joy because of our faith in the living Jesus!

Easter 7

Thought for the day

Although now hidden from our sight, Jesus lives for ever, and in him we can live the Resurrection life even while we are on earth.

Reflection on the readings

Acts 1:15-17, 21-26
Psalm 1
1 John 5:9-13
John 17:6-19

With the Ascension, the earthly ministry of Jesus drew to a close, with the prospect of God's Spirit flooding into the believers, so that in that power they would be enabled to spread the good news down the generations and out to every far-flung community on earth. In our reading from Acts we see the disciples growing up and taking their responsibility seriously, even before the empowering has taken place.

Already, we are told, there are about a hundred and fifty of them, and Peter is the leader. Their first job they see as choosing a Judas replacement, the main criterion being that the candidate should have been an eye-witness to the entire ministry of Jesus. Sensibly they pray for it to be God's choice – not 'help us to choose wisely' but 'show us who you have chosen'. That is an example well worth following.

The elderly John writes in his letter to remind his readers that the eternal life God gives us is invested in his Son, so it follows that those who accept Jesus as Lord will have that life, and those who reject him will not. We are into personal choices again.

Jesus, being human, well understands the kind of world we live in and the minefield of temptations we walk through. As he prayed for his disciples, knowing that he would soon be physically parted from them, Jesus prayed for our protection from evil, and for a realistic harmony and unity. Looking around at our sects and splits, it is easy to see why Jesus was so concerned. Our witness to the glorious, liberating truth is so weakened by our disunity.

Thankfully, we live in an age which is doing its best to refocus on Jesus, so that the great barriers erected through the centuries between Christians may in time crumble to rubble. All this is the work of God's Spirit; the more God's people open themselves to receive that empowering love, the more able we will be to love one another, respecting one another's differences but recognising that we are fellow workers, indwelt by the same Spirit.

All-age talk

Prepare two short straws amongst a few full-length ones. Begin by asking for volunteers. Let all those who have offered come out but explain that as you only need two we'll choose by the fairest way – each pulling a straw from your hand. Those who pull the short straws will be the ones chosen.

Label these two Matthias and Joseph, and remind everyone of the problem the disciples had – there had been twelve of them and now there were eleven. Why wasn't Judas with them any more? Because he had helped get Jesus arrested, and afterwards gone and taken his own life.

So Peter organised the believers to choose a replacement for Judas. Who would they choose? If we were going to choose, what kind of person would we look at? What would that person have to have done?

(Collect the ideas, and reread verses 21 and 22.) Well, there were two possibilities, Matthias and Joseph, both good people, and both having been with Jesus all through his ministry. So how are they to choose? They did it in two stages:

1. They prayed, asking God to show them the one he wanted.

2. They used the straw method, like we used.

In effect, they had decided not to take on the choosing themselves, but felt it was so important that they should leave it entirely up to God's leading. And the one who drew the short straw was Matthias. That didn't mean that God liked Matthias better; it was just that God had another important job for Joseph, and knew that Matthias was going to be most useful for this one.

Although Jesus has ascended into heaven, and we can't see him here any more, he's very much with us *all* the time. When we have difficult decisions to make and important, scary things to organise, we don't have to do them alone. We can do what the disciples did, and keep in touch with God, wanting only what God wants and asking him to show us what that is. We can practise wanting what God wants at all kinds of times, just by saying in our hearts, 'Let your will be done!'

Pentecost

(Whit Sunday)

Thought for the day

The Holy Spirit of God is poured out in power on the expectant disciples, just as Jesus promised.

Reflection on the readings

Acts 2:1-21 or Ezekiel 37:1-14
Psalm 104:24-34, 35b
Romans 8:22-27 or Acts 2:1-21
John 15:26-27; 16:4b-15

As humans we are quite a conservative bunch. Most of us like to hold on to what we are familiar with; to 'our' way of doing things. Since Easter, Jesus' disciples had been learning to let go of the familiar presence of their teacher and friend. He had assured them that he needed to leave them for a while, so that he would be able to send them the Spirit, but before the crucifixion this news had simply made them miserable and threatened, filled with grief. All they could see was a future without Jesus, a prospect that knocked the bottom out of their world.

Now, today, we are celebrating, because we join with the disciples as they are overwhelmed with joy. Whatever they had imagined it would be like to receive God's Holy Spirit, the actual experience hugely surpasses. Far from feeling destitute without Jesus' presence, they now sense him with them more deeply and closer than ever before.

All the things Jesus had patiently tried to explain to them they can understand with a new clarity, as if the light of God has suddenly been switched on in their thinking. All Jesus' urgency for telling people the good news now fills them with zeal they have never known before.

Suddenly the most important thing to do is communicate God's love to those who don't know it. The ability to speak in the different languages of the visitors to Jerusalem is all part of this newly given love for people which cannot wait to let them in on the secret of real freedom. The Holy Spirit, coming like a flame, sets the disciples' hearts on fire with love for God and for other people.

No wonder Peter sees in all this the fulfilling of Joel's prophecy; suddenly it all falls logically into place. He realises that they are experiencing the first wave of a new age, with God's Spirit flooding out into those of all nations; God living in his people in a dynamic, revolutionary way. The offer is available to anyone genuinely desiring more of the living God in their lives.

All-age talk

Cut flame shapes from red and orange paper (shiny paper is specially good), and have these given out to everyone as they come into church.

Remind everyone of how the Holy Spirit came, with the noise of a gale-force wind (the noise of which they can try making), and looking like fire, which split up into flames resting on each of those in the room. (Everyone holds up the flame they have been given, so there are flames all over the church.) That was how it seemed from the outside.

Inside each person, what was going on?

- (Display an exclamation mark.) The disciples were stunned by this display of the power of God. God meant business, and was clearly way outside their control. God was in charge.

- (Display a red rose or a red heart.) They suddenly knew, at first hand, what God's love really meant. They felt full of it, and it made them very happy and excited. They wanted to tell God all about it!

- (Display an empty speech bubble.) They wanted to tell other people all about it too. They wanted everyone to know God

like this, because they knew how wonderful it was. And
God's love in them made them want to share the good news,
rather than keep it to themselves.

God is still pouring out his Holy Spirit on people, every day.
Wherever anyone seriously wants to have the powerful love of
God living in them, the Spirit will come and fill them.

Often we don't really want God that close. This may be because
we are scared of God being really powerful; but we forget that
with power which is full of love and goodness we don't need to be
afraid. Mostly we just aren't bothered enough to take God
seriously. The disciples were spending all day in God's company,
waiting and hoping for the Holy Spirit to come. How much time
do we focus our attention on God?

If we want something really badly, it fills our thinking all the
time. Suppose we really want a computer, or to be a ballet dancer,
or to drive a car. We'll be reading all the advertisements and the
magazines, spending out on lessons and working hard at them,
making sure we're in touch with the experts and so on.

So if each of us, and all of us as a church, are impressed by
today's reading, and serious about wanting a fresh outpouring of
the Holy Spirit, what can we do?

We can really want more of God in our lives. We can want that
when we wake up, all through the day, and when we lay our
heads down on the pillow at night. We can want it so much that
we start listening to God and getting our lives ready to receive his
gift. We can put God at the centre, instead of somewhere squeezed
in at the edge.

And God will come to us, filling us with his Holy Spirit, and
transforming our lives.

Trinity Sunday

Thought for the day

The mysterious and holy nature of the one true God is beyond our understanding, but it is both communal harmony and individual personality, Father, Son and Holy Spirit.

Reflection on the readings

Isaiah 6:1-8
Psalm 29
Romans 8:12-17
John 3:1-17

The festival of Trinity allows us time in the Church year to contemplate the nature of God, and marvel at it. One thing we shall never be able to do, as humans, is to grasp it with full understanding, simply because God is not made in our likeness, but we in his. Often people shrug off the possibility of God because he does not behave according to the limitations of humankind, and they feel he ought to if he is real.

God's reality is of a nature we cannot quantify and contain, rather as our eyes can only perceive certain colours in the rainbow while others are beyond our powers of vision. Isaiah's glimpse of God's holiness and glory is more in the realm of sensing than understanding, and with us, too, the moments when we become fleetingly aware of the depths of God's nature are probably moments of sense and inner assurance, rather than quantifiable knowledge. This is not something to worry about but rejoice in; no matter how much we discover to love and worship in the living God, there will always be the joy of more to explore and other treasure to find, and we can delight in the discovering.

As soon as we try to nail God down mathematically, we are bound to run into trouble, and the concept of the Trinity reminds us that all our models and shapes are only rough guides to help us; the reality is always more and different.

What we do know is that there is more to this life than the seen. As Jesus was helping Nicodemus to understand, even in the seen world there are invisible things like wind. How much more when we are in the realm of the Spirit. If we are open to the possibility of it being so, we shall start to notice it. It's actually the Spirit 'in line' with our spirit which makes the necessary connections.

One of the glorious things about people is their wholesome loathing of being fobbed off with lies as the truth. The Spirit leads us into truth, and God is Truth, so we cannot seek Reality and Ultimate Truth without travelling deeper into the nature of the one true living God. The Son leads us to the Father and the Spirit; the Father leads us to listen to the Son and the Spirit; and the Spirit leads us to the Son and the Father.

All-age talk

Prepare either an OHP acetate or a very large cut-out triangle, as shown.

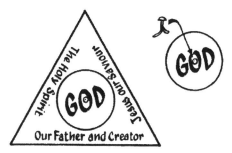

Also have three equal strips of card and three paper fasteners, or bring three equal strips of a large-scale construction toy, with the appropriate nuts and bolts – basically any three things which can construct a triangle.

Start by asking a volunteer to help by making a triangle from the separate strips. As they work, do a commentary on the progress, observing the sides move in all directions until that final join, at which point the triangle is a strong shape, with each two sides holding the other firm. It's such a strong shape that it is used in building – bridges, towers, pylons, roof rafters, for example.

Why on earth are we looking at triangles in church today? Explain that today we are exploring the nature of God. Will we be able to end up by bedtime knowing all about God, then? No! Human brains aren't big enough to cope with understanding our great God completely, any more than your hamster can understand completely what it is to be human.

But as your hamster gets to know you and become your friend, little by little he will understand more about you, as much as a hamster can.

So back to the triangles. Perhaps they can help us understand a little bit more about the great and powerful God of love. (Show your triangle.)

We've seen how strong one three-sided shape can be. Suppose for a minute we look at the threeness and oneness of God as a bit like this triangle. We know that there is only one true God, and here we have one triangle. We know that God is our Father and Creator, Jesus our Saviour and the Holy Spirit. (Turn the triangle round as you refer to each side.) Whichever aspect of God we focus on, we are always looking at God in all his truth and fullness.

And there's another thing. The Son always directs us to see the Father and the Spirit; the Father always directs us to see the Son and the Spirit; and the Spirit always directs us to see the Father and the Son. (Turn the triangle round as you refer to each side.)

Of course, our God is far, far more than a mathematical shape – the God of love and glory is much more than a triangle! But the way a triangle works can help us understand a little more of how, for God, it's no problem to be one God, who is also Father, Son and Spirit. It's as natural for God to be like that as it is for us humans to be able to be in one place and think about being somewhere else, both at the same time.

Sunday between 29 May and 4 June

(if after Trinity Sunday)

Proper 4

Thought for the day

Jesus has the words of eternal life – he sheds light on a right attitude to the Law.

Reflection on the readings

1 Samuel 3:1-10 (11-20) or Deuteronomy 5:12-15
Psalm 139:1-6, 13-18 or Psalm 81:1-10
2 Corinthians 4:5-12
Mark 2:23-3:6

The satisfying thing about rules is that we can achieve a great sense of accomplishment when we have ticked them all off. The accompanying danger is that they can lull us into thinking we have done all that is necessary, simply because we have kept the letter of the law. The spirit of the law is far more open-ended, and cannot 'button up' our ethics in the same way at all.

Today's readings blow fresh air into the stale and hollow rule system which the sacred Law had become. In the reading from Samuel we find God choosing to call to a responsive child in a corrupt religious atmosphere in order to shake things to life again, and in today's Gospel we have instances of Jesus showing by example the Law lit from God's perspective.

The keeping of the Sabbath was considered so important that intricate, detailed rules had been built up around it, till the sense of spending the day celebrating the good creation and joyfully worshipping the Creator was choked in small-print regulations. Jesus directs them to see it again as it really is. He asks them whether it is lawful to do good or evil on the Sabbath, which only allows the positive reply of actively doing good. To be tied down so tightly to the rules that your compassion has to be stamped on, can hardly be in keeping with the generous, caring Lord of Love.

This contrasted with the current thinking, which would probably have let the man's hand stay withered till the Sabbath rest was over. Jesus was not cancelling out the Law, or changing it; he was guiding his listeners back to its original freshness, like recognising that the whole Law is really about building a right and living relationship with God – loving God and loving one another.

In the reading from 2 Corinthians we are given a worked-out example of living by the Law lit up Jesus' way, with the full glory of God. What does such a life look like? We are shown a picture of extraordinary inner joy and vigour in spite of all the hardships and conflicts, dangers and threats. What is obvious is that these lives, rooted in God's grace, are not hemmed in but set free. Jesus has the words of eternal life, valid while we are still living here.

All-age talk

Bring along a piggy bank and some money to put in it. Some people keep their treasure safe in one of these, adding to it each week. (Drop some more money in.) Sometimes people will get an ordinary jar and fill it up with coins, so that soon it's full of treasure. The pot or jar is often very ordinary – it's the treasure inside which makes it special. People in Roman times used to use clay pots to keep their silver jewellery safe – archaeologists have found them, still guarding their treasure!

In one of the letters Saint Paul wrote, he said he thought we were all a bit like clay pots holding special treasure. As people we're just ordinary, but we've got something as Christians which is extraordinary – real treasure. It's being friends with God through Jesus which changes our lives from being ordinary to extra-special, because we're actually holding in us the love of the living God.

What does that look like?

We saw a bit of what it looks like in today's Gospel. Jesus notices a man whose arm is withered and shrunk so he can't use it, and immediately his heart goes out to that man, and more than anything he wants to set the man's arm free to wave and lift things, touch and hold things. His love for the man makes Jesus sad for him having to struggle, and he sets about mending him.

What Jesus doesn't do is look at the man and think, 'Ah yes, a man with an arm which doesn't work. But it's the Sabbath, so that's too bad; he'll have to stay like that – I'm not going to break the rules and heal him today.'

Well, of course he wouldn't think like that, because you can't be full of God's love and yet shut off your compassion. What Jesus did was the Godly, loving thing – he used his power of healing and set that man free, there and then, rules or no rules. And that offended the teachers of the Law. They had become so keen to keep the Law that they'd actually blocked God's light out, and couldn't see that Jesus was keeping the real spirit of the Law completely – love God and love one another.

So here we are as ordinary human pots, holding in us the light of God, and that's going to affect the way we live. We'll have to reach out in love and mercy to those around us, and that might mean we end up offending some people. But who cares? If we're living God's way, then we won't be offending God, and if living that way makes us unpopular sometimes, we'll be in very good company.

Sunday between 5 and 11 June

(if after Trinity Sunday)

Proper 5

Thought for the day

Anyone who does God's will is considered a close family member of Jesus.

Reflection on the readings

> 1 Samuel 8:4-11 (12-15) 16-20 (11:14-15) or Genesis 3:8-15
> Psalm 138 or Psalm 130
> 2 Corinthians 4:13–5:1
> Mark 3:20-35

The terrible thing about sin is the rift and separation it causes between people, and between God and his people. As a result of Adam and Eve's wilful disobedience, the natural relationship between the Creator and his beloved creation, goes horribly wrong, and they are no longer comfortable in God's presence, but hiding from him. So much self-deceit, hidden agendas and complicated destructive living is really to do with this hiding of ourselves from God. So much of Jesus' teaching was showing people how to feel comfortable in God's presence once again.

We see the same, typical human wilfulness in the reading from Samuel, where the people's desire to be like all the other nations and have a king drives them to go against God's will in the matter. And we can all think of wilfulness in our own lives which has resulted in trouble for us and others.

Jesus is the great rift-healer. As Paul writes in 2 Corinthians, there is an ongoing healing for those who live in Christ, which renews us spiritually even as our physical bodies are wearing out. With the eyes of a professional tentmaker he sees physical death as merely a folding-up of one's tent, which has provided temporary accommodation during our journey through earthly life. The permanent house is a spiritual one, prepared for us in God's heaven. Paul adjusts our view to revel in the marvellous reality of what is unseen, rather than wasting time concentrating our attention only on the seen, temporary world.

At first sight today's Gospel does not look like Jesus in healing mode at all. He is being spoken of as using demonic powers to set people free from demons, and his family is concerned for his sanity, hearing the reports about him. These are very serious accusations and Jesus treats them seriously. To be God's chosen One, living out God's love, yet accused of being Love's destroyer, must have given Jesus intense, sharp pain. Surely this was all part of the sword Simeon had predicted, and here is Mary sharing it, just as he said she would.

As Jesus looks into the eyes of those around him, in that typical, straight encounter with people and affection for them, he is cherishing the wideness of close family. In God's love, our family extends and is no longer tied simply to blood and genes. Spiritually we are bound together in God's great family, as close to Jesus as his own flesh and blood.

All-age talk

Whether we live on our own or with others, most of us have family; we may not see them that often, or we may see them every day. Some of them may no longer be alive, but they are still our family. Mothers and fathers, stepmothers and stepfathers, parents-in-law and children-in-law, sons and daughters, grandchildren and grandparents, aunts and uncles, brothers, sisters and cousins, are all family. We share the same genes (and sometimes the same jeans).

In every family there is some thing called a family resemblance – a family likeness. (Some family members may be willing to demonstrate this likeness.) The DNA within our families shows up right across the generations; in my family there's the Morris nose, the Rackett musicality, and the Orme stubborn determination, for instance!

In our Gospel reading today, Jesus says something rather amazing. He's sitting teaching, surrounded by a closely packed circle of faces, people from all kinds of different families and backgrounds, with all kinds of different looks and personalities. They are there because they sense that in Jesus they can get closer to the true, living God than they've ever been before. They are so keen that they are hanging on every word Jesus speaks, listening to him intently.

And as he looks around at them sitting there, and sees in their eyes their love of God, Jesus happily counts all of them – and everyone else who does the will of God – as members of his close family. He is saying that any of us, however ordinary or damaged, whatever natural family we belong to, or are separated from, are close members of Jesus' family!

So you can think of yourself as closely related to Jesus. And that makes all of us in the Church part of the same family, distinguished by the family likeness of doing God's will – living the loving way.

Sunday between 12 and 18 June

(if after Trinity Sunday)

Proper 6

Thought for the day

From small beginnings, and by God's power, the kingdom of heaven grows.

Reflection on the readings

1 Samuel 15:34–16:13 or Ezekiel 17:22-24
Psalm 20 or Psalm 92:1-4, 12-15
2 Corinthians 5:6-10 (11-13) 14-17
Mark 4:26-34

One of the things we all find difficult to do is relinquish power. We may consider that we don't possess much of that commodity, but just listen to yourself and others protesting as soon as our own way of doing something is challenged, or things are suddenly changed without us being told or even our opinion being asked. We bridle!

Today's readings remind us that God is in charge, and can work in all kinds of ways and through all kinds of people whom we may not choose. He goes on working even when we are on holiday, ill, or asleep; though we are important in the growth of the kingdom, the whole thing will not fall apart whenever we are not personally involved. Today we are challenged to recognise that the growth of the kingdom of heaven is not entirely down to our conscientious activity, and we can and should let go and let God.

Samuel was wanting to hang on to Plan A for all kinds of good reasons, but God rouses him to move on in a fresh direction and anoint a new king of Israel. The nudge is sufficient, since Samuel is attentive, but sometimes we seem to need something far more explosive than a nudge before we'll give up on dead issues and agree instead to go God's way forward.

The reading from Ezekiel shows us God acting with typical care and forward planning in a dynamic new way. In contrast to Nebuchadnezzar's worldly empire building, God acts with deep wisdom, startling diversity and breadth of vision, and the power rather like that of a superb orchestra playing softly. God has his power under control and uses it with perfect love and integrity.

Extraordinary as it may seem, we can share in that. As Paul points out in 2 Corinthians, everyone was included in Christ's death so that everyone can also be included in his resurrection life, where our whole focus and aim run in line with what God wants and longs for.

The seed in today's parable does not rely on the farmer's constant attention – it is quite capable of growing wonderfully on its own, simply because it is living seed. Whenever we sow the seed of God's love or his Word in someone's heart, God will continue his work of growth there, using all the circumstances of that person's experience to develop the growing. And what begins so small can grow beyond our imagining. We must never forget that all growth is God's doing. As Christians we are not in the business of empire-building for Christ, but praying for God's kingdom to come.

All-age talk

If possible, have bowls of mustard seeds and invite people to take a seed as they come into church.

Ask everyone to look at the mustard seeds they were given and have a couple of tall people (or children on chairs) to stand back to back, spreading their arms out. In Israel, where Jesus was living, mustard seeds often grow as big as this, and local people will even use the mustard branches for firewood, so that tiny seed really does grow into a spreading tree, and all the birds love to sit in the shelter of its branches. The mustard plant provides spicy flavour, fuel and shelter.

Why did Jesus talk to the people about mustard? He often used things that were all around to help describe spiritual things which cannot be seen. Perhaps there was a shady mustard plant right there where they were sitting, and some of its seeds scattered on the ground.

Anyway, Jesus said that the way God's kingdom grows is a bit like the way a mustard seed grows. It starts off very little, and gradually grows very big. The little seed may be an act of kindness you do which makes someone think to themselves, 'I wonder! She's become a Christian, and it seems to be changing her for the better. Perhaps there's something in this Jesus person after all!' Or perhaps you're the one in the office who insists on honesty, even if you'd gain from being less than honest, and someone notices and starts thinking. Or perhaps someone notices that you aren't that impressed by the labels people are wearing, even though you're cool.

The little seed of God's kingdom is someone opening themselves up a tiny bit to the possibility of God being real and active in their lives. Gradually it grows in them. Perhaps they begin to ask more questions about God, perhaps they read some Bible stories or start coming with you to church sometimes. Then they start to pray! Now that little seed can really begin to grow, because God can lead the person step by step as they get in touch with him more and more. Sometimes the kingdom of God grows gradually as they pick up teaching week by week, or look at God's world with new eyes. At other times there's a sudden growth spurt. Perhaps a verse of scripture hits home and they realise how their life needs to change, or they suddenly sense God real and close to them in a time of sadness or joy.

Perhaps over a few years, or a lifetime, that little seed has grown in the person until they are so full of God in their life that they are standing tall and strong in faith, and many come to them, now, for spiritual help and comfort, like the birds coming to the mustard plant's spreading branches.

How is the kingdom of God's growing coming on in us? Is it still a tiny seed, full of hope but not yet developed very much?

Has it just started to sprout, putting out roots and shoots? Is it not growing very much at all at the moment, or has it recently had a big surge of growth and is excitedly stretching upwards and outwards in the knowledge of God's love and forgiveness? Or is it already tall and strong, providing spiritual shelter for others, scattering other seeds all around, and happy to be full of God's life?

What a world it would be, with churchfuls of people in it, in whom the kingdom of God was growing strong as mustard trees! It could happen. The people could be us.

Sunday between 19 and 25 June

(if after Trinity Sunday)

Proper 7

Thought for the day

What kind of person is this? Even the wind and waves obey him.

Reflection on the readings

1 Samuel 17:(la, 4-11, 19-23) 32-49 or 1 Samuel 17:57–18:5, 10-16
or Job 38:1-11
Psalm 9:9-20 or Psalm 133 or Psalm 107:1-3, 23-32
2 Corinthians 6:1-13
Mark 4:35-41

Although we perhaps know that God is all-mighty, the way we live often shows that we don't take this terribly seriously. Many claiming belief in God speak of him as a slightly ridiculous, inept but well-meaning gentleman, part security blanket and part Father Christmas. Any God with real power, many believe, would act to prevent pain and suffering, and design creation differently so that things didn't go wrong. For the most part God is ignored, much of the time even by his supposed friends and worshippers, and we live our daily lives with an occasional glance in God's direction. Praying is generally the last resort – 'All we can do now is pray'.

Today's readings bring us the shock of ordinary people brought suddenly into close contact with God's power in their ordinary lives. In the Gospel the disciples are floating in their solid, wooden-hulled fishing boat, with its smell of salt, damp and stale fish. The stained and wet sails are straining under the increasing wind, and the ropes creaking. All so normal and familiar.

But as the power of wind and waves increases out of control, and Jesus is woken up in their anxious panic, they suddenly witness a much greater power and authority than anything in the created world. The dramatically hushed and tamed sailing conditions shock the disciples into new questions about Jesus' full identity; they have just witnessed God's power in action, and it shakes them.

Other examples have been shown to us today in the Old Testament reading, of God demonstrating his power and authority. Whenever people glimpse it, they are brought to a new reverence and respect for God, as they suddenly see him in all his awesome greatness, and our condescending, human-sized impressions of him are shown up to be shamefully inappropriate.

The continued readings from 2 Corinthians show us Paul, still dazed from his encounter with the living Jesus, recognising the miracle of God's vitality and power working in the ordinariness of human beings, and the extraordinary effect of this in people's lives. It is, after all, a universe-builder we're talking about, an all-knowing, all-seeing God, whose reality should bring us frequently to our knees in utter wonder and adoration.

All-age talk

If practical, arrange for a couple of people to bring their (well-controlled) pet into church this morning. If this isn't possible, interview a couple of pet owners.

Look at the animals and talk to the owners about what they like to eat, and how they like to play. Then ask them about how their pets behave when they are frightened or feel threatened, and how they calm them down.

It isn't just pets who get worried, angry and upset – it's humans as well. Today we heard about a time when Jesus' friends were so frightened they were panicking, and we saw how Jesus calmed them down. Remind them that Jesus was actually asleep, and the disciples woke him up to tell him to start worrying! With the stormy waves pitching the boat up and down, and the water coming in over the side it was beginning to look like a *Titanic* situation, and there was Jesus fast asleep in the bottom of the boat!

Sometimes we do that, too, if life seems very scary, and everything seems to be going wildly out of control. We scream out to Jesus, demanding that he notices and *does* something, instead of being so calm about it all. It's almost as if we want him to panic as well.

Jesus, once he's been thoroughly shaken awake, doesn't seem to be caught up in the excitement. But he can see that it isn't only the disciples who are churned up – it's the weather as well. And perhaps he sees here a good way to help the disciples understand more about who he is. The disciples are so scared at the moment that they can't take anything in. So instead of calming them down, Jesus calms the wind and the waves. As the howling wind eases and settles quietly again, and the pounding waves flatten back to a gentle lapping around the battered boat, the disciples calm down as well. In this lull they recover themselves and stop panicking.

What does Jesus do next – wait for their applause? Go back to sleep? In fact we find he now starts teaching them, because they are now calm enough to listen. He talks to them about trusting God, even in the middle of raging storms.

Often in life we will find that when we have invited Jesus into our boat – into our life – we don't get so thrown by all the stormy problems (things like quarrels in friendships, loved ones moving away, financial problems, pressure and stress at work). And if we're panicking about them so much that we can't hear Jesus helping us to weather the storm, then often we'll find we're given a breather – a bit of space – where things are calmed down long enough for us to realise that, with God in charge, we don't actually need to be terrified.

Sunday between 26 June and 2 July

Proper 8

Thought for the day

God's power can reach even into death and draw out life.

Reflection on the readings

> 2 Samuel 1:1, 17-27 or Wisdom of Solomon 1:13-15; 2:23-24
> Psalm 130 or Psalm 30 or Lamentations 3:23-33
> Corinthians 8:7-15
> Mark 5:21-43
> (Lamentations 3:23-33 may be used in place of Wisdom 1:13-15; 2:23-24.)

Everything about death looks final. The body we knew laughing, anxious, angry or intrigued is stilled; all the memories and stories locked inside and out of our reach. It seems to be the end of responding, thinking, feeling and moving. Clustered around it are other endings – the cupboards to be cleared, possessions and clothing now redundant; terrible gaps in family, friendships, committees and rotas, the particular pew. The tragedy of death is its terrible finality – it is like a violent rejection of what was previously so very much alive; a slap in the face to life itself. With King David, our gut reaction to death is the grieving of endings – 'Look how the mighty are fallen'.

Yet with God walking this planet in person as Jesus, we discover in his ministry several cases of death's finality being challenged and reversed. Jairus' twelve-year-old daughter had left the living world and yet Jesus speaks into death and calls her out of it, back into the world of life again. She hears his call to her ('Talitha, koum!') and follows it through a journey we can only imagine, emerging to stand up in the world she had left, no longer full of fever as before, but in full health and very hungry.

As with last week's miracle, we might ask why, if Jesus' compassion drove him to do such acts contrary to nature then, does he not continue to reverse natural laws daily and universally on grounds of compassion today? In fact, of course, there must have been many hundreds of other people dying during Jesus' ministry on earth, none of whom were raised from the dead. There are other reasons for Jesus acting like this in these particular situations; reasons to do with signs and pointers to Jesus' true identity.

But we are also challenged by the great faith shown in today's Gospel. In Jesus' encounter with the woman in the crowd, finally healed after twelve years of miserable ill health and uncleanness, according to the law, she is told that it is her faith which has healed her, even though Jesus knows that power has gone out of him. Did her faith draw that healing power out?

Certainly we do need to be expectant, considering God-incidences perfectly possible, allowing God permission for his kingdom to be unleashed in each situation. We choose whether or not to unbolt the door from the inside.

All-age talk

Make a circle of chairs near where you are talking, or a circle of rope – something which is clearly visible.

Explain that this circle is like our life here on earth. How do we get into it? By being born. (Invite a couple of people to make their way in.) While we're here what do we do? We eat, play, work, talk, make friends (and perhaps some enemies), watch TV, learn things and so on. (Everyone can add to the list.) Invite the people in the circle of life to mime some of those things as they are suggested.

How do we get out of the circle of life? By being born backwards? We get out of this life by dying. (The volunteers make their way out of the circle.) Point out that they're not in the circle any more, but they're in a huge space, much bigger than they might have imagined, if they'd only ever known life in the circle. And outside this space is the whole outdoors, stretching outwards and upwards, and full of light and colour, better than anything we could imagine if we'd only ever known the circle as 'life'. Just as the circle isn't the only place, so this earthly life isn't all there is to complete life – Jesus told us that life after our death can be full, rich and wonderful; and it's Jesus who has made that possible for us.

Remind everyone of the story in today's Gospel, about a twelve-year-old girl dying. Everyone is especially sad when a young person dies, because they haven't had a chance to live very long here and enjoy our world. But Jesus brings that young girl back to life again. It's as if from inside the circle of life he calls to her on the outside and she comes back in again, completely better, and hungry. He could do that because Jesus *is* life. When she next died, perhaps after a long and happy time on earth, she closed her eyes on earthly life and heard Jesus calling her name again into life – but this time from heaven, into the life with Jesus that lasts forever.

When we get to the point of our death, Jesus will be there, calling us out into that life, and welcoming us. And because we know his voice, from a lifetime of prayer, we'll be very happy to move towards it and find him, waiting for us there.

Sunday between 3 and 9 July

Proper 9

Thought for the day

If we are not ready to listen to the truth, we will not hear it.

Reflection on the readings

2 Samuel 5:1-5, 9-10 or Ezekiel 2:1-5
Psalm 48 or Psalm 123
2 Corinthians 12:2-10
Mark 6:1-13

Discreet rebellion does not go unnoticed by God. Whatever we proclaim with our lips, whatever we claim to believe, and however cleverly we disguise our rebellion from others, God sees and knows where our hearts really are, and which way we are really facing. This isn't something to make us scared of approaching God. It's actually quite a relief to find there's no point in pretending or trying to impress him. Those who, like me, tend to live in a certain amount of clutter, know there are some people whose visits spur us to a spate of frantic tidying, and others who know us so well that this isn't really necessary – they know and love us well, exactly as we are!

When God has something to say to us which may involve opening us up more to his grace, challenging a fixed or self-centred attitude or behaviour, or a little spiritual growing-up, then he will tell us. But if we aren't ready or prepared to hear what he has to say, then there's no way we'll hear it. Later we might look back and wonder why we couldn't see the obvious! But at the time we're far more likely to react with hostility and defensiveness, rather like those in Jesus' home town. We can hear their indignant, self-righteous wounded egos as they mutter their complaints about Jesus. When they look at the facts, he's not even on a level with them for background; so what right has he to be displaying more wisdom and miracle-working than any of them? It is quite usual to resent holiness, or any other gift, in those close to us. Holiness in strangers is far easier to cope with as we don't take that as personal criticism.

When Jesus sends out his disciples it is in the support of pairs, and, like Ezekiel, they are to preach repentance, whether the people are ready to listen or not. God had prepared Ezekiel for the likelihood of stubborn rebellious natures not taking kindly to the challenge, and now Jesus prepares his disciples in a similar way.

Brushing the dust from their feet is not a vindictive move, but a visual sign – a testimony – that the Gospel of repentance has been offered and refused. It is also important from the disciples' point of view, and ours. There are times when it is right to move on and leave the Holy Spirit to continue working in people's hearts through the subsequent events and conversations, without feeling weighed down by the rejection.

All-age talk

You will need a sieve – either a culinary or a gardening one. Also some appropriate thing to sieve – such as flour or earth.

First talk about the way we tend to hear if someone offers us a second chocolate biscuit, a rise in our pay, or a special discount, but not if we're being told to clean out the rabbit, work late, empty the washing machine or make a dental appointment. As the saying goes, 'There's none so deaf as those who won't hear'.

Explain that what our minds do is to sieve information which comes in through the ears and the eyes. Produce the sieve and start sieving so that everyone can see this process in action. The holes are a particular size so that everything is sorted automatically. Big lumps are not wanted, so they won't fit through the holes. Fine flour or earth can get through quite easily. The rest only gets through if we process it a bit first (breaking it down to a suitable size) and if it can't be broken down (like stones in the earth or a free sticker in the flour) then it doesn't get through the sieve at all.

In just the same way we are selective about what we hear, and mostly that is very useful to us. It stops us turning into nervous wrecks because of the daily news items, for instance.

But sometimes we try to keep out what God is trying to make us hear. Just because it may mean us changing something in our lives, we treat it as a threat, and shut it out, when really it is helping us to get rid of a way of thinking or behaving which is not healthy to us or others, physically, mentally or spiritually. What we need is to have 'God's Word' - shaped holes in our sieves, so that God's Word can always get through.

Sunday between 10 and 16 July

Proper 10

Thought for the day

Those who speak out God's will are bound to be vulnerable to rejection and abuse.

Reflection on the readings

2 Samuel 6:1-5, 12b-19 or Amos 7:7-15
Psalm 24 or Psalm 85:8-13
Ephesians 1:3-14
Mark 6:14-29

Today's readings pulverise any suspicions we might have had that walking God's way is the comfortable option for wimps. We hear story after story of the reality – that those who speak out God's will are quite likely to find themselves rejected and abused, insulted and scorned. Perhaps Bibles should have a safety warning pasted on the front cover: 'Following the God you meet through these pages is usually dangerous.'

We hear of King David dancing with all his might before the Lord in an uninhibited outpouring of love and worship to God as the holy ark is brought into Jerusalem. The glamorous Michal's scorn as she watches him will sound familiar to many of our young Christians at school and university, who often have to suffer the pitying scorn of the glamorous because of their faith. They badly need our constant prayer support and encouragement.

We hear of Amos, told to push off and go back to his farming because he spoke out a message from God which his listeners did not want to hear. Never mind how right and wise God's advice is, those brave enough to speak it, when a community or a relationship needs changing, are bound to be treated as attackers, and are frequently fended off aggressively, at least initially. As a species we do not take criticism positively, but beat it off at all costs, even though it can help us grow. It is a mark of great maturity to be able to welcome criticism in order to learn from it.

In today's Gospel we find John the Baptist has been speaking out that dangerous truth to Herod, pointing out what God's will is and is not. Herod is pulled in two directions – both towards a liberating eternal relationship with the living God, and towards the personal power, wealth, gratification and popularity which spell short-term satisfaction and death. It is the latter he chooses, urged on by Herodias' aggressive resentment at John's meddling in their lives. Yet although John has been beheaded as a true prophet for faithfully speaking out God's word, the disciples are scattered over the countryside in pairs, preaching repentance and the kingdom for all they are worth!

We need to pray for the courage to speak out as God's people, and get on with the work we have been chosen to do, however we are received. All too often the first hint of opposition or waning popularity shuts us up, and we persuade ourselves that we shouldn't mention such things again. But if the early Church had followed a similar line, how many of us would ever have heard the good news of God's love?

All-age talk

As everyone comes into church give them a length of thin wool or string and a paper clip.

Begin by inviting everyone to fix one end of the wool or string into the paper-clip so that they have made a plumb-line. Explain that this can be used to check whether things which are supposed to be upright are as straight as they should be. (They can try out their plumb-lines on the pews and chairs around them, and some volunteers can check other uprights in the building.)

Suppose we were to find that one of our upright walls was actually leaning over – would it be useful to know that? Yes, because then we could get in the workmen and pay them to put it right.

Suppose we just got angry and offended at being told our wall wasn't as upright as it should be? We could tell the person with the plumb-line to go away and not talk about it to us any more. That way we could go on pretending our wall was upright, and we wouldn't have to pay to put it right. But if we did that, the upright wall might go on leaning more and more until in the end the whole building crashed down in rubble.

Plumb-lines for checking how straight and upright things are can be very useful indeed. Being told where things aren't as upright as they should be can also be very useful indeed.

One of the things prophets do is draw our attention to places in our lives or our society or our church community which are leaning dangerously and are nowhere near as upright as they should be. How do people react to being told? We heard today how the people shouted at the prophet Amos to go and leave them alone. They didn't want to hear, because they didn't want the bother of putting things right. We also heard about John the Baptist, who had shown King Herod and his new wife where their life wasn't as upright as it should be. How did they react? By throwing John into prison where they couldn't hear him, and then having him put to death so he couldn't speak out God's truth to them any more. They didn't want to hear it because they didn't want to put things right.

How good are we at hearing God whispering lovingly into our hearts about the places in our lives that should be standing tall and upright but are instead leaning a little, or leaning dangerously? Do we thank him for showing it to us so we can quickly put things right again, or do we get sulky or angry and pretend we haven't heard?

Sunday between 17 and 23 July

Proper 11

Thought for the day

Like a good shepherd, Jesus sees the needs of his people and always responds with love.

Reflection on the readings

2 Samuel 7:1-14a or Jeremiah 23:1-6
Psalm 89:20-37 or Psalm 23
Ephesians 2:11-22
Mark 6:30-34, 53-56

In the reading from 1 Samuel we find the shepherd King of Israel wanting to establish a permanent resting-place for the ark of the Covenant. In a gentle and gracious 'no', God affirms his love and protection of David and of his people during their nomadic history, and his promise of continued leadership and guidance right through into the future. The reading from Jeremiah, in contrast, shows God lamenting the destructive effect of bad leadership of his chosen people. As he sees them scattering in all directions, confused and undisciplined, the promise is made of the plan to draw them back under wholesome leadership, into the peace and settled spirit of God's charge.

In today's section of the letter to the Christians in Ephesus, Paul sets out the important aspect of Jesus' leadership: the breaking down of barriers between people, and the drawing together of those from different traditions and backgrounds into unity through the Christ.

Then in the Gospel we find Jesus doing just that, his heart of God aching to see the vulnerability of the crowds. In Jesus the image of the good shepherd king becomes a practical reality and the people sense it, watching his every move, racing ahead of the boat to be at the other side of the lake when he arrives, ceaselessly demanding as they recognise their need of healing at all levels. They gravitate to the one whose words and works make contact with their deep, unconscious drive to be at one with the living God.

How does the humanness of Jesus cope with such overwhelming demands? Loving with God's love makes him responsive without reserve, and he is never recorded in the Gospels as turning anyone away. However, he is obviously aware of his human need for rest and refreshment, and we do pick up on the weariness and exhaustion of ministry on such a scale. His early morning walks into the hills for solitary prayer are vital to him, and there is evidence that part of his leadership responsibility was aiming to provide periods of rest and retreat for his close disciples and himself. Presumably there were at least some occasions when they managed these oases of quiet, without the crowds catching up with them!

All this enables us to look at the question of demands in ministry, and the provision we make for our own leaders' spiritual refreshment and quiet reflection. We need to look both at the extent of our willingness to put ourselves out for others, and also at the dangers of overworking with insufficient support or rest. We are challenged to see the way crowds naturally flock to where they sense God being proclaimed in the person of Jesus, and check that visitors to our churches are enabled to meet with the living Christ there.

All-age talk

Bring along a crowded diary or calendar, and other gadgets for coping with busy lifestyles, such as a computerised notebook, a laptop, mobile phone, alarm clock or fax message.

Ask a few children to walk up and down pretending to be talking on their mobiles or driving their cars, while you talk about the way we can now continue our office work walking along the High Street or on the train. We can send messages by e-mail or fax so that they get there almost immediately. All this enables us to spend more and more of our time being fully at work if we happen to have a job, with increasing pressure and decreasing space in our lives.

People have either far too much work than is healthy or none at all, and leisure activities often have to slot in some frantic physical activity to compensate for all the physically inactive work of brain and adrenaline. Advertisements shout at us to buy this, choose that, look like them; the newspapers and magazines advise us what to think and how to behave, and often we believe their lies. We are like a scattered flock of sheep racing in different directions, without knowing where we are or where we are going.

(Stop the children and have them sit down very still wherever they are.)

Today we heard in the Gospel about Jesus' busy ministry of teaching and healing, listening and encouraging. When he and his disciples had been hard at work for days, and were really tired and drained, they'd get into a boat to sail across the lake for a bit of peace and quiet – only to find all the crowds had run round the edge of the lake and were already there waiting for them! Jesus didn't send them away and tell them what the office hours were, or put them on hold. He didn't ask Peter to change course and sail off somewhere else instead.

Instead, Jesus saw the lost and struggling lives, the need for reassurance and practical, wise teaching, the longing for healing and wholeness, and the hearts attracted to God but needing help to find him. And seeing all that, he loved them, with the deep affection of God's love; he climbed wearily out of the boat and fed them with the teaching and comforting they so badly needed. From stories like this of Jesus' ministry we know with certainty that God never ever turns any of us away.

None of our needs or wounds or sorrows are hidden from him. Whenever we run around the lake to be there waiting for him, he will step on to our beach and minister to us, because he loves us. Like a good shepherd he is concerned for our well-being and leads us carefully and safely through time into the eternity of heaven.

Sunday between 24 and 30 July
Proper 12

Thought for the day
Out of God's riches, a great crowd is fed and satisfied from a small offering of food.

Reflection on the readings
2 Samuel 11:1-15 or 2 Kings 4:42-44
Psalm 14 or Psalm 145:10-18
Ephesians 3:14-21
John 6:1-21

Great evil and great good do not simply happen out of the blue; both begin in small, barely noticed incidents, whose significance only becomes apparent once the evil or goodness has snowballed. King David had for some reason stayed at home instead of leading his army, when he saw Bathsheba bathing, and from these seemingly little events the sin accumulated. Huge international conflicts can be traced back to a number of small-scale wrongs or misguided attitudes, or an early absence of real communication.

Thankfully the same is true of goodness, and today we are celebrating the way that small acts of generosity and love can be blessed and transformed for great, widespread good. It is like watching a parable of the growth of the kingdom of heaven in action.

First we read about the distribution of twenty barley loaves among a hundred people – a combination of one man's generosity and Elisha's close and faithful relationship with God – so close that he can discern God's will and acts obediently. As a result, many more people are blessed by the original gift than could have been imagined.

The reading from Ephesians reinforces this lavish nature of God's provision. Paul knows from experience that with his power working in us God can do so much more than anything we can ask or imagine, and Paul longs for his readers to take this on board so that they too can live in the fulfilment of God's faithful promises.

In today's Gospel one boy's offer of lunch is accepted with thanks, blessed and used so that thousands are fed. It is always a temptation to look at huge needs and dismiss what we are able to do as being pathetically inadequate so that we end up being too discouraged even to use what we do have. The work of Mother Theresa was sometimes dismissed as being too little to make any difference, but, as far as she was concerned, every little act of loving kindness was something beautiful for God, and infinitely worth doing. That 'little' has been so greatly blessed and brought hope and joy to so many all over the world.

Each of us has a lifetime's worth of moments to offer, each very small but each there to give. Anything that we offer for God to use, however small or insignificant it may seem to be, is gathered up, blessed and redistributed for blessing beyond our imagining.

All-age talk

If you have an ancient building you can direct people to look at how steps or pews are worn away by generations of people simply walking on the step or holding the end of the pew. Or you could show a well-used copy of a Bible, worn out and falling apart just by being handled and read every day. (It is said that Bibles which are falling apart are read by people who are not.) You could show an old and well-loved teddy, threadbare through daily loving.

Each step, each picking up of a book, each cuddling of a bear is in itself only a slight action which we can't imagine would do much. But day by day, over the years, the effect of all those little actions starts to show quite dramatically. Little actions turn out to be very important. Even a smile can spread wider than we might think. There's an old children's poem about that:

Smile awhile, and when you smile
another smiles, and soon
there's miles and miles of smiles
and life's worthwhile
because you smile!

Today we heard about one boy and his packed lunch. What was the point of him offering that when there were so many thousands of people to feed? Perhaps we think he might as well have just eaten it himself! But look at what happened when, instead of that, the boy wanted to offer what he had to share. Jesus used it. He blessed the gift that was offered and then all the people were fed, with some left over.

Those who have been God's friends for a long time will have noticed that God is very good at giving us more than we asked for, and giving in ways we hadn't thought of! But he does need us to offer what we have, whether that's time, money or talents and skills. Basically what we have to offer is ourselves. And when we do that, God can use the rest of our life here in ways we haven't even thought of, blessing people who perhaps we haven't even met yet, and may not meet till heaven. If we offer ourselves at the start of every day, then every day can be used for some wonderful good that wouldn't otherwise happen.

Sunday between 31 July and 6 August
Proper 13

Thought for the day
Jesus is the Bread of Life who satisfies our hunger and sustains us on our journey to heaven.

Reflection on the readings
2 Samuel 11:26–12:13a or Exodus 16:2-4, 9-15
Psalm 51:1-12 or Psalm 78:23-29
Ephesians 4:1-16
John 6:24-35

In our Exodus reading the people were finding their hunger dampening their pioneering spirit considerably, and the provision of quails and manna saved the day, as well as proclaiming God's care for his people.

Most of us start getting irritable and short-tempered when our bodies need food. Complicated or demanding decisions are always best left till after a meal, rather than trying to rush into them when we return home weary and hungry, and in mountain-climbing the hot drinks and food are first on the agenda when setting up camp at the end of the day. We are all deeply affected by the appalling sight of real hunger and starvation. Since we all have bodies which run on the fuel of food, we all instinctively know the importance of feeding, right from screaming our hunger at birth. Food is simply a matter of life and death.

This makes it an ideal image for describing how important Jesus is to us. When he says, 'I am the Bread of Life', we understand the life and death nature of the relationship; it implies that Jesus brings us life, and without him we die. That is why it is linked with the Resurrection – the risen nature of Christ. All we are to do is believe in Jesus and we will be taken with him through death into the fullness of life with God for ever. Believing is attaching ourselves to him so that wherever Jesus goes we end up being taken as well.

What saddened Jesus in today's Gospel was that the people were there clinging to his every move, but for the wrong reasons. They were there for what they got out of it – in their case, being fed with bread and fish. We can sometimes get into the same 'craving rather than believing' mode if we are locked into receiving the spiritual or sacramental gifts for ourselves because they make us feel good. Jesus is not a restaurant where we indulge ourselves and eventually roll out home to bed; he is the Bread of Life, and supplies us with the food we need in order to live out his risen life among the people we are led to.

In Ephesians we are given an inspiring picture of such a life worked out in practical terms, enabled through our spiritual feeding to be built up in a coordinated body, displaying the characteristics of God's loving and humility.

All-age talk

Ask who had a meal yesterday, and express surprise that they are thinking of having another meal today – some have already eaten today and are still planning to eat lunch! They can explain to you that our bodies need food every day for them to stay strong and healthy, and for the children to grow. We run on food like a car runs on petrol.

Produce a loaf of bread. Remind everyone of how Jesus had fed all those people with enough bread and fish, and they had all enjoyed their meal. Now they are all running after Jesus the next day as well. Some of them want to hear what Jesus says, some want to come and be healed, some want to come because it's exciting going where everyone else is going and they don't want to miss out on anything. And lots are going because they remember those nice tuna sandwiches – the meal they ate with Jesus.

Why does Jesus want them to have come? Collect various ideas, and draw out that Jesus wants them to be there because they know they will meet with God if they're here with Jesus.

But Jesus knows all too well why some of them have really come, and he tells them so: 'You're looking for me because you ate the bread and were satisfied.'

And then he helps them to understand how God feeds us not just with bread for our bodies, while we live on this earth for seventy years or so (keep holding the bread), but in another way as well. He gives us spiritual food which keeps us alive through this life and right on into life beyond physical death. With that feeding we won't be finishing as soon as we die, but going on living forever.

The people thought that sounded pretty good bread to have, and asked Jesus if he would give them some, so they could be fed spiritually as well as physically. And Jesus told them (lift the loaf of bread up high), 'I am the Bread of Life!' So it's Jesus himself who we feed on.

What does that mean? Obviously we're not like cannibals, eating Jesus up – he didn't mean that. But if we think how satisfied we feel when we have been very hungry and then eat a good meal, that's how our spirits feel when we spend time with Jesus – contented and satisfied, happy and full of energy and health. And just as we need to keep eating ordinary food every day, so we need to keep spending time with Jesus every day, so that, spiritually as well as physically, we will be growing strong and healthy, and we'll stay that way even when our physical bodies get old and weak, and when they stop working so that we die. Even then we'll be spiritually bounding with life and energy; ready to spend eternity alive in God's company.

Sunday between 7 and 13 August

Proper 14

Thought for the day

Just as bread is the visible form of life-giving nourishment, so Jesus is the visible form of God's life-giving love.

Reflection on the readings

2 Samuel 18:5-9, 15, 31-33 or 1 Kings 19:4-8
Psalm 130 or Psalm 34:1–8
Ephesians 4:25–5:2
John 6:35, 41-51

There are times when we have something important which needs saying, but we know that it will be difficult to say without being misunderstood. Jesus knew that what he was saying would be hard for many to accept or understand, yet he also knew it had to be said. The problem is that, unlike young children, we all carry so much luggage and hurt from our past that our listening is impaired. However good our hearing, we block out and distort whatever we are not wanting to receive, focus on the negatives and recycle explanations as ammunition.

Much of praying and spiritual growth is to do with learning to listen, deliberately putting down our preconceptions, pride and status, so that we are able to take in what God is whispering into the humility of our unladen hearts. And, sooner or later, that will always lead us to Jesus. Our Gospel today homes in on a listening crisis, where the preparatory work could all have been done, if those religious leaders had been practising their Godly listening. Had that been the case, they would have found themselves drawn, like the wise and elderly Simeon, to see what God had been preparing them for throughout their history: to recognise

Jesus as the Bread from heaven – the visible expression of God's life and feeding.

In 1 Kings 19, Elijah is strengthened and refreshed on his journey to the mountain of God, and recognises that the baked loaf of bread and the jar of water are part of God's caring provision for him; even though he is emotionally drained and spiritually burnt out he knows that it is God who is leading and feeding him. How wonderful it would have been if, on hearing those extraordinary words of Jesus – 'I am the bread that came down from heaven' the religious leaders could have seen all the sense and truth of God's plan being worked out in front of their very eyes and in their hearing! But as it was, their habit of loaded listening prevented them from understanding.

The passage from Ephesians continues its practical advice to keep us open to God and able to listen with Godly understanding. There are marvellous hints like not letting the sun go down on our anger, and not letting the devil get even a toehold. There is much talk of shedding whatever prevents us from being built up in the life of Christ. The great news of hope which Jesus proclaims is that full life is possible as we recognise Jesus for who he is, and gladly receive his feeding.

All-age talk

Tell everyone that you are about to show them some vitamin B and some energy, some life-giving essence and some potential penicillin. Have a drum roll or dramatic chords on the organ as you whip out of a supermarket bag a loaf of bread.

But this is just an ordinary loaf of bread – how can something so natural and ordinary be all that clever, invisible, scientific stuff? Well, it is! If we were really hungry we could try it and find out how much better it made our bodies feel. (A hungry person can do this.) We eat our way through loaves and loaves of bread every day because we have found that it does us so much good and comes in a form we can easily take naturally – by eating!

So bread is the visible form of all kinds of goodness and life-giving nourishment. And when Jesus talked of himself being the

Bread of Life, he was describing how he is the invisible God in visible form – in the familiar shape of a human being, who we can talk to, watch, touch and listen to.

So why couldn't the religious leaders understand? Why did they find it offensive that Jesus said this?

- Jesus seemed too normal and familiar – they knew him as their carpenter.
- They thought the Son of God should look greater than Moses.
- Their expectations blinded them to seeing the very person they had been waiting generations to meet, when he was standing there right in front of their eyes.

We too need to make sure we don't miss God in the ordinary. In fact, God made everything, so nothing is just ordinary, and God can speak to us through his creation, as long as we are ready to notice and listen. Here are some examples.

We often see heavy rain, but usually just moan about it spoiling our hair or stopping a match. Suppose we start actually looking at it and seeing there a picture of how generous and fulsome God is; so many individual droplets of rain – or petals in a tree full of blossom!

Or think of the wide night sky describing God's overarching love; the regular days, nights and seasons showing his faithfulness.

In a dog's dogginess and a young child's openness we can see God showing us the importance of being honestly ourselves; when we see weeds and wild flowers growing over a rubbish dump we see God telling us about redemption, and how everything can be made new and beautiful.

All we need to do is train our spiritual eyes to look, so that we don't miss out on anything God is wanting to say to us, even through the ordinary things.

Sunday between 14 and 20 August

Proper 15

Thought for the day

God's wisdom may appear foolishness without the God-given grace to understand.

Reflection on the readings

1 Kings 2:10-12; 3:3-14 or Proverbs 9:1-6
Psalm 111 or Psalm 34:9-14
Ephesians 5:15-20
John 6:51-58

Solomon asks for wisdom because he is acutely aware of his lack of experience and unreadiness for the task of reigning over God's people. Knowing his need makes him able to ask for it. We all need to recognise our ignorance in order to want to learn. In the passage from Proverbs the lady Wisdom calls out to those who recognise that they are simple, and want to increase their wisdom, which is in contrast to the lady Folly, who is encouraging people to drown out any higher calling and indulge their instincts and pleasure drives instead. Too late they will realise that her misleading call was to death, whereas Wisdom will lead her followers into a life of order and inner harmony.

In today's reading from Ephesians, too, we are advised to live wisely, making good use of every opportunity since the times are evil. The inference is that unless we are consciously walking positively in God's direction, we can so easily find ourselves sucked into the foolishness of living contrary to God's will for us. Wisdom is seen as living in inner peace and harmony with the God of our making.

If we are to get anywhere near such a state, we will need to walk expectantly and as disciples, rather than experts defending our position, and feeling offended every time we are tutored or instructed. In our Gospel for today, the religious leaders' status and learning was an enormous block to wisdom. They had too much to protect to risk walking in the nakedness of honesty.

We need to check any areas where we consider ourselves, or others consider us, experts or professionals, since these are precisely the areas where we shall find it hardest to place ourselves in the humility of discipleship.

It is hard for these learned religious teachers to understand his message, hung up as they are on precise detail instead of seeing the whole vision. They would hear Jesus' words not as a wonderful metaphor for God becoming one with his people through his Son, with all the wholesome nourishment and life-giving that the idea of bread contains; rather, they would hear it as a shocking blasphemy, with this wandering teacher aligning himself with the sacrificial Passover lamb and claiming to bring eternal freeing from sin. So they end up rejecting the fulfilment of the very idea they have studied and taught for years – that one day God will be 'with us' in person, and save us from our sin.

All-age talk

Real wisdom is different from knowing lots of facts. Remind everyone of the Brownie story about the wise owl. The children are sent to her because they want to find out who will be the little people who do secret good turns all around their house, and wise owl tells them to go to a pond in the woods and recite a poem. (Any Brownies, present and past, can join in the poem!)

Twist me and turn me and show me the elf;
I looked in the water and there saw . . . MYSELF!

The owl had been very wise because she had been able to help the children understand a deep kind of magic – whenever they did their good turns, they would be not just Imogen and Rebecca, but real Brownies! And they'd go on being Brownies whenever they did their good turns, long after they'd become Guides and grown up and had their own children who were learning the wisdom of the wise owl!

Wise people are good to go to when you want to talk things over, but you don't want to be told exactly what to do. Wise people are those who really listen to you – to how you are feeling inside as well as what you are saying. Wise people think carefully before they speak, and like learning from their mistakes.

We could say that WISDOM is all about

Walking In Simplicity Dreaming Of More

or we could say that to become WISE we need to Wonder and ask questions

Imagine

Seek God

Expect to learn from him.

Sunday between 21 and 27 August

Proper 16

Thought for the day

'To whom else could we go? You alone have the words of eternal life.'

Reflection on the readings

1 Kings 8:(1, 6, 10-11) 22-30, 41-43 or Joshua 24:1-2a, 14-18
Psalm 84 or Psalm 34:15-22
Ephesians 6:10-20
John 6:56-69

Most choices we make in life are fairly unimportant. It will probably make little difference whether we choose vanilla or raspberry ripple, ten o'clock or ten fifteen, chrysanthemums or asters. But the big important decision, which drives everything else we decide, is the direction we choose to face as we walk through life.

In our reading from Joshua, the significance of this commitment is made thoroughly clear to the people, since Joshua wants to be sure that everyone really knows what they are voting for, together with the potential cost as well as the benefits. Having laid out the facts, Joshua then gives the lead. He is not opting out of leadership and suggesting that either choice is as good as the other but offers one direction as choosing life, the other death, and takes his stand on the good choice as he declares:

'As for me and my household, we will serve the Lord.'

The people wholeheartedly agree, basing their commitment on their actual experience of God's consistent loving care of them.

Similarly, in the reading from 1 Kings, we witness the consecration of the temple, in which King Solomon is again making a great national statement of commitment to the one true God whose name the house bears.

In a genuine but over-enthusiastic desire to allow freedom and engender mutual respect, our own age tends now to distrust any absolutes, preferring to think of all truth as relative and a matter of individual choice. In such a climate it takes courage to profess our faith in Jesus Christ, and we may often find ourselves in the minority, or actively disputing widely accepted moral principles which run contrary to God's law of love.

So we hear with empathy today's Gospel reading, with many disciples walking away from Jesus now that he claims such a close relationship with the transcendent God. It is too much for them to come to terms with, and they conclude that Jesus has overstepped the mark. We too are faced with the same challenge. Either Jesus, as a good and gifted human being, has overreached his sanity, or he is speaking the truth. If the latter is so, he must indeed be the Holy One of God, with all that this implies for us in terms of commitment.

All-age talk

Have a show of hands for a few choices – Who's for football, who's for rugby? Who's a lark and loves the early mornings, who's an owl and loves to stay up late? Who's a 'dog' person, who's a 'cat' person?

All these are a matter of choice, and happily we are all different so we all like to choose different toppings on our pizzas, different music to listen to and different colours to wear. It's wonderful and important that we are all different.

But there are some things we can't choose, because it's been decided that there is a collective good way of going on. So we all drive on the same side of the road whatever part of the country we're in; we all go to school and learn how to read and write and do maths and science; we all pay taxes on what we earn so everyone, both poor and rich, can use schools and hospitals and so on.

In our first reading, from the Old Testament, Joshua wants the people to decide, before they go in to the promised land, whether they really do want to serve the Lord their God or not. He makes it quite clear that they will only be choosing wisely if they do choose to worship God, as he is real and powerful, and the other gods are not. It's a little bit like asking a football team if they are going to choose to play with a football or a matchbox in an international match. There really isn't much point in playing with anything other than the real thing!

In the Gospel we heard of some of the crowds choosing not to walk with Jesus any more because he seemed to be making out that he was the Holy One of God. Jesus asked his disciples if they were going to turn away as well, and Peter spoke for them all, and for us as well 'Lord, who else could we go to,' he asked, 'seeing that you are the one with the words of eternal life?'

When we know that God is real, and that Jesus really is the Holy One of God, what else can we do but make the sensible, wise choice and commit ourselves to following him? That's the wisest, most important choice we make in the whole of our life.

Sunday between 28 August and 3 September

Proper 17

Thought for the day

We need to be careful never to replace the timeless commands of God with man-made traditions.

Reflection on the readings

Song of Solomon 2:8-13 or Deuteronomy 4:1-2, 6-9
Psalm 45:1-2, 6-9 or Psalm 15
James 1:17-27
Mark 7:1-8, 14-15, 21-23

In the reading from Deuteronomy the people are given reasons for valuing and upholding the Law of God as encapsulated in the ten commandments. One reason is that a community living according to such a Law will look very impressive to all the surrounding peoples, and point to the nation being full of wisdom and understanding. Another reason is that such a relationship with the living God will make all observers respect the obvious greatness of a nation so greatly blessed. However, this does depend on the people actually keeping the Law, and passing it down through the generations. That is crucial.

When we come to the passage from Mark, we find that a very human corruption of truth has been eating away at that wonderful ideal. We always find it so much easier to reduce vibrant truth to rigid, narrow rules. Insidiously the rules surrounding the truth take over in importance and are given permission to reign through the name of tradition, which is then reverenced, tragically at the expense of the original glorious, liberating vision. It is not just in Jewish religious teaching that this happens, but everywhere.

Jesus, with the clear insight of the Son of God, sees the terrible reality gap and its consequences. So corrupted has the perception of the Law become, that the very teachers are preventing the truth from catching hold of people's imagination, and in many cases the real meaning has been turned completely on its head. Jesus is not so much turning the world upside down by his teaching as turning it right side up again, the way God intended it to be.

Far from not keeping the Law, Jesus is reverencing it with his whole being, while the teachers have let go of the essence of God's truth and are left hanging on to scraggy handfuls of dry rules.

The reading from James is particularly helpful today since it comes from the Jewish tradition, with the fresh life of the Spirit breathed into it. Like the ancient prophets, the writer grounds God's truth in compassion and practical caring, coupled with a rigorous checking of personal purity so as to live in the wide freedom of God's law of love, which is altogether more demanding but also infinitely more fulfilling.

All-age talk

Probably quite a lot of us washed before we came out today. Why do we keep ourselves clean by regular washing? (Collect ideas and reasons.) Conclude that there are good reasons for washing. It's all to do with keeping healthy as well as being pleasant to sit next to!

Our Gospel reading today was talking about what makes us unclean. If we are talking about our bodies, what sort of things make us unclean, or dirty? (Collect a few ideas.)

Now it was traditional for Jewish religious people to do lots and lots of washing. Some of this was to keep everything clean and healthy, and, having lived as wandering nomads in hot desert country, all that was very important. But there was another kind of 'being unclean' which wasn't to do with bodies but souls. Sin is your soul, or spiritual nature, being unclean and in need of a good clean-up. They believed that eating certain foods or not following special rituals would make you unclean.

But whereas it's *outside* things that make our bodies unclean and in need of washing, Jesus explained that with our souls it's thoughts and wants from deep *inside* us that often lead us into sin, making us unclean. Like what, for instance?

- Like when we have mean, unkind thoughts;
- when we feel like hating or despising people because they've got what we want;
- whenever we want what we know is wrong and against God's way of living;
- when it seems like a clever idea to lie our way out of trouble;
- when doing something unselfish seems too much hard work and we can't be bothered with it.

When we are baptised, we're dunked in water, partly as a sign that we're being washed clean from sin. (And in some churches, the priest washes his hands just after the bread and wine are brought to the altar, as an outward sign that he wants God to wash him clean of sin, ready for this special part of the service.)

So if those wrong and bad thoughts and drives make us sin, so that our souls are unclean, how on earth can we get clean again? Can we scrub our souls with soap and water, or soak all our nastiness away in a hot bath? No, we can't. But there is a way of getting our souls clean without leaving any stain of sin at all. It's a two-stage washing process, rather like putting stuff out for the laundry because we know it's dirty, and then having it washed clean. And it's called *repentance* and *forgiveness*.

Once we realise that our souls are messy and dirty with sin, and that makes us sad, we bring all of it to Jesus, tell him how sorry we are and how we would love our souls to be completely clean again. That's repentance.

What Jesus does is to take our souls and soak away all the sin in a wonderful bath of forgiveness, that leaves us feeling free and happy and spiritually clean.

Sunday between 4 and 10 September

Proper 18

Thought for the day

Jesus comes fulfilling the hope of healing to wholeness; he shows that mercy has triumphed over judgement.

Reflection on the readings

Proverbs 22:1-2, 8-9, 22-23 or Isaiah 35:4-7a
Psalm 125 or Psalm 146
James 2:1-10 (11-13), 14-17
Mark 7:24-37

In the Old Testament prophecies describing a healing Messiah, we sense the huge waves of longing for the whole nation to be restored and beautiful in God's sight; in full and vigorous health morally, elementally, physically and spiritually. Everything is pictured as bursting into new life and vitality through the direct touch of God's presence.

The reading from James picks up on the kind of healthy attitudes which are free from prejudice and discrimination, recognising that in the fullness of God our thinking is to be reworked until it reflects God's character, and we celebrate the triumph of mercy over judgement.

Today's Gospel shows Jesus acting all this out in person. He doesn't advertise for custom, so as to force the events to fit the promises of scripture; on the contrary, people drag their loved ones to him and beg him to work God's healing in them. Even as he sighed, 'Ephphatha!', longing in love for the man's ears to be opened, it is as if he is longing for the ears of the whole people of God to be opened so that they may hear and understand.

Immediately before this healing, which exactly matches with the expected touch of the Messiah, we are given another healing which can sound initially offensive to our twenty-first-century ears. The woman asking for her daughter to be healed is both a Gentile and a foreigner, and Jesus' reaction to her seems to go against what we expect of the Saviour of the whole world. Surely this was a wonderful opportunity for him to show the Jewish community that God's healing is for everyone? Perhaps Jesus wanted to voice the traditional Jewish attitude on behalf of the people so they could see how God intended to overcome such barriers.

Certainly Jesus' first priority was obedience to the Father. Since he knew that his mission was to bring the good news to the Jewish people, he was hesitant about the timing of this outreach, just as he had said to his mother at Cana, 'My hour has not yet come.' Always he was communing with the Father, keeping exactly in step with him, however that might look from the outside. The wonderful thing is that God uses this woman to reassure his Son. As she gives him the picture of crumbs dropping as the children eat, Jesus sees how much in line this overflow of blessing is with God's will, and gladly restores her daughter to health.

All-age talk

Bring along a couple of different masks and ask volunteers to come and put them on. Point out how Farouk has now turned into a fierce tiger, and we might be scared of him; Mazin is now a clown and looks even funnier than usual! Thank the volunteers and restore them to their normal identities.

One of the things that all grown-ups do is to put on different masks for different people. We need to learn from the children, especially the very young children, how not to. What sort of masks do grown-ups wear? Not usually animal or clown masks, but masks all the same!

We put on a special voice for people we want to impress, we wear special clothes and try to give the other person the impression that we are efficient, cool, witty, deep or dependable. Why do we do that? Because we know that most people are influenced by outward appearances, and most people are fairly judgemental. If we can persuade them that we are worth respecting, then we reckon they will be more likely to listen to us and take notice of us.

Is that how we want it to be? Think instead of young children, who simply act as themselves, and haven't yet learnt the game of pretending who they are. You can see in the direct look in a young child's eyes that there is something there which grown-ups call innocence, because they are real; and we all regret losing that in all the clever pretending and wearing of masks.

As Christians, we are called to break that destructive cycle. We are *not* to judge from outward appearances, or just be friendly and respectful to wealthy, important-looking people. For us it's different because we know that every person we set eyes on is made and loved by God. And if we treat every person with the respect and love which they deserve as God-made human beings, they won't feel that they need to put on masks when they are with us. We will be joining Jesus in allowing people to be who they are, so that they are helped to wholeness and integrity.

Sunday between 11 and 17 September

Proper 19

Thought for the day

Loving obedience to God is shown by Jesus to be a quality rich in courage and wisdom, a quality to be highly respected.

Reflection on the readings

Proverbs 1:20-33 or Isaiah 50:4-9a
Psalm 19 or Wisdom of Solomon 7:26–8:1 or Psalm 116:1-9
James 3:1-12
Mark 8:27-38

Obedience is currently rather a despised quality, and certainly not one which most people would strive to develop. Rather the opposite, since it has connotations for us of being somewhat immature and not yet our own, independent person if we claim to place any store by it. Not surprisingly children pick this up in adults and copy it. Children learn discipline and self-control from disciplined, self-controlled adults, who value obedience themselves.

The passage from Proverbs speaks of wisdom being the willingness to listen to advice and take it, and to accept rebuke so as to learn. That is all part of obedience, the getting into a position where we can hear and accept a superior's teaching. Those who refuse the offer are considered simple and foolish, in terms of eternity.

As the prophet in the book of Isaiah speaks of the figure of the Servant in complete loving obedience to God, his hearers would understand that here is someone of perfect wisdom and harmony with God, humble and courageous enough to do what is required as Saviour, whatever the personal cost. Though the people might well rebel in full-blooded human style, they recognised the importance and good sense of obedience.

In the letter of James the early Church is roundly chastised by the exasperated elder who has presumably come across yet another disaster caused by ill-disciplined tongues! And he's right – that small organ is capable of so much harm, and we'd do well to take James' passionate outburst to heart, not least in the conversations immediately following our worship each week. Again, it's our dislike of living obediently. If only God would turn his back for a minute while we say or do what we know he'd tell us not to!

But our example is Jesus, and today we meet him at the point when his disciples are beginning to grasp who he is, so he starts to explain what this will involve. It's too much for his friends. If Jesus isn't going to protest, then they will. Satan is quite happy to use well-meant persuasion to tempt us away from obedience. Thankfully Jesus stands firm, and lays out the obedience needed for all potential followers. Are we prepared to take him up on it?

All-age talk

Ask for some volunteers and spread them around in the aisle. Explain that all you want is for them to do as they're told. Then give a series of instructions, such as right hand in the air, stand still, run on the spot, stretch arms out to the sides, touch your toes, touch your nose, and so on. Hardly give them time to think. Finish by telling them to go back to their seats and everyone can give them a round of applause for giving us such a stunning example of perfect obedience.

Point out that it's quite easy to be obedient when someone's shouting out instructions, and the things aren't too hard. But if you had told them to push everyone off their chairs, or give all their money to the vicar, would they have rushed to be obedient and carry out the instructions? Hopefully not! God forbid that we should be so keen to obey anyone that we fall in with any dangerous or wrong instruction. Teachers often come across children who have done something really stupid, and give the excuse that their friend told them to. Is that a good excuse? No, of course it isn't, because we have to think when we are asked to do anything, and refuse to do it if it seems selfish, dangerous or wrong. (It isn't just children, either – grown-ups will give as an excuse that everybody else does it, which is just as foolish an excuse, since everybody else could well be doing something dangerous or wrong.)

So where have we got to with obedience? That we are not meant to leave our brains and consciences behind. That means we are measuring every instruction up against the one we really trust to know what is right and good – underneath all the other obedient things we do there is a deep solid rock of obedience to God. That is what keeps us obedient wherever the instructions we are given are sensible and good, because measured up against the solid rock of our God we can see clearly that it's right to do what we're told here. In being obedient we are also being obedient to God.

And it's also what stops us obeying foolish, dangerous or wrong instructions which we might get from other people. Because when measured up against the solid rock of our God we can see clearly that to obey in those cases would make us disobedient to God.

Obedience to God is what matters more than anything, and Jesus showed us that.

Sunday between 18 and 24 September

Proper 20

Thought for the day

The truly great in God's eyes are those who are prepared to be last of all and servant of all.

Reflection on the readings

Proverbs 31:10-31 or Wisdom of Solomon 1:16-2:1, 12-22 or
Jeremiah 11:18-20
Psalm 1 or Psalm 54
James 3:13–4:3, 7-8a
Mark 9:30-37

Plato reckoned that the only people suitable for leadership and positions of power were those who would never want to do it. The corrupting influence of power is clear for all to see, and we can all think of people in positions of greatness who are there through their ambition rather than their suitability for the office! In today's candid Gospel the disciples are not spared the gaze of the world at their petty arguing about which of them is most important, carrying most status. As we recall our own (probably private) conversations about what people think of us, we can humble ourselves with them as we listen to Jesus' teaching.

The kind of values we usually set store by are upended by Jesus' criteria for greatness. Being the last of all and the servant of all is, for a start, likely to go unnoticed and unappreciated most of the time. But we usually would expect praise and acknowledgement for humble service, and grumble if it wasn't forthcoming. Jesus is talking about enjoying working for others without recognition; keeping such service secret as far as possible.

The little child is a dramatic visual aid of the vulnerable and those of lowest status, without rights or wealth or power. And

Jesus is suggesting that we consider ourselves servants with fewer rights than these little ones. We are to gather up all our ambitions about wealth, power and status, which are bound to affect our attitudes to others, and scatter them on the wind, leaving us free and unburdened, so that we can simply serve others in humility and love. We have the shining example of such a life in Jesus himself.

All the battles and strife which James talks about stem from this drive to be considered best, or to be better than other people. Often we ground this drive in our desire to possess money, things, qualifications, people, or any kind of trophy. Sadly, none of it impresses God, and none of it helps us fulfil our true selves, even though Satan persuades us that it will give us what we crave. As James suggests, we need to stand up to Satan and then we will find he slinks away, and we are already totally valued, so there was no need to strive after any of those things. Loving and service, in simple humility, is what gladdens the heart of God, who already loves us completely.

All-age talk

You will need to bring along a Christening gift of some kind (Peter Rabbit bowl, silver spoon or locket), a 5 or 10 metre swimming badge, an item of school uniform, several cups or trophies, a graduation certificate or gown, and a driving licence, a few brown envelopes and a clock.

Ask for a volunteer to help take on a whistlestop tour of a lifetime. Work through a person's life (you can call them the name of the volunteer), presenting them with the trophies which mark each stage of the climb to power and greatness. As a baby they are presented with special presents. As they grow up they start doing clever things like swimming and riding bikes. They wear special clothes to show they're old enough and clever enough to be going to school and learning loads more things every morning. Perhaps they have a hobby – in sport or music – and they do so well that they keep winning cups and trophies for it. As they get older still, they're off to university, and a few years later, here they are at their graduation. It's congratulations time again. And then there are the driving lessons and the practice and the extra insurance, and suddenly it's the test, and a smart new driving licence. All they need now is the car to drive. But the work's going well and the money's coming in, so they can buy all the things they've always wanted, and here are the bills to prove it.

And then, after a good many years of work, this highly respected person is old enough to retire. They have become a powerful and important pillar of society.

The volunteer is now loaded. Help unload them and thank them for their assistance.

We all have ambitions; we all hope our lives will turn out like our dreams. We want to be successful, liked, appreciated, fit and good-looking. And often we secretly want to be best. Jesus sees all of our dreams, even the secret ones. He knew what the disciples had been muttering about on their way as they walked along. They probably hoped he couldn't hear, because, like all of us, they had a strong suspicion that discussing who had most status was not really Jesus talk. Jesus really didn't care if the important people disapproved of him. He wasn't out to impress anybody, or work his way up, or gain status – he was just there to get on with the work of loving people to wholeness.

And that's what he wants for his followers as well. He wants us to have that freedom, so we can get on with what's really important, instead of wasting our time and energy empire-building in our particular area, impressing people, or collecting status symbols to wear or drive in. What do they matter when we compare them with God's values? Let's learn to be happy and content with nothing but being last, being unnoticed and the servant of all.

Sunday between 25 September and 1 October

Proper 21

Thought for the day

Don't let your body lead you into sin and risk exchanging eternal life for eternal punishment.

Reflection on the readings

Esther 7:1-6, 9-10; 9:20-22 or Numbers 11:4-6, 10-16, 24-29
Psalm 124 or Psalm 19:7-14
James 5:13-20
Mark 9:38-50

Nobody talks much about hell. We have moved away from the graphic fire and brimstone images of the medieval artists, and tend to pass over Jesus' teaching about it. But sometimes we have to address it, and today is one of those days.

Jesus had a lot of hard sayings for his disciples to swallow. They needed to understand and accept, for instance, that God doesn't rigidly limit his spirit to work within the Church. Joshua had been just as offended by the seventy elders all prophesying, and Moses had to remind him that as far as he was concerned he'd be happy for the whole community to be filled with the Spirit of God. God doesn't limit his power to those of specific groups. We, too need have no problem with Christian work being done by those outside the Church.

And then there is the hard but dear teaching on the importance of self-control. Jesus is not pretending temptation is easy to cope with. He knew from personal experience that it was agonisingly difficult. It is always a struggle to resist temptation, and fighting it can feel as drastic as chopping off hands or feet, or plucking out eyes. Even hearts, if they are causing us to sin and distracting us from God. It is because we don't take temptation seriously enough that we so often fall into sin. Jesus, in his agony in the garden, as he watched and prayed desperately to resist the temptation to opt out of the work of salvation, urges Peter and the others to do the same, so that they will not fall when the onslaught of temptation engulfs them, but they slept instead.

The reason for Jesus' urgent concern for us is that sin has eternal terrible consequences that we can barely imagine. It is forfeiting eternal life we are talking about, and some kind of eternal punishment which certainly fills Jesus with horror to think of. If he was taking it that seriously, then surely we would be wise to do the same. We are called to be preservers – like salt – working at preserving souls for a glorious eternal life which is God's will for us all. We can't do that if we are allowing our own bodies and attitudes to lead us deep into sin. Neither can we kid ourselves we are preservatives unless we are actively committed to helping others towards the kingdom.

All-age talk

Bring along some salt and a slice of ham. Explain that salt is often used as a preservative, to keep food fresh and good, and stop it going off. We tend to use freezing for this, but if you haven't got a freezer, salt works very well. Ham and bacon are salty because they have always been a way of preserving pork. When it's salted it lasts, and it still tastes good. (Give the ham to some volunteers.) At the end of today's Gospel, we heard Jesus saying to his disciples that they were to be like salt – not preserving food, but working in the world to preserve people for eternal life. Presumably he was thinking that if people didn't have preservative, they'd go rotten. Sin is what makes people go bad and rotten, not just in this bit of life that we walk about on earth and in time but for ever. And that's a terrible thought and we wouldn't want it to happen to anyone at all, would we?

That's why God badly needs some volunteers living in this world, and this parish, going to the local school, shopping in the local supermarket, working wherever you work and belonging to the clubs you belong to. God needs us to work as spiritual salt among all the people you meet and work and live with, helping to keep people fresh and alive for ever, and preventing them from going bad and rotten from sin. Who's prepared to volunteer as God's salt? Let's hope we *all* are!

So how can we do it? First, and most important, we've got to make sure we're still salty ourselves. If we're letting our bodies or minds lead us deep into sin, then we're not going to be much good at preserving other people, are we? We're more likely to infect them with our sin – even our secret sin. So Jesus tells us to sort out our own sin with God. We need to ask him to help us clean our life up and keep it clean, so we're really salty salt, useful as God's preservative in the world. Get that done, however much it hurts and however difficult it seems – even if it feels as painful as chopping off a hand or a foot. Turning from sin hurts, but it won't kill your eternal life, like the sin will.

Once we're really salty, we can spread around us the peace which only God can give. We'll be treating people with God's love, able to talk with them about the freedom of being forgiven, introducing them to our wonderful friend Jesus, by the way we live and obviously enjoy his company. And we'll be fighting for good and against all that we come across which is evil. We'll be active in making our society more responsible and wholesome because of us living in it.

Is all this an idealistic dream? Could we really make a difference? The good news is that in God's power and strength we really can be salt; all of us here can join the work of preserving life, knowing that through our willingness to be salty, people will be saved for the joy of eternal life.

Sunday between 2 and 8 October

Proper 22

Thought for the day

Human beings are made responsible for the care of creation but are subject to God in all aspects of their lives.

Reflection on the readings

Job 1:1; 2:1-10 or Genesis 2:18-24
Psalm 26 or Psalm 8
Hebrews 1:1-4; 2:5-12
Mark 10:2-16

In the reading from Job we are shown a man who recognises and accepts his place under God, and who will not be persuaded to curse his creator on account of his sufferings. To Job they, as well as the joys of life, are part of the deal and we have no right to expect all sunshine.

In the Genesis reading we look at the more ancient and primitive of the creation stories, with Adam being taken around the freshly made world, naming the animals and thus being established as responsible for the care of creation. No animal being suitable as a helpmate, woman is created from Adam, though for this 'birthing' Adam is anaesthetised and spared the pain! (Floating ribs would have become separated in skeletons seen around at the time of writing, possibly giving rise to the idea of woman being created from a spare rib.)

The deep truth of the story lies in God creating people who are given responsibility while remaining subject to God, their creator. The ' God with man and woman' teamwork is established right at the start of history. It is just as fresh and definite now, and we must not shirk that responsibility, under God, to care for the universe we inhabit. We are not called to dominate it and squeeze it dry for our own short-sighted indulgence, but to be careful stewards in every generation.

That careful stewardship extends to our own lives as well, and all our relationships, particularly marriage. Choosing life partners is a serious matter for God and us to consider carefully together; and the upholding of marriage is the responsibility of the whole community. Jesus takes his disciples back to this basic established pattern when he reinforces the importance of lifelong faithfulness in marriage. We cannot tear these verses out of the Gospel simply because they are at variance with society's norms. Jesus is describing God's good intention for those called to marriage to live in the security and comfort of lifelong partnership under his banner of love.

Of course there will be cases where, due to our hardness of heart, our wrong choices or through other pressures, the ideal falters and relationships break down irreparably. Those are occasions of deep sadness for the whole community, for a recognition of our brokenness, for repentance and forgiveness. They do not alter the wonderful provision God has made for us.

All-age talk

Invite people to share what jobs they are responsible for, including household chores, professional responsibilities and so on. Have people of all ages contributing so that it is clear that we all have responsibilities of some sort, whatever our age. You could also draw attention to those responsible for particular jobs in church, making it an opportunity for everyone to thank the flower arrangers, servers and choir, cleaners and pastoral team.

Point out that right from the beginning, when Adam was naming the animals, God has made us human beings responsible for looking after this world and each other. That is the important job that God has given us to do. If we all did our bit and everyone acted responsibly to the planet and to one another, under God's guiding hand, we would find that our life together here would be greatly blessed. People would have enough to eat, and many disasters and much suffering would be avoided.

So why doesn't that happen, when it seems such good sense for us to live according to the Maker's instructions?

The trouble is that we all let our own wants and selfishness get in the way. If we, as rich nations, started acting more responsibly, then things we've become used to getting cheaply would be more expensive, and we might have to make do with less. Our greed stops us acting responsibly. So does our short-sightedness, when we want 'lots, now!' instead of considering those who haven't yet been born.

It's even the same in our friendships and marriages. If we are responsible in these, we will be caring for the other person and looking after their needs, sensitive to their feelings and wanting to help them. If one or other or both stop doing that, the relationship becomes hurtful and wearing instead of rewarding. The answer may not be to get out of the friendship or marriage, but change our way of behaving with each other, talking things over with each other and with God, learning to be responsible again. It is grown-up and sensible to know that life can't always be happy, and the person we love can't always agree with us. Giving one another space, understanding that we all have bad days, forgiving one another and working at our friendships – all this is part of being the responsible people God created us to be.

He doesn't expect us to do it without help. God is there with us in all the bad patches as well as the easy rides, and as a community we are to look after one another properly, making sure we're all OK and coming to the rescue whenever someone isn't.

Sunday between 9 and 15 October

Proper 23

Thought for the day

The word of God is living and active, piercing right to the heart; only with God is it possible to be saved.

Reflection on the readings

Job 23:1-9, 16-17 or Amos 5:6-7, 10-15
Psalm 22:1-15 or Psalm 90:12-17
Hebrews 4:12-16
Mark 10:17-31

The prophet Amos urges his hearers to seek the Lord and live, implying that unless they actively seek God and his goodness, truth and justice, they will find themselves unable to inherit God's blessings in their lives or their nation. The alternative Old Testament reading from Job shows us in contrast a God-fearing, upright man who is steadfastly seeking God with all his heart, even though he feels surrounded by thick darkness and unable to find him. Even in the darkness and silence, Job continues to seek, trusting that God knows where he is and will eventually reveal himself.

Seeking God is a quest that alters our whole outlook on life. It isn't a casual hobby, or a weekend interest. While we actively seek God, we will be listening and looking attentively, and this will move us to question our own motives for doing things, and the way we behave. We cannot be seeking God, for instance, if we are trampling on all that is right and good, despising those who tell the truth and crushing the poor. If we are honest and serious in our search, the very seeking will begin to change us, by changing our hearts.

The writer of Hebrews has obviously seen and experienced this process and likens the power of the word of God to a sharp sword – or perhaps for us the image of a surgeon's scalpel – with its precise, clean cut, enabling the healing work to be done. Once the thoughts and attitudes of our hearts are being transformed, through God's power, then the impossible business of conquering sin becomes a distinct possibility; hope is in sight for us at last!

The young man in today's Gospel is keen. He comes running up to Jesus, wanting to know how he can inherit eternal life. Typically, Jesus doesn't answer directly, but picks up on the young man's thinking, as shown in calling Jesus 'good'. His seeking has already led him to recognise goodness in this preacher, and Jesus helps him further along, to look at what God's ideas of goodness are, and where that challenges the young man's life. When he moves away frowning, it isn't that he disagrees with Jesus, but that he has just realised he is right.

Like the young man, we who seek will find Jesus challenging us, and then we have to choose whether to go on with the search, or press cancel.

All-age talk

Beforehand set up a kind of treasure hunt, like this. Prepare the following envelopes, numbered clearly, and place them all around the church.

1. Contains the reference Amos 5:14 and a Bible with a bookmark in the right place.
2. Contains a charity envelope with a description of the need for fresh water in many villages, or an immediate crisis concern.
3. Contains a flag of our nation.

Ask for a couple of volunteers, old enough to read, and send them off to search for envelope number 1. When they bring it back, ask them to open it and look up the reference in the Bible. This was part of our first Bible reading today, and in order to understand what seeking God involves, we're doing it. The prophet knew that seeking God actually changes us, helping us to find God. Already our search has led us to pick up a Bible and read it. All of us need to do that – it's no good having a Bible at home if we never open it up and read it! As we heard in our second reading today, the word of God is living and active. If we are really seeking God, we'll have to find out what the word of God says, every day.

Ask for another couple of volunteers to search for envelope number 2. They open it and show the contents. Either describe the needs in the present crisis, or explain how (Action Aid) is trying to provide the basic need of fresh water for villages in Africa and India, where the children die because the water is so bad. We have fresh water there in our taps all the time! What can we do to help these people? Produce a labelled bucket and announce a retiring collection as we show our love and concern. God is leading us to see with his eyes of compassion and love.

Another couple of volunteers search for envelope number 3. Inside is the national flag. Invite people to think about their country – the things that make them happy about it and the things which sadden them. As we seek God's goodness, truth and justice, we'll find that we notice things that need to be changed. Our country needs us to stand up for what is right and fight what is evil. Are we doing that, or leaving it to other people?

The young man in the Gospel was seeking God, and Jesus helped him. The next stage of that young man's journey into God would be to change things in his life. If we set out to seek God, we must expect the same.

Sunday between 16 and 22 October

Proper 24

Thought for the day

Even the Son of Man himself came not to be served but to serve, and to give his life as a ransom for many.

Reflection on the readings

Job 38:1-7 (34-41) or Isaiah 53:4-12
Psalm 104:1-9, 24, 35c or Psalm 91:9-16
Hebrews 5:1-10
Mark 10:35-45

Job has continued to seek God through the bleakness and silence, and now it is as if God suddenly throws open the door so wide that Job almost falls over. With the joy of an answer comes the humbling question of what right any of us have to expect to understand, or to challenge the great Creator of the universe, the One who is the ground of our being.

In the Isaiah reading we have one of the extraordinary prophecies about God's suffering servant, which we, in the light of the Gospels, see as so perceptive in grasping the inevitable suffering of God's Saviour, Jesus. The writer of Hebrews helps us to understand it. Although the Messiah figure for many was seen as a national leader who would establish his reign and drive out oppressors, the more spiritual Messianic dream was that he would be a priestly king, mystically anointed with the power of Yahweh himself, taking on the suffering of the people with God's blessing, so that they may be saved.

Humans find it so hard to break away from the power and hierarchy models of thinking. Even though James and John have spent two or three years living and working with Jesus, have gone out on mission preaching the kingdom and experiencing many miracles, being dragged off to meals with rich and poor, socially elite and social outcasts alike, they are still thinking in worldly terms of greatness and status.

I suspect they might, at the time, have protested at that, and believed they were asking to sit at Jesus' right and left for noble reasons, like feeling themselves so close to their master, and wanting that to continue for ever. Who knows. Jesus is wonderfully forgiving of their inane suggestion, so alien to all he is. We can imagine him shaking his head helplessly as he says, 'You don't know what you're asking!' James and John are like so many of us, arrogant in our ignorant enthusiasm.

Today's message is really to do with that humble obedience which comes through suffering and persevering when the going is tough, and eventually makes us wise enough to listen with our hearts to what is really important.

All-age talk

Have three chairs placed in front of the altar, in the obvious place of honour. Prepare three 'Reserved' signs.

In the Gospel today we watched two of Jesus' disciples – James and John – coming up to him with a question they wanted to ask. They wanted to make sure Jesus would give them what they wanted, so instead of starting with the real question, they first said, 'We want you to do for us whatever we ask.' Perhaps we try that one with parents or spouses, or the boss sometimes. Like this.

Invite a child and adult to come and read the following script:

Child Dad, you love me, don't you?

Dad Yes, son.

Child You'd give me anything I wanted, wouldn't you?

Dad Mmm . . . maybe I would.

Child Well, can I have this really good educational computer game?

Dad No.

Child Oh, but Dad, you said . . .

Dad I only said maybe!

Child Oh well, it was worth a try.

Jesus didn't say yes either. He asked James and John what they wanted, and was pretty gob-smacked by what it was. Invite two children to read out James and John's question – have it printed out in large, clear letters for them: 'Let one of us sit at your right and the other at your left in your glory.'

What on earth was Jesus to say to that? Point out the three chairs, and have someone place a reserved sign on the main, middle one. Who was this place in glory reserved for? Jesus. Had he pushed for it or even asked for it? No! He was given it by Almighty God, his Father. It was being a servant and being willing to give up his life for us all that brought Jesus to reign in glory. If James and John were to be granted their wish (invite them to go and sit either side of the main seat), what would it show about them, and about Jesus? (Collect ideas. It might show that they were the most important of the disciples, that Jesus liked them better than the others, that pushy people get their way in God's kingdom, for instance.)

Jesus pointed out to them that those places are not his to give anyway as they have reserved signs on them. (Invite someone to move James and John off the thrones and place reserved signs on them.) No one, not even Jesus, knew who they are reserved for. It could be for someone here! What we can be sure of is that the people they're reserved for would be the very last people to ask to sit there, or count themselves more worthy than anyone else!

Jesus tells us that we are all here to bother about serving others, not to bother about being served. Even Jesus himself, the Son of the living God, came as a servant, and gave up his life for the good of others. That's the example we're to follow, not resigning ourselves to it, grudgingly, but happy to have the honour of giving up our lives to serve others in love.

Sunday between 23 and 29 October

Proper 25

Thought for the day

In Jesus, God gathers his scattered people and opens their eyes to see.

Reflection on the readings

Job 42:1-6, 10-17 or Jeremiah 31:7-9
Psalm 34:1-8, 19-22 or Psalm 126
Hebrews 7:23-28
Mark 10:46-52

In the reading from Job, the vision of God's tender and comprehensive care of all creation, and his love in bringing it all to being, results in Job recognising God's true greatness at a deeper level. In new reverence and humility he bows before God, who gathers him up and lavishes his blessings on this honest and suffering man.

In the passage from Jeremiah, the prophet longs for the people to find again a close, personal relationship with the living God. No more empty, formalised religious practice, but a real reverence and tender returning to the Lord who loves them. He describes it as if it is happening, with streams of scattered people, all with their needs and frailty, being drawn from the ends of the earth, weeping and praying as they realise who they are, and whose they are.

The writer of Hebrews reinforces this joy of finding in Jesus the Saviour who meets our needs, providing for us what we by ourselves cannot achieve. Only Jesus, as the go-between, priestly figure of all time, is holy, blameless, pure, and set apart from sinners, yet willingly taking their part.

The Gospel reading catapults us into the kingdom longed for by the prophets. Here, in the dusty main street on the way out of Jericho town, we find the promised Christ going about his healing business of giving sight to the blind. Bartimaeus is anxious not to miss out on this opportunity, and it is his faith, Jesus tells him, which heals his sight. In the reality of this beggar, happy and freed from blindness, choosing to follow Jesus, we glimpse the wider vision of the whole of the world returning, with tears of joy running down their faces, to the God who never gives up on them and longs to gather them to himself.

All-age talk

Begin by asking people to imagine a child who has gone outside to play. She has been learning to ride her bike, and is quite good at it now, with a few wobbles. She's happy out there, riding up and down, until she takes a corner a bit steeply, brakes sharply, and she and the bike crash down. The child has a nasty graze on her leg, and is upset and a bit frightened by the fall. All she can think of is getting back home, to the person she knows will make it all better, and there she is, limping up the road, with her leg bleeding, crying out for her mum as she goes.

Most of us have been there. Whenever we're badly hurt, even when we've grown up, there's a young child inside us limping back home, crying, to the place we feel safe, and to the person we know will look after us and make it all better.

It's a good picture of our loving parent God, who is always there, waiting for his hurt and limping children to walk back home to the one who can and does make it all better, however old or young we are, and however we got our wounds; What that walk back home shows is that the child trusts. What our walk back to God shows is that we know and love and trust God to help us.

In today's Gospel we met a blind man called Bartimaeus. He knew he was blind. He knew he missed out in life because he couldn't see. When he heard that Jesus was passing by, he shouted and kept on shouting, so he wouldn't miss his chance. Never mind if the disciples told him to be quiet, he knew this was too important an opportunity to miss, and he shouted hard until Jesus himself heard him. That gave him the chance to do his 'limping home' – he made his way to the person he knew could help him. And, sure enough, Jesus did just that.

All Saints' Sunday

Sunday between 30 October and 5 November

Thought for the day

Great is the rejoicing in heaven among the saints of God as they worship their Lord in glory.

Reflection on the readings

Wisdom 3:1-9 or Isaiah 25:6-9
Psalm 24:1-6
Revelation 21:1-6a
John 11:32-44

When we have the handed-down stories of the saints, and the stained-glass pictures of them with sun streaming through and bathing us in coloured light as we kneel, praying, it is perhaps inevitable that we think of the saints as a different breed from ourselves. With all the noble things they did and persevered at, it's somehow hard to imagine them doing ordinary things like getting irritated by the length of queue at the checkout, or shouting at the children. We rather imagine them unruffled by the things which give most of us grey hairs, sailing through their deep, spiritual sufferings, helped by some saintly gene we haven't inherited.

Perhaps the most important thing we celebrate today is that, however we have since reworked their lives, and however beautiful their monuments, saints begin as ordinary as the rest of us, and it is just as possible for all of us to be saintly as it was for them and everyone else in their class at school. But would we want to be? Even the word 'saintly' has unfortunate connotations for some, suggesting an insufferable 'goody goody' character and a loss of contact with reality to be avoided at all costs.

Wrong again. Real saints have their feet fixed firmly in the real world, loving and appreciating it. They are people taking the

'Love God; love one another' code seriously, and you can't do that from an ethereal distance. Loving means getting involved, getting hurt, seeing the funny side (sometimes), learning from your embarrassing mistakes and all your experiences. These are real, ordinary people with their individual ways and habits, and lots of times in their lives when they had no idea what the next step should be.

The point is that they became saints through living ordinary lives, closely in God's company. The refining of lives takes place through living, and no one can side-step that requirement. As Jesus said, if we try to protect and shield our life we end up not keeping it safe but losing it. It is those who daily give it joyfully away who end up gaining the heavenly life which lasts for ever.

All-age talk

Give everyone a sweet which is wrapped in coloured cellophane (or just clear cellophane). This is a special present to everyone to celebrate All Saints' Day. Ask everyone to unwrap their sweet, eat it while they listen to the talk, and keep the wrapper carefully.

We are tasting the sweetness of our All Saints' gift. What makes a saint is someone who tastes the sweetness of God's amazing love and savours it, enjoying it and thanking God for it. Living like that is what transforms their lives, so that when people are with them they know they are in the presence of God. They can detect God's peace, God's love and God's joy.

Now invite everyone to straighten out their wrapper and look at it. When we look straight at it we notice all the sticky bits and fingerprints. When we look not at it but through it, we see beyond all those. That's how saints are with their view of life. They are here in the real, ordinary world, some of it bright and breezy, and some of it heavy with sadness, and a bit messy. But they keep looking through all the experiences of this life, using them to help them understand more and more of the love of God which shines through it all.

We are all called to be saints, set apart as friends of Jesus, walking through this life in his company and dying in his company. What about after that? Our readings today tell us about all the rejoicing that goes on in heaven for those who have gone faithfully through earthly life. It's difficult to describe heaven in ordinary language because heaven is so wonderful that it breaks the vocabulary barrier, and no one can find quite wonderful enough words to give us the full picture.

But we do have some idea. Some of the joy of heaven spilt out into the sky above the shepherds' field near Bethlehem the night Jesus was born, and that was full of angels singing and praising with great delight. Whatever it looks like, we can be sure that there will be a glorious sense of welcoming love and homecoming waiting for anyone who has spent their earthly life close to Jesus, loving God and loving those sharing the earth with them.

Fourth Sunday before Advent

(For use if the Feast of All Saints was celebrated on 1 November)

Proper 26

Thought for the day

To love the living God with heart, soul and strength, and to love our neighbour as ourselves means far more than any sacrificial offerings.

Reflection on the readings

Deuteronomy 6:1-9
Psalm 119:1-8
Hebrews 9:11-14
Mark 12:28-34

We might wonder why a scribe, highly educated in the law, should ask Jesus the seemingly obvious question: 'Which is the first among all the commandments?' Surely he knows that? But, as in any discipline, the simplest-sounding questions are often the most complex to experts, and the Jewish academics spent much time puzzling over the huge number of accumulated laws, so it had become hard to see the wood for the trees. Genuinely this scribe is wanting to search out right priorities – or indeed to establish whether any prioritising would be insulting to God.

Jesus' answer, coming after the discussions with those out to trick and test him, responds to this scribe's honest searching with perhaps the most powerful statement of faith ever uttered. Here is the Son of the living God, standing among his own people, in direct line from the patriarchs, prophets and King David, proclaiming the Shema: 'Hear, O Israel! The Lord our God is the one Lord!' To all Jewish people, this expression of faith is profoundly precious, a kind of 'passport into paradise' for every child of Abraham, spoken three times every day by every believer.

What must it have sounded like, in this context, spoken by this voice? I would love to have been there!

All the love, all the obedience, all the authority, inspired the scribe to recognise, with fresh understanding, the wonder of those words, and the following summary of the law. We can hear in his excited response that he has seen the fresh colours of God's law again, as if the accumulated varnish from generations has been cleaned away, and the original beauty and brightness is startlingly visible.

Right back in the Deuteronomy reading, the significance and importance of this statement and law was urged upon the people. They were to wear it, tie it on gates and attach it to door-posts, passing it on to their children and grandchildren so as to ensure its continued obedience, and the psalmists meditated on the joy and blessing resulting from keeping God at the heart of our lives.

The writer of Hebrews, speaking to a Jewish audience, explores the work of Jesus in terms of Jewish sacrifices, right at the heart of their worship of the one true God. Time and again the priests needed to offer sacrifices on behalf of the people; in Jesus, both high priest and sacrificial victim, the total sacrifice is accomplished once and for all.

All-age talk

Beforehand ask three people to practise saying the same sentence, each emphasising a different word so that the meaning is slightly changed.

- WE go to church on Sunday – (as opposed to other people)
- We go to CHURCH on Sunday – (that's our destination)
- We go to church on SUNDAY – (rather than another day)

Also they need to practise saying the same sentence meaning something different.

- Yes, I believe so – (but you're not at all sure about it)
- Yes, I believe so – (automatically because it's written for you to say, but absent-mindedly)

- Yes, I believe so – (after much thought and with deep conviction)

Begin by pointing out how jokes can be really funny if you tell them right, but fall completely flat if you don't. How we say things is as important as what we say. Somebody can be saying nice things but you know they really don't like you and are trying to be nasty. Your friend could say the same things and you'd be happy and pleased instead of upset.

Invite the sentence-speakers to the front and invite everyone to spot the difference in what they are saying. (We go to church on Sunday.) Through stressing different words, they changed the meaning, even though the words stayed the same.

In the Gospel today we met a well-educated person, who had been quoting the scriptures every day of his life for a good number of years. He was thought of as fairly expert in his field of understanding God's law. He's been sitting listening to Jesus discussing the matters of law and faith with other experts, and he's impressed. He thinks it sounds as if Jesus really knows what he's talking about. He's so impressed that he asks Jesus a question, addressing him very respectfully as Rabbi, or Teacher. And the question he asks is this (have a volunteer, or everyone, read it out clearly and loudly): 'Which is the most important of the Commandments?'

The trouble was there were so many commandments now (as you speak, gradually unroll a very long roll of paper labelled 'Commandments') that it was all rather complicated and confusing. The scribe needed some help to sort it all out.

And what Jesus does is this. He recites the special statement of faith which every Jewish person knew by heart from childhood. It was this (everyone reads it out clearly): 'Hear, O Israel! The Lord our God is the one Lord.'

Just imagine how God's Son, a Jewish young man, would say that! The scribe could hear, in the way he said it, all Jesus' complete trust in God. He could tell it meant everything to Jesus, and he wasn't just rattling it off by heart. He meant it, completely and joyfully. And that got the scribe excited about his own faith – Jesus' love of God was catching!

When we talk about Jesus, does our love for him show?

Third Sunday before Advent

Proper 27

Thought for the day

When we are called we need to respond with obedience so that many may be brought to repentance.

Reflection on the readings

Jonah 3:1-5, 10
Psalm 62:5-12
Hebrews 9:24-28
Mark 1:14-20

It's 'Take two' as far as Jonah is concerned, following the first calling which had resulted in his marching smartly away in the opposite direction, with fairly drastic consequences. Typically, God's call hasn't changed when he eventually gets Jonah's attention again; he just quietly repeats into Jonah's heart what Jonah knows is the right thing to do. And this time he obeys God's calling, with the result that the people of Nineveh come to a dramatic, collective repentance, and are saved from destruction.

The psalmist urges us to put our trust in God, who is rock-like in his firm faithfulness and protection. In comparison, all else is considered air-headed rubbish, bound to disappoint and let us down.

The passage from Hebrews continues to show us how Jesus the Christ draws to completion and fulfilment all the sacrificial history of God's people. The tent of the Holy of Holies was set apart from the camps in the desert, and it was a sacred, holy occasion when Moses entered the tent. The writer sees Jesus' entry into heaven as the real fulfilment of what that image of the tent was saying. He looks forward to the second coming which will not be dealing with sin, since that is now accomplished, but rather the bringing-in of promised salvation.

The Gospel swings us back to Jesus first striding out into ministry, announcing the coming kingdom of God and urging repentance and belief in the good news. No sooner has he started to alert people, than he begins to gather workers for the harvest, calling fishermen from casting and mending their nets to reaching people and mending them through God's love. Their obedience to his call is vital for the saving of many.

All-age talk

Begin by giving out a few messages as if they are notices, rather like this. 'Is Ali Holden here? I've got a message from Molly, your neighbour's dog. She says when you next take her for a walk could you go past the swimming pool as there are some good smells around there. And then there's another message . . . this is for John Bendkowski. It's a message from the rope you used to climb the tree, asking for another high-level outing as it enjoyed the view.' (Use inside information so that the messages match up with real life.)

What do we reckon – are those messages true or not? Does Ali take a dog called Molly out for walks? Did John use a rope to climb a tree? Yes! Then what makes us think the messages aren't quite right? It's because common sense tells us that dogs and ropes can't send messages like that, even if they wanted to. Today we are looking at the way God calls us, and how we can work out whether it's really God calling us, or not.

What first alerted Ali and John to the messages given out? It was their names: When God calls us, he gets our attention and speaks directly to us. Sometimes what happens is that we hear a reading at church, or read a passage of the Bible at home, and suddenly a particular bit hits home, and we know it's meant specially for us. It's as if it has our name on it. God spoke into Jonah's heart so that Jonah knew God had a message for him, whether he chose to obey it or not. The fishermen heard Jesus calling directly to them as they worked in the fishing boats. So one thing we can learn about God's call is that it feels personal to us.

The next thing to look at is this: is this the sort of message that God would give? With our messages from a dog and a rope, we knew they didn't ring true, so we could laugh at the messages and not take them seriously. But what other things might make us suspect that a call is not from God at all? If it's to do with anything unkind, violent, selfish, greedy, lazy, deceitful, or evil, then the call we think we are hearing is not coming from the God of truth and love. But if we feel God is calling us to something loving, selfless, thoughtful, kind, courageous, honest, or good, then it's likely that God is speaking into our hearts, and we should listen carefully.

Then what? The first time Jonah heard God, he chose to run away from what he was asked to do. That ended up with him being tipped overboard and swallowed by an enormous fish! The second time God called, Jonah chose to do what God wanted him to do, even though he really didn't like the idea very much.

When Andrew and Simon Peter, James and John heard Jesus calling them, they got up straight away, left everything and followed him to do what they were being called to. If we hear God calling us, and we choose not to listen, or not to obey the call, the terrible truth is that people who might have been helped won't be; people who might have been saved might not get the chance God wanted them to have.

So we need to be ready to hear God calling in the quiet of our hearts, check with our experience of God that the call is true, and then be prepared to obey the call, going bravely wherever God is leading us.

Second Sunday before Advent

Proper 28

Thought for the day

We are to be on our guard; great anguish will accompany the last days, but all that is good and loving, wise and true will be saved and celebrated for ever.

Reflection on the readings

Daniel 12:1-3
Psalm 16
Hebrews 10:11-14 (15-18), 19-25
Mark 13:1-8

As the darkness crowds further into each day for those of us in the northern hemisphere, we have a powerful reminder of the gathering evil which it is foretold will accompany the heralding in of the last days. Jesus smelt it with the nose of a prophet, and although no exact dates can be given, he is very concerned for his disciples to understand the importance for them and us to be on our guard. We do indeed need to take great care as we walk and drive through our time on earth. All around us are subtle and powerful temptations to steer us off course, and distract us from our calling.

As we begin to experience the effects of our shrinking world, and recognise our interdependence, we are aware of the opportunities provided for mutual damage and instability as well as positive partnership. Large-scale damage of evil is increasingly possible and harder to prevent.

All is not gloom and doom, however. For those already living the risen life, the fear of annihilation is actually irrelevant, and the last day should fill us with excitement and hope, rather than terror, since at that time of accomplishment, all goodness, love, wisdom and truth will be revealed for what it is, shining and beautiful, and lasting for ever.

The psalmist describes his spiritual inheritance as if he is walking around the pleasant farmland which he knows will become his own as soon as he comes of age. He is pleased with the patch God has chosen for him and enjoys it in the present as well as for the future. Perhaps that gives us a model to work with.

We know and are thrilled that Jesus Christ has secured salvation for us, and our hope for that last day is not in our own ragged and scarred lives, but in the victory of the cross. The reason for being on our guard in these last days is not that the promise of salvation may suddenly be snatched away from us, but that in all the evil we may choose to throw away our hope of salvation. If we stay faithful through all the troubles which there are bound to be, we have nothing to fear at all, but rather a celebration to look forward to.

All-age talk

Bring along a well-loved and very well-worn companion – teddy or pyjama case. Introduce him to everyone and point out how we can all see just how well loved he is! He bears the signs of being well loved. Probably most of us older ones feel a bit like this – loving has worn us to the shape we are, a bit threadbare and squashed maybe, but perhaps a little wiser and softer and less selfish as a result. Although we know from experience that loving hasn't always been easy, we can say with certainty that it's well worth living lovingly.

Our readings today are helping us to look forward to the end of time, when the sky is wrapped up and the moon folded away. It can sound very frightening, to think of everything we know coming to an end.

Whenever there are terrible disasters and famines and wars it can feel as if things are spinning out of control – even out of God's control. Is the end going to be some huge ghastly mistake, brought about by our greed and selfishness?

The Bible reassures us that, however it may look as evil grows and temporarily gains the upper hand, God is always ultimately in charge. As we know, God's way is not to crash into our blundering and force us to change so that disasters are prevented. He has given us that great gift of free will, so that we can choose good or evil in the small and large decisions of life. He longs for us to choose the good that will bring us blessing and peace, but is always there weeping with us in the chaos and suffering that evil leads to, ready to redeem it for good.

And it is that buffeted and battered loving which will last and last for ever. The prophet Daniel gives us a lovely picture of that. All those who have guided others in the right path, he says, will shine like the stars of heaven for ever. All the wise leaders will show up brightly for all to see. If we have set ourselves to live lives of faith and love, there is no way we need be frightened by the last days. After the feeding of the five thousand Jesus told his disciples to gather up the fragments so that nothing is lost. That's how it will be at the end; every scrap of goodness and love will be gathered safely in, so that nothing of it is lost.

Christ the King

Thought for the day

Jesus Christ is the everlasting King whose kingdom is not of this world, but grows in the hearts of his people and lasts for ever.

Reflection on the readings

> Daniel 7:9-10, 13-14
> Psalm 93
> Revelation 1:4b-8
> John 18:33-37

It is always difficult to describe heavenly things in terms of our human experience, but Daniel tries to give a faithful account of his vision of the one he calls the Ancient of Days, sensing the everness of his wisdom and power, his piercing integrity and all-knowing perception. Images of rivers of fire, throne and vast crowds worshipping help to give us some idea of God's glory as the source and sustainer of all. Daniel witnesses the moment of one like a son of man entering heaven and receiving the authority and dominion which are his for ever.

We who have met Jesus in the Gospels, and heard him refer often to himself as 'Son of Man', recognise the one who enters heaven as the Lord and Saviour who loved us enough to die for us. The Gospel for today refers us to Jesus' conversation with Pilate, just before his crucifixion. Jesus tells the Roman governor, who represents the worldly power and authority of the whole Roman Empire, that his kingdom is not of this world. He is not therefore a threat to the authorities in terms of violent uprising and revolt. The kingdom of God is a lot more powerful, far-reaching and long-lasting than any empire!

In the reading from Revelation we are back in the world of vision and prophecy, written for those who had witnessed the crucifixion and resurrection of Christ, the outpouring of God's Spirit in tongues of flame, and the business of living as followers of Christ in an often hostile world. There will come a time when Christ the everlasting King will appear in all his glory, and every eye shall see him.

The Church's year has come full circle. We began last Advent by preparing ourselves for the coming of Jesus, both at his birth into our world and at the second coming. We have walked with Jesus through his life and ministry, led mainly this year by Mark's dynamic Gospel account. We have watched Jesus and listened to him, sorrowed and rejoiced with him. We have seen the gradual understanding of the disciples and their transformation through the gift of the Holy Spirit. And now, as we celebrate Jesus, King of all ages and nations, born for this, living and dying and rising for this, we proclaim the basic Christian belief which will enable us to press forward into our Advent preparations: Jesus Christ is Lord!

All-age talk

Beforehand prepare a long length of lining paper on which the alphabet is written clearly. Fix it up where everyone can see it, or ask people to hold it. (Please don't make them hold it high or their arms will drop off!)

Claim that on this sheet you have the whole of the Bible, the complete works of Shakespeare, every love letter ever written, every postcard and Christmas letter ever sent. You also have the names of every person and every place.

At this point a pre-arranged person walks out to protest. Preachers are supposed to tell the truth and here you are telling porky pies. You can't possibly have all that on this sheet of paper. You've only got a few letters!

Meet the challenge by inviting them to find their own name from the sheet, which they spell out letter by letter, and have to admit that they are on the sheet after all. Get someone else to find 'To be or not to be' and 'Come, Lord Jesus'. These are also found to be there.

Our God is like A to Z – the beginning and the end of everything, all thoughts and ideas all creation, all love, all hope, all existence. That's why we worship God – God has always been. God is, at this very moment now. (Pause for everyone to become aware of that amazing fact.) And God will always be, for ever. God's kingdom is wherever Jesus reigns as our King. And that means wherever people say, 'Yes!' to Jesus, 'I really want to be in your kingdom!'

And we know what being in Jesus' kingdom is like; don't we? It's full of love and joy and peace, full of forgiveness and patience, full of hope and healing. Today it's as if we've brought out our flags to wave as we celebrate Jesus as our wonderful, everlasting King, who sets our lives dancing!

YEAR C

Advent 1

Thought for the day

The gathered hopes of generations remind us to get ourselves ready, so that Christ's return will be a day of excitement and great joy.

Reflection on the readings

Jeremiah 33:14-16
Psalm 25:1-10
1 Thessalonians 3:9-13
Luke 21:25-36

Today is filled with a sense of expectancy. It's rather like knowing that when you come of age you'll inherit a fortune, or that in another few years your ISA account will mature. Only this is rather more mind-blowing than mere financial hope. The promise is there and stands secure, and God, being faithful, will keep that promise. Eventually, when the time is ripe, he will gather up all the goodness and honour and patience and long-suffering that has been grown throughout the ages, and bring things to completion.

This week's readings speak to the deep-seated longings of humanity for right and justice to triumph. They speak to our yearning for a final end to all the cruelty and misery of our world, some of which we all know from first-hand experience. Of course, it is serious and sombre stuff to be considering the winding-up of all the created universe as we know it, and it is very necessary to be reminded of our need to be ready by the lives we are leading.

Yet running through the readings is a clear, bright shaft of strong and exhilarating hope, which we can catch and make our own. God is familiar with our world. He too hears the cry, generation by generation, of those who find faith in a good God impossible because they are overwhelmed by the sorrows and tragedies screaming at them. But ultimately, as Christ has already shown us on the cross, and in his risen life, it is good that triumphs, and God's harvesting at the end of time will be a glorious celebration of all that is just, right and loving. This is not wishful thinking but hope, in all its integrity.

All-age talk

Have ready a good supply of inflated balloons on strings. These will be needed later.

Bring out three sweets or apples and explain that three people are going to get them. Give them out completely randomly and then ask if that was fair. Agree with them that it wasn't fair, and often life seems unfair to us. (This is something that all ages know about.) Explain how our world is full of injustice and sometimes cruel and terrible things happen which don't make sense.

Now ask anyone who would like a balloon to raise a hand. Invite these people to come and collect a balloon and return to their seats. You will need them to gather with their balloons later on, when you beckon them.

As Christians we don't have to pretend the bad things aren't there, or try to work out easy answers that don't make sense. God knows there are sad and bad things happening in our world as well. They happened just the same when Jesus was walking around in Galilee. A tower fell on some people and killed them. The people asked Jesus to explain it, but he didn't. He felt very, very sorry for anyone who was ill or whose child had died, and, instead of explaining why, he set about comforting them and doing everything he could to make things better. So that's what we need to do as well while we are alive.

But Jesus did tell us that life wouldn't always be unjust. One day, he said, everything as we know it will finish, and on that day everything you, and everyone else, have ever done which is good or kind, or helpful, friendly or honest will be gathered in, like harvest, and kept. (As you say this, gather all those with balloons together in the centre.) It will be an exciting and very beautiful harvest!

Let's make sure that we grow plenty of love and thoughtfulness and honesty and integrity in our lives, however old or young we are, so that whenever that last day comes, we'll be helping to make it a bumper harvest.

Advent 2

Thought for the day

It had been prophesied that there would be a messenger to prepare the way for the coming of the Messiah. Now John the Baptist appears with his urgent message of repentance.

Reflection on the readings

Malachi 3:1-4
Canticle: Benedictus
Philippians 1:3-11
Luke 3:1-6

Today we read one example of many references from the prophets to a messenger who will prepare people for the coming of the anointed one, the long-awaited Messiah or Christ. It is typical of God's provision for his people. All teachers and builders know the necessity for thorough preparation and the way this so often involves chipping back to the solid foundations and making good. Anyone in advertising knows that people may need telling the same thing several times before they are likely to do anything about changing their favourite product.

So God, knowing human nature affectionately and realistically, tells us beforehand what he will do, and then provides John who himself points towards someone else. Hopefully there will be those who, having heard the prophecies, will already be waiting expectantly, ready to latch on to what the messenger is saying. There will be those who, through John's urgent message, will be sorting their lives out so that when Jesus' ministry begins, their hearts will already be attuned to receive what he has to say and eventually to recognise who he is.

And what about us? Paul's prayer, similar to that in the letter to the Thessalonians last week, is rather like the image of carrying a very full mug of tea from the kitchen back to bed, carefully holding it so that nothing spills and nothing is lost on the way. We are in the privileged position of having read the prophesies, seen them fulfilled in John the Baptist, and having met Jesus through the Gospels and his living presence. So in a sense we are like the full mug of tea. What we now have to do is make the journey to death and the second coming without losing a drop of what we have been given.

At another level is the recognition that it isn't enough to hear John's message once. It does us all good to use each Advent as a fresh chance to look at our lives and habits, and sort them out; to be ruthless about anything which is impairing our walk with God.

All-age talk

Beforehand arrange for a local builder/decorator to be interviewed, preferably in working clothes and carrying his tools.

Introduce the guest, and ask his advice about a structural problem (either real or imagined). When the builder talks about the importance of all the 'making good', suggest that surely he could just smear some more plaster over the top, and wouldn't that be as good? Or put on thick wallpaper to hide the cracks? Let the builder explain what will eventually happen if the real problem isn't sorted out.

Thank the guest builder and have a couple of the children bring him a mug of tea as it's time for his tea break.

While the builder drinks his tea, explain how what is true for walls and windows is true for us as well. If we have been mean or a pain, or lazy, or if we've been telling lies or living lies, or if there is anything at all in the way we behave which is not right, loving and honest, then we are like a building with bad cracks and damp. As the builder told us, the only way to put it right is to have the wrong things cleared away, and then be built up soundly again.

God can do that in us if we want. He will help us put our lives right, however bad a state they are in. Tell him you are sorry you tell lies, and want to be more honest. He will help you become an honest person who others can trust. Tell God your sister/ father-in-law / colleague winds you up and you hate all the rows and want to be more able to cope. God will help you improve those relationships. Tell God you find it hard to share your toys or your money, and want to be more generous. He will help you do it.

But we can't put anything right until we see that there is a problem. It was only when the damp and cracks were noticed that the builder was called in.

John the Baptist spoke about 'repentance'. That means he is saying to us: 'Look at your lives; see those cracks and damp patches; and get them sorted out.'

Advent 3

Thought for the day

Our period of preparation shifts from repentance and forgiveness to the freed exhilaration of hope, as the momentous truth of God's immanence begins to dawn on us.

Reflection on the readings

Zephaniah 3:14-20
Canticle: Isaiah 12:2-6
Philippians 4:4-7
Luke 3:7-18

Over the first two weeks in Advent we have been focusing our attention on putting our lives straight, and this may well have been a very challenging and painful task. We may still be wrestling with its implications.

The shaft of hope has always been present in all this. But now it is as if the forgiveness we are receiving, resulting from real repentance, has enabled that shaft of hope to flood us with unexpected light and joy. From the viewpoint of forgiveness, the coming of Christ, both as we look back to Bethlehem and forward to the last day, is not something to fear, but to anticipate with great delight and enthusiasm.

There is Zephaniah's image of light-hearted and liberated singing and dancing, with something of the flavour of the street parties which celebrate peace after war. And there is Paul's signing-off message as he draws to a close his letter to the Christians at Philippi, the sense of God's closeness throbbing through the words. Everything is going to be all right; they can rejoice and go on rejoicing, whatever the immediate sufferings, because God has them ultimately safe.

And the people are enthusiastically taking up John the Baptist's challenge, and throwing themselves into giving up the behaviour they'd probably always known was wrong, but which they had never had the desire to address before.

In the gathering momentum some of them get over-enthusiastic, and how easily John could have been tempted to go along with their misguided assumptions.

Thankfully his own rigorous self-awareness keeps him humble, and he is able to use their questions to point their expectations in the right direction – towards the Christ.

All-age talk

Bring with you a sealed envelope containing an invitation to a very special party or wedding. The date for the celebration needs to say 'to be arranged'.

Tell everyone how you have received this letter, and it looked so exciting that you thought you'd bring it to church and open it there. Invite someone to come and help you open the envelope, and someone a bit older to read it out. Show your excitement and start planning what to give as a present, and what to wear, getting suggestions from people and scribbling it all down on a list. Such a lot to think about!

Then stop as you ask to check the date of the celebration. Realise that it only says 'Date to be arranged'. *Date to be arranged!* That means you have no idea when to get ready. It might be ages to wait. It might be next week! Suppose it's next week!

Come to the conclusion that the only way you can be sure to be ready is to get ready straight away.

Put the invitation down and pick up a Bible. As you flick through the pages talk about how you are sure there is an invitation to a party somewhere in here as well. Find the Zephaniah reading and discover that it's the one we heard this morning, with all the dancing and singing in it.

It's going to be quite a day, and we'll need to make sure we're ready for it. But what was the date again? Look and find it's another case of 'Date to be arranged'. Only God knows the actual date. That means it could be a long time ahead or it could be very close, so the best thing to do is to get ready straight away.

What kind of presents would be in order for this party?

Collect ideas like loving kindness, peacemaking, compassion, forgiveness, goodness and self-control. If we start now, we can grow those in our lives.

What kind of clothes would be suitable?

Clean clothes and good habits like honesty, faithfulness, humility, just or fair behaviour, and thoughtfulness. If we haven't got any yet, we can go to God's wardrobe and he'll make them to fit us perfectly. And if we have got them, but haven't worn them lately, now is the time to get them out and put them on again. These clothes get more and more beautiful as you wear them.

The second coming will be a wonderful celebration, and whether we are alive here or the other side of death, we will all be able to see it and take part.

Advent 4

Thought for the day

When we co-operate with God amazing things happen.

Reflection on the readings

Micah 5:2-5a
Canticle: Magnificat or Psalm 80:1-7
Hebrews 10:5-10
Luke 1:39-45 (46-55)

It is not only Mary and Elizabeth who are pregnant in today's readings. The whole atmosphere this week is full of expectancy and the sense that what we are looking forward to has already begun to be fulfilled. It may be hidden but it leaps within us.

The prophet Micah speaks of events far greater than he imagines, and we, with our knowledge of the Gospel, can pick up on the image of a shepherd saviour being brought to birth and establishing a reign of peace. The writer of the letter to the Hebrews reminds us not just of Christ's birth but also of his death. As an unborn child already has the DNA pattern for the potential adult, so we are given here a kind of spiritual antenatal scan of Jesus, stretching back into the longing and forward to the sacrificial giving which secures our future.

There is enormous strength in the capacity to set aside something precious to you in order that a greater good may be enabled to happen. We marvel at Jesus laying aside his glory; laying aside his garments to wash the disciples' feet; laying aside the law – all in obedience and out of love. It is a hallmark of true Godliness.

So when we find human beings like Mary willing to lay aside so much in obedience and out of love, we are watching the most real and beautiful of human nature; God and humanity co-operating together for the good of the world.

Today we are given the chance to press the pause button as Mary and Elizabeth meet, with their unborn children within them, and wonder at what can happen when we allow God to work in us and with us for the good of the world.

All-age talk

Try a kind of Mexican wave, first with one side of the church and then the other. The side not involved can enjoy the effect. Row by row, starting with the front row, everyone stands together and then sits together. The row behind gets up as soon as the row in front of them has sat down. Point out that for this to work they all needed to co-operate with one another and also with you, in agreeing to try it in the first place. Today we are watching what can happen when people are willing to co-operate with God.

Last week we found John the Baptist challenging people to sort out their lives and giving them some practical advice. Those who went away and did as John suggested found that once they had started to co-operate with God their lives took on a new sparkle and freshness many had lost. Those of us who took last week's teaching to heart and started looking seriously at what needed changing in our lives will also be here this morning with a new lightness in our step and a more positive sparkle in our lives because co-operating with God is very exhilarating and liberating. Working together with God sets us free. (And if we haven't yet got round to that there is still time for us to shake ourselves awake and use Advent profitably.)

Mary was one of those people who had decided to work together with God. And that meant that God could use her. So he did. It was through Mary co-operating with God that Jesus could come into the world.

Mary and Elizabeth are both pregnant. Mary is expecting Jesus, and her cousin Elizabeth is expecting John the Baptist. It's the same John the Baptist we met last week when he was grown up, teaching people by the River Jordan. Today we have a flashback to before he was born. Any mothers here will know that exciting feeling when the baby you are carrying first moves. Luke tells us that the unborn baby John was so excited at sensing the unborn Jesus, brought along in Mary, that he leapt about in his mother's womb!

Never before had God come among his people so closely. And now his birth into the world was less than a year away. No wonder Elizabeth and Mary were so excited. Having agreed to co-operate with God they found themselves being used for such an extraordinary and important job that they could hardly believe it. And they weren't even rich or powerful! They probably weren't even that well educated!

When anyone (and that includes you and me) says to God, 'I want to spend my life working together with you', God takes us up on our offer. If we don't opt out as soon as he asks of us things we may not want to give, he will be able to work with us in our lives to do amazing things. Imagine if everyone here in church decided to work with God. He could get us making waves in our community which would completely transform people's lives.

Christmas Day

(Set 1)

Thought for the day

Emmanuel – 'God with us' – is born at Bethlehem into the human family. Now we will be able to understand, in human terms, what God is really like.

Reflection on the readings

Isaiah 9:2-7
Psalm 96
Titus 2:11-14
Luke 2:1-14 (15-20)

The rejoicing Isaiah speaks of is a deliriously abandoned relief. After years and generations of oppression and injustice, this coming day is filled with evocative images of the security of a good harvest, the elation of overcoming an enemy in battle, and the freedom of slavery yokes being triumphantly shattered.

Typically, God brings about this longed-for day amid all the noise and confusion of ordinary life, with the census crowds jostling for space in the Bethlehem streets, the usual mix of noble and base behaviour, and in the context of unsettling circumstances. It is as if God is proving a point by acting out his name 'Emmanuel'; as if he is emphasising beyond doubt that he is truly with us in the untidy and muddled world we really inhabit. Nothing special is expected to be laid on, because he is not coming to meet us on our best behaviour, but on our real behaviour.

It is only when we are ourselves before God that he can truly be born in us. And if that place is crowded and dusty, or insecure or dark or full of questions, then he will be feeling very much at home.

All-age talk

You will need to borrow a mobile phone (unless you have received one as a Christmas present!) and a helper who is expert at sorting out OHPs.

Begin by telling everyone you want to show them something on the OHP, and then find that you can't work the equipment properly. Before anyone rushes to your aid, produce the mobile phone, delighted that this is an opportunity to use it to get in touch with an expert. Pretend to use the phone to get through to the expert, and have a mock conversation with them about how to work the apparatus, during which the expert suggests coming to help in person.

Welcome the help and pretend to talk through their (speedy) journey, which can be from anywhere in the world. As you get to guiding the expert down the road and into the church your helper arrives in person, mobile phone to his/her ear. (They have been standing hidden somewhere at the back of the building.)

The expert is able to get the apparatus going, and you enthuse about how much more helpful it is to have them there in person. You can now show the OHP acetate, which says: 'EMMANUEL = God with us in person.' The helper can point out that you've just been saying that it's much more helpful having them there in person. Is that what Emmanuel means?

You can then draw out the similarities – that with Jesus being born into the world as one of us, we have God with us in person to help us live good lives, make good decisions and guide us in all the tricky places. It's not that things won't ever go wrong any more, but it does mean we can always be in touch with the one who can help us sort things out. And that is a truth well worth celebrating in style! Suggest that over the Christmas festivities we live out this truth to one another. It will mean being generous-hearted, thankful, available and willing to meet people where they are, whether that is a group of friends at a party, or relatives we find it less easy to relate to. Welcome God in person to your home this Christmas and enjoy yourselves in his company.

Christmas 1

Thought for the day

Jesus' perception and understanding of his purpose and work begins to take shape throughout his childhood.

Reflection on the readings

1 Samuel 2:18-20, 26
Psalm 148
Colossians 3:12-17
Luke 2:41-52

It is significant that the young Samuel is clothed in the priestly ephod. Although Eli's sons are treating the Lord with contempt by their behaviour, this young child is innocent and clothed in a symbol of purity. In this climate of right living and integrity the child's family is blessed and Samuel himself grows in favour both with God and people.

The reading is linked with the passage from Colossians where we are reminded of our calling to be Christians and the clothing that entails. It is a clothing with those qualities of good Christian living which are so often lacking in our world, and often dismissed or despised. Yet, as people sense things moving out of control, and the extent of violence and the breakdown of trust shock us into taking stock of our direction, there is also a yearning for the possibility of these qualities of compassion, kindness, humility, gentleness and patience. Samuel is a symbol of hope in any corrupt society.

As we celebrate the Incarnation it is important that we also have this picture of a gradually developing recognition in the child Jesus of his life's work and purpose. Like Samuel he knows he is set apart, and throughout his early childhood Mary, Joseph and Jesus must have talked together about the events surrounding his birth. Now, at the annual Passover visit to Jerusalem, with Jesus come of age in the Jewish tradition, he is starting to see the prophecies and hints of scripture adding up, and the vision of his role and purpose sharpens into focus.

Mary, scolding him in her anxiety for his safety, points out that she and his father have been worried sick, searching for him. Jesus, with the enormity of his life's work flooding into consciousness, has spent the past few days beginning to grasp what it means to be God's son, and cannot understand why they should be searching for him when he is at home in his Father's house. Capital letters are not always audible! No wonder Mary and Joseph couldn't understand what he was saying to them – they hadn't been part of this emerging revelation taking place in the temple.

It is rather comforting to read that Jesus went back to live according to their rules, nursing his vision as Mary nursed her experiences, treasuring them but not imposing them on anyone. Not even sharing them until the time was right. God will always go with us at our own pace and in ways that we can cope with. That is all part of what Incarnation means.

All-age talk

Beforehand cut out two simple white cloth tunics like this one to fit a three- or four-year-old and a larger one for a twelve-year-old.

Invite a couple of toddlers and their parents to the front and interview them about the coats or jackets the children are wearing. Admire them and ask where they were bought, and what size was needed compared with their last coat.

Tell everyone how Samuel was brought to the temple when he was able to feed himself, and every year his mum brought him a new linen coat she had made. Every year he needed a slightly bigger one as he grew older. Produce your linen ephod lookalike and dress the toddler in it. As you do so, explain that it was worn as a sign of coming before God with a clean heart and mind. Priests all wore them, too.

When God came to earth at Christmas as a baby, it was like him putting on the clothing of being human, and it was God's way of showing how much he loves us and is with us. It also helps us to see what God is like, because we cannot see God, but in Jesus we can see how God behaves. We can see that he enjoys people's company, wants to help them and shares their sadness and joy.

And Jesus didn't suddenly arrive on earth as a grown-up. He was born as a baby (draw attention to the size of someone very small in the congregation) and grew to be a toddler and a child (use other people of appropriate ages to demonstrate), so by the time he was a grown-up twelve-year-old he had experienced all the sort of human things that we experience.

Use the larger tunic with the word 'Humanity' written on it to clothe a twelve(ish)-year-old. All twelve-year-olds start asking questions about God and themselves, and so did Jesus. Part of wearing humanity meant that he developed as a human person and now he was grown-up he was fascinated to know who he was and why he was alive, just as we are. Those questions are important, and need to be asked. They are a sign of growing up.

The answers for Jesus (and the answers for us) didn't come all at once. But that visit to the temple seems to have been a very important one for him. He began to understand that he was on earth to carry out God's purposes. That was why he was wearing the clothing of humanity. Perhaps for some of us this Christmas is an important one for finding out God's purpose for us in our lives. We need to come into God's presence wearing the clothes of honesty and openness, and ask our questions.

Christmas 2

Thought for the day

Christ is the way God tells people about himself.

Reflection on the readings

Jeremiah 31:7-14
Psalm 147:12-20
Ephesians 1:3-14
John 1:(1-9) 10-18

Jeremiah lived his dream. He hated standing out against the rulers, priests and people, but because he knew it had to be done, he did it, and suffered imprisonment, torture, derision and rejection because of it. Yet through all this the great vision of hope shines clear, of a time when, with a new and direct relationship with God, the remnant will be restored and comforted, led by a good shepherd. Rather like Jesus, Jeremiah's message was as much his life as his words.

In the letter to the Ephesians, Paul takes up Jeremiah's prophecy and sees it fulfilled in the community of the followers of Christ. Through Christ we can have this new and direct relationship with God, and so receive the grace which makes forgiveness and a new start possible.

John's introduction to his Gospel draws all this together, as he speaks of Christ as the Word – the Message – of God, always present and part of him, and proclaiming God clearly, as a living Message, as he walked about on earth. Today we are given total cinema, so to speak. We are looking at the past, present and future all at once so that God's purpose, and its fulfilment, are seen together. That is the extraordinary truth of the Incarnation: God was, God is, and God will be. And we can see it in the person of Jesus.

All-age talk

You will need a hair-drier or a fan, or a lit candle to blow out.

Start with a riddle. You're thinking of something which is all around us, pressing against our faces and bodies at 15 pounds per square inch. It goes in and out of us all the time we're alive, and there's lots of it right in front of our eyes. What is it? (Air.) But we can't see it, so how do we know it's there?

Put on the hair-drier or fan, or ask someone to blow the candle out. When air moves, we can see what it does. When we try to hold our breath we realise how much our bodies need air to live.

God is here as well, and we can't see him. No one has ever seen God while they are alive on earth. So how can God tell us what he is like, when we can't see him?

There are ways we can see what God is like by what he does and by what he creates. If we look at the world we can see that God must be generous, imaginative, careful, clever, organised, hopeful and happy to let us work with him.

But God had an even better idea. If he could walk among humans as a human, then all the humans who lived at the time or at any time afterwards would be able to see exactly how God behaves. We could see it in our own human language. The language of doing, thinking, feeling and speaking.

In the Gospel today Jesus is talked about as being the Word, or the Message of God. When we look at how Jesus lived and died, we are looking straight at God, even though we can't see God with our eyes.

And what do we see? John describes Jesus as being 'full of grace and truth'. Have this written up on a sheet. Around it you can add other people's ideas. Head the page 'Jesus is' and display it for the rest of the service.

Epiphany

Thought for the day

Jesus, the hope of the nations, is shown to the world.

Reflection on the readings

Isaiah 60:1-6
Psalm 72:(1-9) 10-15
Ephesians 3:1-12
Matthew 2:1-12

Beginning with one person (Abraham) and developing to embrace one family and eventually one nation, God has painstakingly planted the seed of salvation and nurtured it until the whole earth is involved. Isaiah had sensed that day in terms of a sunrise dawning with the light of day on a world of darkness, with all the hope and joy and relief that a new day can bring after a long, dark night. Probably this was one of the prophecies these magi had read as they studied the signs of the sky and wondered about life's meaning. And perhaps it was then that they felt stirring in them a profound calling to be, in person, those visitors who could symbolise the light dawning on the wider world. Certainly they must have been inspired by a powerful sense of urgency and necessity to make such a journey. And as they travelled, both physically and spiritually, towards Bethlehem, bearing the gifts laid down in those ancient scriptures, perhaps they were drawn by much more than a star. Jesus later proclaimed that anyone who sets out to search always finds.

Paul also knows himself to be commissioned to explain God's nature to the Gentiles. He is overwhelmed by the extraordinary way that the Christ has enabled us to approach the great and awesome God with freedom and confidence – as one of the family.

And for all of us who are Gentiles, the feast of the Epiphany is particularly one to celebrate, since it marks the truth that we too are part of God's salvation and can share the light of dawn.

All-age talk

Beforehand arrange for a knitter to bring a completed garment to church, together with a ball of wool and needles. Also prepare a large paper cut-out of a similar garment, which is folded up so that the first bit that would be made is the only piece showing. Alternatively use the actual garment, folded up at that point.

Begin by showing everyone the wonderful garment that the knitter has made and asking how long it took to make and who it is for. What did it look like at first, when they started making it? The knitter can show the ball of wool and needles, and do a couple of stitches. Hold up the needles with these stitches and point out that it doesn't look much like a jumper/scarf yet! But the knitter went on working at it, knowing that one day it would be ready.

God knew that one day everything would be ready for Jesus to come into the world, but he, too, took a long time making things ready. He started by calling one person, Abraham. (Show the folded garment, but don't refer to it – it is there to be a visual reinforcement of what you are saying.) Over the years God went on to prepare all Abraham's family. (More of the garment is revealed.) Until over more years that family became one nation. (Reveal some more of the garment.) But God's plan still wasn't finished. He went on to include not one nation but all the nations and everyone in them. (Shake the whole garment out and display it.) Today is called the Epiphany because the word 'epiphany' means 'showing' or 'revealing' or 'manifesting', and when those wise men arrived at Bethlehem with their presents, God was showing or revealing himself not just to Abraham or his family, not just to the whole nation of Israel, but to all the rest of us in the world as well.

Whatever country you come from, whatever you look like and whatever language you speak, God is saying to us today that he is there for you and no one is left out. You don't have to have the right ancestors to know God. You don't have to pass any exams to know God.

We sometimes get so interested in the presents the wise men were bringing to Jesus that we forget what brought them there in the first place. It was God who called these wise men from other nations to be there when Jesus was still a baby, so he could welcome them as well. They were there representing all the nations, so when God welcomed them he was welcoming each of us.

The Baptism of Christ

Thought for the day

Jesus is baptised, and God confirms his identity and his calling.

Reflection on the readings

Isaiah 43:1-7
Psalm 29
Acts 8:14-17
Luke 3:15-17, 21-22

Choosing names for our children is an important job, and one which most family members are more than happy to help with! Using one another's names in conversation is an important way of emphasising our concern for one another as precious and unique. To lovers the name of the beloved is deeply emotive. To be known by name indicates a closeness of relationship which as humans we value. It was hearing her name spoken that made Mary Magdalene realise she was in the presence of the risen Jesus.

As the Isaiah passage reminds us, God has called each of us by name; he knows and loves us as individuals, with our own particular mix of gifts and problems. The redemption he brings is personal and answers our particular deepest needs. It is good to celebrate this on the day we remember the Baptism of Christ, since each person's Baptism is not only their decision to commit themselves to Christ, but also God's calling to each by name.

We are told that at Jesus' Baptism the Holy Spirit descended on him in bodily form like a dove, as he stood praying. God was confirming Jesus' identity as his Son, with whom he was well pleased, and affirming his calling as Saviour of the world.

All-age talk

Using a flipchart, OHP or large sheet of paper and thick pens, collect everyone's suggestions about what water can do. Some of the suggestions can be drawn rather than written, so that the non-readers can also join in.

Read through all the suggestions to celebrate them, and talk about how Baptism picks up on these qualities of water and uses them to teach us spiritual things. When we are baptised we are 'drowned' to the old ways, given new life, washed clean, and refreshed. If it is practical, have water in the font and pour it as you explain each quality and its spiritual meaning.

Remind everyone that today we have heard about Jesus being baptised, and as he was praying the Holy Spirit came upon him, looking rather like a dove flying down to rest on him. And God told Jesus that he was God's Son, and God was well pleased with him.

Point out any dove symbols there are in the church – in carvings, pictures or windows – and have a cut-out dove shape (you can use the picture below) to show everyone. The dove has become a sign or symbol for the Holy Spirit because of what happened at th ⌐ ·· ⸍ ⸏

When we are baptised God calls us actually by name to follow him, and sets us apart to love and serve him through the whole of our life. We can only do that with the gift of the Holy Spirit, so that is what we are given. The more we use it, the more it will grow. The sign of the dove will remind us. Whenever we see a dove or a pigeon, or a wild goose, it will remind us that we belong to God, and have chosen to follow him.

Epiphany 2

Thought for the day

As a marriage celebrates the beginning of a changed, new life for the bride and groom, so our loving, faithful God has chosen us and is ready to transform our lives for the good of the world.

Reflection on the readings

Isaiah 62:1-5
Psalm 36:5-10
1 Corinthians 12:1-11
John 2:1-11

Today the nature of our relationship with God is expressed in terms of marriage. Starting with our experience of the best in human love, we can use this to imagine the totally loving, totally faithful nature of our God. Really, of course, it is the other way round: being made in the likeness of God we share, in part, his capacity for faithfulness and loving which is often expressed in the decision to marry the object of our deep love and affection.

At a marriage celebration there is in many cultures a symbolic change of name, to signify that there has been a fundamental life change and that the two are now one. In a similar way God first loves us and chooses us, and then calls us onwards into so changed a life in him that it is often referred to as being born again into a new life.

The passage from 1 Corinthians explores how this new life in the Spirit manifests itself. Paul is anxious to make it clear that there is no rigid format for our new life. It is as varied and diverse as we are, reflecting all the richness of individual gifts. But for all the differences there is a bond of unity, because all these gifts are expressions of the one Spirit. We can get ourselves unnecessarily worked up about the distribution of such gifts. If, instead, we keep our eyes on Jesus, the gifts can be received and valued wherever and however they happen to show up.

The transformation of our lives could not be shown more dramatically than in the Gospel event of the water being transformed into wine at the marriage in Cana. The ordinary is turned into the remarkable through contact with and obedience to the word, or Word, of God.

All-age talk

Beforehand ask someone in the congregation who still has their wedding dress or bridesmaid's dress to bring it along. Several people could do this – they won't have to wear them unless they want to! Ask a happily married couple to be prepared to talk about their wedding day.

Introduce the people and their wedding dresses, bringing out how special they are because of it being such a special day in their lives. Talk to the married couple so that they show how their love for one another brought them to marriage and how the wedding day emphasised the important step they were taking. If there are couples soon to be married, this would be a good time to pray for them as they start their new life together.

Through the prophet Isaiah, God tells his people that his love and faithfulness are a bit like that of a devoted bride and groom. We have been loved and called, and chosen to live a new life together with our God. He will take us just as we are and gradually change us into being more richly ourselves than we could ever be on our own.

Today's Gospel was all about something changing. Water was changed into wine. That happens naturally every year as the rain falls and gets drawn into the vine to make grape juice, and then the grape juice is fermented carefully to make that new drink – wine. But that wedding day in the town of Cana was different because the change happened straight away. Ask the married couple if they had ordered enough wine for their wedding, and then go over the wedding story and the way Jesus transformed the whole situation. John, who wrote this account, tells us that it showed the disciples they could put their trust in Jesus.

That is true for us as well. Whatever has gone wrong in your life, whatever makes you really sad or angry or disappointed, God will take and change so it can be used for good. Nothing you have to suffer will ever be wasted if you stick with Jesus, and do as he tells you.

Epiphany 3

Thought for the day

The meaning of the scriptures is revealed to the people.

Reflection on the readings

Nehemiah 8:1-3, 5-6, 8-10
Psalm 19
1 Corinthians 12:12-31a
Luke 4:14-21

Sometimes we may be reading a very familiar passage of scripture, yet for the first time it seems to shoot out at us with great significance and we realise with a shock that it is exactly what we needed to hear. When this happens it reminds us of the way the scriptures are much more than historical data and fine literature. They are also in-breathed with God's presence so that through them we can be given God's guidance.

As the law was read out to that ancient crowd in the square in front of the temple, we can imagine their emotions: sorrow and grief as it suddenly dawned on them how they had neglected their spiritual heritage, the yearning to put things right, and the joy that at last they were able to see things more clearly. It seems to be a hallmark of God's way of doing things that instead of condemnation, he gently brings us to see for ourselves what and where we are wrong, and gives with this insight a joy and excitement at the prospect of putting things right.

In the Gospel we see another congregation, gathered and attentive as the scriptures are read. But there is a difference, which Jesus must have been aware of even before he started his teaching. These people were his own people, the people he had grown up with, representative of the chosen people of Israel. They are privileged to be hearing the scriptures explained by the Word of

God in person. And yet whether or not they were able to receive him and what he said would depend on where they were spiritually as they sat there that morning. Jesus cannot but reveal to us the truth, because that is his nature. If we are to recognise it as the truth, we need to make sure we are open and receptive.

The Church is a body of people, rich from its diversity of types and gifts, and strong when it recognises its unity in Christ. When as a body we are open and receptive, the life of Christ in us can speak out love and truth to the world. But wherever individual members lose their receptiveness to Christ, the whole body is seriously weakened.

All-age talk

Begin by telling everyone you are going to drop a pin. Ask people to raise their hand if they hear it. (If the building is large, choose something slightly noisier to drop.) Point out how they all listened to be able to hear it. Today we are thinking about careful listening. Tell everyone you are going to drop the pin again, and this time ask them to notice what their bodies are doing to hear such a little sound. When you have dropped the pin, collect some of the things people have noticed. (These might include things like concentrating, waiting, being very still, cutting out our own noises, putting our better ear forward, turning our hearing aid up a bit.)

Today we are told that God is often revealed or shown to us through the scriptures – through the words in the Bible. (Hold a Bible and open it as you talk about it.) In our first reading we heard how all the people gathered in the square in front of the temple and had God's law read out clearly to them so they could really understand it. And when they heard it like this, they couldn't wait to start living the way they knew God wanted them to live. The reason they heard God's voice that day was because they were really trying to listen, like us trying to hear the pin drop.

When Jesus went to preach at his local synagogue he taught the people that the prophecy from Isaiah was coming true that very day. The ones who were listening as carefully as you listened for the pin dropping would have been very excited. Jesus was giving them a very strong clue about who he really was. And it isn't every day you have the promised Messiah turning out to be someone you grew up with!

The trouble is that lots of them weren't listening at all. And in our lives we are often so busy and preoccupied with things that don't really matter that we make too much noise to hear the still, small voice of God telling us really important things about what is right and what is wrong, and how we can live good lives, full of honest, loving behaviour.

God will always whisper what is good and true and loving to help us. We won't hear an actual voice because God can speak straight into our hearts and minds, so we will just know, suddenly, that what we are doing is very good or very bad, very thoughtful or rather selfish and unkind. Once we know, we can stop the wrong behaviour and change it. But we do need to get used to listening so we can hear God clearly.

Epiphany 4

Thought for the day

At eight days old, Jesus is presented in the temple, and at the Purification is revealed to Simeon and Anna as the promised Saviour who is able to reveal to us our true selves.

Reflection on the readings

> Ezekiel 43:27–44:4
> Psalm 48
> 1 Corinthians 13:1-13
> Luke 2:22-40

This week is the last in the series of 'showings', or Epiphany. Simeon and Anna are wonderful examples of the elderly faithful who have stayed spiritually flexible and alert throughout their long lives. Simeon has been told by God that he will see the Messiah in person before he dies, and we can imagine his excitement as on this particular day he feels drawn to go to the temple court. His trust in God is such that he will not be thrown by anything unexpected, and as soon as he sees this unremarkable little family walking in with their new baby he knows beyond all doubt that this is the child he has been waiting all his life to see.

As the wise men were in a sense representative of all Gentiles, so Simeon and Anna are representative of the faithful remnant of Israel, watching and waiting with Godly living and a hopeful heart. Typically, God nudges them to be there at exactly the right time to witness God's Son being presented in God's dwelling-place, the temple.

Ezekiel's vision of a guided tour around the temple reminds the people in exile of their glorious heritage, and it is interesting to have this particular passage today. We are bound to pick up echoes of only the prince being allowed to enter by the holy gate, as we hear of Jesus being carried in and recognised by those who are wise and mature in the Spirit. God's glory is expressed both in the awesome beauty of holiness and in the immanent vulnerability of a human baby.

Simeon has no problem with Jesus being the light for the whole world because he has never allowed legalism to hide or quench the flame of truth. But this perception also enables him to see something of the inevitable, 'suffering servant' role the Messiah will have as he reveals people to themselves. Some will find this the key to new life, while others will prefer to reject the light of truth. Simeon can see that an intrinsic part of saving through love and truth is making enemies and meeting conflict and suffering; suffering that this young woman, his mother, is bound to share.

The beautiful and familiar Corinthians passage in praise of love speaks of Godly love that has no limit, the kind of love exemplified in the life of Jesus. The closer we stay to Jesus, the more loving we shall become ourselves, and the more our potential selves we will become.

All-age talk

Today is a good opportunity to celebrate the elderly faithful and build relationships between young and old.

Beforehand arrange for an elderly man and woman to sit at the front with a microphone to answer a few questions put to them by the children about what life was like when they were children. Gather the children round their feet and introduce the elderly people. Since they have been alive a long time they have picked up lots of wisdom. They have lived through things the younger ones here have heard about in history. Invite the children to find out what it was like being a child 70 or more years ago – they can ask about clothes, toys, school, church or food, for instance. After a few questions thank the volunteers and have the children escort them back to their seats.

In today's Gospel we heard about Joseph and Mary bringing the baby Jesus into the temple. All Jewish families did this when their first son was born. They came to give a present, or offer a sacrifice to God and dedicate the child. We've had two wise, elderly people answering questions today. And when Mary, Joseph and Jesus came into the temple there were two wise elderly people there. Their names were Simeon and Anna. They had both loved God all their life, and if any of us do that, we will end up wise and lovable in our old age. You can't love God all your life and end up crabby and narrow-minded.

Jesus didn't have a big label tied round his swaddling clothes saying 'I am the Messiah'. Joseph and Mary didn't wave flags or shout to everyone, 'Look! This is the baby you've all been waiting for!' From the outside he looked just like any other baby, and Mary and Joseph looked just like an ordinary, fairly poor set of parents, rather dusty after the journey.

So how did Simeon and Anna know that this baby was the one they were waiting for?

Simeon had been told that he would see the promised Messiah in person before he died. He had been listening to God all his life, and because he was used to listening to God, he was able to recognise that this particular baby was the Messiah, God's chosen one.

When we spend a lot of time with another person we get to know how they think, and we understand them better and better. If we spend time with God every day, starting from today, and carry on doing that right into our old age, we will get to know him better and better, and it won't be long before we are able to hear what he speaks into our hearts. It is astounding that the powerful creator of this universe is happy to communicate with individuals like this, but that's God for you. He's hoping there will be some wise and faithful elderly Christians in the future – twenty, thirty, forty, fifty, sixty, seventy or eighty years from now. There could be. It could be us.

Epiphany 5

Sunday between 3 and 9 February (if earlier than 2 before Lent)

Thought for the day

God calls his people and commissions them.

Reflection on the readings

> Isaiah 6:1-8 (9-13)
> Psalm 138
> 1 Corinthians 15:1-11
> Luke 5:1-11

We can be driving along the motorway without a care in the world until we glance at the petrol gauge and discover that we are about to run out of fuel. Suddenly we are anxiously watching the miles to the next service station, and at the first opportunity we drive in with great relief to sort things out. Similarly, it is only when we suddenly catch sight of God that the meanness of our lives sharpens into focus and we cannot wait to put things right. Before we noticed, we were quite happy to carry on as we were.

It is when Isaiah sees that vision of God in glory that he is suddenly aware of the lack of righteousness and integrity both in his own life and his society. It is when Simon sees the signs of God's power in the catch of fish that he feels completely unworthy to be in the company of Jesus.

At this point it is always God's nature to reach out and never to condemn. Isaiah has his guilt taken away by the angel's burning coal from the altar, and Jesus rescues Simon, telling him not to be afraid. Our God is full of compassion and mercy, and will never take advantage of us at moments of weakness or vulnerability. The realisation is necessary for restoration to happen but, the moment we see the problem, God helps and enables us to put things right.

Only after this does God commission us, involving us and working with our consent each step of the way. All three characters in our readings today – Isaiah, Paul and Simon – have been made so acutely aware of the need that they enthusiastically agree to work with God. I love this characteristic of God's; the way he almost gets us thinking his commission is our idea! Sometimes after prayer about something we will get a sudden and unexpected good idea which we can't wait to put into practice. It may well be that God was speaking silently into our hearts.

As a result of God's commissioning, the good news is spread. Those who have recently had their eyes opened are still excited by what they can see, and their excitement is infectious, so they are particularly effective at spreading the news.

All-age talk

You will need a mirror. First do a spot of face-painting on a volunteer, writing their own name in mirror-writing across their face. Then show them their face in the mirror. They will be surprised at what they look like because it isn't their familiar face looking back at them. Yet it is their own named self they are looking at.

Whenever Jesus met up with people he seems to have been able to show them who they were; what they were really like. By the things he said, the stories he told, and by the signs and miracles he did, people were able to look at him and suddenly see something about themselves they hadn't realised before. Some suddenly realised that they were lovable and important, when they had always thought they were rubbish. Others suddenly saw that they were living very mean, selfish lives, and knew they wanted to change.

In the event we hear about today, Simon Peter has been fishing all night long without any success at all. It's possible that Jesus had watched them, and noticed how they carried on even when they were tired and disappointed. Perhaps Jesus brought that into his teaching, and the fishermen would have sat up on the beach and thought, 'This man really knows what it's like to be a fisherman like me, working all night with nothing to show for it!' So when Jesus suggested they try again, Simon was doubtful, but willing to give it a go. The huge catch of fish, coming suddenly after all that time they had worked in vain, must have given Simon a shock. It was a bit like looking in a mirror and seeing who he really was for the first time.

He saw that this man Jesus, who had been sitting in Simon's own fishing boat talking to the crowds, was different from anyone he had ever met before. His goodness, his wise teaching and his knowledge of where the fish were, all made Simon suddenly ashamed. We don't know what it was in Simon's life that went through his mind. It might have been some particular sin he still felt guilty about, or it might have been remembering all the general meanness and selfishness, or the bad temper he knew he had.

The important thing for us to look at is how Jesus helped him see himself, and then said, 'Don't be afraid, follow me.' That is what Jesus does with us today as well. So be ready for it. If something makes you suddenly see yourself and you don't like everything you see, Jesus will not be standing at your elbow, saying, 'There's no hope for you, then, is there? You might as well give up.' He will be there, speaking into your heart words of love and comfort and hope: 'Don't be afraid of what you really are. Come and follow me.'

Epiphany 6

Sunday between 10 and 16 February (if earlier than 2 before Lent)

Thought for the day

The challenges and rewards of living by faith.

Reflection on the readings

Jeremiah 17:5-10
Psalm 1
1 Corinthians 15:12-20
Luke 6:17-26

It is always noticeable how much less you spend if for some reason you can't get out. Shops rely on our habit of browsing and getting what we don't particularly need. Several times an hour on radio and television we are persuaded to invest in all those things we cannot possibly live without, and the social pressure to wear or use or play with particular brand-name items is very strong. The young, and the insecure, are particularly vulnerable.

Such consumerism is a symptom of our trust in things and systems and wealth and power. We bank on all this bringing us happiness and fulfilment. And although the actual items change across the centuries, the basic problem is exactly the same now as it was in the days of Jeremiah. Through him God spoke to his people of the foolishness of living with our faith in things which cannot ever satisfy and which stunt our spiritual growth.

The lovely image of a strongly rooted tree near the water, so that its leaves are always green, shows up the blessings to the whole community, as well as the individual, that spring from right living, based on trust in God. Psalm 1 also reflects on this valuable fruitfulness of well-rooted lives.

Jesus' teaching in today's Gospel comes after the resentful anger of the teachers and Pharisees resulting from his healing on the Sabbath, and after the apostles have been chosen and called. Luke sets the beatitudes on a level place with a large crowd, and Jesus is looking at his disciples as he speaks. We can only guess at what was going through the minds of these people. They have given up their security and their earning potential, they have no idea where their next meal will be coming from, and they have glimpsed the hostility they are inviting by committing themselves to walking around with this leader.

Jesus speaks into their possible misgivings and natural concerns, reassuring them that although they have chosen poverty, insecurity, insult and rejection, they have indeed chosen wisely and bravely, and the rewards of living by faith are great and lasting. In contrast, those who cling to the material, intellectual or even religious security, which stunts their growth and anchors them to the ground, can never be swept up in the wind of the spirit and experience the fullness of joy God longs to provide.

The quantity of our possessions does need looking at, and we cannot sweep such teaching comfortably into the realm of attitudes towards our wealth and lifestyle. If we are really living by faith in God it is bound to affect our comfort. If we know we have given up anything or any relationship for the sake of living God's way, then today's Gospel is reassuring and comforting us that we have chosen well and in the long term the tears will be wiped away.

And if we discover that much of our happiness is linked with things, or systems, or other people's praise, then today's readings challenge us to choose the risky vulnerability of living instead by faith in God.

All-age talk

Beforehand gather a selection of brand-name items relevant to each age group in the congregation.

Begin by displaying each item and drawing attention to the brand name to impress people. Talk about how we are sometimes made to feel we have to have a particular thing in order to be thought normal or worth anything. Sometimes we are teased if we haven't got them. Sometimes we go out shopping to cheer ourselves up, thinking that having more will make us happy. Sometimes we spend money we can't afford to keep up with our friends or neighbours.

Put all the items into a carton labelled 'Very Important' and close the lid. Explain that Jesus turns our ideas of what is important upside down. As you say this, turn the carton upside down. Today we have heard Jesus telling the people that trust in what you can buy and possess is not the good thing the advertisements say it is, and these things don't give us long-term happiness at all.

So what does he offer instead?

Jesus says that we will be much happier if we trust in God rather than in things people say about us, and things people make and sell. Getting stuck in the 'wanting something else' mode or the 'everybody else does it' mode just ends up making us dissatisfied and greedy and selfish, which doesn't bring happiness to us or those we live with. But if we put our trust in God, all the riches of the kingdom of God will be ours. We'll enjoy the lovely and surprising ways God provides for our needs. We'll be able to see what is good and right, and want to work enthusiastically again instead of just going through the motions. We won't be frantically running to keep up with the latest fashion. We won't be so anxious about material things.

Jesus doesn't say we'll have lots of comforts or fame or money if we live like this. In fact he says we will run into insults and people will think we're crazy, and they will laugh at us and make life difficult for us. We can't say we haven't been warned!

But the rewards far outweigh the disadvantages. Putting our trust in God will enable us to live as free, contented and generous-hearted people – the kind of people we would, deep down, probably prefer to be.

Epiphany 7

Sunday between 17 and 23 February (if earlier than 2 before Lent)

Thought for the day

Jesus teaches us to love our enemies and forgive those who sin against us.

Reflection on the readings

> Genesis 45:3-11, 15
> Psalm 37:1-11, 39-40
> 1 Corinthians 15:35-38, 42-50
> Luke 6:27-38

The last time the brothers had seen Joseph they had just sold him to some traders and they were about to tell their father that he had been killed by wild animals. No wonder they are afraid when Joseph turns up in this position of power and authority.

Surely he is bound to want revenge? But no. Instead we find him overjoyed to see his brothers again, and able to recognise the good that has come from a terrible situation. There is no bitterness or harboured resentment, and it is a mark of Joseph's closeness to God that he is able to behave like this.

So often we insist on carrying grudges, and they weigh us down. They imprison us and prevent us from knowing inner peace. In advising us to forgive those who sin against us, and to love our enemies, Jesus is actually setting us free from the chains we clank around with us, sometimes for years.

Jesus would not have been talking simply to a group of friends and sympathisers at this point. Among his hearers there were no doubt some who regarded Jesus as their enemy, so this teaching was very close to the bone. While your heart is filled with hurt and anger and hatred towards someone, the last thing you want to do is love and forgive them. It can be a real battleground as we wrestle with our rage and disappointment and frustration, and it is important that we don't pretend these feelings are not there. To squash such emotions deep down inside us and sit on them is in no way forgiveness. Yet neither are these very real emotions an excuse for permitting us to behave badly.

We do need to recognise and acknowledge them, asking for God's grace to transform what is going on inside us, and then face the battle which may be long and difficult. But if we really want God's will to be done in us then we are playing on the winning side, and victory over revenge, resentment and hatred will eventually come. That victory is a cleansing and wonderfully refreshing desire to forgive. And it melts the hatred away.

All-age talk

Beforehand ask the children to make lots of paper chains.

Remind everyone of what Jesus teaches us in today's Gospel: to love our enemies and forgive those who sin against us. How on earth are we supposed to do it? Surely enemies are people you hate? Why does Jesus tell us to love them, then?

Ask a volunteer to run and skip around a bit and talk about how life can feel when we are happy with ourselves, and everything is going well for us. But sooner or later we get into a mood with someone, someone upsets us and annoys us, someone else winds us up, someone makes our life a real misery, someone lets us down and spoils our plans, someone hurts a person we love, or someone steals from us a close friend or a marriage partner, or our dignity in old age. (At each suggestion, drape a chain around the volunteer until s/he is smothered in chains.) And if we haven't forgiven these people who have sinned against us and hurt us, we end up still carrying invisible chains which weigh us down. The volunteer can walk around bowed down with the heavy chains.

So when Jesus says to us, 'Love your enemies and forgive those who wrong you', he knows it is hard, but he also knows it will set us free to live fully again. Every time we say (and really mean it) 'I forgive you for what you did', a chain drops off. (Pull a chain off the volunteer.) Every time we wrestle with our feelings of hate for someone and ask God to help us sort things out, a chain drops off. (Pull off another chain.) Pull off the remaining chains, with everyone saying 'I forgive you!' for each one.

Jesus doesn't like to see us weighed down with heavy invisible chains of hate and resentment and bitterness against people. He wants us to be free to enjoy life, and he will always help us to do the forgiving. Forgiving is not easy; it's very hard work. If you know there is someone you are finding it very hard to forgive, ask God for the grace to forgive and then work at the forgiving. Don't live with the chains any more.

Second Sunday before Lent

Thought for the day

'He commands even the winds and the water and they obey him.'

Reflection on the readings

Genesis 2:4b-9, 15-25
Psalm 65
Revelation 4
Luke 8:22-25

As humans we are naturally curious about who we are and where we came from. We first wonder about these things when we are toddlers and are still thinking about it a lifetime later. Today's creation story is the older and more primitive of the two in Genesis. What truth does it proclaim? How does it help us in our understanding of the human story?

We find here that God is in charge, and his provision is both complete and flexible. He moulds the man and other creatures from mud, starts a garden, and operates on the man so that both he and the woman are of the same material; they are one flesh. There is a sense of a child creating a world in a sandpit – with all that care and overall vision deciding where things should be and how they should be done. There is close, practical involvement and good communication. God and humankind are working together. There is the energy of youth and the wisdom of age. So in this ancient story we can sense the truth of God's power, authority and sheer goodness, together with his intimacy with the humans he creates.

When we are living in harmony with the God who created us, there is indeed an inner peace which not even the best relaxation CDs can imitate, nor the best whisky provide. It comes free and holds us firm through the turbulence of a lifetime and beyond.

It is interesting that when the disciples in the storm wake Jesus in their terror of the life-threatening wind and water, he first calms the storm and then challenges their own inner storm of panic. 'Where is your faith?' he asks. We no doubt sympathise with the disciples here! Surely we are allowed a bit of panic at such times? But Jesus is drawing them to such a deep, secure knowledge of God's protective indwelling that they don't need to lose it completely even when threatened with death. If we think of the radiance of Stephen as he was stoned, for instance, we can see how such faith transforms our reaction to any disaster.

What the disciples began to understand through this experience in the boat, was the link between this extraordinary friend and teacher they had discovered, and the God of all creation.

All-age talk

Borrow a toy farm set, or a play-mat with animals, houses and cars to arrange on it. Also borrow any remote control vehicle.

Set the youngest children arranging their landscape in a space where they can be seen. Then have the remote control vehicle demonstrated in the aisle. As it is directed to run in different directions, talk about the kind of control the demonstrator has over the vehicle; the vehicle has no choice in the matter. Look at the kind of control demonstrated in the children arranging the animals and buildings. Here, too, they are deciding for the animals what is the best place for them to be. These decisions may be sensitive and based on what the animals would probably like best, but still they have no choice, and must remain in the pond or looking over a fence where they are placed, unless the children decide they need a change.

What about our behaviour in this service? We mostly all sit/stand/kneel in all the right places very obediently, though no one can make us join in attentively if we choose not to, and we could, of course, choose to be very disruptive and spoil it for others.

The Bible tells us that God cared about the people he made. As soon as Adam was made he was invited to help God and share in his work. God would bring the animals to Adam, and Adam named them. (Take some pictures or animal models to the children and let them name them.) The gardening was not drudgery, but wholesome and rewarding work, with God and people working together.

This is a picture of us all living in harmony with God, obeying him, and living as he suggests is right and good for us. It isn't remote control, with God making us do what he wants. It isn't God doing what is best for us whether we want the best or not. It is God loving us and inviting us to work with him. He lets us choose whether to live this way or not. He hopes we will choose what he knows will make us really deep-down happy, but if we choose ways that mess things up for us or others, he won't stop us. He will just be there ready to dry our tears and help us try again when we realise how foolish we have been.

Sunday next before Lent

Thought for the day

God's glory makes Moses' face radiant, and it transfigures Jesus as he prays on the mountain. Our lives, too, can become increasingly radiant as the Spirit transforms us.

Reflection on the readings

Exodus 34:29-35
Psalm 99
2 Corinthians 3:12–4:2
Luke 9:28-36 (37-43)

Those who are not committed Christians will often express disappointment at the selfish or immoral behaviour of churchgoing Christians. They obviously expect that our faith should make a big difference to the way we look, think and behave. I find this quite encouraging. Obviously it needs to be recognised that the Church is a 'school for sinners' and for those who know their need of God, rather than for the perfect. But it also suggests that those who make such remarks hang on to a belief in God's transforming power. And they are right to, because God can and does transform his close followers.

Moses, communing as a friend with God, comes away from the meetings with his face radiant and wears a veil to cover it. The veil prevents the people from seeing the glory of God which terrifies them, and Paul sees this as a foreshadowing of the way the people cannot or will not discern the glory of God revealed in Jesus. When we recognise Jesus it is as if the veil is finally lifted, and as we draw closer to God in this new relationship, the Spirit can begin to transform us until our lives begin to shine.

So why don't they? Sometimes they do and we don't notice. It is quite likely that if you told someone you had seen God's love in the way they behaved they would be surprised. It may be that people have seen his radiance in you on occasions. You cannot spend your time regularly in God's company and work at living his way without it changing you and making you beautiful. But we also have to recognise that half measures are not good enough, Jesus always presents us with this challenge: 'Who do you say that I am?' What we reply has a lot to do with recognising the glory shown in the Transfiguration, and that will affect how we decide to spend our time and money and choices.

All-age talk

You will need a hand mirror.

Begin by asking everyone if they have noticed how people often look like their pets, particularly dogs! Perhaps they choose a pet which reflects their own character. Today we are looking at how spending our lives with God makes us more and more like him.

Use the mirror to catch the light and throw it on to people's faces. Mirrors are excellent at spreading light around, because they are able to reflect light. In the first reading today we saw Moses, who was a close friend of God. He was the person who led the people of Israel out of Egypt, where they had been slaves, and through the desert to the promised land. When Moses had been on a mountain in God's company and was given the Ten Commandments, he came down from the mountain with his face glowing and radiant. Like a mirror, he was reflecting some of the glory of God.

Sometimes if people are really happy – a bride and bridegroom getting married to the one they love, students hearing they have passed all their exams really well, or children on their birthday – we talk about them looking radiant, or glowing with happiness. How we are feeling and thinking inside changes the way we look.

When Jesus was on earth, three of his close friends were on a mountain with him when he was praying, and they saw him not just with a radiant face, but completely shining, or transfigured. What they were seeing was the glory of God in Jesus, who was and is completely at one with God, his Father. They heard God's voice explaining who Jesus was and telling them to listen to him.

Not like listening to music in the background, but really attentive listening, like you would listen to instructions for flying an aeroplane if you were the only person on board able to bring it safely to land.

When we live our lives close to Jesus like this, listening to his quiet voice guiding us, talking over our problems and happiness with him, and working at living a good life, then gradually our faces will start to show some of God's glory, and our lives will start to shine, reflecting God's loving nature like mirrors (flash the light again) reflecting the light.

Lent 1

Thought for the day

Following his baptism, Jesus is severely tempted out in the desert, and shows us how to overcome temptation.

Reflection on the readings

Deuteronomy 26:1-11
Psalm 91:1-2, 9-16
Romans 10:8b-13
Luke 4:1-13

We often use temptation as an excuse for sin. It is Satan's whispered lie that when temptation gets too strong we have no hope of resisting and can somehow plead diminished responsibility. So it is quite an eye-opener to watch Jesus in action. After all, the temptations are exceedingly powerful, and the stakes are so high. If the powers of darkness can sabotage God's plan of salvation almost before it has started, then humankind will be gloriously and utterly lost and God will have failed. Arrogance, as well as deceit, is a hallmark of Satan.

So how does Jesus deal with these temptations, and what can we learn from him to help us when we too are severely tempted?

One thing Jesus doesn't do is enter into an argument with Satan. He would lose, because temptations are always cleverly constructed and entirely logical, with enough truth in them to make them appear plausible. What Jesus does is to recognise the motive under the scheming and address this instead, reaching into the secure promises of God and holding firmly on to these.

Using the vulnerability of Jesus' hunger, Satan subtly grafts this on to a challenge to his role and authority so that we can barely see the join. Jesus refuses to get drawn into this, and recognises that the fast is making him vulnerable, so he encourages himself with God's words which affirm what he is doing and its value. In the next temptation Satan attempts to take Jesus' pondering over his mission and his urgent longing for the coming of the kingdom, and to distort this into the need for a quick and immediate answer, which Satan offers to provide. Jesus recognises Satan's apparent generosity for what it is, and reaches into the firm law of God to deliver another simple one-liner: We are to worship only God. End of story, end of negotiation.

In the final temptation, where Satan again homes in on Jesus' longing to draw people to recognise God at work among them, the longing is manipulated into the possibility of bypassing the expensive and time-consuming method of salvation by love. Discerning that Satan's 'helpful' suggestions are really about denying God's sovereignty and total righteousness, Jesus reminds himself as well as Satan of the command not to put God to the test.

All too often we let ourselves get drawn into Satan's arguments. Think of those times your conscience will whisper that you shouldn't be doing what you are, and all the justifications pour into your mind. If we take Jesus' example, we will refuse to listen to these plausible arguments, and reach instead for the deep truths we know of God, recognising that Satan will use our vulnerable areas, and try to distort our noble ones. If we stick firmly with the truths of God, they will reassure and affirm us enough to resist temptation. Contrary to what Satan tells us, temptation can be resisted and overcome.

All-age talk

On matching sets of three graded sizes of card, from A5 to huge, write these two messages, with the print and thickness increasing with the card size.

I want it and I want it now.
Love God and love one another.

Begin by explaining that Jesus went into the desert after he had been baptised, and had a very hard time out there being tempted. We all know what it feels like to be tempted. It's when we want something or want to do something which we know is wrong. (Show the middle-sized 'I want it and I want it now' card.) Ask someone to hold this card, but don't make them stand with their arms in the air for ages.

Jesus was being tempted to turn the stones into bread so he could eat them, but he knew that this would be using his power in a selfish way. He remembered that he loved God and he loved other people (display the largest 'Love God and love one another' sign). Ask someone else to hold this up.

As you can see, the love for God and other people stayed bigger than the temptation, and so Jesus was able to stand firm and not let the temptation get the better of him.

Whenever Jesus was tempted he always remembered that his love for God and other people was much stronger than the 'I want'. Put these signs down.

Now let's see what happens with us. First we get a little temptation inside us. (Give one helper the smallest 'I want' sign.) It isn't very big and we remember the right way to live (give the other helper the middle-sized 'Love God' sign) so we don't give way to the temptation.

But as we think about it more, this happens. (Exchange the small 'I want' for the middle-sized one.) And now there's a battle going on inside us, because the 'I want' is the same size as the 'Love God'. If we're not careful the 'I want' will get even bigger! (Swap it for the largest 'I want' sign.) And when we let the 'I want' get bigger than the 'Love God', even for a minute, we're in danger of falling into temptation, and doing or saying what we really know is wrong.

Jesus shows us how not to do this. As soon as you feel a little 'I want' coming on (show it), remember that you love God and you love other people more than you want what is wrong. (Display the middle-sized 'Love God' sign.) And if the 'I want' gets bigger in you (show the middle-sized 'I want') think hard about how you and God love each other (show the largest 'Love God' sign) so that the 'I want' is less strong and you can fight it; and instead of giving in and doing or saying what you know is wrong, God will be helping you to stand up to temptation and win.

Lent 2

Thought for the day

If only we will agree to put our faith in God, he will fill our lives with meaning and bring us safely to heaven.

Reflection on the readings

Genesis 15:1-12, 17-18
Psalm 27
Philippians 3:17–4:1
Luke 13:31-35

On those occasions when you know the answer on a TV quiz programme and those on the panel don't, it's quite likely that you will be calling the answer out to them. The frustrating thing is that of course they insist on taking no notice of you, oblivious to your offers of help!

I sometimes wonder if God must feel the same frustration with us when we so often live oblivious to his offer of help and guidance. Not exactly like the TV panel, who actually cannot hear, even if they want to, but more like parents who must watch their child getting deeper involved in an unhealthy relationship which they know will end in misery, while their misgivings are dismissed as nagging, or simply ignored.

Jesus had so often longed to gather up the people of Jerusalem as a hen gathers her chickens to safety under her wings, but there is no way he will force his love and help on anyone, and if people refuse to come, he will always let them go the way they choose.

Yet the benefits from putting our faith in God are so remarkable. Today we see Abram believing God's promise in spite of its unlikeliness, and experiencing the power and greatness of God as the covenant is ratified. Psalm 27 is full of hope despite difficult circumstances because of the psalmist's trust in the faithful God. Such faith anchors us. It roots us so deeply that we are able to open up and live vulnerably. It enables us to stand firm through all circumstances and be less thrown by whatever life flings at us.

All-age talk

Beforehand collect some 'special offers' from your junk mail during the week and from local shops. Also make one sign that says, 'Not today, thanks!' and another that says, 'Yes, I'll go for it!' Ask everyone (or just the children) to shout out the words on the signs whenever you show them.

Start by talking about the special offers in your collection, referring to those which people of different ages in the congregation might find interesting, amusing and completely ridiculous. Ask a volunteer to display the general view of people about various offers by holding up the appropriate sign. Point out that in all these special offers we are free to choose whether to take advantage of the offer or not, and if it's something we really want and like we're likely to say, 'Yes, I'll go for it!' If we don't think we need the item on offer then we don't think it's worth having and we're more likely to say, 'Not today, thanks!'

Jesus' special offer to us is extremely good value. He offers to make himself at home in our lives and set us free from all the things that imprison us, so that we can really live to the full, not just now, but after death as well. For ever, in fact. How much does it cost? Nothing. Or rather, everything, but Jesus has already paid the complete cost for us.

As it's such a good offer you'd think that everyone would rush to take him up on it. (Display the 'Yes, I'll go for it!' sign.) But today's Gospel tells us that there have always been lots of people who have refused the offer and turned it down. (Display the 'Not today, thanks!' sign.) In our Gospel reading we see Jesus really sad. What has made him so sad is that he has been longing to give people the love he knows they need and yet they won't let him give them this free gift which could make their whole lives rich.

Perhaps we don't think we need God's love and help. Perhaps we are afraid to accept because it seems just too good to be true. Perhaps we think it can't be possible because we don't think we're worth something as good as this. Whatever the reasons, lots of us humans end up saying 'Not today, thanks!' to the best special offer ever. That means losing out on all the good things God is hoping to give us during our lives on earth and our lives in heaven. Things like joy and peace of mind, contentment and fulfilment, a sense of really being alive and living life the best way there is.

Abram was a 'Yes, I'll go for it!' person. He took God up on his offer and believed God would put his action where his mouth was. As a result his life was greatly blessed. And God did keep his promise to make Abram's descendants as many as the uncountable stars in the sky.

God will never force us to say 'Yes, I'll go for it!' when we really want to say 'Not today, thanks!' But before anyone says 'Not today, thanks!' to God's special offer of his freely given love, they would be wise to think it over very carefully. It's such a fantastic offer that the only wise thing to say is, 'Yes, I'll go for it!'

Lent 3

Thought for the day

We have God's invitation to come and drink freely of his Spirit, but if we keep refusing his offer it can eventually be withdrawn.

Reflection on the readings

Isaiah 55:1-9
Psalm 63:1-8
1 Corinthians 10:1-13
Luke 13:1-9

When we are seriously thirsty we are no longer bothered about the choice of drink, but simply desperate for water. In extreme thirst the body shrieks for water, and a nomadic desert people would be well used to the power of such thirst. So the image of 'spiritual water' is a strong one, drawing on our life-and-death human need which is both physical and spiritual.

The invitation is not confined to the material or spiritually rich; it is freely available to everyone. Instead of wasting our time and money on poor-value substitutes we might as well go for the real thing: God himself.

So far it is all good news. But there is also a serious shadow which we have to address. God is no fool. He is wise to all our excuses for rejecting his offer. For all kinds of reasons we continue to invest in values and lifestyles and spending and habits which sell us short and bankrupt us spiritually. Sometimes we half convince ourselves that God doesn't notice, or even doesn't mind; that his understanding of why we do the things we do is so tolerant and accepting that we can mostly live as we like, especially if we are being 'true to ourselves'.

In today's reading Jesus is at pains to point out the dangers of living and thinking in this way. Of course it matters. Of course

God knows exactly what we are doing and how we are living. And if we go on and on refusing to accept him on his terms, the truth must be faced that his invitation can be withdrawn.

Lent is an excellent time to look carefully at what our real response to him is, and act on what we see.

All-age talk

Have some different varieties of bottled water and some cups, and offer drinks to a few people around the church. Ask some to describe what it feels like to be really thirsty – when your mouth feels like sandpaper, and all you can think about is the drink you long for.

God says to us, 'I am like a drink of water to you when you're really thirsty. I can quench your thirst, make you feel better, keep you alive, refresh you and comfort you.'

What we need to do is take what God offers us. We need to say, 'Thanks, Lord God. I'll accept what you are offering and drink deeply from you.'

Sometimes if we're thirsty we're not too fussy about the source of the water. (I was so thirsty once in Spain that I drank from a fountain and spent the rest of the holiday regretting it!) Some water isn't clean and can make you very ill. With water we need to make sure we can trust it. And it's the same with spiritual water, too.

Suppose we are thirsty to understand who we are, why we are alive, why there is so much evil and suffering and why things go wrong. There are lots of people offering us easy answers or giving us things to take our minds off this deep thirst. Some of those things (like drugs and alcohol abuse, and materialism) are bad for us.

The only way to be completely and safely satisfied – physically, mentally and spiritually – as the whole wonderful human being you are, is drinking in God's Spirit. Don't be distracted. God is pure, faithful, true and full of love; the best drink there is.

Lent 4

Mothering Sunday

Thought for the day

While we are here in this life, given one another to care for, we can learn the lessons of mutual love and support and shared suffering.

Reflection on the readings

Exodus 2:1-10 or 1 Samuel 1:20-28
Psalm 34:11-20 or Psalm 127:1-4
2 Corinthians 1:3-7 or Colossians 3:12-17
Luke 2:33-35 or John 19:25-27

Both Moses and Samuel were marked and chosen to be spokesmen for God, and today we see the love their mothers have for them; love that extends to the letting go, but is in no way an abandoning or cutting-off.

And in the Gospel we see another side of motherhood, just as real and recognisable. It is the path of shared suffering which all parents will relate to. However old we and they get, our mothers still suffer our hurts with us. Pain that hurts us hurts them too. Simeon could see this shadow in Mary's future, and in John's Gospel we glimpse that tender reversal of roles that happens to many of us as we age, and find that, instead of caring for our children, they have started to take care of us. Jesus shows such loving care as he gives Mary and John one another to love and look after.

One of the greatest gifts God gives us in this life is one another. Together we walk through the years, learning to listen and scold, to encourage and forgive; learning to give and accept, to protect and let go; learning the responsibility of helping those dependent on us and the humility of enforced and unwelcome dependence on others.

And through all of it God gives the companionship and the joy of humans loving one another. There is a place for mothering in all relationships, including, of course, God's relationship with us.

All-age talk

Ask for two volunteers of about the same height (or several pairs of volunteers) and tie the ankles of each pair together. They can practise walking three-legged around the church. As they do so, point out how difficult it is until you get the hang of walking in step with one another. This is one of the most important lessons we can learn in life.

We are all given other people to live with. People in our families like brothers and sisters, mums, dads, grandparents, aunts, uncles and cousins. Is it easy, just because we are related? No! Sometimes it's very good fun, like when we're all getting on together and making one another laugh, and listening to what the others are saying, and the others understanding when you come home fed up.

At other times it's very hard living with those close to us. Like when everyone wants something different and no one wants to do the washing-up, and so on. That's a bit like when we get in a tangle of feet in the three-legged race and trip one another up. When we start to think it would be a lot easier to live on our own without other people around.

What Saint Paul suggests is that we need to live in step with one another, learning to do things like forgiving one another, being patient, letting someone else have the best sometimes, co-operating instead of getting at each other's throats all the time. That's the Christian way. That's Jesus' way. It may also mean comforting one another, sharing one another's suffering. It's really learning to love in the way Jesus talked about love.

When we live like this, we and the people we are joined up with, in our families and at school and at work, won't need to keep tripping one another up. We'll be able to live more supportively, enjoying one another as God meant us to.

Lent 5

Thought for the day

When we are privileged to share in Christ's suffering, we also share in his new life.

Reflection on the readings

Isaiah 43:16-21
Psalm 126
Philippians 3:4b-14
John 12:1-8

Today we become aware of the shadow of the cross as we draw closer to Holy Week and Easter. There is a sense of the inevitable sadness and suffering approaching as we sit with Jesus and his friends, and Mary anoints his feet with the pure nard as if lovingly and lavishly preparing him for death.

Yet, although there is sadness, this is not a time of despair or hopeless resignation. Far from it. Even as Judas dismisses Mary's act as sentimental extravagance, we know that this suffering will be the gateway to something of vital importance. The echoed words of the prophet – 'forget the former things – I am doing a new thing' – bring with them a wonder and excitement for the gathering momentum of Jesus' time on earth.

This is to be greater even than the great escape story of Exodus. This rescue will be God acting in an extraordinary way, breaking completely new ground.

Paul, writing to the Christians at Philippi, gives us such a catalogue of sufferings as to make anyone considering following Christ think again. Why commit yourself to something which will lead you into such discomfort and insult? Yet Paul sounds anything but resentful. He is so impressed by what he has gained in Christ that he's more than happy with the hardships. This suffering is positive and full of hope.

All-age talk

Have some perfumed oil burning throughout the talk, a shell showing the mother of pearl, and a dish of smoothed beach pebbles. Ask for a volunteer and fasten a string of pearls round their neck. Let them walk up and down to show everyone.

Explain how pearls come about, a bit of grit or sand getting inside the shell and rubbing so it hurts. The way the mollusc deals with this is to coat the grit with layers of mother of pearl and in the end something beautiful results from the pain.

Look at a pebble. The beauty often comes from the violent battering and explosive forces of molten rock, which has been worked on by the waves and sand to smooth those scars to beauty. Today we are shown how God can turn terrible suffering into something very beautiful.

We join Jesus with his friends at a celebration meal, knowing that there is suffering ahead. That's never nice or comfortable to think about. We can get some idea of what that felt like if we think of how we feel when we are dreading something. You may be dreading a visit to the dentist or a maths test, or an operation or moving house. You know it has to be done, but that doesn't take away the unease and dread. Jesus knew the suffering would be terrible, but he knew it would be worth it because through it people would be set free from their sin.

At the meal, Mary, one of Jesus' friends, smoothes some sweet-smelling oil on to Jesus' feet – rather like aromatherapy. It was very expensive stuff, and you're probably wondering why she did it. Judas certainly thought it was a waste of money. She did it because she loved Jesus. And she loved Jesus because through him she knew God accepted her as she was and forgave her and loved her. (We all long to be accepted as we are and forgiven and loved. When we are, we blossom; when we're not, we shrivel up inside.)

In Jesus' country it was usual to anoint the body of your loved ones with fragrant oil when they had died, so when Mary poured that sweet-smelling ointment on Jesus' feet she was looking ahead to when he would have to suffer and die out of love for us. Loving us was going to be very painful and cost his whole life, but it would be turned into something beautiful because through Jesus dying we can all know for certain that we are accepted as we are, forgiven, and loved completely.

Palm Sunday

Thought for the day

As Jesus rides into Jerusalem on a donkey, and the crowds welcome him, we sense both the joy at the Messiah being acclaimed, and the heaviness of his suffering which follows. Jesus' mission is drawing to its fulfilment.

Reflection on the readings

Liturgy of the Palms:
Luke 19:28-40
Psalm 118:1-2, 19-29

Liturgy of the Passion:
Isaiah 50:4-9a
Psalm 31:9-16
Philippians 2:5-11
Luke 22:14–23:56 or Luke 23:1-49

It is no accident that the Isaiah reading, the Psalm and the passage from Philippians prepare us to hear the Gospel narrative of the Passion with our hearts as well as our ears. They have been chosen to work on our understanding and bring us to the point where we sense deep truths and echoes of hope, right in the centre of the gruelling and disturbing events of the Crucifixion. And even before these readings we will have joined with the crowds of Jerusalem in waving our palm branches and celebrating Jesus' entry into the city. It is a day of mood changes and can feel quite emotionally draining.

The Isaiah passage introduces us to the concept of the Saviour being a vulnerable, suffering servant, obedient to God's will, and utterly faithful to his calling, in spite of the rejection he receives and the way his mission is misinterpreted. Then the Psalm expresses firm trust in God's loving goodness which continues for ever. This is not a shallow feel-good factor, but a steady pulse of assurance which works in the bewildering and distressing times, as well as the times of relief and light-hearted happiness.

The letter to the Philippians focuses our attention on the amazingly generous nature of Christ's humility. With the Isaiah passage fresh in our minds, we realise that Jesus is taking on that suffering obedience of the loyal servant which is bound to bring with it rejection and worldly failure and misunderstanding.

So when we come to the story of the Passion in today's Gospel, all the echoes from Isaiah, the Psalm and Philippians are there, enabling us to grasp something of the cosmic proportions of what we are witnessing; something of the extraordinary love and provision, gracious humility and total faithfulness of our God.

All-age talk

Ask about football matches people have watched which have been really memorable and exciting. If you happen to have any players in the congregation, ask them to talk about a particularly memorable moment of triumph, and how it felt to have the spectators sharing the exhilaration.

When Jesus rode into Jerusalem all the crowds were on his side, cheering, waving and singing, pushing for the best view, and excited not just with Jesus as a hero but at what was a turning point for their side – their country. There would have been some there on that first Palm Sunday who saw it as a political statement, others as religious revival, others as a festive carnival of some kind.

So why did Jesus ride into Jerusalem on a donkey?

He was doing something the scriptures had said would happen to the promised Messiah. This meant he was giving a very strong hint to the people about who he was. He was saying that the Messiah had now come and was entering the holy city of Jerusalem as a king. But instead of all the rich clothes and grandeur of an earthly king, Jesus was riding on a very humble animal that was often piled high with people's luggage and shopping. It was a bit like using a shopper bike rather than a Rolls Royce, stretched limo or BMW.

All the crowds that day cheered Jesus, but a few days later, once he didn't look like a winner any more, many of the same people had turned against him and were yelling for his blood.

What kind of supporters are we? Do we support our team only when it's doing really well, or do we hang in there even after a run of lost games? Do we stick with our friends even when they go through a bad patch? Do we keep trying even when a marriage gets shaky? And, perhaps most important of all, are we happy to sing God's praise in church on Sunday but ignore him or deny him by our behaviour and language and choices during the week?

These are Palm Sunday questions which we need to ask ourselves today.

Easter Day

Thought for the day

It is true. Jesus is alive for all time. The Lord of life cannot be held by death. God's victory over sin and death means that new life for us is a reality.

Reflection on the readings

Acts 10:34-43 or Isaiah 65:17-25
Psalm 118:1-2, 14-24
1 Corinthians 15:19-26 or Acts 10:34-43
John 20:1-18 or Luke 24:1-12

Throughout the whole world today Christians are celebrating the most extraordinary event. Death, the most final thing we know as humans, has been the setting for the greatest regeneration story of all time. Jesus of Nazareth, handed over to the Roman authorities for execution and a cursed death, has been raised to a kind of life never before experienced. He has a body, the scars are still visible, he talks, listens and eats. Yet he is no longer bound by space or time.

In Christ's risen nature we sense the stirring of that new life described by Isaiah, freed from all the tragedy and pain of mortal life, and full of hope, joy and overwhelming fulfilment. But the Resurrection stories are about people who are emotionally confused and drained. The exhausting events of the past week have them seeing but not recognising, wondering and agonising but not immediately able to make sense of anything. And that is so human and reassuring for us to read.

So often it takes us years of living before we eventually grasp something of God's involvement in our journey or our pain. So often the evidence of his real, loving presence is staring us in the face, and yet we assume any number of other factors are responsible, much as Mary assumed Jesus was the gardener. And Peter was wallowing so deeply in his own misery and pessimism that he probably wouldn't have noticed Jesus if he had been standing there next to him. It may well have been that Jesus was!

With great gentleness and courtesy Jesus holds back on revealing the full power and vibrancy of his new life, so as to lead people at their own pace to recognise the astounding truth. He lets them see only what they are capable of assimilating, for he loves them, and has no desire to scare or overwhelm. That is just as true for us today. The more we seek this risen Lord, the more of him we will notice, recognise and delight in.

All-age talk

Take along a few Easter cards you have received, and show them around, describing the pictures on them. There are probably some fluffy new chicks, young lambs skipping about in the spring fields, lots of flowers, and some decorated eggs. And we probably all gave and received a chocolate Easter egg today. So all this says that Easter is a happy, festive occasion, in tune with the new life of springtime, with all the new birds, animals and flowers.

What else? Some cards have a garden with an empty tomb, and three crosses on a hill in the distance. Others have made all the flowers into the shape of a cross. So what do these cards tell us about Easter? They tell us about another kind of new life, which doesn't happen naturally every time winter is over, but only ever happened once. It wasn't an ordinary thing at all. It was so completely amazing and impossible that people are still talking about it two thousand years after it happened! Do you know what it was? (Let them tell you.)

Well, that's impossible, surely? People can't come back to life again. It just doesn't happen. The fact that it actually did happen – that Jesus really did die on the Friday, and he really was alive again on the Sunday – shows us that Jesus must be more than a human being. He must be God as well as human. And he must be still just as much alive now as he was then. No wonder we want to celebrate and give one another flowers and cards and Easter eggs!

Spring is nice to celebrate, but this is the most wonderful event ever. It means that nothing, not even death itself, is out of God's reach for saving and transforming.

When you eat your chocolate eggs, and open your Easter cards, remember what we're really celebrating today: Jesus is risen. Alleluia! (Everyone can shout back: 'He is risen indeed. Alleluia!)

Easter 2

Thought for the day

Having seen Jesus in person, the disciples are convinced of the Resurrection. We too can meet him personally.

Reflection on the readings

Acts 5:27-32
Psalm 118:14-29 or Psalm 150
Revelation 1:4-8
John 20:19-31

People will often say, 'If I hadn't seen it with my own eyes I'd never have believed it!' Sight is the sense we trust most for evidence and proof. There are many who assume God does not exist because they cannot see him with their eyes, and it is interesting that God has chosen to withhold from us that very proof of existence that we prize most highly. It's almost as if he is challenging us to be less dependent on this sense because our very mastery in sight can blind us to other kinds of perception.

The disciples had the women's eye-witness account to trust, but they didn't trust it. They were only convinced of the Resurrection when Jesus suddenly appeared right there in the room with them, talking with them and fully alive. We may think we are convinced of the Resurrection, but supposing the risen Christ suddenly appeared visually in the middle of our worship, and spoke to you, and looked you straight in the eye. I suspect our conviction would suddenly rocket, and we would be bursting to tell everyone about it.

In the reading from Acts we find the apostles doing just that, and getting themselves into a lot of trouble as a result. They argue that they cannot possibly stop teaching people about the risen Jesus because it's too important to keep quiet about. They are not saying, 'Some people believe that . . .' but 'We know this is true because we have actually witnessed it'.

The really exciting thing is that we can also meet the living Jesus personally. We may not be able to see him visually, but there is no doubt that he is with us in person whenever we gather to pray, whenever we share the bread and wine at Communion, and whenever we 'wash one another's feet' in loving service. Sometimes his presence is full of peace, sometimes reassuring, challenging or affirming, and as we become more attuned to his company, we come to realise that sight isn't the most important proof after all.

All-age talk

Beforehand place a CD in your pocket.

Begin by telling everyone that you have got an orchestra in your pocket and asking them if they believe you. Then show them the CD. Now they have seen with their eyes they know exactly what was in your pocket. And now that they understand what it is, they can see that you were right – you did have an orchestra in your pocket, but not in the way they expected!

Jesus had told his friends that he would have to suffer and die before rising to new life, and they hadn't understood what he meant. Even when Jesus was dying, nailed to the cross, they didn't realise that this had to happen if we were to be saved from sin and death. Instead they felt miserable and let down and lost and confused. They didn't believe because they hadn't seen for themselves. (Put the CD back in your pocket.)

Then, on the first Easter evening, Jesus was suddenly there with them. He was alive, talking with them and they were so excited and overjoyed to have him there again. Now that they had seen him they knew it was true that he was alive. (As you say this bring out the CD from your pocket again, but don't refer to it. It will simply help them make connections.)

But it was also different from what they might have thought. Jesus wasn't exactly the same as before. With this new life he was able to be there without having unlocked the doors. He could appear and disappear. But he was a real person, not a ghost. He didn't make the disciples feel scared; he filled them with peace and happiness.

At last they began to understand what he had meant when he had talked to them about dying and rising again. They began to understand that God's love had to go right through death, loving and forgiving the whole way, so as to win the battle against evil. When Jesus came through death and out into the light of new life, he was like a butterfly coming out of its chrysalis – the same but completely different, free and beautiful.

Thomas and the others needed to see Jesus with their eyes for quite a few times after the Resurrection. They now had to learn that he was always there with them, even if they couldn't see him.

Easter 3

Thought for the day

Those who know Jesus and recognise that he is the anointed Saviour are commissioned to go out as his witnesses to proclaim the good news.

Reflection on the readings

Acts 9:1-6 (7-20)
Psalm 30
Revelation 5:11-14
John 21:1-19

This week the readings invite us to see the consequences of the Resurrection both from a heavenly and an earthly point of view at once, which is a very three-dimensional experience! In the passage from Revelation we see through the eyes of the visionary the ecstatic and eternal welcome given by the inhabitants of heaven to the triumphant Lamb of God, who has proved worthy of all honour, glory and praise through his total sacrifice, self-expending and loving obedience.

From the earthly point of view we have the disciples, so wonderfully human and well-meaning and bumbling, going back to the safe place they came from as a natural reaction to the trauma and turmoil of the present. We recognise the symptoms, as we remember our own tendency to settle into old established behaviour patterns if God's new direction for us is proving too challenging or too open-ended.

So, typically, our God makes his appearance in a place we will be bound to meet him: the place we are fishing in. And as Jesus sets up his camp breakfast on the beach, he gives those friends he loves so fondly the opportunity to discover him, recognise him, and recommit themselves to his way of living. Gently and deliberately Jesus leads Peter to undo those denials and face the dangerous consequences of commitment realistically. There is a maturity about Peter's commitment now which is quite different from his previous enthusiastic claim that he would never forsake his Master. This commitment is quieter, and made with more self-knowledge. Peter is growing up.

Saul, too, receives his commission, and the fiery zeal of his desire to cleanse the Jewish faith of these dangerous heretics crumples in the shining light of Jesus' heavenly presence that he experiences on the Damascus road. Once again, Jesus has made his appearance where Saul has chosen to ride.

Whenever Jesus meets us and challenges us, we become his witnesses and are drawn into a commission which carries great responsibility. Those who have not met Jesus will judge him by the way we behave and speak.

All-age talk

Beforehand prepare some masks from thin card, and mount them on sticks so that they can be held up in front of people's faces. Here is the pattern.

Begin by asking for two volunteers (of different age groups) and giving them a brief interview: What is your name? What is your favourite colour? What do you enjoy doing? How did you get to church today?

Explain that it's nice for us all to know who these people are, and suggest that we all get to know the name of someone in church today. We may see them there regularly but have never actually discovered their name!

Notice how Jesus made a point of calling Simon Peter by his name in today's Gospel. 'Simon, son of John, do you love me?' And in the reading from Acts about Saul meeting Jesus on the Damascus road, again Jesus calls him by his name: 'Saul, Saul, why are you persecuting me?' And on the first Easter Day when Jesus met Mary in the garden he called her by her name, and that's when she recognised him as Jesus.

Produce the 'happy' mask and ask for a volunteer to 'wear' it. Talk about the way we sometimes pretend we're different from the person we really are, because we think God and other people will like us better. This person is pretending to be happy. But if we are pretending, and God knows that inside we are really feeling very grumpy or sad, then the mask we are wearing makes him sad. This person is pretending to be very holy and good. But if we are pretending, and God knows that inside we are feeling angry and resentful, then the mask we are wearing makes him sad.

Jesus wants us to trust him with our real selves, even the bits where we make mistakes and get our lives in a mess. He speaks to us by our real name and will spend our lifetime teaching us who we really are. (Take the mask away.)

Easter 4

Thought for the day

Asked if he really is the Christ, Jesus directs his questioners to look at his life in action and see for themselves that he and the Father are one.

Reflection on the readings

Acts 9:36-43
Psalm 23
Revelation 7:9-17
John 10:22-30

With the benefit of hindsight we might wonder how people could fail to make the connection between Jesus' way of living and the promise of the Messiah. Surely for anyone fortunate enough to witness the miracles of healing, the teaching and the grace and wisdom of this man, the truth must have been obvious?

But in fact we often fail to notice the obvious, often because what we see is not what we were expecting, and our preconceived ideas can be most effective at blinding us for a while. We must also bear in mind the enormity of the implications for those who met him of Jesus being the Christ. It was vital that such a claim should be very thoroughly checked out and no rash decisions made. Jesus respects where we are all coming from, and his sensible advice to study the facts is a recognition, both of our need to make sound judgement and of the value of using the minds God has given us.

So, if we take Jesus' advice to his questioners and look at the signs and miracles, what do we see? We find deep compassion and love for people. We find the power of forgiveness being used to liberate imprisoned souls from guilt which has weighed them down for years. We even find the authority which can reach into death and pull people out. And, when we look at Jesus' followers, continuing his work in the power of the Spirit after the Resurrection, we see those same powers at work. Peter's approach to Tabitha has close connections with Jesus' raising of Jairus' daughter. Peter is clearly allowing the living Jesus to work through his own body in order to restore this woman to life. It is exactly the same power as we saw in Jesus' own physical ministry on earth.

The evidence points us in the direction of recognising, in the person of Jesus, the Christ or promised Messiah, at one with God the Father, and willing to rescue us as our Saviour. It directs us to see the truth of the Resurrection, as we see Jesus continuing his work through the members of the Church, his body. The Resurrection has made it possible for that life to be spread all over the world and all time.

The readings from Revelation during this Easter season continue to give us glimpses of resurrection life in the context of eternity, where there is lasting healing and total wholeness.

All-age talk

Begin by explaining that you are going to pretend you have just arrived from outer space, and you're going to work out what the climate is on planet Earth. Walk around picking up on the kind of clothing people are wearing and using that to give you clues about the weather outside. Point out that as humans we are quite good at working things out from signs and clues. What can you tell about the faith of the people who built this church, for instance? (People can share their ideas aloud, or with one another in pairs.)

Signs and clues help us to learn about life and make up our minds about the truth of things. If you claimed that you had just had a bucket of water thrown over you, you would expect people to be more likely to believe you if you were soaking wet, and less likely to believe you if you were completely dry. Show some muddy football kit belonging to one of the children. What was Sam doing yesterday, do you think? Is it more likely to be ballet or football?

Today we heard about some people who came up to Jesus at the feast of Hanukkah and asked him to tell them plainly whether he was the Christ they had been waiting for. Jesus told them to look at the signs and work it out for themselves. Let's look at those signs and see where they lead us. Ask for suggestions and then draw the ideas together. Jesus healed the sick, opened the eyes of the blind, gave the deaf their hearing back, and showed people in lots of ways that he loved them and enjoyed their company. And that's just what the scriptures had said the Christ would be like! So the signs lead us to recognise that Jesus really is the promised Messiah, or Christ.

Easter 5

Thought for the day

Christ, breaking through the barrier of sin and death, allows us to break into an entirely new way of living which continues into eternity.

Reflection on the readings

Acts 11:1-18
Psalm 148
Revelation 21:1-6
John 13:31-35

Today's readings continue to help us see events from several viewpoints at once. Rather like those remarkable holograms which burst into three dimensions from a flat surface, we are seeing the Crucifixion and Resurrection of Christ from beforehand, afterwards and in eternity, and these viewpoints, clustered together like this, throw into relief for us the powerful and cosmic significance of those events.

In the Gospel reading, just after Judas has gone out into the night, Jesus looks ahead to the imminent suffering, degradation and failure, and paradoxically claims that the Son of Man is about to be glorified. This is followed by the command given to his disciples to love one another. It is in their self-giving love that people will recognise their allegiance to the God who is glorified by this total expending of self about to be displayed on the cross. God will be glorified by the living-out of forgiving love without limit.

The reading from Revelation enables us to see from heaven's point of view, standing aside from the confines of time, and looking with the eyes of the visionary. There are images of accomplishment and victory over all evil for all time. There is the beginning of what is new, as if we are watching with the shepherds the self-emptying of God in the baby on manger straw, and the sense of that full completion at the end of time when all tears will be wiped away for ever. And stretched across time and space is the God of life, focused in the stretching-out of Jesus' arms for us on the cross.

Barriers crumble in the face of such love, and we see an example of this ongoing process in the reading from Acts, as Peter proclaims and celebrates his realisation that God's saving love is not confined to the Jewish people but is freely available to us all, however distant in years or miles we may be. As Christ breaks through the barrier of death, all new things become possible. If we are resurrection people, our lives will act this out and gather others into the kingdom through the way we refuse to live by the old order of sin, the old prejudices, the old values. Love, though expensive, is the new way to live, and we are to spread it liberally and lavishly without boundaries or exceptions.

All-age talk

Beforehand ask a family to help you by providing a couple of clothing items which are now too small for their child to wear. Or you could borrow a cub/brownie sweater which once you would have been able to get into. Also find a sprouting acorn, or a similar example of life bursting out of confines.

Begin by talking about the way we grow out of our clothes. Sometimes we like a sweater or jacket so much that we want to go on wearing it even when it's a bit short or tight, but eventually we realise that we just can't get into it any more, and we'll have to hand it down to someone younger or smaller. As you talk about this, use the children and their skimpy clothes to illustrate how silly it looks and how uncomfortable it feels to wear something which is much too small for us, and then try the same garment on someone it fits to see the difference.

Remind everyone that we are spiritual as well as physical, and we can grow out of things spiritually as well. Some of the early Christians thought that it wasn't right for non-Jewish people to be allowed to join the Church. Today we heard how Peter realised that was like wearing a sweater which was too small, and God's ideas were much bigger than they had thought. He wanted everyone to be part of his love, with no one left out. So the early Church very sensibly took off that outgrown idea.

When we are very young, we are taught to pray prayers we can understand. That's wonderful. But if we are still praying like a three-year-old when we are thirteen or twenty-three, or fifty-three, we are wearing skimpy spiritual clothes that we have really outgrown. Unless we realise that, and take them off, and find ways of praying that fit, we won't be able to move forward where God wants us to go.

Take a look at the acorn. Acorns are lovely to hold and play with, just as they are. But the oak tree can't become its huge, leafy self unless it breaks out of the acorn, and leaves that behind.

Jesus gives us all a rule, or command. We are to love one another. As soon as we start this kind of responsible, caring love for one another, we are bound to start growing. Sometimes the growing hurts. Sometimes the growing feels exciting. Sometimes the growing is hard work. And always the growing will be breaking out of where we were before. This means that, like children growing taller year by year, we will not be able to keep wearing the same old spiritual clothes. God won't let us get set in our ways because he goes on having exciting plans for us right through our lives, no matter how old we get.

Easter 6

Thought for the day

The continuing presence of God, as Holy Spirit, leads us, as Jesus promised, into a personally guided outreach to all nations.

Reflection on the readings

Acts 16:9-15
Psalm 67
Revelation 21:10, 22–22:5
John 14:23-29 or John 5:1-9

During this time between the Resurrection and the Ascension Jesus continues to prepare his friends for something which is completely beyond their experience. In today's Gospel we hear how he introduces them to the idea of God's personal involvement through the power of the Holy Spirit.

The prospect of having to carry on without Jesus in person among them must have been bleak and daunting to the disciples. Jesus speaks into those fears and assures them of this faithful presence once he has gone from their physical sight.

There is a section of the Bayeux tapestry which is called 'William encourages his soldiers'. This strikes me as a somewhat wry comment, as the picture shows William encouraging them by jabbing at their backsides with a sharp weapon! Forceful encouragement, indeed. But there is in this image an acknowledgement that fear can prevent us from doing what we know is right, and at such times a prod or two sharpens our determination to get the better of our fear.

When Jesus has given us full assurance of God's presence, we are told not to let our hearts be troubled. I suspect this has a sharper edge which is often missed, and we are actually being told not to allow ourselves to be perturbed or shaken by circumstances. Satan can so easily sidle in through our fear, self-doubt and trepidation, and start whispering the lie that whatever we are facing is far too difficult and we are bound to fail. We can prevent that, in God's strength, by refusing to allow such undermining fears access.

In the Acts reading we can see the promised guiding power of the Holy Spirit in action. God's close involvement with his people means that, whenever Christians are attuned to him and make themselves available, they will be led at the right time into the right circumstances where they can be best used for the work of God.

There is an urgency about outreach. We have before us that great vision of all peoples gathering to acknowledge their Creator, and worship the one true God, and whenever we pray the kingdom in, in the Lord's prayer, we voice our longing for the vision to be accomplished. Yet there is still so much to do, so many lives to touch, and each of us has only a lifetime.

Dare we waste any more of it with our own priorities?

All-age talk

First fill the space of the centre aisle with chairs and obstacles. If yours is a fixed pews building, have people to sit down as obstacles in the aisle. Remind everyone of how, in today's Gospel, Jesus was talking to his friends at the last supper they had together before he was crucified. Jesus knew his friends were dreading the future without him being there with them. Perhaps they thought it would be a bit like this.

Ask for a volunteer and blindfold them, twizzle them round and send them off down the aisle. As they walk hesitantly, bumping into the obstacles, you talk about Jesus' friends thinking that living without Jesus around would be like trying to get round the difficulties of life blindfolded, and with no one to help or guide them.

Rescue the volunteer and remove their blindfold. As this person knows, you don't feel very safe all on your own and unable to see where the obstacles are. It is frightening and could be dangerous. Sometimes our life can feel like that, and it isn't a comfortable place to be.

What Jesus wants his friends to know is that God doesn't have that in mind for them at all. Although Jesus knew he wouldn't be there physically with his friends for ever, he promised them that they (and we) would have a personal guide right there with us. Let's see how that changes things for us.

Blindfold the volunteer again, but this time appoint a sensible, caring guide who steers them round the obstacles, talking to them and helping them along. (You may want to have primed this person beforehand.)

Watch them together, and then talk alongside the rest of their journey about God's Holy Spirit being with us to teach and explain things to us, to guide us and help us through the dangerous parts of life, so that we are not left alone, but working in partnership with our loving God.

Ascension Day

Thought for the day

Having bought back our freedom with the giving of his life, Jesus enters into the full glory to which he is entitled.

Reflection on the readings

Acts 1:1-11 or Daniel 7:9-14
Psalm 47 or Psalm 93
Ephesians 1:15-23 or Acts 1:1-11
Luke 24:44-53

The Ascension marks the end of Jesus' appearances on earth and his physical, historical ministry. It is also a beginning, because this moving away from the confining qualities of time and place means that Jesus will be present always and everywhere. It also means that the humanity of Jesus is now within the nature of the wholeness of God. Our God has scarred hands and feet, and knows what it is like to be severely tempted, acclaimed and despised.

In a way, it is at the Ascension that the value of all the risk and suffering involved in the Incarnation becomes apparent. The saving victim takes his rightful place in the glory of heaven, and only that can enable God's Holy Spirit to be poured out in wave upon wave of loving power that stretches to all peoples in all generations.

Amazingly our own parish, our own congregation, is part of this glorious celebration with its far-reaching effects. Each of us, living squashed into a particular time frame lasting merely a lifetime, can be drenched in the power of that Spirit, and caught up in the energising nature of it.

As we celebrate the Ascension we, like the disciples, are expectant with joy at the prospect of the gifts God has in store, and yet still mulling over the breathtaking events of Easter. It is like being in the still centre, in the eye of the storm.

All-age talk

Begin by staging a Mexican wave, which runs through the whole church or assembly. Point out how it only worked so well because all of us as individuals were working together as a unit of energy.

Remind everyone of the events leading up to today, giving them a whistle-stop tour of Jesus' life, death, Resurrection and post-Resurrection appearances. Explain how the disciples needed that time to get used to Jesus being alive and around, though not always visible or physically present.

Now they were ready for the next stage in the plan. Jesus leads them out of the city and he gives them his blessing, telling them to hang around Jerusalem without rushing off to do their own bit of mission work. (Enthusiasm is wonderful but it can sometimes make us race off to start before we've got everything we need.) The disciples have got to wait because God is going to send the Holy Spirit to empower them and equip them for the work they will be doing. This will make it possible for the news of God's love to spread out through the world like our Mexican wave.

When Jesus had finished giving the disciples their instructions and his encouragement, we are told that the disciples watched him being taken into heaven, until a cloud hid him from their sight. Those are the only practical details we have, so we don't know exactly how it happened. But we do know that the disciples were in no doubt about where Jesus had gone, and they were full of joy and excitement as they made their way back to the city to wait for the Holy Spirit, as Jesus had told them to.

A lot of years have gone by since Jesus ascended into heaven – about two thousand years. But that isn't much if you aren't stuck in time as we are, and God isn't stuck in time. He's prepared to wait to give us humans the chance to turn to him in our lives, and we don't know the date when Jesus will return. We do know that in God's good time he will come back, and everyone will see his glory together, both the living and those who have finished the earthly part of their life.

In the meantime, we have been given the Holy Spirit, so that God can be with us in person every moment of our life, helping us and guiding our choices, steering us safely through temptations, and teaching us more and more about our amazing God. All he waits for is to be invited.

Easter 7

Thought for the day

Jesus lives for all time in glory; we can live the fullness of Resurrection life straight away.

Reflection on the readings

> Acts 16:16-34
> Psalm 97
> Revelation 22:12-14, 16-17, 20-21
> John 17:20-26

As we reach the final part of Jesus' great prayer before his arrest, recorded with perception and empathy by John, we cannot fail to be moved by the heartfelt yearning shown there. Jesus truly loves this untidy band of companions, and longs passionately for them to become bound to their God and to one another as they have already begun to in his company. And then we suddenly find that we, too, are being prayed for by our Saviour on the night before he dies. We are the ones who have come to believe through the witness of the apostles, and the years between melt away as we become aware of the personal handing-on in succession, one to another down through the generations from these friends to whoever it was who introduced us to Jesus.

There is a great air of excitement in the readings today, because we don't have to wait to start living this new Resurrection life Jesus promised. Pentecost is only a week away, the Lord reigns, Jesus in glory is also close with us, and the joy of living the risen life is infectious, as the marvellous reading from Acts shows.

In these days before celebrating Pentecost we see the effects of Pentecost, graphically described by Luke. It seems that Paul and Silas were at first content to let the slave girl direct people to the truth about them, but as it went on for days they must have found it getting to them. The imprisoning effect of this spirit on the poor girl must also have been increasingly obvious. Ironically, it is for liberating someone that the friends are beaten black and blue and thrown into prison.

And what do they do? They sit bruised and bleeding in the painful stocks and sing their hearts out, praising God! That is living the new life. That unquenchable, bubbling joy in real, lasting things is what other people notice and are attracted to. That night it changed the lives of the jailer and his entire family, and quite possibly some of the other prisoners as well.

All-age talk

Beforehand ask a few people to bring awards they have been given. These should include things that probably lots of others have as well, such as a five-metre swimming badge and a driving licence. There may also be a darts cup or a music certificate.

Begin by showing the awards and talking briefly to the award-holders about how these have been well earned, and give us an idea of the standard that has been achieved, so they are something to celebrate. Probably lots of us have similar awards that we have been honoured with, which is well worth celebrating. (A round of applause may be in order.)

When Jesus entered heaven, about forty days after he had come back to life on the first Easter Day, the whole of heaven gave him a hero's welcome. They said he was worthy to receive power and wealth and wisdom and strength, honour and glory and praise – everything good they could think of.

They wanted to honour him like this because Jesus had managed to do such an incredible thing. He had lived a human life and gone on loving all the way through it without once giving in to temptation, turning against God's will or putting his own wants first. Through loving people enough to die for them, he had been able to break the hold death has over all of us, so we can live freely and happily in God's company. (Another huge round of applause for Jesus.)

Now go back to the swimming badge. This badge proves that Susie is able to swim. What God is saying to us today is that Jesus has won the victory for us, so we are all able to live this incredible new, free and happy life in his company – the sort of life we saw Paul and Silas living, as they sang their hearts out in the middle of a very nasty situation.

It is as if there's a wonderful pool just waiting for us to enjoy, but perhaps we're only holding our badges at the edge of the pool, instead of getting into the water and using them. Let's plunge into the life Jesus has won for us and enjoy it to the full!

Pentecost

(Whit Sunday)

Thought for the day

As Jesus promised, the Holy Spirit is poured out on the apostles and the Church is born.

Reflection on the readings

Acts 2:1-21 or Genesis 11:1-9
Psalm 104:24-34, 35b
Romans 8:14-17 or Acts 2:1-21
John 14:8-17 (25-27)

In the ancient story of Babel a deep human puzzle is explored. Why is it that, whenever we let our skills and gifts divert us into pride and ambition, we end up bickering and losing our capacity for mutual co-operation? It is a story which provides a useful foil to the events of Pentecost.

For here we have God's answer, and the Babel story turned on its head. God's Holy Spirit, residing in our whole being, opens up the possibility of living as God intended – in harmony with our Creator. That new relationship is bound to spill out into our relationships with one another, and work against the destructiveness we know so well and despair of overcoming.

As the force of the Spirit, coming in great power, surges like wind and fire into the place where the apostles are expectantly waiting, they are completely drenched in the waves of God's energising love. 'Drenched' is perhaps an odd word to use in the context of tongues of flame, but in terms of the Holy Spirit it makes sense, because air (breath or wind), water and fire – those raw experiences of natural power – are all linked with the physical expressions of the presence and power of God among his people.

It is God's nature to warn us ahead of time if something is coming up that he wants us seriously to attend to. The disciples have taken Jesus' prophecy to heart, and have been waiting watchfully and prayerfully for the last nine days since the Ascension. So often we miss God's voice because we are not expecting to hear it. We miss the outpouring of his Spirit in our lives because we are not expecting him to act. Yet as soon as we set ourselves faithfully and expectantly to ask for it and wait for it, God honours the honesty of our longing, and makes his presence known.

All-age talk

Beforehand make five red, yellow and orange flame shapes (about 30 centimetres high) and hide them around the church.

Begin by asking for examples of flames, such as on a gas hob, bonfire, forest fire, log fire, candle, acetylene torch, fire-eater, house on fire, match, oil lamp, steel works, steam engine, lighter, Bunsen burner. Draw people's attention to the tremendous power of some of these and the quiet, gentle nature and soft light of others. Fire is something we all have to respect, as it can burn and destroy as well as giving us light and heat.

Send the children off to search for the five flames that are hidden in the church, and tell the adults about our need to seek out the Spirit expecting to find, just as the children are doing now. They trust that what they have been told to search for will be there, and it will. We need to believe that if we seek God we will find him – and we will.

When the children return with the five flames, you can remind everyone of the way the Holy Spirit is described as being like tongues of fire, with the sound of a rushing wind. (You can get everyone to make this sound as the flame-carriers run round the church.)

Like fire, the Spirit can be strong and powerful in our lives. (The first flame is held up.) Sometimes the Spirit is gentle and quiet, whispering deep into our needs and telling us what is right. (The second flame is held up.) Like fire, the Spirit is warming, spreading love and a real desire to put things right, and stand up for goodness and truth. (The third flame is held up.) Like fire the Spirit is purifying, burning away all that is evil and selfish in us, so that we can become like pure refined gold, glowing with the light of God's love. (The fourth flame is held up.) And, like fire, the Spirit is enlightening, shedding light for us on the Bible, our conversations and relationships and the events of our lives, so that we can see God more clearly through them. (The fifth flame is held up.)

Trinity Sunday

Thought for the day

The unique nature of God is celebrated today, as we reflect on the truth that God is Creator, Redeemer and Life-giver.

Reflection on the readings

> Proverbs 8:1-4, 22-31
> Psalm 8
> Romans 5:1-5
> John 16:12-15

The actual word 'Trinity' does not occur in the Bible, but that is not to say it is not mentioned. As we get to understand the nature of God more and more, it becomes clear that we are wrestling with understanding something quite beyond our human experience. Even though God can make himself and his will known clearly to us along the way of life, there is no way that we will ever be able to grasp exactly who God is and what he is like, at least during our time on earth.

But that's no reason for not trying! Trying to get to grips with the truth about God's nature is all part of our journey into the depth of his being, and as such is immensely valuable. Our readings today are a good starting point.

First we have the poetry of Proverbs, expressing something of the 'community' of God's nature; the way that Wisdom, described as a personality, has been present from the very beginning, and was part of the creative loving process that brought all things into being. There is a sense of harmony and shared delight, along with the everlasting 'now', which we, being time-trapped, find hard to imagine.

Psalm 8 catches the song of Proverbs and dances with it, amazed at the nature of creation and the attitude of God towards it. Humankind is so privileged in having the ability to marvel.

In Romans we sense the orchestration of God; the way that in Jesus it all comes together, and we as humans can be drawn into God's life-giving power which transforms our attitudes to the trials and troubles we are likely to face. God is both transcendent and immanent.

So, when we read in John about Jesus referring to the Friend – the Spirit who will take his followers by the hand and lead them into the truth – in the same breath as he speaks about the Father and himself sharing all things, we can begin to glimpse something of the dynamics of God. Rather as you may look at a speck of microfilm and see it first as a dot which then explodes into a wealth of information when properly viewed, so our initial glimpses of God are going to burst into a dynamic, unimaginable richness which is sensed and worshipped, rather than understood.

All-age talk

Beforehand prepare a cake. Also get together two eggs, a bag of sugar, a bag of flour and some margarine, and a mixing bowl, cake tin and wooden spoon.

Set the cake tin down and tell everyone that today we are going to have a cake, because today is an important day, Trinity Sunday. So we are going to have a Trinity cake. Ask various helpers to bring the eggs, sugar and flour and margarine and place them in the cake tin.

Proudly present the cake, inviting everyone to take a slice, and let the children point out to you that you haven't got a cake at all. You've just got the ingredients. But isn't a cake just ingredients, then? Let them help you understand that you'd have to mix them together and cook them before you had a cake.

Now let it suddenly dawn on you that it's a bit like that with the nature of God. God is the Father who created the world, Jesus Christ who saved us, and the Holy Spirit who gives life to the people of God. But they aren't separate from each other, any more than these separate ingredients are a cake. To be a cake all the ingredients need to be co-operating and working together. Then they become something which is not just eggs, flour, sugar and margarine. Produce the real cake and point out that you wouldn't say, 'Have a slice of eggs, flour, margarine and sugar with your cup of tea.' You'd call it by its name: a cake.

In the same kind of way, when we talk about God we are talking about our Maker, and we're talking about the risen Jesus who has rescued us from sin and death, and we're talking about the Holy Spirit who brings us into new life. We know that the word 'God' means all three persons in a wonderful harmony, a community which is still One.

Give the Trinity cake to whoever is in charge of refreshments after the service, so it can be shared out then.

Sunday between 29 May and 4 June

(if after Trinity Sunday)

Proper 4

Thought for the day

The good news we have been given is not just for us, but to pass on to the rest of the world.

Reflection on the readings

1 Kings 18:20-21 (22-29), 30-39 or 1 Kings 8:22-23, 41-43
Psalm 96 or Psalm 96:1-9
Galatians 1:1-12
Luke 7:1-10

When Jesus commissioned his apostles to go out and make disciples of all nations, he was not breaking with Jewish tradition but taking it one stage further. There had always been the understanding amongst God's chosen people that eventually through them the whole earth would be blessed, and all nations would come to realise that the God of Israel was the one and only God.

We see that in Psalm 96 today, in the fervent prayer of King Solomon, and in the story of Elijah and the prophets' competition when, as a result of what the people saw, they spontaneously turned to worship Elijah's powerful God who had shown himself to be listening and active. All these writings from the Old Testament assume that the truth is for everyone to share.

In the letter to the Church in Galatia it is clear that Paul has been putting into practice the command of Jesus to preach the good news to all nations. He had founded this church community during his first missionary journey, and encouraged the pagans to accept the sovereignty of the living God in their lives. Now he is finding that some of them are being persuaded that in order to become proper Christians they must also be brought under the Jewish Law. Passionately Paul writes to prevent the new freedom in Christ from being clawed back into the past confines of the legalistic traditions of Judaism.

In contrast, we find the army officer, who is not even Jewish, displaying a degree of faith that Jesus finds amazing.

Today's readings raise questions for us about who we should be evangelising, and what expectations we should have concerning rules and traditions, in view of where the unchurched are coming from. What shines out clearly is that outsiders are best persuaded of the truth about God by the behaviour of his followers and the amount of access they allow him into their lives.

All-age talk

Bring with you a newspaper, a TV remote control, a mobile phone, an airmail letter and, if possible, a trumpeter (failing a real one, a recorded version will do nicely).

Begin by picking up the newspaper and reading out a few headlines. Talk about this being one of the ways we use to get other people to hear our news. People used to use a town crier. (You could ask a loud-voiced volunteer to demonstrate. The news they bellow is written on a piece of paper: 'There is only one real God. He made us and he loves us!') Pick up the remote control and explain that now we don't have to shout so loud because we invite the town criers into our homes and sit them in the comer to tell us the latest news. We can even switch them off!

Another thing people used was a trumpeter. (Have this demonstrated briefly.) That got people's attention so they would listen to what you were saying. Now we have this to get people's attention, and get them listening to us. (Demonstrate the mobile phone.) People used to send their news by pigeons, and now we send it on a metal bird. (Show the airmail letter.)

What has stayed the same all through the years is that people always want to pass on their news. And today we are being told that the news the town crier shouted to us (they can do it again) is such good news, not just for us but for everyone, that we need to make sure we pass it on. Like honey or peanut butter, we are not to keep the good news to ourselves, but spread it!

We can tell people about God's love by behaving in a kind and loving way, by being generous with our time and money, by praying for our friends and for difficult situations, by living by God's rules, and by bringing our faith into the conversation instead of only mentioning it among our church friends. And who knows, God may also call some of you to tell the good news as newspaper reporters, in government, on television or as a famous sports star. However you do it, do it!

Sunday between 5 and 11 June

(if after Trinity Sunday)

Proper 5

Thought for the day

Our God is full of compassion; he hears our crying and it is his nature to rescue us.

Reflection on the readings

1 Kings 17:8-16 (17-24) or 1 Kings 17:17-24
Psalm 146 or Psalm 30
Galatians 1:11-24
Luke 7:11-17

Look at a picture of any person's face and you will see that one side speaks more of the hope and happiness and the other side more of the pain and suffering they have known. Although there is widespread expectation that we should be happy in life, the truth is that life is always a mixture of light and deep shadow, and our calling as humans is not so much to be happy as to be real.

God reaches down into our deep shadows and feels with us in the grieving and emptiness there. We see examples of that practical compassion in the readings from Kings and from Luke. With great tenderness, God provides not only for his friend and servant, Elijah, but also for the widow in Zarephath and her son. The flour and oil which never run out are like a sign of God's faithfulness to his people which also never fails.

As God's close friend, Elijah has that same love for people, which is poured out in prayer as he pleads for the child's life. Love is like a channel that cuts through any situation and allows God's healing to happen. Even those who have not received physical healing witness to the way that, through the prayers of faithful people, God has healed their anxiety or their attitude, and enabled them to face their suffering courageously. Many sense that they are being 'carried through' a difficult time.

When Jesus sees the heartbroken widow, with her dead son being carried out of the house, we are told he is filled with compassion, and it is out of this loving that he acts, speaking right into death and calling the young man back, for a while longer, into earthly life with his mother.

In a sense God calls all his people out of death. He calls us into the possibility of a life in which we are no longer living to the old rules of selfishness, but are freed to walk tall in the light and life of God's loving.

All-age talk

Bring with you a pair of balance scales. These can be either a heavy-duty kitchen type or a children's educational toy. You could even use a small portable seesaw and have two children to demonstrate it. It's the balancing of weights that matters.

Demonstrate the scales or seesaw with the help of some children, reminding everyone of the way the scales are balanced when there is the same weight both sides. Sometimes our lives can feel like a seesaw or a pair of scales. We might be really happy, and everything is going well, and our team is winning, and we passed our driving test on the eighth attempt, and our operation was successful, and someone has just changed our nappy and fed us. However old or young we are, we all know what it feels like to have the 'joy' side of the scales full up.

Other times we may feel that everything is against us. Our best friend is moving away to another town, our team has lost for the third time running, the washing machine floods the kitchen, and you fall over and graze your knees. Sometimes the pain is so deep that we can hardly bear it – like when someone we love dies, or we are suddenly let down by someone we thought we could trust, or we are faced with serious illness. We all know what it feels like to have the 'sadness' side of the scales full up.

We heard today about the way God looked after a widow and her son and Elijah, and made sure there was just enough food for them so they didn't starve to death in a terrible drought. And we heard about another widow, beside herself with grief, whose dead son was brought to life by Jesus and given back to her.

So does it look as if our God is only interested in us when the happy side of our scales is full to bursting? No, it proclaims loud and clear that our God is tenderly interested in us all the time, during those terrible times of sadness we sometimes have to go through, as well as the times of great joy we dance through. And that is because he really loves us.

Sunday between 12 and 18 June

(if after Trinity Sunday)

Proper 6

Thought for the day

God has the authority and the desire to forgive our sins completely and set us free from guilt.

Reflection on the readings

1 Kings 21:1-10 (11-14), 15-21a or 2 Samuel 11:26–12:10, 13-15
Psalm 5:1-8 or Psalm 32
Galatians 2:15-21
Luke 7:36–8:3

Most of the time it is not so much a falling into sin as a sliding into sin that happens. Ahab did not simply wake up one morning and decide to have Jezebel sort Naboth out, and David was not the kind of person to stick one of his men deliberately in the front line to have him out of the way. We slip gradually towards committing the terrible wrongs by not paying attention to the top of the slide – sins of pride, greed, laziness and self-indulgence, for instance – which if unchecked will start us sliding further and further into wrong values and wrong behaviour.

Since the slide is often so gradual, we may not notice what is happening, and our readings today show us some examples of the ways God does his best to draw our attention to what needs putting right. Being in the position of God's spokesperson at such times is an unenviable job, but a very necessary one. We may well prefer to wriggle out of the responsibility with the excuse that we don't want to be judgemental. But to avoid alerting someone to a downward slide in their lives is actually unloving behaviour. Provided we ensure that we do it in love, and without being judgemental, it is one of the kindest acts we can do.

Once our attention is drawn to the wrong we have done, or the wrong attitudes we have allowed to become habits, we are faced with a choice. Since it is never pleasant to be faced with criticism, and we have probably put considerable energy into persuading ourselves that our behaviour and attitudes are justifiable, we may wish to go on the defensive, and reject what we have been shown. If we choose that route God is unable to put things right for us.

If, on the other hand, we are honest enough to see some truth in what has been said, we can take that great and difficult step of breaking down our defences before God and acknowledging that we need him to sort things out. God is the only one with the authority to forgive sin completely, and he is very good at it. The other thing about him is that he loves doing it, and will help us as much as possible.

The only way of crawling back to the top of the slide is recognising and acknowledging before God what is wrong, taking full responsibility for it, and expressing our shame and sorrow – our desire to stop and change. It is those who have known the incredible release and joy of God's forgiveness in large measure who have great love for the one who has let them out of their prison.

All-age talk

During the week record a few well-known parish voices, perhaps from choir practice, children's ministry planning, or the scout or brownie meeting. If you can have some photographs taken at such things, these can be displayed as people come into church. You will also need a length of string with a Lego person tied on one end, and a pair of scissors.

Begin by playing the tape and letting people experience the 'Good heavens, that's me!' factor. Remind everyone of how you feel when a raffle ticket is called and you suddenly realise it's the same as the number staring at you from your own hand, or when you catch sight of yourself unexpectedly in a mirror when you're out shopping.

Ahab, David and Simon were all given that shock in our readings today. They had all done wrong, and yet hadn't really recognised it. Now, suddenly, they are shown the truth about themselves, and it isn't a pretty sight.

Like them, we don't always know when we've done wrong or sinned. We might have had a little tug of conscience but quickly stamped it out so we could go on doing what we wanted to be doing! If you're in doubt, think to yourself, 'Am I happy for God to see me saying this, or doing this, or thinking this?' And if you're not happy with God seeing how you behave at school, or with particular people, or at work, or at your club, then the way you are behaving is probably wrong, and you need to change it.

Sometimes we will need to point out gently to one another where we are wrong. That's all part of loving one another and helping one another to live God's way.

Show the piece of string with a Lego person tied on the end. Explain that whenever we fall into sin, we cut ourselves off from God (cut the string and let the person drop). God longs to put things right, but he can't, unless we call out to him and say, 'I've fallen down! I'm sorry!' As soon as we turn to God like that, and ask him to forgive us, he ties us on again so we're not cut off any more. And the funny thing is we end up closer, if anything, because being forgiven is so wonderful that it makes us love God more than ever.

Sunday between 19 and 25 June

(if after Trinity Sunday)

Proper 7

Thought for the day

God is close through all our troubles, and can bring us safely through them.

Reflection on the readings

1 Kings 19:1-4 (5-7), 8-15a or Isaiah 65:1-9
Psalms 42, 43 or Psalm 22:19-28
Galatians 3:23-29
Luke 8:26-39

In the readings today there is no shortage of heartaches. And for many people, it comes as a relief to find that Christianity addresses the pains, troubles and heartaches of life, not by telling us these things shouldn't matter; not by giving us good advice on how to get out of any pit we are in; but by providing a person who is prepared to climb down into the pit with us. For that is what we need at such times, and all we can cope with.

Let's look at Elijah who had so courageously challenged the prophets of Baal, and is now drained and vulnerable, probably exhausted, and temporarily crushed by the powerful dominance of the scheming Queen Jezebel. It looks to him as if everything he has lived and worked for has fallen about his ears, and that, as many of us know from experience, is a desolate place to be.

I love the way God deals with Elijah. First the practical, sensible caring: Elijah is taken to a safe place and given sleep, food, more sleep and more food! Thank heavens for all those practical caring Christians who act out this kind of loving without any questions or deliberations or advice at this stage! Then he is given space and time to come to God at his own pace. We are in such danger of trying to rush healing, with all the counselling piled on at times of heartache, forgetting this need which our God always remembers. Any grief takes time, and we must be prepared to give others that time.

Then comes the close contact, when Elijah is ready for it. Gently God brings him to state the ache, and that may need to be stated more than once. God only continues when he can see Elijah has no further need to state it. Now Elijah is ready to move forward, so it is only now that God gives direction, encouragement and assurance.

What heartache there must have been in the country of the Gerasene people over this wild man, and what turmoil and terror in the man himself. Jesus, with the honesty of love, makes contact with the agonised being trapped inside the horror. The healing holds its own horror, as the drowning pigs give us some idea of the power that had been strangling the sanity of the man. And the people cannot cope. Yet Jesus again gives a commissioning to the released man, knowing that the people need their time and space to come gradually to understand and receive his teaching.

There is much here that we can learn about our own encounters with those whose hearts are heavy.

All-age talk

Bring with you a small loaf of bread, a pillow, a calendar and a clock, writing paper and envelopes, and a briefcase. Place these prominently around the church.

Begin by reminding everyone of how our God hears us laughing and being happy, and is happy for us. He also hears us when we are crying and feeling sad, and his heart goes out to us, and he feels sad for us and quickly comes close to comfort us with his presence. Even if everyone else has let you down and rejected you, God never has and never will.

All of us will have some sad times in our lives, and today we are going to look at how God looks after his friends when they are going through a rough time. So even if you are in a really happy phase at the moment, it's a good idea to be prepared! And if today you are feeling a bit like Elijah, exhausted or chucked out, vulnerable and unable to see any hope, then God offers his help straight away.

Ask someone to go and find something to eat, and something to sleep on. As they go, explain how God is very practical, and starts by providing our practical needs – in this case, sleep and food. As the body of Christ, we church people can do that for one another.

Ask someone else to collect things to do with time. As they go, tell everyone that God gave Elijah time, and he didn't rush him. So we mustn't rush one another to get over a heartache either. People whose loved ones have died, or whose marriages are broken, for instance, need time, and we, in love, must give it to them, just as God does.

Ask someone to find some things for helping us keep in touch. While they are fetching them, talk about the way God was in contact with Elijah, and we are helped in our troubles if God's people make a point of keeping in contact through the dark days, and don't leave us feeling isolated. That's why sympathy and get-well cards, short visits and short phone calls can be so comforting. People need to know that we are all praying for them, too.

Ask someone to find something you might carry to work. As they collect it, talk about the way God knows when we are ready to move forward, and gives us a job to do. The job he gave the healed wild man in the Gospel today was to tell the people in the area about what God had done for him. Elijah was told to go back and continue his former work of being God's spokesman. The job God gives is one that only we can do, and it may well put to use the experiences we have suffered, so that they are turned into opportunities for good.

Leave all the objects out to remind people.

Sunday between 26 June and 2 July

Proper 8

Thought for the day

When we are called to follow Jesus, that means total commitment, with no half-measures.

Reflection on the readings

2 Kings 2:1-2, 6-14 or 1 Kings 19:15-16, 19-21
Psalm 77:1-2, 11-20 or Psalm 16
Galatians 5:1, 13-25
Luke 9:51-62

Both the readings from Kings describe Elisha's calling, first to be Elijah's servant and disciple, and then his successor. In each case the cloak is an important sign of authority and acceptance, and Elisha chooses to take up the mantle, with all the commitment that this involves.

In the reading from Luke other people are called to follow Jesus, and not everyone is prepared to do this. Others enthusiastically offer to come with him, and Jesus has to dampen their enthusiasm somewhat by bringing them down to earth, and making them count the cost of the commitment before they decide. The practical living arrangements, for instance, and probable lack of home comforts, need to be looked squarely in the face before the choice is made.

It is not everyone's calling to wander with Jesus around the countryside, preaching and healing the sick. Equally valid is the ministry of those chatting the good news among their own people in their own towns and villages, and of all those living by God's values in commerce and industry. What binds all these people together, though, is the decision made to commitment.

In the baptismal promises the Church continues to place people on the spot. What commitment to Christ entails is stated clearly, so there may be no misunderstanding, and the candidates are free to choose whether to commit themselves or not. But, having made the choice, there is no getting away from the fact that they are committed to living differently.

As Paul explains to the Galatians, it is for *our* freedom that Christ has set us free, and to settle back into former sin patterns will only enslave us. Living as committed Christians we need to check constantly that we are still walking in step with the Spirit. Paul gives us a whole list of examples to check our behaviour against, so that we can adjust our direction accordingly.

All-age talk

You will need someone who can do gymnastics or dance. Ask them to prepare a sequence of moves which need total commitment in order to work, such as somersaults and cartwheels, pirouettes and arabesques.

Begin by asking the gymnasts or dancers to perform their demonstration. Briefly interview them, thanking them and asking whether they could do these things first time, or whether they had to practise. Draw attention to the commitment that has to be given to anything you want to do really well. You can't 'half do' some of those moves, or you'd probably fall flat on your face.

As Christians we are called to that same kind of commitment. We can't 'half do' it. When we commit ourselves to following Christ, it's going to affect the way we talk, the way we behave with our friends and our enemies, the way we spend our time and our money. It's going to affect all our thinking and the choices we make. So it's a bit like deciding to do a double somersault, or a triple pirouette – it takes a lot of dedication and courage to launch off.

Elisha, in our Old Testament reading today, watched his teacher and master being taken to heaven, and was then chosen to be Elijah's successor. He had been a loyal and hardworking student, and now he was off to carry on his master's work for God. But, of course, he wouldn't be left alone to cope on his own. God was going to be his strength.

Imagine if you were just launching yourself into a triple somersault and all your strength suddenly wasn't there. You'd certainly notice it was missing! In fact, you wouldn't be able to do any of those clever moves without strength.

In our Christian life, God's Holy Spirit is the strength. He enables us to do those triple somersaults of caring love for those we don't much like, and the double pirouettes of co-operating when all we want is our own way. Real loving is very hard work, and it takes lots of dedication. With God's strength we can do it, and then we will be moving freely and beautifully through life, in the way God called us to, and knows will make us, and others, truly happy.

Sunday between 3 and 9 July

Proper 9

Thought for the day

In Christ we become a new creation.

Reflection on the readings

2 Kings 5:1-14 or Isaiah 66:10-14
Psalm 30 or Psalm 66:1-9
Galatians 6:(1-6) 7-16
Luke 10:1-11, 16-20

At first Naaman is most reluctant to take the necessary steps for his skin to be made new. Elisha's instructions are far too low-tech and simple for a man of his standing and intelligence. It's all rather an insult. Yet he was anxious enough to be healed. The skin disease was both irritating and unsightly, and judging by the changes of clothing packed for the journey, Naaman was a fastidious man.

Happily his servants are able to persuade him to put his pride away and try the recommended cure, and he is totally thrilled with the result. We sense his joy and relief as he comes up out of the water with skin as clear as a young child's.

God can give us all that 'fresh as a young child' sensation, as we allow him to make us new creations, born of the Spirit. Paul, writing to the Galatians, sees that a constant battle is going on between our sinful nature and our spiritual nature, and inspires us to go for the better deal of the spiritual nature, which brings joy and lasts for eternity. It is bringing people to enjoy this new creation which is the whole point of our ministry, says Paul, and the religious traditions and habits matter only in so far as they help to make us aware of our need of God's nursing and bathing. The really important thing is being made new.

And there are so many tired and disillusioned souls, all struggling to save themselves, and suspecting their frenetic attempts are actually doomed to failure, if they dared stop for a minute and look. Jesus sees it as a huge harvest, ripe for gathering, but with far too few workers; and people remain trapped in their distracted existence as a result of meeting no one able to offer them the freedom of God's new life.

So today offers us both great hope and a great challenge. Who are the workers to be?

All-age talk

Beforehand write out clearly on different colours of paper, six or twelve (depending on numbers of children expected) healings that may well have taken place when the seventy were sent out. (For example, a blind woman got her sight back; two children were dying of a disease, and now they're playing outside; a young man can now walk again; a boy who stuttered can now speak clearly; a family feud has been sorted out.) Give these to different adults to hold in different places around the church when the talk begins. Also give each adult some food to give the children who come to them. Some will be given a sweet each, some a bun each, and some a piece of dry bread.

Begin by reminding everyone that Jesus sent out seventy of his disciples in pairs, to different towns and villages. Let them suggest some reasons for the disciples being sent in pairs. (Friendly; supportive; safer.) So you are going to send people out around the church in pairs, on a mission to find a notice the same colour as the slip of paper you give each pair.

Before they go, tell them to be careful, travel light, not stop to speak to strangers on the way, eat what they're given, say 'Peace be with you' to the person holding their colour, and tell them the kingdom is very near. Get the pairs to repeat the instructions. As they go off around the church, some people can try to make some of the older ones talk on their way. As they reach their paper, the adult there can remind them of their message, if necessary, and give them their food and the notice. The pairs return to you and you can enthuse with them over all the wonderful things that have happened.

Thank them for all their hard work, and tell everyone about Jesus wanting everyone to be made like Naaman in the Old Testament story today – restored and like a new person. But we're still short of workers in this harvest of people. We need to pray that God will send more workers. And we need to make ourselves available, in case it's us he can use!

Sunday between 10 and 16 July

Proper 10

Thought for the day

Straighten your lives out and live by God's standards of love.

Reflection on the readings

Amos 7:7-17 or Deuteronomy 30:9-14
Psalm 82 or Psalm 25:1-10
Colossians 1:1-14
Luke 10:25-37

It is in today's Psalms that God's standards of loving are clearly and beautifully stated. These precepts of defending the cause of the poor and oppressed, upholding right judgement and caring for those in need, are like a strong heartbeat pulsing underneath the events and stories of the other readings.

Amos, burning with God's indignation at the corruption and idolatry of the practices in the northern kingdom, sees the lives they have built like a leaning wall that ought to be straight and true. Not surprisingly his words, spoken as an outsider from the southern kingdom, and critical of a civilisation which has brought comfort and wealth to many, are received with anger and verbal abuse. It's never an easy life being a prophet. Amos bridles in response. Surely they didn't think he would have chosen to come to their country? Their refusal to listen to God's warning simply proves the extent of their spiritual deafness, which is bound to bring about their destruction.

In the reading from Luke, Jesus is also facing opposition. The seventy-two have recently arrived back, and there has no doubt been an angry backlash from those towns denounced by Jesus for their refusal to receive the message brought to them. The law expert is smugly deprecating as he leads Jesus into a trap, which

Jesus neatly sidesteps, dropping the man in instead. Perhaps he was hoping for Jesus to agree that 'neighbour' only refers to those within the law – such as the denounced Capernaum, for instance?

The story Jesus gives by way of an answer forces him to look with God's measure, or plumb line, at attitudes and assumptions which need a thorough overhaul. The right words may still be in place, so that love for God and neighbour can be glibly quoted, but the spirit of those words has dried up inside and left only the empty shell.

In contrast, Paul is full of thankfulness at the lush growth of the Christians at Colossae, and he prays for that to continue to flourish. For us, too, there are many signs of re-growth and regeneration in the Church, which is wonderful to see. We need to ensure that walls are regularly checked as we build, so they can stay true to God's priorities and values.

And when any prophet speaks out, and what they say is uncomfortable to hear, it is wise to listen carefully, in case the unpalatable is the truth. Prophecy is rather like a surgeon's scalpel: it's worth putting up with being sliced open if it's going to lead to healing and life, rather than death by default.

All-age talk

Bring with you an egg cup, a whole egg in its shell, and a boiled egg which someone has eaten, so that just the shell is left, with a spoon hole at one end. Put this into the egg cup upside down so that it looks like a complete egg ready to eat. You will also need an egg spoon.

Begin by talking about those times you've desperately needed help, like missing the bus when you're already a bit late, or being caught in a downpour on your way to school, and you're hoping one of your friends will happen to drive past and see you. Perhaps the man who had been mugged in Jesus' story felt a bit like that, if he was still able to think after the beating-up he'd been given. Perhaps in the daze of his injuries he heard each set of footsteps coming nearer, and hoped that now he'd get some help. But no, the footsteps quickened up when they got nearer and then went off into the distance again. And the man still lay there, unable to move.

Perhaps he had almost given up hope when the Samaritan, a foreigner, stopped and came to peer at him to see what was wrong. Perhaps, as he swayed in and out of consciousness, he was half aware of being carefully given first aid, of being comforted and reassured that he was going to be all right. Those are good things to feel and hear, when you're in great need. You have no power at such times to make anyone care for you, so all you can do is rely on other people choosing to treat you well.

And that's what we're being taught today: that as Christians we are people called to treat others well, whether we're told to or not, whether anyone sees us or not, whether we want to or not. Why? Simply because our God says that this is the right and good way to live.

In our first reading Amos the prophet was sent to tell the people in Israel that the way they were living was disgusting by God's standards. He said they needed to sort out their values and behaviour to bring them in line with their calling as God's people. They didn't like being told that at all.

And the man in today's Gospel, to whom Jesus told his 'good neighbour' story, could recite the rules he was supposed to live by off by heart: 'Love the Lord your God with all your heart and with all your soul and with all your strength and with all your mind. And love your neighbour as yourself.' But for him and for lots of others, those words are like this boiled egg. It looks wonderful and full of goodness. But if I start to dig into it (do that) with my spoon, I find that all the inside is missing, and there's nothing of any goodness there at all.

We must be brave and dig into the words we sing and pray together today, and look at what we find inside. Perhaps there will be rich meaning, and you will know that the words your mouth says are backed up with the way you live. Perhaps you will find the words are just a shell, and your life doesn't back them up at all. If so, come to God today and ask him to fill the shell with new meaning. He can do that, and he's waiting for you to ask.

Sunday between 17 and 23 July

Proper 11

Thought for the day

Against impossible odds God has reconciled us to himself, in Christ.

Reflection on the readings

Amos 8:1-12 or Genesis 18:1-10a
Psalm 52 or Psalm 15
Colossians 1:15-28
Luke 10:38-42

This week we are given a near-lethal dose of the bad news about human nature. The prophecy from Amos is particularly bleak and depressing because it paints such a true picture of the familiar materialistic, self-orientated world we know, both in society and in the secret places of our own hearts.

What hope can there possibly be? As humans we hold on to a vision of what it ought to be, and how we ought to live, but the disturbing truth is that we seem unable to haul ourselves above the selfish nature that drives us. We may see glimpses of nobility here and there in good men and women doing better than the rest of us, but the main tide is in the other direction, with no real possibility of widespread goodness. In Amos we read of that terrible prophecy of a famine, worse than thirst and hunger, which speaks of us being abandoned for our failure and locked out from all hope, as people struggle and search for the word of the Lord but never find it.

Into this misery and helplessness strides Paul, through his letter to the Colossians, like a being from a new and different dimension, shouting to us over the centuries that we need not despair. Someone has done the impossible, and through Christ

Jesus, stretched out between earth and heaven in love, God has been able to reconcile all things to himself. Far from being abandoned, he has been searching through the rubble and debris of our human situation and has come in person to rescue us.

All-age talk

Beforehand make a pair of large card ears, about 30 centimetres high, and a pair of large card hands, about the same size.

Start by asking for two volunteers, one of whom holds the ears to the side of her head, and the other who has the hands fixed to her own hands with large rubber bands. Remind everyone of the two people in the Gospel for today, both very good friends of Jesus. Their names were Martha and Mary and they were sisters. Jesus often went round to the home where they lived with their brother Lazarus, and they all enjoyed one another's company.

(Alice) is like a cartoon picture of Mary, because what she liked to do was sit and listen to Jesus and she could listen to him for hours. She probably liked listening to all sorts of people, and may have been the kind of person people could talk easily to because they could see she was interested in them. Mary's idea of cooking a meal was probably beans on toast, and she probably didn't notice the dust creeping up until she could write in it.

(Laura) is like a cartoon picture of Martha, because what she liked best was doing things for people and making sure they had clean shirts and well-balanced meals. Her idea of cooking a meal would be something like roast chicken with all the trimmings. If you wanted something done, you'd ask Martha.

Now people sometimes get upset by today's Gospel because they think Jesus is saying that everyone ought to spend their time listening like Mary, and that busy, practical people like Martha aren't somehow as good. But, of course, Jesus isn't saying that at all. His own life was full of work and activity, travelling, preaching, teaching and healing, and none of that would have got done if he hadn't been a doer.

But he also spent hours late at night, or early in the morning on his own with God, talking things over and quietly listening. And he knew that this was a really important part of the doing. He knew we need to keep the right balance between input (the ears) and output (the hands). On that particular visit to Martha and Mary's house, the listening was more important than the doing. What we all have to do is notice when we need to listen, and be ready to stop what we're doing and listen.

All of us need to set aside a quiet time to be with God morning and night, every day. It doesn't have to be long, but it has to be there. If we neglect that, our ability to discern right behaviour will start to slip, and we risk sliding into the kind of life that hurts God so much. Spending time quietly with God is not an optional extra for people with time on their hands, it's an absolute necessity, as well as being refreshing, rejuvenating and problem solving! (If there is a parish or diocesan weekend planned this year you can mention that as well.)

Sunday between 24 and 30 July

Proper 12

Thought for the day

Keep asking for God's Spirit and he will keep pouring out his blessing on you.

Reflection on the readings

Hosea 1:2-10 or Genesis 18:20-32
Psalm 85 or Psalm 138
Colossians 2:6-15 (16-19)
Luke 11:1-13

It is not God's will that anyone should be lost; God longs for all of us to be saved. Each one of the inhabitants of Sodom and Gomorrah was part of God's loving creation, and made in his image. Each person in Israel was known and loved. Those in every generation, who deliberately turn away and feed their selfish nature until they can no longer hear God's prompting, are all cherished and of God's making.

Today's readings remind us of that immense parental tenderness that God has for us. He creates us full of potential and watches over our spiritual growth, ready to bathe us in his light, and drench us in his Spirit. The tragedy is that we so often refuse to let him give us the gifts necessary for our growth.

In the Genesis reading we are given this lovely example of the close relationship shared by Abraham with his God. He is full of respect, and perfectly understands the justice of the threatened destruction, but he feels with his God's love the terrible sadness of waste, and pleads for mercy on behalf of those cities. How his pleading must have made God's heart sing, for here was a man loving in the broad and generous way he longed to see in all his creation.

The passage from Paul's letter to the Colossians urges his readers to let their growth in faith continue to flourish in Christ so that their lives overflow with thankfulness. It is not a question of everything happening at the beginning of our journey when we first commit ourselves. To grow, and to remain in close fellowship with God, we need constant filling up, feeding and guiding on a daily basis. The Bible, prayer and communion are gifts provided for us to use, and without taking God up on these gifts, our spiritual growth will weaken and become stunted.

In the Gospel for today, the disciples ask Jesus to teach them to pray, and the guidelines they are given have been valued by Christians of all denominations and traditions through the centuries. Luke links this teaching on prayer with a whole passage encouraging us to ask for what we need, and ask persistently. God will never force himself on anyone; he waits for us to invite him into our lives, and that is why it is so vital that we do ask and seek and knock at the door.

If we look at many of his acts of healing, we find Jesus often gets people to state what they want; that is part of the healing because God likes to work in partnership with us, not as a take-over bid. So he wants us to wake up each morning and ask that the kingdom may come, that we may have our daily needs provided – both physical and spiritual – and that we may have our sins forgiven and be guided safely through temptation. That way we shall be actively seeking the God who made us and loves us, and has ready all the gifts we need to bear fruit.

All-age talk

Bring along some strips of bedding plants, or a packet of seeds and a flourishing plant of the same or similar variety.

Proudly show the results of your horticultural exploits, and talk about what your hopes are for the seed or the tiny bedding plants. You don't really want them to stay as they are because, although the pictures on the labels show wonderful flowers or fruit, at present they are only dry dusty things, or boring leafy things, in spite of your recent planting efforts. What you are hoping is that they will eventually grow and flourish, until they flower and fruit as you know they can if all goes well.

That's how God feels about us. When he plants us into life, he knows we have lots of potential, lots of good possibilities. Since he loves us, he really hopes that we will grow, spiritually as well as in our bodies. He doesn't want us to stay the same as when we first begin in our Christian life, because he knows that if all goes well we shall one day be full of flowers and fruit that will help the world.

If I want my little plants to grow I will have to give them things like water and food, and make sure I give them plenty of light. And, being plants, they will just sit there and let me give them the things they need to grow nicely. I also need to talk to them!

God wants to give us lots of things to make us grow. He wants to drench us in his Spirit, warm us with the light of his love, and feed us with his word and in communion. He also wants to talk to us! But because we are humans, and not plants, we sometimes turn away from his light, and put up huge umbrellas against the rain of his Spirit, and refuse to let him feed us, and block our ears to stop ourselves hearing what he says. And when that happens, we stop growing and we wilt and weaken, and we never get to bear any fruit.

Today God is saying to us, 'Let me give you the gifts you need to grow as Christians; keep asking me for them, keep looking for me, and I promise that you will receive everything you need to grow into strong, healthy plants with beautiful flowers and fruit.'

Sunday between 31 July and 6 August
Proper 13

Thought for the day

True richness is not material wealth; true security is not a financial matter.

Reflection on the readings

Hosea 11:1-11 or Ecclesiastes 1:2, 12-14; 2:18-23
Psalm 107:1-9, 43 or Psalm 49:1-12
Colossians 3:1-11
Luke 12:13-21

Our culture runs on consumerism, and one of the side-effects of that is an encouragement of greed and increase in the daily temptation through the media to us that security, happiness and peace of mind come from possessions and self-indulgence. It is a myth which has enough truth in it to be dangerous. It undoubtedly helps to have enough to live on, but the wisdom of Mr Micawber holds true, all the same: living within our means is happiness where finances are concerned, and sixpence over that is misery! Many know the misery of accumulated debts resulting from the pressure to live beyond our means and spend what we actually haven't got.

It is a short step from being told that we haven't got something to believing we need (rather than want) it, especially if we can see others who already have it. The 'if only's' set in, with their accompanying sense of discontent and resentment. Equally dangerous is the possession of financial 'security' which can kid us that we have no need of God, so that we shut down our spiritual antennae and grow increasingly oblivious to the needs of others and the glaring inequalities. The preoccupation with protecting what we own is good news for the insurance and home security firms, but bad news for the soul.

Today's readings point out the foolishness of living in this way, and the wisdom of living with our security in the eternal things. Now that Christ has given us a new life, our insurance – or perhaps I should say 'assurance' – is kept with Christ in heaven. The whole yardstick of life is changed, and our time here recognised as only the first part of our full and lasting life. When we really grasp the implications of what Jesus has done for us, it is bound to alter our outlook on what is important to possess and what is of only minimal value.

It is not so much a question of giving away our possessions as changing our attitude to them and recognising them for what they are – pleasant comforts to thank God for, but lent to us to use, as good stewards, and in no way altering our real wealth and security.

All-age talk

You will need the packing boxes for various consumables, such as a computer, electronic game, microwave, brand-name shoes, or luxury biscuits. You will also need such things as a CD, gardening and teenage magazines, and a film carton. Choose the items to suit the interests of the people in your congregation, and have enough for one person to hold all at once with great difficulty. Finally, you need a pocket Bible and a tiny spray of flowers.

Remind everyone of the story Jesus told us in the Gospel today, about the farmer who thought that having a bumper harvest, and therefore a financial windfall, meant total security, so that he could just do as he liked and take no care of his soul. His greed had made him foolish. As it happened, he was going to die and face God that very night, and he wasn't in the least prepared for death.

Ask for a volunteer to help you explain something. Explain how all the advertisements tell us that if we get a particular brand of yoghurt or car or shampoo, everyone will like us and fancy us, and we'll be really happy. Sometimes we get taken in by this lie, and start wanting to have things so we'll be safer or happier or better liked.

Go through the things we like to get, piling the packages into the arms of the volunteer as you talk. When they are completely loaded up, and have no hands left to hold anything else, point out the problem with all this 'having' being important to us. It means that when Jesus offers us his Word and his Love (offer the Bible and flowers), we simply haven't room to take it, and we turn it down, because our minds are too full of what we've got and what we want, and how we're going to hang on to what we've got.

And that is a tragedy that lasts not just for a few years but for ever. We need to put down our wanting and having, so that we can take the really important wealth that God offers us. (The volunteer is helped to unload, so they can hold the Bible and flowers.) These are the things which will make us content and happy and secure, whether we have all the other good things or not.

Sunday between 7 and 13 August

Proper 14

Thought for the day

Have faith in God, and get yourself ready to meet him.

Reflection on the readings

Isaiah 1:1, 10-20
Psalm 50:1-8, 22-23
Hebrews 11:1-3, 8-16
Luke 12:32-40

The Gospel reading for today begins with such an affectionate reassurance. It is God's good pleasure and delight to give us the kingdom; everything is in hand, and nothing can ever tear us apart from the God who loves us. The only way separation can happen is by us choosing to walk away ourselves. So our God has us safe and expectant, knowing that there are great things in store for us both in this world and the next, even though we cannot see them.

And that is the faith God looks for in his people: believing the hope as a fact and trusting that what God has promised will indeed happen. The reading from Hebrews recalls the extraordinary faith of Abraham, God's close friend, in the way he was prepared to launch out into the unknown on many occasions, simply because God told him to. Not only did he believe that God had authority which asked for obedience; he also knew that God's responsible, caring nature would ensure that placing himself in the hands of his Lord was a sensible and safe thing to do.

So Abraham's faith determined how he lived. That always happens; you cannot trust the one true God and go on behaving with corruption, deceit, injustice or self-glory which you know to be totally alien to his nature. But it is, of course, perfectly possible to pretend you have faith, and go through the rituals of words and worship, while your eyes stoically avoid God's gaze, and your life proclaims that you actually despise the one you claim to worship.

It was exactly this which so wounded the heart of God about the people of Israel, to whom Isaiah was sent. How could God accept their offerings when they were living a lie? Hypocrisy and corruption creep up on us insidiously, minor detail by minor detail, so that we end up fooling ourselves that wrong is right. Sometimes we can fool others, too. But God we do not fool, and his reaction is to try to shake us out of the lie we are in, because he hates us being there and knows it causes all kinds of stress, whether we recognise that or not.

Having faith means looking seriously at the God we claim to believe in, and checking that our lives, in every aspect, in secret and in the open, are lined up with those qualities of truth, love, integrity and right action which are hallmarks of God and his friends.

All-age talk

You will need a pair of swimming flippers. Have ready a couple of large freezer labels with the words 'I believe in God' written on them.

Ask for a volunteer to walk up and down the church, so that everyone can see the way this person normally walks. Now give them the flippers to wear. As they are being put on, explain that today's readings teach us about how our faith in God affects the way we live. Remind them of Abraham and the way he was ready to get up and go when God asked him to, even though he didn't know exactly how the move would work out. He trusted God to want the best for him, and had faith that God would look after him.

Now that the volunteer is wearing flippers, is he going to walk in the same way as before? Well, let's see. As the person walks up and down, point out that we can all see the effect the flippers are having on the walking – it's a very distinctive flipper walk! Put the freezer labels on the flippers, explaining that when we decide to walk with faith in God, that is going to affect the way we walk through life. It will give us a very distinctive faith walk. The readings today tell us the kind of things to expect. We will be stopping doing what is wrong and learning to do what is right. We will be noticing the needs of those around us and in our world, and making sure we help out with our time and prayers and money. We will be building up treasure in heaven by our loving kindness, patience, honesty, thoughtfulness and self-control.

Sunday between 14 and 20 August

Proper 15

Thought for the day

When we fix our eyes on Jesus our lives will reflect his nature.

Reflection on the readings

> Isaiah 5:1-7 or Jeremiah 23:23-29
> Psalm 80:1-2, 8-19 or Psalm 82
> Hebrews 11:29–12:2
> Luke 12:49-56

Many parents have high hopes for their children. Musical toys are given encouragingly to offspring who start singing in tune before they can talk. Balls to kick around are bought partly for fun and partly to foster any latent talent. Financial sacrifices are made for children showing potential in particular sports or arts. It would be cynical to think that all this is 'pushy parent syndrome'; mostly it shows the natural pride and delight of parents in the children they love.

God, too, has high hopes for the children he loves. He delights in our progress, and looks out for the seeds of gifts he has given us to blossom; he loves to watch us using these gifts for the good of the world. Today we sense God's sadness as he looks for the good and wholesome we are capable of as his creation, and finds instead destructive selfishness, bloodshed and cries of distress. We all know the aching disappointment of an attempt which has failed, in spite of the lavish care we have invested in it. Sadly we have to recognise that sometimes our behaviour, both collectively and individually, disappoints our parent God.

Such behaviour and attitudes are a waste of our life. The writer of the letter to the Hebrews urges us to get rid of everything that hinders and entangles us, so that we can run the race more easily and comfortably. And the best way of doing that is by keeping our sights fixed on Jesus. It is noticeable throughout history that whenever people have done this they have been enabled to bring about great good, both within the Church and in society. It is when their eyes swivel round to fix on other things that corruption, distortion of truth, and injustice start taking over. Rather like bindweed, they can look attractive, but throttle the life out of whatever they climb over. And the roots need to be totally eradicated to prevent strong re-growth. Jesus warns his followers that the path of righting deep-rooted wrong will not be straightforward or without radical disturbance and upheaval, not only in individuals, but also in families and nations and church communities.

All-age talk

Beforehand prepare a number of heavy carrier bags and a rucksack, and have a sack or strong dustbin bag. Label the bags 'I want my own way', 'It isn't fair', 'So what?', 'I'll never forgive them' and 'No one will notice'. Also bring the local school's PE kit.

Begin by showing everyone the PE kit and draw from them what it is, who wears it, and why we do PE dressed like this instead of in our best clothes, or in bridesmaids' dresses, or Mickey Mouse suits. Establish that it's more practical and comfortable to wear light clothes like this which don't get in the way of our running and jumping.

Refer to the letter to the Hebrew Christians in which following Jesus through our lives is said to be a bit like running a race: we need to look where we're going. That means keeping our eyes on Jesus and his way of living. This will keep us on the right track in our own lives, reminding us to be honest instead of telling lies, thinking of other people's needs instead of just wanting our own way, and sharing our ideas and fears with God instead of ignoring him most of the time.

But often we run our Christian life in very unsuitable clothes. At this point ask for a volunteer, and load them up with all the bags, explaining what each represents, and how we weigh ourselves down with all this luggage. As you hand over the sack for them to stand in, point out how difficult we make it for ourselves by hanging on to all these attitudes which make Christian living extra hard. The volunteer can try running to prove the point.

Today we are being given a useful tip for Christian living: get rid of all these unhelpful habits (name them as you take them from the volunteer), so that we are free to run God's race-track uncluttered and 'light'. Then we can concentrate on Jesus, and learn to live his way – the way of love.

Sunday between 21 and 27 August

Proper 16

Thought for the day

God sets his leaders apart to challenge prejudices and assumptions, and alert people to the truth.

Reflection on the readings

Jeremiah 1:4-10 or Isaiah 58:9b-14
Psalm 71:1-6 or Psalm 103:1-8
Hebrews 12:18-29
Luke 13:10-17

The crippled woman, who made her way into the synagogue on that Sabbath day, would have had her eyes, as always, fixed on the floor in front of her. Her bent back meant that she had to put up with a very narrow field of vision. When Jesus released her spine to move from its locked position, she could at last look ahead, up and around with a wonderful new freedom, which thrilled her and set her praising God. Her life would have changed completely now that her 'outlook' had been so freed.

Others in that congregation were equally locked, with a cripplingly narrow field of spiritual vision. They had reduced the keeping of the Law to a complicated set of detailed rules, and had spent so much energy focusing on these that they could no longer see the spirit and essence of the Law, guiding people to love God and love one another. When they were faced with the possibility of being released from their narrow field of vision, they could see it only in terms of broken rules.

Not only Jesus, but also all the prophets of the Old Testament and all those commissioned from the New Testament down to today, are called by God to speak out and challenge people's assumptions and prejudices – to straighten the spiritual backs of the narrowly visioned. God longs for his people to be free, and wherever people have become spiritually jammed, God raises up someone to offer them release and a fresh start.

Today we are urged to take God up on his offer of release and new vision, and not to miss out on the possibility of our whole life and outlook being transformed just because we have become used to living and behaving in a particular way. As the crippled woman found, it's worth straightening up.

All-age talk

Bring along a couple of long scarves tied together.

Ask a volunteer to help you explain today's teaching, and get them to stand on the scarf. Wind the scarf round the back of their neck, and join the two ends so that the volunteer is forced to stand bent forward, looking down in a fixed position. Looking sideways is quite difficult, and looking up and into people's faces is almost impossible. Remind everyone of the crippled woman in today's reading from Luke's Gospel, whose back was set into this position so that she had lived the last eighteen years of her life looking down at her feet, unable to see the world properly, or have a face-to-face conversation.

What Jesus did was to release her from this locked position. When he saw her he felt so sorry for her and longed to set her free. And when he placed his healing hands on her back and told her she could now move again (untie the scarf), she found that she could stand upright, and see all around and look into people's faces again! That felt wonderful, and she praised God for all she was worth.

Now ask for another volunteer, and tie them up in the same way. Explain how people can be just as crippled and stuck in their thinking and living, even though their bodies look and work quite normally. Habits of grumbling about everything, wishing for things we can't have, or being so set in our ways that when God asks us to help someone we see it as impossible because it doesn't fit in with our plans – these things can mean that spiritually we are stuck and unable to look up and around. So can spending all our time thinking of one thing, whether that is a hobby, an addiction, an ambition, our health or fitness, or even a person. If we haven't looked up to God's face for ages, we might find we're stuck in the 'head down' position.

God is offering to release us from such crippling habits. He is the one who can put his healing hands on our lives (untie the scarves) and set us free again. It feels so good, and no one needs to stay trapped any longer.

Sunday between 28 August and 3 September

Proper 17

Thought for the day

When we live God's way, both individually and as a community, we will be greatly blessed.

Reflection on the readings

Jeremiah 2:4-13 or Ecclesiasticus 10:12-18
Psalm 81:1, 10-16 or Psalm 112
Hebrews 13:1-8, 15-16
Luke 14:1, 7-14

In the reading from Jeremiah there is a powerful image of a broken, leaking well. God grieves because his people have chosen to reject the life-giving springs of his pure water which never dry up, and decided instead to do their own thing and build these wells which are cracked, so any water they collect quickly runs away. The wells of their own making are vastly inferior and they don't work; yet still the people choose to trust these, rather than God's blatantly superior offer.

Often when people are first converted, they are bursting to tell people about the God they have just discovered, and can't understand how anyone could not want what they have found, even though for years they themselves have also been struggling with leaking wells without realising the reality of God's alternative. The more Christians there are gossiping the good news among their own contacts in a regular, informal and friendly way, the more chance there is of people hearing about God's offer at the point when their hearts are ready to listen.

It was at a 'Sunday dinner' equivalent, as one of the guests, that Jesus brought the conversation round to what people needed to hear, spoken anecdotally and through the after-dinner stories. They described a way of thinking that was quite radical, turning accepted values upside-down and suggesting a way of living which could liberate people and transform them.

The reading from Hebrews provides us with some good, practical guidelines for living God's way, both as individuals and as a community. All the behaviour described is a natural result of loving one another as brothers and sisters – as 'family'. We are advised to pray imaginatively for prisoners and all those who suffer – 'as if you are there with them'. There is a great sense of the importance of community, with the mutual care and respect that results from being bound together in love. Perhaps we need to recover some enthusiasm for community again, and recognise that in God's way of living, individuals have a calling and a responsibility to be members of a corporate unit of loving: the Church of God.

All-age talk

Bring along a front door mat (if possible with 'Welcome' on it), an oven shelf, a first-aid box and temperature chart, a white flower, a purse or wallet, and a stone or piece of local rock. Also ask a happily married couple of many years if they would mind standing up at one point in the talk to help people focus on faithfulness. Place the objects (but not the married couple!) on a table at the back of the church, so that people pass it as they walk in, and start wondering.

Begin by asking everyone which they think would be better for drinking from – a fresh water spring that even bubbles out during dry weather, or a well which is cracked and leaks so the water doesn't stay in it. When they choose the spring, remind them of how sad God was about his people turning away from his excellent offer of life, and choosing instead a way of life that would be about as useful to them as a leaking well. He got his prophet, Jeremiah, to tell them how he felt, and hoped people would realise their mistake and make a more sensible choice: to live God's way.

The letter to the Hebrews, or Jewish Christians, gives them some good, practical guidelines for living God's way, and we are going to look at these guidelines today. They are all about loving one another.

Ask a volunteer to go and fetch from the back table something which reminds them of people coming to visit your home. When they bring back the welcome mat, explain that we are told to 'practise hospitality', which means making people welcome, making them feel at home, being interested in them, and giving them our full attention when we listen to what they say. This may be at home, or with passengers on public transport, or with visitors to our church or school or workplace. Make every visitor to your home feel valued and loved.

Let someone fetch the 'prison bars' (oven shelf), and hold them up in front of their face. We are told to keep in mind those who are in prison, and pray for them by imagining we are there in prison with them. Imagining it can help us pray. Some people are in a real prison with bars, others are imprisoned by their bodies or their disappointments or their fears. All of these people need us to pray for them and befriend them.

Ask someone to find something which reminds them of being unwell and being made better. As they come back with the first-aid box and temperature chart, explain that we are told to pray for all those who are ill or in pain, and look after them however we can.

Now ask the married couple to stand and celebrate with them the joy of being together. We are told to honour marriage, and help one another keep our marriages healthy and strong. God wants us to be faithful to one another in all our friendships and family relationships, even when it gets difficult. As someone fetches the white flower, explain that it is a sign of purity, and God wants all our relationships to be honest and pure, with nothing we are ashamed of or need to hide from other people.

The next object to be fetched is the wallet or purse, and this reminds us that God wants us to live free from the love of money. Money is very useful, and it's good that we can have enough to live on and be able to give presents to one another and so on. But love of money is not good, and only makes us greedy, mean and resentful. You can have a love of money whether you are very rich or very hard-up, so we need to check that and get into the habit of being satisfied with what we have instead of always wanting what we can't get.

There is only one object left, and that is the rock or stone. Like solid rock under our feet, God is firm and strong and will never forget us or let us down. 'I will never leave you; I will never forget you' (Deuteronomy 31:6).

Sunday between 4 and 10 September

Proper 18

Thought for the day

Following Jesus is expensive – it costs everything, but it's worth it.

Reflection on the readings

Jeremiah 18:1-11 or Deuteronomy 30:15-20
Psalm 139:1-6, 13-18 or Psalm 1
Philemon 1-21
Luke 14:25-33

No sooner have you missed paying a credit card bill than invitations to get further into borrowing start crashing through your letter box. We live in an age of plastic or electronic money where the planning of our finances is pressurised to include living beyond our means, and many discover, too late, that they have over-reached themselves and are heavily, and dangerously, in debt. Jesus' words from today's Gospel hit home to us very powerfully. It is so easy to start enthusiastically committing yourself financially to a new bathroom, car or double-glazing and regret your decision once the 'pay later' date has arrived in the present.

Although Jesus' words sound very strict and demanding, they badly need to be taken on board. It is essential that no one is given the impression that following Jesus is all easy and happy, with no real cost involved. Part of spreading the good news is ensuring that people are properly informed of the small print. In fact Jesus would not have it in small print, but large letters, so there is no doubt about what is required in the way of commitment. God wants us to make a well-informed, well-considered decision; becoming a Christian, like undertaking marriage, should never be done lightly or carelessly.

Placing God at the very centre of our lives means deliberately placing him at the centre of our thinking and working, our emotions and feelings, our energy and ambitions and in the centre of every relationship, and every decision. Just as when you look at the world through a coloured filter, everything is coloured, so when we take the decision to follow Jesus, everything is coloured by that commitment.

So far, so demanding! Of course, the wonderful good news is that when we take this step we can trust God to lead us into the very best, most fulfilling life possible. The lovely Psalm 139 celebrates the intimate knowledge God has of us, and every stage of our growing. Never will he demand of us less than we can, in his strength, give. Never will he push us too fast or overload us too quickly. In partnership with Jesus we can look forward to a lifetime of growing, blossoming and fruiting, in an environment of total security, warm affection and the knowledge of being precious and valuable.

All-age talk

Bring along some catalogues with items which would appeal to the different ages and cultures of those likely to be present. Read out several of the items on offer, and ask people to raise their hands if they think each is a good offer. The more varied and unusual, the better. You might try, for instance, the latest sports car, an electronic game, a lawn mower and a Disneyland holiday. Would the items still be good bargains if you had to give up eating, hobbies or driving in order to pay for them? Establish that if something is important enough, we are prepared to give things up for it. If we're not prepared to change our habits to pay for it, we won't be able to have it.

We are called to follow Jesus. We are offered a fulfilling and rewarding life, inner peace and joy, and life that lasts for ever, even beyond our bodily death. That's quite an offer. But what does it cost? What would we have to give up to pay for it?

Have a long and a short piece of card, or two sticks, and show the long vertical one on its own. This looks like the word 'I'. Place the shorter piece across it. Following Jesus costs us the cross – it means deciding to give up the 'I want' way of living, and putting the sign of God's love (the cross) right at the centre of our lives. (Hold the cross you have made against your own body.)

That means that following Jesus is going to cost us quite a lot. It isn't a cheap, throwaway thing like a paper cup. We need to think very carefully about it before we decide to go for it. Is it worth it?

Yes, it certainly is! God made us, so his way is exactly right for us. No one but God can give us the lasting peace and happiness and complete forgiveness we long for. With God we can become more and more our true selves, selves we can face in the mirror and love. With God we can reach out to other people, and be brave enough to stand up for what is right and loving. Although our life as Christians may lead us into some difficult or dangerous situations, we will always have our friend Jesus with us, and that makes it all possible and all worthwhile.

Sunday between 11 and 17 September

Proper 19

Thought for the day

Jesus does not avoid the company of sinners but befriends them.

Reflection on the readings

Jeremiah 4:11-12, 22-28 or Exodus 32:7-14
Psalm 14 or Psalm 51:1-10
1 Timothy 1:12-17
Luke 15:1-10

Today's readings take us on a journey from near despair to strong hope. We begin with the Jeremiah passage, where we look the human condition full in the face and recognise the human capacity for making wrong, self-centred choices, excelling at mastering the skills of evil, and sidling away from the responsibility of Godly living, preferring to indulge in the pursuit of personal comfort and the easy life. Ancient Judah could equally be the world in the twenty-first century.

How does a totally good and loving God cope? In Jesus we find out: God comes to the rescue, in person, searching out the lost, untangling them from the messy situations they have got themselves into, and carrying them safely home. The whole of heaven rejoices over each and every one.

In his letter to Timothy, Paul cites himself as living proof that God is indeed merciful and ready to forgive sinners, wherever they are coming from. He, after all, was actively persecuting the followers of Jesus when God alerted him to the truth and transformed his life. Many of us know the same truth in our own lives – I used to be a passionate atheist and now here I am writing this book! The Lord is an excellent shepherd and can find any bedraggled sheep, no matter where they have wandered off to, or how muddy and unsavoury they have become.

God will always search for us because he loves us, and doesn't want any of us to be lost. But it is still up to us whether or not we agree to be rescued.

All-age talk

Gather a mixed group of 'sheep', and appoint a shepherd who is given a crook. Talk about the way the shepherd looks after sheep, finding fresh water and fresh grass, and protecting them from the dangers of wolves and bears. Sometimes a sheep will wander off on its own. (Send one of the sheep to go off and hide somewhere in the church, ensuring that enthusiastic sheep are prevented from going right outside.)

Jesus thought the way we wander off from living good lives was rather like sheep wandering off and getting lost. He loves all of us, and doesn't want any of us to be lost, so, like a good shepherd, he checks that all the rest of the people in the church are OK. (Are they?) Then he sets off to search for the one who has wandered off.

As the shepherd searches for the lost sheep (tell him/her to wait with the sheep when it is found), give some examples of what makes us wander off from God. Perhaps other things crowd God out and take over our life; perhaps we want to disobey God's rules and please ourselves; perhaps some tragedy in our life shakes our faith, and we think God has caused the pain instead of realising that he is weeping with us. Whatever it is, once we realise we are a long way from God, we feel very lost and alone. Sometimes we have got ourselves trapped in habits we can't break out of on our own.

Thankfully Jesus, our good shepherd, is out looking for us, and he will search and search until he finds us. We can help by bleating – which is praying, calling out to God from where we are.

It is very good to be found. As the shepherd brings the wandering sheep, hand in hand, back to the flock, talk about how wonderful it is to know that we are forgiven, and that God loves us enough to forgive us even when we ran away from him. When the sheep comes back to the flock everyone can clap, as, with all the angels of heaven, we celebrate the truth that our God is such an excellent rescuer, full of understanding and mercy, and willing to give up his life to get us back home again.

Sunday between 18 and 24 September

Proper 20

Thought for the day

If you cannot be trusted with worldly riches, or even small amounts of money, then you will not be trusted with spiritual riches either.

Reflection on the readings

Jeremiah 8:18-9:1 or Amos 8:4-7
Psalm 79:1-9 or Psalm 113
1 Timothy 2:1-7
Luke 16:1-13

Today's readings remind us that the way we deal with worldly finances and possessions should be scrupulously honest, fair and wise. It should be directly affected by our spiritual values, and reflect our beliefs completely.

The story of the cheating manager and his cunning way of avoiding trouble has the rich man praising him for his cleverness. This does not mean that Jesus is advising us all to follow the manager's example, of course, but it certainly highlights the zeal given to worldly affairs compared with the laid-back attitude so often given to eternal and spiritual matters. If we were to take the same trouble over our spiritual journey as criminals invest in embezzlement, the results would be dynamic in the extreme.

Jesus also picks up on our need to be responsible with our worldly affairs. It is no good excusing ourselves from such responsibilities on the grounds that we are only interested in spiritual things. Jesus is always practical, and realises that the way we manage our weekly budget, our expenses and our life-decisions is important. If we can't manage these honestly and sensibly, we are likely to be irresponsible about the important things of life as well.

Jeremiah was deeply saddened by his own people using their privileged position as a cover for ungodly behaviour. The closer we get to God's way of thinking, the more saddened we will be by the lack of integrity we see around us. We are bound to start noticing people's misdirected 'worth-ship' and longing for a change of direction. This sadness and yearning is all part of walking in step with the God who loves us and desires that sinners should turn and live.

All-age talk

You will need to prepare this talk with another adult. The two of you will be bosses, standing at either end of the church.

Begin by asking for a volunteer who doesn't mind doing a few jobs. This person stands halfway down the church, and you introduce them to the two bosses they are to work for this morning. They are to serve both people as well as they can.

First one boss gives an order, such as to put three chairs out in a line in the middle of the church. As soon as this is done, the other boss gets annoyed that the chairs are arranged like this and tells the servant to put only two chairs out, facing different ways. The first boss tells the servant to put a hymn book on each chair. The other boss tells the servant to put the hymn books away and put a kneeler on each chair. Continue the orders so that the poor servant is running about the church pleasing no one.

Thank the volunteer, and explain how Jesus said in today's Gospel that it is impossible to serve two bosses like that. Either you end up loving the first and hating the second, or hating the first and loving the second. It is the same with trying to serve God while we are still bound up with materialism, money and possessions. (Have two signs: 'God' and 'Worldly Riches'. These can include appropriate symbols, such as a cross and some money.) It simply can't be done. While God is whispering to your conscience to live simply and generously, Worldly Riches is insisting that you get the latest fashion in clothes or music. While

God is expecting you to commit time to prayer and Bible reading, Worldly Riches is expecting you to commit that time to reading the latest magazines and watching the latest videos.

If we choose to serve God (display the 'God' sign) we have to choose not to serve Worldly Riches. (Tear up the 'Worldly Riches' sign.)

Sunday between 25 September and 1 October

Proper 21

Thought for the day

Wealth can make us complacent so that we fail to notice the needs of those around us.

Reflection on the readings

Jeremiah 32:1-3a, 6-15 or Amos 6:1a, 4-7
Psalm 91:1-6, 14-16 or Psalm 146
1 Timothy 6:6-19
Luke 16:19-31

On the face of it, Jeremiah's purchase of the field was likely to be a complete waste of money. Had he been thinking only in terms of financial gain, it would hardly have been considered a wise investment. But since God had just spoken to him about using it as a sign of hope, Jeremiah was happy to go along with God's priorities. These took precedence over all his plans and ambitions.

Amos underlines for us the danger of being comfortably well off; the very comfort can cushion us from feeling for the poor and needy until we barely notice their suffering. So often this goes along with a sense of well-being which lulls us into thinking life is like this for everyone else too. We can become so cut off from the real world that we actually believe the needs are not there. It is this blindness, and the injustice of the situation, which angers the God of love and compassion. He feels for the ones who get despised and ignored, simply because they possess less.

Paul has more good advice for young Timothy. He, too, recognises that many sins can get traced back to the 'love of money' rootstock, and advises Timothy to stay well away from it, pursuing instead the kind of riches that are good and eternal. God is by far the better bargain!

The parable of the rich man and Lazarus focuses our minds on the seriousness and urgency of this whole question. We are not to know when our opportunities for living thoughtfully and generously will run out; it would be sensible to sort it all out now, while we still have the chance. As we take stock of how we are living, we can hold in front of us the picture of this wealthy man who did nothing particularly evil, but neglected to notice the needs of those he probably saw every day.

All-age talk

Arrange for the following items to be in church today, giving different people responsibility for them, so that they will emerge from various people all over the congregation: a pair of sunglasses, some well-known expensive brand of sun cream (the bottle can be empty), a luxurious, squashy cushion, a bottle of champagne (or a champagne bottle) in an ice bucket, and a CD player with some easy-listening music in it ready to play. At the front of the church you need one of those comfortable sun-loungers. Arrange for another person to walk quietly to the middle of the aisle with a begging bowl and sit down there.

Get the sun-lounger out and invite someone to be cosseted and pampered for a few minutes of the morning. They can lie on the lounger, and various people from all over the church bring them all their comforts. Enthuse about each item as you make the volunteer really comfortable. Leave them snoozing in luxury as you pose the question: 'Is there anything wrong with living in wealth and luxury, and pampering ourselves?'

In itself, no, there isn't. Of course it is good to have times of rest and relaxation, and it is fine to enjoy the good things of life. But if we use wealth to cushion ourselves from the real world, shield our eyes from the harsh glare of suffering, protect ourselves from feeling people's pain, block out the sound of people's crying, and deaden our sense of duty, then we run the danger of rejecting all the needs, and not feeling we have any responsibility to do anything about them anyway. (Hold a 'speech bubble' of card over the volunteer, which says, 'What problems?')

In Jesus' story, the rich man was probably a nice guy, and there is no mention of him doing anything really evil. But he simply hadn't noticed the beggar who sat at his own front gate every day. Point out that all the time we've been enjoying indulging ourselves up here, there has been someone begging down there.

It's all too easy for us to ignore the needs. Jesus reminds us to check that our lack of poverty doesn't prevent us from doing the practical caring love we are called to.

Sunday between 2 and 8 October

Proper 22

Thought for the day

God hears our distress and our crying, and feels it with us.

Reflection on the readings

Lamentations 1:1-6 or Habakkuk 1:1-4; 2:1-4
Lamentations 3:19-26 or Psalm 137, or Psalm 37:1-9
2 Timothy 1:1-14
Luke 17:5-10

Today's readings are full of laments and heartbroken crying. Our faith is not a fair-weather faith, but speaks into our pain as well as our joy, into our darkest valleys as well as our hilltop experiences. It is both crucifixion and resurrection. God never does nothing when we pray; he may not come charging into the situation and sort it in the way we would like, but in his time, which is the best time, he will redeem it for good, and while we are waiting he will provide all the courage, inner peace and hope we need.

The important thing for us to establish as we cry is God's position in the suffering. So often when there are national tragedies we hear people crying, 'How could a loving God let this happen?' as if God were there orchestrating the evil or, even worse, watching it with his arms folded. This is a terrible distortion of the truth, for the real God of compassion is neither tyrannical, nor aloof and unconcerned. Nor is he well-intentioned but ineffectual. He is actually there suffering alongside the broken-hearted, sharing their grief and distress and ready to comfort them by being there. The costly gift of free will is matched by the costly gift of loving redemption.

At the same time, as today's Gospel reminds us, there is no room for spiritual self-pity. We have no built-in rights for everything in our lives to run smoothly and easily, and Jesus is forthright in talking of the servant who simply accepts the work and weariness as part of his duty, without expecting any special payment or privileges. If following Christ brings us hardship and suffering, that is no more than we were told to expect, and we are asked to accept it as such, always on the understanding and conviction that we will be provided with whatever grace and strength we need to cope and triumph over the difficulties.

All-age talk

Bring along a football, a musical instrument, a cross and a Bible. Choose someone to come out and give them the football, telling them that you are letting them borrow this so that you can watch them on television, this week, playing in the next (Liverpool) game. Give someone else the musical instrument and say you'll be looking forward to hearing them on Classic FM tomorrow morning, then.

Are these things really possible? Why not? Obviously it doesn't really happen like that. Just having a football doesn't mean you can get out there and land the goals against fierce opposition.

For that you need lots of training and lots of skills. Just having a musical instrument doesn't mean that you can join a top orchestra and get all the notes and phrasing right. For that you need years of training and practice, and a musical gift.

We know about this in football and music, but we sometimes forget it when it comes to our faith, even though it's still true. Give someone the cross and the Bible. Just because they now have these things doesn't mean that they have arrived as a Christian, and can now make all the right decisions, and be perfect in every way. Living Christ's way will take us a lifetime of training and practice, and we are bound to make mistakes and get into scrapes along the route.

So when the going gets hard work, and we find it's a challenge and a struggle to live by God's rule of love, we mustn't get discouraged. Jesus never promised us it would be easy all the time. All training, whether it's in tackling or goal defence, vibrato on the violin or overcoming the break on the clarinet, forgiving wholeheartedly or conquering self-indulgence – all these things are difficult to learn and require dedication and perseverance.

When you are finding it's hard being a Christian, don't give up or decide it's too difficult; go to God and ask for some more help. Throughout your whole life he will provide all the training, practice and gifts you need for the work he asks you to do, whether that work is preaching to thousands, or helping your next-door neighbour.

Sunday between 9 and 15 October

Proper 23

Thought for the day

God can always use even seemingly hopeless situations for good.

Reflection on the readings

Jeremiah 29:1, 4-7 or 2 Kings 5:1-3, 7-15
Psalm 66:1-12 or Psalm 111
2 Timothy 2:8-15
Luke 17:11-19

The people of Jerusalem have been taken into exile and forced to live far from home in the city of Babylon. They are aware of the unpleasant truth that this is at least partly their own fault, and in his letter to them, speaking out the word of God, Jeremiah urges them to think and act positively, so that through their presence in Babylon the city may be blessed. We have probably all known at some time the misery of being rejected and isolated. Whether we are in that place through our own fault or through circumstances beyond our control, it is still a bleak and painful place to be.

Some of us will have known the haunting suspicion that we could infect others, either physically or emotionally; most of us can only guess at the terrible sense of chronic isolation and terror experienced by those with leprosy.

Jesus meets the ten lepers in their community of isolation, outside one of the villages, and all their years of suffering pour out poignantly as they plead for pity from their contamination zone. Jesus, ever practical, tells them not that they are healed, but that they are to go and do what healed lepers have to do by law – show themselves to the priest. It is typical of Godly direction to use the existing framework so as to bless as many people as possible.

Paul, writing to Timothy, is actually chained up in prison, but quite content to be there as anywhere else because he knows that although he is chained, the good news is not, and can bring anyone blessing, wherever you happen to spread it.

This is rather heartening, because it means that all of us can blossom with God's love where we are planted; we don't have to wait until we are in a 'better' situation, or get discouraged because we only meet those in the office or on the bus each day. The wholesome goodness of the Gospel can be brought to those we meet – by us!

All-age talk

Ask for ten volunteers and dish out 'bandages' for them to wear on arms, legs and head. Explain that they are lepers and, because the disease is thought to be very catching, they can't stay with everyone else here but must go and sit somewhere else. Direct them to a place separate from the rest of the congregation. As they go, tell everyone how the lepers of Jesus' day had to leave their homes and live right away from the villages and towns, and look after themselves. How must they have felt? Lonely? Left out? Guilty? Unacceptable? Frightened?

We may not have the disease of leprosy, but there are lots of people in our world, in our country and in our town – perhaps even in our church – who feel lonely, left out, guilty, unacceptable and frightened, like the lepers. People cry themselves to sleep and wake up feeling sad about the day ahead. People who have lost contact with friends, or whose loved ones have died, try hard to be cheerful when they have a big ache of sadness inside them. Lots of people are hurting, and longing for their life to be different.

That's how these ten lepers felt that morning when they saw Jesus walking along the road on his way to a village. They couldn't come too close to him, but they came as close as they could, and shouted to him, 'Jesus, Master, have pity on us!' (This can be written on a sign so the ten 'lepers' can shout it out.) People still cry out to God in their hearts like this. Does God hear?

He certainly does! Jesus shows us what God is like, and what Jesus did was to tell the lepers to go and show themselves to the priest. Why ever did he tell them that? Because if you were a leper and you were healed, you had to show yourself to a priest, so he could check you over and pronounce you fit and well.

Send your lepers off to the priest, who has ten cards saying, 'I declare this leper is now CLEAN. Signed: Revd. *John Hayward.*' Tell them that when they have their certificate of health they are free to join the other people in the congregation.

If any of the volunteers decides to come and say 'thank you' you can of course use this and praise it. However, since they haven't actually been healed of anything, they will probably all sit down in their places. Tell everyone how one leper (choose one) came back to Jesus to say 'thank you'. All the others had been keen to talk to Jesus when they needed something, but they forgot him once he had sorted them out.

Let's make sure that when God answers our prayers, we don't forget to say thank you – even if his answer is not the answer we expect.

Sunday between 16 and 22 October

Proper 24

Thought for the day

Don't get side-tracked; always pray and don't give up.

Reflection on the readings

Jeremiah 31:27-34 or Genesis 32:22-31
Psalm 119:97-104 or Psalm 121
2 Timothy 3:14–4:5
Luke 18:1-8

I have a half-finished tapestry somewhere in the back of a cupboard, which has been in that state for years. Whenever I rediscover it, I make the decision to keep it, as one day I may have the time to finish it. Even as I put it back in the cupboard I know this is unlikely; the commitment simply isn't there, as my tapestry doesn't rank high enough in my order of priorities.

For many people, faith in God is similarly packed away, and brought out and looked at from time to time. Their prayer-life is haphazard and irregular, with long gaps of inattentiveness punctuated with occasional attempts to open up the communication channels. For whatever reasons, building a deep relationship with God is simply not a high priority at present. If it were, the commitment would show in a regular and more persistent prayer pattern.

Whereas my tapestry remains much the same sitting in the cupboard, relationships are dynamic and do not store well without attention. It is always rather sad when a close friendship subsides into the printed Christmas letter category. Although this can be a valiant effort to avoid losing touch completely, it is a poor substitute for the daily contact and shared lives. And so often our prayer-life and Bible-reading, if similarly rare and impersonal, result in a very stilted relationship with God, which is such a poor substitute for the rich, vibrant companionship he has in mind for us.

We live in a rather fragmented and disjointed culture, which doesn't help. Many young children are now entering school with a marked increase in poor listening and concentration skills. Persistence in anything, whatever it is, does not come easily. But prayer, like our heartbeat, needs to be regular and constant, a quiet rhythm pulsing faithfully under all our other activities. We also have a responsibility to keep up our study of the Bible so that we, like Timothy, are thoroughly equipped for every work.

All-age talk

Bring along (or ask someone else in the congregation to bring) something which you have made or are making, which requires lots of persistence and perseverance (such as a garment or model, diary or recipe). Talk about the struggle you have had keeping going with it.

Use parts of the church building, particularly if it is an ancient one, and draw everyone's attention to some piece of stained glass or carving, and all the persistence and hard work that went into making it. Emphasise the value of doing these things, even though they are difficult.

Jesus tells us to keep going with our prayer, and never give up. Suggest a pattern of praying when you wake up, before you eat a meal, and before you go to sleep at night, showing large posters of logos for these (as below). Or they can be shown on an OHP. If we get into a prayer habit like this, we will be deepening our friendship with God, and getting to know him better.

There is another good habit we need to have as well as praying, and that is reading the Bible every day. There are lots of books and schemes to help us, and we can choose one which suits our age, interests and experience. Show a few of these. If we don't know much about the Bible there are people in the parish to talk it over with.

However we read it, it's important to pray and read God's word in Scripture so that we really can have God's law of love remembered in our minds and written on our hearts. That way we will be ready for any jobs God asks us to do, and we will be better able to hear him speaking into our lives.

Sunday between 23 and 29 October

Proper 25

Thought for the day

When we recognise our dependence on God we will approach him with true humility and accept his gifts with joy.

Reflection on the readings

> Joel 2:23-32 or Ecclesiasticus 35:12-17 or Jeremiah 14:7-10, 19-22
> Psalm 65 or Psalm 84:1-7
> 2 Timothy 4:6-8, 16-18
> Luke 18:9-14

We all want to be independent, and any parent can remember the battles which mark the route! One of the hardest things for the ageing is having to gradually relinquish their independence, and many struggle on with great difficulty rather than asking for help. This kind of pride in our independence as humans is good and healthy. The danger comes when we lose touch with where we have come from, and forget that as created beings we are fundamentally dependent on our creator and sustainer, God himself.

The readings today express the praise and thanksgiving which result from recognising God's lavish showering of gifts on his people. There is so much to be thankful for, and the whole pattern of seasonal rain and growth work as a visible sign of God's Spirit drenching and soaking us as it is poured out over us in life-giving abundance. Even those of us who have long been city-dwellers can appreciate the image of rain and growth.

To receive such a drenching we need to be like the earth, open and vulnerable, and ready to accept a soaking. It isn't any coincidence that the word 'humility' means 'earthiness'. And we simply can't be earthy if we are working on the principle that we have no need of God, or of anyone's help, and can manage perfectly well on our own, thank you.

While the Pharisee in today's Gospel is going through the motions of communicating with God, he is really affirming his own independent worth and has no concept of his deep need of God at all. It's like insisting on protecting our earth from rain; and if we do that, nothing can grow. In contrast the tax collector, complete with questionable morals and principles, at least recognises his basic dependence on God, and his need of God's mercy. It is this honesty before God that Jesus recommends.

All-age talk

Involve a couple of children in constructing a tower, using building blocks or large packing case cartons. When it is really high, suggest that now they won't need the big block at the bottom any more. Take it away, and of course the whole lot falls down. Be surprised, and protest that you only took one brick away! Then point out that it was the important brick you took – the foundation stone – and everything else depends on that.

Our whole lives depend on God. It's God who gives us life for a start, and provides our planet with what we need to live on. It is God's rain, sunshine and earth which we use to grow our wheat for bread and pizzas. We might sometimes forget to think about God, but he never ever forgets to think about us. He looks after us through our whole lives as we grow up and get old.

We heard another of Jesus' stories this morning, with some more cartoon-type characters. There's Pharisee Ferdinand and Tax Collecter ⊤ '

Both of them have gone to pray. Let's look again at how Pharisee Ferdinand prays. (Display the picture, while a pompous voice reads the part. He needs to sound really smug.) Let people give their ideas of what's wrong with his prayer.

Let's listen in on Tax Collector Ted. (Show the picture, and have someone saying his prayer. This should sound quite genuine.) Comment on the way this person knows he needs God's mercy. And it was this person, Jesus said, who went away right with God, rather than Pharisee Ferdinand who did lots of good things but didn't have any idea of how much he depended on God, thinking that doing good things could earn him a special place in God's kingdom all by himself.

We owe our whole life to God. Let's not kid ourselves that we don't need him.

All Saints' Sunday

Sunday between 30 October and 5 November

Thought for the day

In Christ we are chosen to be God's holy people.

Reflection on the readings

Daniel 7:1-3, 15-18
Psalm 149
Ephesians 1:11-23
Luke 6:20-31

There are occasions when you are caving of suddenly finding yourself in huge, lofty underground caverns with the most beautiful rock formations and colours that take your breath away. And you realise that there would be no easy way of seeing these wonders; the tight and terrifying passages you have just squeezed through are an essential part of the experience.

Perhaps this is a little like the pattern of our spiritual experience, too. We are all chosen in Christ to be saints, and part of the glorious life awaiting God's chosen ones in heaven is the challenging and often uncomfortable journey towards it. You cannot have one without the other, and the expectation of that promised, but unimaginable destination can actually make us happy to be spiritually crawling through mud, or holding our breath through sumps.

Nearly all of us share the forgotten but impressive experience of birth through a narrow and uncomfortable tunnel out into the breadth and light of this world, and many mothers find that the pain of the birthing process is different from other pain because of being positive and full of hope. They are in no way denying the pain, but seeing it (at least with hindsight!) in a wider context.

It is in the wider context of eternity that the Beatitudes make sense, and that our attitude to earthly pressures and persecution lightens. Even these times catch the light of God's love and glory, and so become not just possible to bear but reasons for rejoicing, as they mark out and confirm our route.

As we celebrate today the many who have persevered on this route and now cheer us on, we catch the excitement again of our calling, both individually by name, and as the entire Church of God.

All-age talk

Bring with you something to inflate, such as a beach ball, or a travel neck-cushion, or a balloon.

Begin by playing a snippet of *When the saints go marching in,* reminding everyone that today we are celebrating the festival of all the saints marching into heaven, and we also want to be among that number.

But what is a saint? You may have some windows with particular saints on. If so, you can briefly draw people's attention to these, and any saintly connections your parish has. Emphasise that although these may be importantly fixed in stained glass now, in their lives they were ordinary people. We may well have lots of saints sitting here now, because we are *all* called to be saints, or God's holy people.

How can you spot a holy person when you meet one? The way they think and talk and behave makes you realise that they are full of God's loving spirit. Show your inflatable. It was designed to be full of air, so at the moment, without air in it, it isn't really able to be properly itself. Ask someone to breathe into it to inflate it. Can we see the air that has been breathed in? No. Can we see the difference it makes? Yes! It has turned this ball/cushion/balloon into what it was designed to be, so now it is really itself, and also very useful.

We can't see the loving Spirit of God either. But whenever people are filled with it, they are able to be more fully their true selves, and it shows in their love for God and their love for others. Lots of inflatables have a valve which stops the air coming in until it is deliberately opened. With us, too, there has to be a definite decision to open up to God's in-breathing of his Spirit. What the saints have done and are doing is keeping that valve open, so that they can be filled with the Spirit, and topped up whenever they get a bit deflated.

One saint – Paul – whose letter we heard this morning, wrote about the whole church being filled with the Holy Spirit of God. The Church isn't supposed to have loads of deflated Christians and one or two saints here and there who are full of God's loving Spirit. The idea of the church is that *everyone* in it is full of the breath of God!

Let God fill you up with his life, and make you into the person he knows you can be. We'll all look different shapes, and we'll all be useful to the world in different ways, just as a beachball is useful for throwing around but not so good as a pillow or a camping mattress. But as God breathes his loving Spirit into us more and more, we will become more and more our true selves – holy people the world needs, marching into God's kingdom with all the other saints.

Fourth Sunday before Advent

(For use if the Feast of All Saints was celebrated on 1 November)

Proper 26

Thought for the day

Jesus came to search out the lost and save them. Through him we come to our senses and make our lives clean.

Reflection on the readings

> Isaiah 1:10-18
> Psalm 32:1-7
> 2 Thessalonians 1:1-12
> Luke 19:1-10

With all the hurt of a parent who expects honesty from a child he loves and finds instead that he is living a lie, God's indignation burns. Perhaps we too have felt the pain of discovering that someone, who has been speaking pleasantly to our faces, has been ridiculing or insulting us behind our backs. The deceit hurts as much as the actual offence.

God cannot bear hypocrisy. All through the Bible, both in the Old and the New Testament, we find this loathing of falsehood and pretence; we get the impression that he would prefer an honest sinner any day to the mealy-mouthed obsequiousness described so well in Dickens' Uriah Heap. In Jesus' day it was the hypocrisy of the Pharisees which most often drew his harshest words.

The Isaiah passage for today makes it quite clear that no efficient worship or complex rituals of sacrifice will ever be acceptable unless they are matched by pure and honourable lives and the awareness of sin. Our worship must simply express the outpouring of our love for God which, as a matter of course, shows itself in our loving behaviour to one another day by day.

Psalm 32 beautifully expresses that wonderful feeling of freedom and lightness that comes when we finally get round to admitting where we are to blame, so that God can at last do something about it and sort us out. Why, we wonder, did we take so long pretending it wasn't a sin!

Perhaps Zacchaeus had spent considerable time and effort persuading himself of all kinds of good reasons for living the life he did, but there was always the deep-down nagging suspicion that there was a better way. Certainly he made quite an effort to see Jesus once he knew he would be in the area, and Jesus, always in touch with his Father's viewpoint, noticed the first tentative reaching out and responded to it.

So it is with us. As soon as we make the first tentative move to desire honesty and cleansed thoughts, God will pick up our longing and run with it, bringing us into contact with help and encouragement or challenge, just as we need it. Real and expensive sacrifices may well need to be made, but we will find we are making them out of choice, without resentment, and over the years God will keep his promise to restore the years the locusts have eaten.

All-age talk

Bring along some wallpaper, paste and brush, and also some foundation make-up.

Introduce these items, talking about what a difference they can make to the look of a room or a face, and how we carefully choose and apply them. The people of Israel were taking great care over their worship, and what it looked like, and we do as well. Point out the colours and clothing, candles and music that we take care in choosing to make our worship beautiful.

So if all this is in God's honour, why was he disapproving of it? The trouble was not in the actual colours and shape of the worship, any more than there is anything wrong with decorating our walls and faces. The big problem was that the people of Israel were pretending to show they loved God, through their worship, but their lives showed that they couldn't care less about his laws of love. They were saying one thing with their worship and something else with their lives.

That was a bit like using nice wallpaper to cover up a crumbling wall with holes in it and damp stains. Before long the underlying badness is bound to show through, and the nice wallpaper won't put the wall right at all. It's a bit like having a spot and smothering it with foundation cream to cover it up. It certainly won't help the spot get better, and may even make it worse.

Zacchaeus knew something was wrong in his life. When Jesus came to his house, he helped him to sort out the problem properly, instead of just covering it over and hoping it would go away. Sin never goes away unless we deal with it properly. It isn't any good trying to make it look pretty or covering it over with excuses. Like Zacchaeus we need to invite Jesus in and deal with it.

Then our worship will be honest and truly reverent, as we pour out our love for the God who has saved us from sin. And however beautiful we make our worship with colours and music, the most beautiful thing about it, as far as God is concerned, is the state of our hearts, which he can see right into.

Third Sunday before Advent

Proper 27

Thought for the day

Life after death is not wishful thinking but a definite reality.

Reflection on the readings

> Job 19:23-27a
> Psalm 17:1-9
> 2 Thessalonians 2:1-5, 13-17
> Luke 20:27-38

When you have a favourite author, it is disappointing to get to the end of the last available novel she has written; my mother, with considerable enforced reading time, felt quite lost after the Cadfael books ran out. On one occasion I read *War and Peace* straight through twice because I couldn't bear to finish it!

When we set off on the journey of discovery into friendship with God, there is no problem of getting to the end of him, or having to break our relationship with him simply because our physical body has stopped working. We can carry on enjoying his friendship, and an ever-deepening understanding of his nature throughout the whole of eternity. There is no end to God, and, through the redeeming work of Christ, there need be no end to us either, so we can look forward to life beyond death and enjoy the prospect of living in God's company for ever.

The Sadducees had decided that the idea of resurrection wasn't workable and therefore couldn't be true. As so often happens, they were judging God's ways by human limitations. They worked out this complicated problem to make Jesus realise how silly it is to think there can be life after death. Faced with this conundrum he will surely have to admit that they are sensible and right in their belief.

What Jesus does is to show them that they are asking the wrong question. Resurrection life is not a tangled continuation of the earthly order of things, but a new and different experience, just as real but with whole new dimensions of possibility.

It is rather like arguing that caterpillars couldn't possibly fly. In their present state and with their present limitations it is indeed impossible, but the freshly emerging butterfly proves that flying is a perfectly natural progression from leaf munching. Few of us would ever guess that a caterpillar could turn into a butterfly, and similarly we have little exact idea of what our resurrection life will be like. What we do know is that it will be fulfilling and rewarding, full of joy, peace and love.

In the meantime we are to stand firm and stick to the teachings we have been handed down faithfully through the generations in an unbroken line which can be traced back to Christ himself. That will enable us to discern the false rumours from the truth, and we will be ready to enter the glorious heritage of resurrection life in heaven.

All-age talk

Bring along some tasters of a particular cheese, tiny chunks such as those you find in most supermarkets from time to time. Bring also a block of the same cheese, labelled.

Show your tray of tasters for the cheese you have brought to recommend. Suggest that people try a taster of it to see whether they like it. Since these tasters came off the main block of cheese, you can guarantee that they will taste as good as the main block. Discuss their findings briefly.

Although we haven't been to heaven, God gives us lots of little 'tasters' which help us find out what it is like. Whenever we sense Jesus giving us peace of mind or joy, or the lovely knowledge that God really loves and cares for us, we are getting a taster of life after death. Jesus lives in heaven so when he comes into us, he doesn't leave heaven behind but brings it with him. So the more we live in God's company and follow Jesus, the more of heaven we will have in our lives even before we die.

Explain that lots of people think Christians are crazy believing that there is life after death. Since they can't see beyond death, they don't think there can be anything like heaven. If I had never seen the yellow daffodil flowers in spring, I would probably think people were crazy burying dry bulbs in their earth at this time of year. But because I have seen what happens to those bulbs, I trust that they won't just rot in the ground. If I were a caterpillar, I would probably laugh at anyone suggesting that one day I would be flying about with colourful wings. It isn't true that the only real things are those we can see.

It is sometimes difficult to trust that what we can't see is still there, but we make the effort to do it whenever we drive in fog, walk along looking around instead of at the path under our feet, or wash our backs. So it is quite possible. And Jesus has told us that there really is life after death, and lots of people saw him alive after he had died. So we aren't crazy for believing there is life after death; we happen to know it's true, and we've already tasted little bits of how lovely it is.

Second Sunday before Advent
Proper 28

Thought for the day

There will be dark and dangerous times as the end approaches, but by standing firm through it all we will gain life.

Reflection on the readings

Malachi 4:1-2a
Psalm 98
2 Thessalonians 3:6-13
Luke 21:5-19

The Gospel for today makes terrifying reading. The seemingly solid beauty of the temple seems to have triggered in Jesus a vision of the world from outside time. Like a speeded-up film we scan the great cosmic cycles and seasons, natural disasters and human agonies, as the earth labours towards its time of accomplishment.

Amongst the terror, distress, upheavals and ructions are scattered the bright lights of individuals who are unperturbed and faithful; those who are not drawn into the panic but remain steadfast, strong as rocks in their perseverance.

We may well wonder how we could ever survive; what hope there could possibly be of us joining the number of those who will win eternal life by their endurance. Certainly Jesus is anxious to stress that it will not be an easy ride, nor a natural consequence of setting out with enthusiasm on the Christian journey. We can't take our salvation for granted and then sit back with our feet up.

We are warned of what to expect to enable us to be prepared, and the important truth is that we shall not be doing all this on our own or in our own strength. We will be yoked up with Jesus, sustained by his power and provided with the right words and the necessary courage. Only one second at a time will be expected of us!

There is no way church congregations or individual Christians will be able to shut their doors and hide away from the troubles and threats of the world. Our place is right in the centre of the action, getting involved, and standing up for what is right and just, whatever the personal consequences may be.

All-age talk

Prepare some large card road signs, and a cereal packet which is labelled 'The last age' on the front and has 'Warnings and advice' with a copy of today's Gospel stuck on the back. Bring these along, together with a packet of cigarettes, and something packed in a plastic bag with the warning of suffocation printed on it.

Begin by asking volunteers to hold the road signs at intervals down the aisle, and ask a couple of people to 'drive their car' among the signs. Talk them through, getting people to say what the signs mean as they come to them, and encouraging them to react appropriately. (If a roundabout sign is used, for instance, they can drive round an imaginary roundabout.) Point out how useful the signs are in warning us so that we are better prepared as we drive.

Show the cigarette packet and read out the warning on that, and on the plastic bag. Lots of things have warnings and good advice printed on them – hair colouring, pain-killers, frozen pies and skateboards – the manufacturer wants customers to be warned of any dangers and know how to avoid them.

Now pick up the prepared cereal packet, and show the 'product name'. Today's Gospel is doing the same thing. It's offering us some warnings and advice for living through this: the last age. We are in the middle of this at the moment. It's the time between Jesus dying on the cross and coming to life again and going to heaven (which has already happened) and the Day of Judgement, or the Second Coming, which will mark the end of things as we know them. (That hasn't happened yet.)

Jesus knew this would be a very difficult and dangerous age to live in, and he told his disciples to watch for the signs and be prepared. (Turn the packet of cereal round and show the warnings and advice.) Compulsive cereal packet readers will find it may put them off their breakfast. It's the section of Luke's Gospel that we've all just heard this morning.

Pick up on some of the phrases to remind people, and help them see that these things are indeed happening in places all over the world. The signs are there. So what are we to do about them?

Our job as Christians is to stand firm and not get fazed when these terrible things happen, but be in there helping, comforting and doing our best to show and proclaim God's love by our words and actions, even when we get laughed at, despised or persecuted in the process.

Perhaps you are thinking that sounds very hard. Well, you're right, it is very hard and we may feel like giving up. But God promises to be there with us through it all, and will make sure we have all the courage we need to do it. We are warned and prepared specially, because God wants us to be able to stay firm to the end and be saved.

Christ the King

Thought for the day

This Jesus, dying by crucifixion between criminals, is the anointed King of all creation in whom all things are reconciled.

Reflection on the readings

Jeremiah 23:1-6
Psalm 46
Colossians 1:11-20
Luke 23:33-43

In the passage from Jeremiah we have that wonderful image of God, gathering up all the scattered sheep from where they have bolted in terror and confusion, and bringing them carefully back to their pasture. Good shepherds are appointed to tend them so that they will not be afraid any more. The idea of a Shepherd King touches a deep chord in us; there is a rightness of balance, a wholesome combination of authority and practical caring, which rings true and speaks of safety and security. The tradition is already there in David, the shepherd boy made king, and now it is given even more powerful meaning.

God's great rescue plan is extraordinarily focused at the crossing of two rough pieces of wood, designed for use in Roman executions. Yet it is as if those two pieces of wood, which form the cross on which the Shepherd King hangs dying, extend onwards and outwards across the whole of human experience, the depth of human suffering and the height of human joy. They stretch out to unite our deepest needs with the most complete fulfilment; they draw together all things from all generations and cultures, into that point of reconciliation at the point of complete love.

The cross becomes a throne, where the kingdom of forgiving love is seen in action; costly forgiveness serenaded with insults and sneers. The attendants, finding the innocent Jesus beside them, sharing their hours of deserved agony, are representative of us all. Wherever our wanderings have taken us we need only turn our head to see him there suffering with us. We too can react either in disgust at this terrible vulnerability of God's love, or we can allow the acceptance and forgiveness to work its healing in us, long before we can understand the full implications.

Today we look back over the unfolded story of God's redeeming love that we have explored during the past year, and the journey brings us firmly back to the cross, which fixes and anchors everything.

Being a cross, it also points us to look forward, to a deepening understanding of the Incarnation as we approach Advent and Christmas once again.

All-age talk

Beforehand prepare a flock of large card sheep. Numbers will depend on your congregation; there need to be at least six.

Begin by talking about the way sheep get easily scared, and will scuttle away a few metres and then stop and eat, and then scuttle away again and eat again. That's why they can easily get lost, because they don't realise how far they have scuttled! Children with little experience of sheep may have noticed a similar 'scuttle, eat, scuttle' pattern in rabbits, who also get scared very easily.

Introduce your flock of sheep, with a volunteer holding each one. Those who are holding them can give them names, or they can be given the names of the children. All through the Bible we read that people are rather like sheep. We get scared (though we usually try to hide that and pretend we aren't scared at all) and we tend to wander off and get lost, and we follow one another into all sorts of rather silly and dangerous places and ideas.

Like sheep, we need a shepherd, and our first reading today told how God was angry with the leaders of his people because they had been bad shepherds, and made the sheep scared, so that they had all scuttled off and got lost. (Send the sheep to do that now.)

God promised that he would be sending his people a king – a good king, whose kingdom would last for ever. Ask for a volunteer and place a crown on their head. But he also knew that his people were like sheep, so this king would not be the kind of king who bosses everybody around and makes them give him all their money so he can be the richest person in the world. God decided that this king would be a shepherd. (Give the king a crook.) And he would go and search for all the lost sheep and bring them safely back to their pasture again. (Send the shepherd king off to do that.)

When the shepherd king has brought all the sheep back, explain that Jesus, the Christ, is our King, and he is the sort of king who knows us each by name, and searches for us when we are lost, and looks after us when he has found us.

In the Gospel today we heard that even when Jesus was dying on the cross he was still searching for lost sheep, right up to the moment he died. Two criminals were being executed with him that day, and one of them, only hours before he died, turned to him and asked for help. Straight away Jesus assured him of forgiveness; he had just brought another sheep back home to its pasture.

Ask the shepherd king to stretch out his arms. Point out that when Jesus, our King, was on the cross, his arms were stretched out like this, so he was in the shape of a cross, and this is the shape of welcoming love.